THE WORKERS OF TIANJIN, 1900-1949

天津工人

GAIL HERSHATTER

The Workers of Tianjin, 1900-1949

STANFORD UNIVERSITY PRESS
Stanford, California
1986

Stanford University Press
Stanford, California
© 1986 by the Board of Trustees of the
Leland Stanford Junior University
Printed in the United States of America

Published with the assistance of a
special grant from the Stanford
University Faculty Publication
Fund to help support nonfaculty
work originating at Stanford.

CIP data appear at the end of the book

Calligraphy by Carma Hinton

To my parents,
Evelyn Chohat Hershatter and Richard Hershatter,
and to the memory of my grandmother,
Gittel Brook Chohat

ACKNOWLEDGMENTS

This social history of the Tianjin working class could not have been written without my having the opportunity to live and conduct research in the People's Republic of China. I am especially grateful to those who aided me in my work at a time when assisting foreign scholars was a sensitive and often frustrating endeavor. The Nankai University History Department hosted me for two years and department members did their best to accommodate my voracious demands for material. Professor Wei Hongyun acted as my advisor; Long Jingzhao spent countless hours arranging access to archives and factories. The staffs of the Tianjin History Museum and the Santiaoshi History Museum permitted me to examine parts of their archival holdings. Li Shiyu was an invaluable source of information about every aspect of Tianjin customs. Xing Guangwen shared his family with me. Wang Yufeng, Pan Hangjun, and Lu Xinmin answered endless questions about Chinese idioms and taught me much about Chinese life as well. Linda Grove, at Nankai in 1979–80, was generous with advice and research materials. After I left China, the staffs of the ILO Archives and the World YWCA Archives in Geneva, as well as Professor H. D. Fong, helped me fill in pieces of the story that the Chinese materials had not covered.

This book has taken shape with the prodding and encouragement of many teachers, colleagues, and friends. Harold Kahn and Lyman Van Slyke, my advisors at Stanford, were meticulous in their comments on the initial project and the dissertation; they remain for me models of eloquence, precision, and human-heartedness. Helen Chauncey, Emily Honig, and Randy Stross patiently waded through initial drafts of the material and forced me to sharpen both my thinking and my presentation. The Stanford Women's History Dissertation Group—Antonia Casteñeda, Estelle Freedman, Gary Sue Goodman, Gayle Gullette, Lois Helmboldt, Emily Honig, Joanne Meyerowitz, and Vicki Ruiz—read several chapters and helped me to understand gender divisions within the working class.

Many scholars in the China field have squeezed all or part of my bulky manuscript into their busy schedules. Among them I would particularly like to thank Joseph Esherick, Chris Gilmartin, Susan Mann, Elizabeth Perry, and Margery Wolf. My colleagues in the Williams College Department of History, Peter Frost, Michael Smith, Tom Spear, William Wagner, and James Wood, have done their best to ensure that this study is comprehensible to non-China specialists. At Stanford University Press, Jess Bell and the anonymous reader finally convinced me that the last chapter had to be written. Muriel Bell painstakingly edited several versions of the book. Office Services at Williams College reproduced the final manuscript with remarkable dispatch.

Funding for my research was generously provided by the Committee on Scholarly Communication with the People's Republic of China, an Office of Education Fulbright-Hays Doctoral Dissertation Research Abroad Grant, and the Mrs. Giles Whiting Foundation. Williams College funding aided in the revision of the dissertation and manuscript preparation.

Finally, I want to thank four people for their unique contributions: Randy Stross, for his unrelenting pursuit of every inconsistent argument and unclear phrase; Sankong Fang, for aiding with computer graphics and making sure that I knew why various computers reacted the way they did; Sarah Brook Fang, whose entertaining presence enlivened the tedious process of copy-editing; and Emily Honig, for the hundreds of hours spent talking about most of the ideas in this book before and while they assumed written form.

G.H.

CONTENTS

THE WORKERS OF TIANJIN, 1900-1949

China and the Making of Working-Class History

In 1963, the British historian E. P. Thompson published *The Making of the English Working Class*. A study of tremendous breadth, it was at the same time intricate, almost intimate. It traced the history of the English working class from 1780 to 1832, a period in which "most English working people came to feel an identity of interests as between themselves, and as against their rulers and employers."[1] More than a major contribution to British history, Thompson's work was a call for a new kind of labor history: a history that concentrated less on the formal activities of unions and working-class parties, more on class formation in all its dimensions. Thompson, drawing on the work of Karl Marx, was particularly concerned with the process by which a class-in-itself became a consciously active class-for-itself.

Thompson criticized any attempt to define class "almost mathematically—so many men who stand in a certain relation to the means of production." Rather, he wrote in an oft-quoted explanation,

The finest-meshed sociological net cannot give us a pure specimen of class, any more than it can give us one of deference or of love. . . . Class is a relationship, and not a thing. . . . If we stop history at a given point, then there are no classes but simply a multitude of individuals with a multitude of experiences. But if we watch these men over an adequate period of social change, we observe patterns in their relationships, their ideas, and their institutions. Class is defined by men as they live their own history and, in the end, this is its only definition.[2]

Thompson devoted much of his book to an analysis of the ways of thinking, habits, and modes of association that British artisans brought with them into the formative period of industrial capitalism. These factors (which can be grouped under the term "tradition" if it is recognized that tradition is neither unitary nor static) provided resources that workers drew on to respond to their changing conditions of work and leisure under capitalism. Further, Thompson was at pains to show that this working class in the making was not simply a passive group, reacting to the imperatives of expanding capitalism. Rather, he saw the working class as an active agent in its own formation.[3]

Thompson's work was in part a reaction to the political and scholarly constraints of Stalinist Marxism. In the two decades since the publication of his book, both scholarship and politics (at least within the academy) have developed in directions congenial to his work. A generation of younger scholars, many of whom were active in the New Left and its various successor movements, have turned their attention to the history of working people in Britain, continental Europe, the United States, and to a lesser degree the Third World. Many of these scholars share neither Thompson's Marxist orientation nor his penchant for detailed narrative. But virtually all begin by quoting him, and their work manifests a serious attempt to use and further develop the kinds of questions he raised.

What have these historians (and a scattering of historically minded sociologists) accomplished? Broadly speaking, they have extended Thompson's work in five ways, which are frequently interrelated or overlapping.[4] First, they have extended it geographically. What Thompson did for the English working class, others have attempted to do for France, Italy, Russia, and the United States. Their work has accomplished more than a simple geographical transposition of Thompson's concerns and methods to other places. Whereas Thompson was able to build on a well-developed historiography of the English industrial revolution, those who study other nations have often had to write this history as they went. Their focus has generally been more narrow than his, limited to a particular industry or a particular locale.[5] This extension of Thompson's work has added an explicit comparative dimension to working-class history. Scholars have had to ask, for instance, how successive waves of immigration affected the making of a United States working class, and how continuing ties to the land shaped the consciousness of Russian industrial workers.[6] The experience of artisans in different times and places has been an especially fruitful point of comparison. Thompson saw artisans, whose position was threat-ened by the factory system, as the creators of working-class radicalism. Subsequent studies, especially of France, have explored the causes of ar-tisan radicalism in various cities and trades.[7]

In extending Thompson's inquiry to other places and times, scholars have also expanded the methodology of working-class history. Thompson's strength was in the meticulous collection and elegant exposition of con-ventional written sources. His successors have benefited from the methods of historical demography and the capabilities of the computer. They have pored over marriage registers, death certificates, census counts, and police reports, emerging with new accounts of working-class migration, family structure, and occupational mobility.[8] Thompson might be hesitant to ac-knowledge some of these scholarly progeny, since in their fascination with numbers they sometimes ignore his warning that the working class cannot be reduced to a series of statistical relationships. Yet their findings provide more than a false sense of precision; they help us reconstruct the lives of those who joined no workingmen's societies and left no written records. They make it possible to ask Thompson's questions about a larger and more diverse population of working people.

This enlarged working population includes many women, and a third extension of Thompson's work has begun to address their experience. As in other areas of women's history, scholars have had to do more than simply apply standard questions to the female experience. They have had to revise old concepts and develop new ones. The concept of the family wage econ-omy, for instance, has enabled historians to ask how women contributed both to capitalist production and to the reproduction of the labor force. Questions have been raised, though by no means exhaustively answered, about the changing nature of women's work, its effect on the social con-struction of gender roles, the reasons for women's relatively low valuation in the labor market, and the involvement of women in working-class poli-tics.[9] Frequently the new understanding of women's role in the working class has forced a revision of long-held orthodoxies. For instance, the analysis of outwork ("putting-out") industries, in which women played a prominent part, has altered the view that capitalist industry grew in a lin-ear fashion, with large-scale factories displacing all older forms of produc-tion. Rather, it appears that the home manufacture of matchboxes and knit goods survived alongside the factories and indeed helped them prosper.[10] As the investigation of women's work proceeds, it can be expected to gen-erate further insights into the not-so-linear logic of capitalism.

A fourth extension of Thompson's work has returned to the question of worker militancy and tried to explain it. Some historians have focused on the structure and traditions of the working class, others on the cumulative political experience of workers or on long-term economic changes. They have looked, with Thompson, at the struggle of employers to impose industrial discipline on new generations of factory recruits, and on workers' hardy resistance to that discipline. They have traced the process wherein workers "learned the rules of the game" and began to fight "not against time, but about it."[11] In general, these historians have tried to explain strikes not as sudden outbursts, but as natural extensions of the collective association of workers in their everyday lives. And they have traced the growth of collective association to a variety of sources: common roots in the countryside, common experiences in the factory, common dialect and customs, common problems in times of war and economic crisis. Historians investigating worker militancy are eclectic in their methods; some prefer computer correlations and Kondratieff waves tracing long-term economic cycles, whereas others look to the complaints of employers and the memoirs of working-class intellectuals. But they share a Thompsonian belief that workers' activity, and the consciousness that informs it, cannot be explained by reference to immediate political events alone.[12]

A final extension of Thompson's work, one that has caused a great deal of academic controversy in Britain, concerns the relation of working-class culture to economics and politics. Thompson has been criticized for reducing "class" to "class consciousness and class organization," ignoring its "rootedness in economic relations." In his determination to avoid mechanical applications of theory, critics argue, he has shunned all theory and indeed all abstraction.[13] Further, many of Thompson's followers stand accused of reducing the history of the working class to a depoliticized notion of "culture." Where Thompson emphasizes consciousness to the exclusion of other factors, these authors gloss over class consciousness and ignore ideology. Critics argue that such an approach isolates the working class from the larger society of which it is a part, and therefore cannot make sense of such events as revolutions. These critics have called for a return to the study of working-class politics, not narrowly conceived as organizational history, but broadly conceived as one part of the history of classes under capitalism. Although the polemical exchange sparked by their criticisms has thus far generated more heat than light, they have set themselves a task that Thompson himself would probably applaud: the integration of working-class history, in all its aspects, with a larger history of society.[14]

Faced with this rich and imaginative body of scholarship, the product of twenty years' effort by many historians, the student of China feels first inspiration and then despair. A year before the appearance of E. P. Thompson's work, the French scholar Jean Chesneaux published his study of the Chinese labor movement from 1919 to 1927. Twenty years later, in 1982, Lynda Shaffer's monograph on the Hunan labor movement of the early 1920's appeared. In the intervening two decades, several local studies on the Canton labor movement and a number of articles by the Tokyo-based China Labor Movement History Research Group added to the literature on movements of labor protest. Yet the making of a working-class history of China has definitely not kept pace with that of other nations, including those, like the Soviet Union, where access to materials has been similarly problematic.[15] This silence, while frustrating, is not inexplicable. Simply put, the attention of China historians has been focused elsewhere. Both inside China and abroad, historians of the modern period have concerned themselves with the pivotal event of the twentieth century: the 1949 revolution. This has led them back to the nineteenth century, to investigate the effects first of Western and later of Japanese imperialism. It has led them to the Chinese countryside, to explore the dynamics of the rural economy and analyze the peasantry as a source of social revolution. It has led them to twentieth-century Chinese universities, the wellspring of much highly visible political activity. But it has not generally led them into the factories, much less the artisans' workshops or the homes of Chinese workers. For understandable reasons, workers have gained attention chiefly when they intersected with large national movements of anti-imperialist or revolutionary protest, as they did in the mid-1920's and the late 1940's. In periods of political quiescence, their activities were less visible, and they have remained uninvestigated by China historians, shadowy onlookers at the main events.[16]

Yet inconstant militance on the part of Chinese workers is in itself an important historical circumstance. It forces our attention outward, to an examination of how the working class interacted with other classes in society. To understand quiescence it is necessary to explore the relationship of workers to the dominant classes, relations between the dominant classes themselves, the exercise of violent and nonviolent political power, and the question of hegemony. One direction for investigation is thus outward, into the larger society that helped to structure the actions and thinking of workers.[17] In current research on Beijing local politics, David Strand has begun to pursue this line of inquiry, finding that "modern union activity was one strategy among several used by workers to protect and promote their interests—'vertical mobilization' being at least as strong as 'horizontal mobilization' in this regard." Mark Selden suggests that the scope of inquiry must be further expanded to include the "study of the nature of the state, its legal structure, its power and penetration, and its relationship to social classes. . . . State power fundamentally shaped both the terrain on which the working class fought and the outcome of the struggle."[18]

A second direction of investigation is inward, into the working class itself, for a closer look at the connections between consciousness, organization, and action. These connections are not mechanical. As Eley and Nield point out in a discussion of German workers, workers' failure to organize may not "denote satisfaction with the status quo, or absence of class consciousness. Passivity may indicate 'a correct assessment of objective possibilities.'"[19] This investigation into consciousness in turn leads us backward in time and place, to the villages from which most twentieth-century Chinese workers came. How permanent was this working class? What looked in China like the helter-skelter urbanization of new treaty port cities may actually have been a complex process of movement in and out, in which important components of the urban population were not a permanent part of city life. Here again, the connections between rural origins and militance cannot be derived from a predictive model, but must be investigated in all their messy specificity. Mobility, transience, and rural conservatism might have made workers less committed to an urban situation and thus less militant. But continuing ties to the countryside could also increase militance if rural networks were brought into the factory and reshaped to suit new survival strategies. What is important is the use workers made of their rural ties in historically specific times and places.[20]

Finally, the investigation of worker militance pushes us forward, into an investigation of the visionaries and social organizers who tried to organize in Chinese workplaces. The ideologies these people brought with them have been much discussed in the historical literature. But their acceptance or alteration by the working class, and their effect on working-class consciousness, are not well understood. Nor do we know much about the political strategies worked out by the laborers themselves, drawing both on older traditions of protest (rural and urban) and on lessons learned in the urban workplace, independent of outside organizers.[21] Thus, even a working class that is quiescent most of the time can tell the historian a great deal about the larger society, about the links between consciousness, organization, and action, about the revolutionary process, and ultimately about the development of class itself. Current research on Chinese workers has just begun to refocus our questions so that they are organized not around the discrete events in a beleaguered labor movement, but around the workers themselves and their emergence as a class in relation to other classes.[22]

Most of the history of the Chinese working class has yet to be written. For the historian, this is both a problem and a pleasure. It is difficult and sometimes tedious to assemble a portrait of a city in which to locate the workers one is studying: errors of omission and commission become virtually unavoidable. On the other hand, it is possible to range more widely than in a field where every event and trend has been picked over and analyzed by others.

This volume tells the story of the workers of Tianjin, North China's most important industrial city in the first half of the twentieth century. When I began this study in the spring of 1979, I expected to devote most of my time to the female textile workers of Tianjin. The discovery that very few such workers existed (in contrast to better-studied Shanghai) was my first lesson in the need for regional specificity. My research was further hindered by the lack of any study, in English or Chinese, devoted to the urban history of modern Tianjin. Chapters 1 and 2 piece together this background. The former focuses on the physical growth and fragmentation of the city, the latter on the vagaries of local capitalist development, as influenced by imperialism and regional disorder.

As my research progressed it became more inclusive, much against my will. The Tianjin working class was deeply fragmented, with significant numbers of handicraft workers, freight haulers, and casual laborers in addition to the millhands I had hoped to study. The material commanded an attentiveness to fragmentation, divisiveness, a changing sexual division of labor, and growth that proceeded in a distressingly nonlinear fashion. Chapter 3 sketches the divisions between different sectors of workers, but also traces the commonalities most of them shared: connections to the countryside, close bonds to kin, a marginal and transient position in the urban economy.

The three case studies that follow concentrate on themes specific to each sector. Chapter 4 discusses the use and abuse of apprenticeship in the ironworking and machine-making trades. Chapter 5 explores corporatist organization and gang alliances in the transport industry. Chapter 6 records the struggle of cotton millowners to impose industrial discipline using, among other tools, the sexual division of labor and the sexual vulnerability of women millhands. Despite the diversity of these working situations, certain themes recur: the importance of cross-class alliances, for instance, and the ubiquitousness of institutionalized violence as a means of settling conflicts. Chapter 7 explores the ways workers used their scant leisure time to reinforce and expand the networks of connections that protected them in the city. Markets, amusements, holidays, and rites of passage became not an area *between* politics and work, but settings for the elaboration of cultural patterns that informed *both* politics and work.[23]

Everything in these chapters suggests that patterns of labor militance must be viewed not as a sharp break from "normal" working-class behavior, but as an extension of it. Chapter 8 pieces together the history of organized labor activity in Tianjin. When elite political control weakened, or when political activists targeted workers for organization, then protests erupted in Tianjin's larger factories. The most effective organizing made use of existing alliances between workers. Strikes, however, were one survival strategy among many; they should not be taken as the only reliable indicator of working-class consciousness. This volume is a study of workers in enterprises of many sizes, between as well as during periods of militance. It argues against a structure of inquiry that permits workers to troop on and off the historical stage at twenty-year intervals, meanwhile waiting in the wings passive and unseen.

CHAPTER ONE

The Shaping of Tianjin

Alexander Michie, a nineteenth-century resident of Tianjin, has left us a vivid description of the city and its occupants:

The city of Tientsin was one of the dirtiest, most repulsive, and busiest commercial cities of China, the mart of the North, and the people were reputed to be the most turbulent, predatory and wicked race in the Empire, so much so, that for many centuries past and even to this day (1888) the inns of the province, the capital, and of the neighboring provinces also, often have a notice on their gates: "No men of Tientsin admitted." Undiscovered crimes in other cities were generally debited to Tientsin "bullies." At the same time, however, they were shrewd business men, and a Peking proverb says that "Ten oily-mouthed Pekinese cannot get around one tonguey Tientsinner." But, in many ways, the ill-appearance was deceptive. Though the streets were horrible quagmires at all times, impassable after a few hours' rain, and between the hours of sunrise and sunset, blocked with the enormous traffic carried on in cattle drays, carts and wheelbarrows, great and luxurious houses were numerous; there was a large and influential official society, the guilds were splendid and powerful, and scarce any city in the Empire contained more numerous and better endowed charitable institutions, such as orphanages, schools of the poor, refuges, food distributaries, etc.[1]

The site of Tianjin, low marshy land traversed by a serpentine and capricious river, often flooded, plagued with locusts in bad times and mosquitoes in good, was not an auspicious location for a city. Yet by Ming times (1368–1644) it was a major transshipment center for grain and salt and a strategic defense area. As the gateway to Beijing it was visited by foreign delegations in the eighteenth century and assaulted by foreign armies in the nineteenth. After its opening as a treaty port in 1860, it often appeared to be a cluster of separate cities, as nine foreign powers each built a separate concession area. The native city expanded and outlying villages became industrial districts. By the 1930's, second only to Shanghai in the volume of foreign trade, Tianjin had become the largest center of industry and commerce in North China.

The physical development of the city reflected the development of its social landscape, and in this sense the fragmentation of Tianjin into discrete sections is telling. It was a city divided. Foreigners, civil officials, warlords, compradores (Chinese employees of foreign traders), small merchants, and gangs each had their own sphere of influence. Their relationships were complex, but it was the separateness of these ruling groups that gave Tianjin's economy its distinctive character.

The splintering of Tianjin's economy into separate sectors, sectors defined by the multiplicity of ruling groups, profoundly influenced the development of industry. Capital itself was splintered and diffused. A succession of powerful people invested in medium- and large-scale manufacturing, yet no stable group of industrial entrepreneurs emerged. The result was industries that were perpetually short of capital, as well as extremely vulnerable to changes in the city's political structure.

The local economy was fragmented in another way as well. Because of its helter-skelter growth as a treaty port, Tianjin had enterprises of every form and scale. Facilities for docking and export-processing crowded one another along the waterfront. Large mechanized cotton mills sprung up at the same time as tiny handicraft workshops. In Tianjin a range of historical capitalisms existed side by side, with no sign of linear development from small-scale production to factory system.

The urban history of Tianjin, and of its brief period of capitalist development, has been little explored. Yet this setting was crucial to the formation of the working class, which like the city itself was fragmented, tied to the North China rural economy, and chronically beset by problems of economic and political instability.

THE SETTING

Over the centuries the North China plain, pushed by movements of the earth's crust and layered with mud and sand dumped by the many rivers that traverse it, has gradually extended itself outward into the sea. Tianjin lies in the northeast corner of this plain, 100 kilometers southeast of Beijing. The area, flat for 100 kilometers around, is barely above sea level and is thoroughly waterlogged. Depressions where shallow lakes form are surrounded by marshy expanses of reeds; inadequate drainage has been a problem well into modern times.[2]

Five rivers (Daqing, Nanyun, Beiyun, Ziya, and Yongding) flow into the Hai River at Tianjin and run beyond it to the sea at Da Zhi Kou. They bring both fertile silt and the danger of floods, particularly in the intense rainy season between June and August, when Tianjin receives 75 percent of its annual rainfall. In a 1917 catastrophe, two summer typhoons pounded the area and dikes on all five rivers eventually burst, inundating 15,000 square miles of the province and leaving more than six million people homeless.[3] A British resident of Tianjin at that time wrote:

The concessions rose out of a great sea of water that might have been likened, had there been a background of hills, to Peitaiho Beach or Venice. When the wind was high the breakers were heavy and frequently broke over the back walls of the Travers-Smith houses. Early in the floods, which came in the latter part of September, all manner of vermin, snakes and even domestic animals were to be seen swimming in the water or clinging to trees, tops of gravemounds and walls.

[In the surrounding area] farmers went about in junks and attempted, by submarine harvesting, to save some of their crops. Thinly clad the younger of them would take a reaping knife and dive through the ten feet or so of clear water to the bottom, cut off a few stalks, and come up for air. By this painfully slow process they saved a small part of their crops.[4]

Tianjin's warm, wet, flood-prone summer season is followed by a brief autumn and a long bleak winter. The rivers are frozen from the end of December until February, and there is little snow. Winds blow unimpeded from the Mongolian steppes across the deforested North China plain. One folk rhyme popular in Tianjin warns of winter's dangers: *La qi La ba dongsi lia sa.* ("On the seventh and the eighth [of the last lunar month, corresponding to parts of January and February], two or three will freeze to death.") A more optimistic rhyme divides the time from winter solstice until spring plowing into ten groups of nine days each:

Yi jiu er jiu bu chu shou	First and second, hands we hide
San jiu si jiu bingshang zou.	Third and fourth we walk on ice.
Wu jiu he kai, liu jiu yan lai	By the fifth the rivers open
Qi jiu ba jiu he bian kan liu	Sixth the wild geese arrive.
Jiu jiu jia yi jiu geng niu	By the seventh and the eighth
bian di zou.	Willows on the riverbank.
	On the ninth and add one more
	Cattle plowing everywhere.[5]

But while spring is warm the wind increases, kicking up sand, small stones, and tree branches, and hurling them through the air.

A final scourge is insects. Passing through Tianjin by water on his way to Beijing in 1793, Lord Macartney complained that his party was "much troubled with mosquitoes, or gnats, and stunned day and night [by] obstreperous cicadas."[6] Of more concern to the local peasants was the periodic invasion of crop-eating grasshopper swarms. A Dutchman who visited Tianjin in 1655 observed:

> Toward night the people were gathered in troops to defend their country against the grasshoppers, who visit them annually about this time [June]; being brought by an easterly wind in such mighty swarms; that in a few hours they devour all before them, if once they alight; to prevent which, the inhabitants march to and again through the fields with their colours flying, shouting and hallooing all the while; never leaving them till they are driven into the sea, or some river, where they fall down and are drowned.[7]

Despite this inhospitable environment, human settlement flourished in the Tianjin area from Neolithic times.[8] By the Song period (960–1279), fortifications ringed the area, defending against intruders from the north. The name "Tianjin" dates from the early Ming period, when the imperial rulers founded Tianjin Garrison (*Tianjin wei*). The name was derived from the future Yongle emperor's having crossed the Hai River there, hence Tian Jin or "heavenly ford" (the ford of the Son of Heaven).[9]

Perhaps reflecting its military importance, Tianjin was known in common parlance simply as "Wei" or "The Garrison." A sneering folk rhyme, which dates from the Qing (1644–1911), categorizes the inhabitants of Beijing, Tianjin, and Baoding as follows: *Jing youzi, Wei zuizi, Baoding fu de gou tuizi* ("the slick operators of Beijing, the fast talkers of Wei, and the hired thugs of Baoding").[10]

Wei's fast talkers evidently put their skills to good commercial use. By the mid-Tang dynasty (618–906) Tianjin, located at the juncture of two sections of the Grand Canal, already had become an important transshipment point for rice and satins from the south. Official grain passed through Tianjin on its way to the capital well into the Qing period. Trade with Shanghai, Fujian, and Guangdong was carried on by fleets of junks during the eighteenth and nineteenth centuries. They brought not only grain but also foreign goods and foreign opium. Merchants from the interior sold their products in Tianjin and bought opium with the proceeds; just before the Opium War, Tianjin was the central point for drug shipments into North China. The production and storage of salt was another important commercial activity. In the early Qing period the government-run Changlu salt administration moved to Tianjin. Wealthy producers and merchants made their homes in the city from the seventeenth century onward.[11]

Tianjin's role as granary and saltworks for the region, and the need to protect this strategic transshipment center, led to the proliferation of government offices within the city. In the eighteenth century all the prefecture and county offices in the region, as well as the salt administration and grain offices, were located in Tianjin. The continued growth of an official class to be served and a merchant class with money to spend encouraged the development of petty commerce. Long-distance trade, meanwhile, was financed by an elaborate remittance system run by bankers from Shanxi province.[12] Soldiers, grain, salt, and above all trade shaped the early economy of Tianjin.

TIANJIN IN 1816

A foreign traveler visiting Tianjin before the opening of the treaty port in 1860 probably came by ship to Dagu, on the coast, and then traveled up the Hai River by junk.[13] Since passage up the serpentine river took about two days, he had ample time to notice the "huts with mud walls and thatched roofs" along the suburban banks.[14] Sorghum, corn, yellow millet, kidney beans, and rice were cultivated intensively right up to the water's edge, while cucumbers, watermelons, apples, pears, plums, and peaches were also visible on the shore. Along the banks, local peasants wove the tops of sorghum stalks into mats, while the bottoms were used for fuel and for banking up loose soil along the river's edge.

As the junk approached Tianjin, pyramids of salt about 15 feet high lined the banks, covered with matting to protect them from the rain.[15] The entrance to the city was undramatic, marked only by "the gradual crowding of junks till they become innumerable, a vast population, [and] buildings though not elegant yet regular and peculiar."[16]

The rarity of foreign guests made their arrival in Tianjin a public event. Hundreds of Tianjin citizens would stand in the water to get closer to the vessels that conveyed the foreigners, while others scrambled to the tops of the salt mounds. Henry Ellis, who traveled to Tianjin with the Amherst Mission in 1816, exclaimed that he "had not before conceived that human heads could be so closely packed; they might have been by screw squeezed into each other, but there was often no possible vacancy to be observed."[17] Foreigners entering the city ran a lengthy gauntlet of such scrutiny, for Tianjin appeared to be "about the length of London."[18] It took two-and-a-half hours to get from the first outlying row of houses to the main anchorage just east of the walled city (see Map 1).

At anchor the foreigner might have a hard time telling where the river ended and the shore began, since the water's surface was scarcely visible for the crowd of junks. There was even a bridge of boats crossing the river

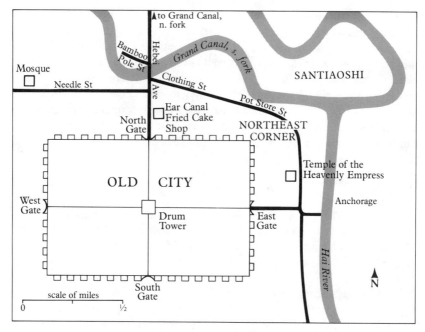

Map 1. Tianjin, 1816

"for the convenience of the people, but which occasionally separated to let vessels pass between them." [19] Thousands of sailors and their families lived permanently on these boats; most of them were engaged in trade along the internal river network rather than in oceanic shipping.

As soon as he stepped ashore, the visitor would gain a fair idea of the commercial life of the city. Most merchants lived outside the city walls to the north and east, desiring to avoid both the marshy dampness within the walls and the depredations of the officials whose offices dominated the city proper. Some of their establishments, "having shops for the retail of merchandize, or working places for manufacturers, were open to the street." [20]

Residences were "chiefly built of brick, of a leaden blue colour. Few were red. Such as were used in the smallest and poorest dwellings, were of a pale brown. Those last mentioned had been exposed to no other heat than that of the sun." Houses were usually one story, occasionally two, but their interiors could only be guessed at, for they were "shut towards the street by the outward wall; and even when the gate is opened, a skreen of masonry fronting the entrance, and considerably exceeding it in width, intercepts the view." [21] No matter how elegant the dwelling, its only water was supplied by itinerant water-sellers, and sanitation conditions were such that one visitor from London (itself none too clean in this era) felt that "our olfactory nerves will have been so saturated with stench, that the absence of smell will probably overpower us when restored to a pure atmosphere."[22]

Making his way up the west bank of the river just outside the city wall, the explorer traversed an area crowded with pharmacies, butchers' shops, and millers' shops. Many shops carried more than one type of merchandise; one of the most common foodstuffs, "a black mass looking like caviare, proved to be soy mixed with salt, with something to give the mixture consistency."[23]

At the northeast corner of the old city the explorer could turn off the road bordering the east side of the city wall, which though narrow was regular and paved with large stones, and venture onto the even narrower North Temple Street (Gongbei Dajie). The temple that gave the street its name was consecrated to the patron saint of sailors, the Heavenly Empress (Tianhou).[24] Built in 1326, it stood on the west bank of the Hai River so that sailors coming upstream could have an unobstructed view of it. In front were two flagpoles about 25 meters high, where banners flew to hearten approaching sailors.

The road to the temple was short but sometimes impassable because of the crowds, especially during the annual procession in the spring. Each year on the birthday of the Heavenly Empress, her image was removed from the temple and paraded through the streets. It was accompanied by stiltwalkers, floats, lion dancers, entertainers in the garb of the Eight Immortals, and women carrying strips of red cloth with which to petition the goddess for a son. Most of the populace of Tianjin turned out for this parade and for the market held at the same time. Because special tax exemptions were granted by the government for the occasion, ships came bearing merchandise from as far away as Fujian, birthplace of the Heavenly Empress.

After joining the festivities, the foreign guest could retrace his steps back down North Temple Street, passing on his way the largest group of money-conversion shops in the city. Back at the northeast corner of the city wall, he could turn right and explore the area just north of the city, following Pot Store Street (Guo Dian Jie) until it ran into Clothing Street (Gu Yi Jie) and then out to the southern spur of Hebei Avenue. Clothing Street specialized in the sale of medicine, cloth, and provisions for the dead, including burial clothing and wooden pillows for the head and feet.

A right turn followed by several days' journey would bring the traveler to Beijing, but a quick jog to the left brought more immediate rewards: a visit to the Ear Canal Fried Cake Shop (Erduoyan Zhagao Pu). Its unappetizing name was derived not from the contents of its fried cakes, which were filled with a sweet red bean paste, but rather from the alley off to the side, which was so narrow that residents compared it to the inside of an ear. The fried cake shop, like many other shops in this district, was run by Chinese Muslims. Their community was centered in the northwest corner of the city; their mosque and the many shops selling mutton distinguished this quarter from other districts of Tianjin.

Retracing his steps north, the explorer passed Needle Street and Bamboo Pole Street, both bustling with merchants and buyers. A very short hike would bring him to the southern fork of the Grand Canal, which in this era was still crowded with junks from the internal shipping trade. If he were really intrepid he might continue up the road about fifteen minutes to the northern fork of the Grand Canal. Unbeknownst to him he would pass on his right a spit of land called Santiaoshi (Three Stone Slabs). Lined with docks for small river boats, it was later to become Tianjin's most famous ironworking district.

But a less energetic stroller would turn back at the southern canal and work his way back down to the northern gate of the walled city. He would turn left along the wall, which was described by one author in 1739 as resplendent with "vermilion balustrades and white battlements slicing through the lofty clouds."[25] From there it would take him only a few more minutes to return to the northeast corner and thence safely back to his ship at its crowded berth.

Even without visiting the narrow alleys of the walled city, the visitor had covered most of Tianjin's thriving commercial area. Having observed the sailors and shopkeepers, he could fairly report to his shipmates that he had seen the most important sectors of Tianjin at work. But old Tianjin was soon to be swallowed up by a larger, more complex city, a treaty port in which many emergent groups coexisted uneasily.

TREATY PORT TIANJIN

Twentieth-century visitors to Tianjin found a greatly changed city. The Treaty of Beijing was signed by a defeated Qing government at the close of the second Opium War in October 1860. One of its provisions made Tianjin a treaty port. In the 90 years that followed the city was transformed. The population of the city proper grew from about 60,000 in 1860 to more than 1.7 million in 1947. By 1927 it was the fifth largest Chinese city, by 1935 the third, and by 1947 the second.[26]

A tiny but significant minority of the new residents were foreigners, ensconced in one of the nine concessions that the foreign powers demanded and built in Tianjin between 1860 and 1902. Under their energetic ministrations the villages on both sides of the Hai River grew into the economic center of Tianjin, while the old city became a commercial backwater.

But Chinese, too, had an active role in the building of modern Tianjin. Modernization-minded Qing and Republican government officials built up the Hebei and Honqqiao districts. Commercial capitalists developed the downtown area southeast of the old city. Transport bosses ran the riverside warehouses and divided municipal streets into territorial strongholds. Workers crowded into suburban factories and inner-city workshops. Entertainers, prostitutes, and thieves practiced their arts in the south city.

Tianjin in 1930 was too large to cover easily on foot, and most of its inhabitants were not inclined to try. Foreigners and wealthy Chinese seldom ventured outside the concession areas. Shopkeepers had little occasion to leave the central city. Apprentices in every trade were not permitted to leave their workshops. For the industrial worker or the peasant newcomer in search of work, the boundaries of Tianjin were defined by networks of family and fellow-townsmen, and by the factory walls. Even the mobile transport hauler did not transgress the boundaries of the territory controlled by his guild, unless he was prepared for a violent struggle with his rivals. Geography and social structure created formidable barriers; few Tianjin residents saw the city whole.

Yet a foreign visitor in 1930 might want to tour the diverse collection of urban environments that made up Tianjin. Because of the city's radical expansion, this tour would barely overlap with the area covered in 1816. It was in the outlying areas that most of Tianjin's new urban builders made their homes, and it was there that the Tianjin working class took shape.

Like his predecessor more than a century earlier, the 1930 explorer might start his tour with the banks of the Hai River (see Map 2). The river was both stimulus and impediment to Tianjin's development. Stimulus because in all North China only Tianjin was easily accessible from the coast and also convenient to internal river transport. Impediment because its tendencies to freeze and to silt up periodically disrupted shipping.[27]

Beginning in the second decade of the twentieth century, icebreaking boats swept the river every winter. The silting problem proved harder to solve. A joint Sino-foreign Hai River Conservancy Commission, founded in 1897, dredged and straightened the river, but by 1927 it had silted up again until it was only 12 feet deep. Not even steamers of small tonnage could navigate in such a shallow channel, and all boats had to unload at Tanggu and transfer their goods to barges.[28]

Nevertheless, it was along the Hai River that the city's development was most noticeable. The earliest concessions (British, French, and American) were built on a long strip of land less than a quarter mile wide along the

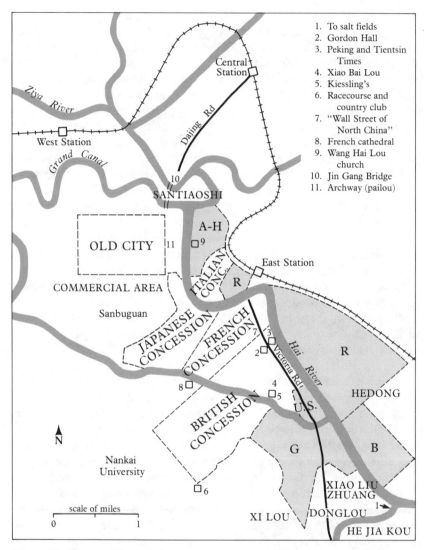

1. To salt fields
2. Gordon Hall
3. Peking and Tientsin Times
4. Xiao Bai Lou
5. Kiessling's
6. Racecourse and country club
7. "Wall Street of North China"
8. French cathedral
9. Wang Hai Lou church
10. Jin Gang Bridge
11. Archway (pailou)

Ziya River

West Station

Grand Canal

Central Station

Dajing Rd

SANTIAOSHI

OLD CITY

COMMERCIAL AREA

Sanbuguan

A-H

East Station

ITALIAN CONC.

R

JAPANESE CONCESSION

FRENCH CONCESSION

Hai River

Victoria Rd

R

HEDONG

BRITISH CONCESSION

U.S.

N

Nankai University

G

B

XIAO LIU ZHUANG

scale of miles

0   1

XI LOU

DONGLOU

HE JIA KOU

Map 2. Tianjin, 1930. The shaded areas represent former foreign concessions within the city: the Austro-Hungarian (A-H), the Russian (R), the Belgian (B), the German (G), and the United States (U.S.; came under British control in 1902).

west bank. Before construction began "the site of the British Settlement was a long stretch of vegetable gardens, with here and there a cluster of squalid mud houses . . . and . . . chiefly fields of *gaoliang* [sorghum] and pools." The French settlement was scarcely more imposing, "a wretched terrain given up to pools, cabbage gardens, storing fruit and vegetables, and a rowdy, sinful, and criminal population." [29]

Over the next 70 years the Purple Bamboo Grove (Zi Zhu Lin), as this unpicturesque area was called, became a bustling collection of docks, warehouses run by foreign firms (*yanghang*), customs offices, and export-processing factories. A new round of concession-granting at the turn of the century added a Japanese settlement to the north and a German settlement to the south. Facing them on the east bank of the river were the Austro-Hungarian, Italian, Russian, and Belgian concessions.

The traveler might begin his explorations at the south end of the concessions. Although both banks of the river were far less built up than the area upstream, four of Tianjin's six large cotton mills and a dozen tiny breweries were found here. Millhands from villages all over North China had turned southeastern suburbs like Xiao Liu Zhuang, He Jia Kou, Xi Lou, and Dong Lou into sprawling settlements of one-story houses. Married women who did not go out to work in the mills spun wool at home for sale to merchants. On the east bank of the river and slightly to the north, in the Hedong district, tobacco workers and more millhands made their homes. Downstream to the south were the salt fields, still productive in the twentieth century.

A few blocks west of the riverbank was the main thoroughfare, which changed its name at every concession boundary. In the ex-German concession it had once been Kaiser Wilhelmstrasse, but was redubbed Woodrow Wilson Street after World War I. Twenty minutes' walk in a northward direction and it became Victoria Road, pride of the British concession and the most important commercial area in Tianjin.

Many of the streets and buildings in the British concession were named after people who had made their careers in the "opening" of China. Elgin Avenue, Parkes Road, and Napier Road alternated with streets named for cities in the mother country (London, Cambridge, Windsor, Greenwich, Limerick, Oxford) and for other areas of British influence in Asia (Hong Kong, Singapore, Colombo, Canton). The seat of the British Municipal Council, turreted Gordon Hall, was named for General Charles "Chinese" Gordon, who had helped suppress the Taiping Rebellion and later drew up the plans for Tianjin's British settlement. Gordon Hall was situated in Victoria Park, "the evening resort of the elite of Tientsin. Here the regimental band play[ed] at stated hours, usually between six and eight o'clock, if the weather [was] fine." [30]

Racecourse Road led southwest to the racecourse and country club, which featured a parquet dance floor supported by springs underneath. The foreigner in search of entertainment had other choices as well, depending upon his financial resources and his tastes: the posh red-brick Tientsin Club diagonally across from Victoria Park for the businessman, the bars along Dagu Road for the foreign troops stationed in Tianjin, the Empire Theatre a few blocks west for family entertainment, the houses of prostitution near the American barracks for those who cared to visit, and of course Kiessling's, a combination German bakery and restaurant, for residents in search of fine pastries and hearty stews.

But the center of economic life in Tianjin was on and near Victoria Road. Less than a block to the west on Meadows Road was the palatial colonnaded administrative office of the Kailuan Mines, one of the largest foreign investments in North China. Farther north, extending into the French Concession, were the banks that gave Victoria Road its nickname, "the Wall Street of North China." Among them were the Hong Kong and Shanghai, the Yokohama Specie, the Russo-Asiatic, the Chinese-American Bank of Commerce, the Banque de l'Indochine, l'Epargne Franco-Chinoise, and the Banque Belge pour l'Etranger.

On this same street the traveler could also find the headquarters of the *Peking and Tientsin Times*, an English-language daily paper founded in 1902. By 1920 Tianjin had at least 13 foreign-language newspapers, including five British, one American, one French, and four Japanese journals. Several of the major Chinese-language newspapers, a few of them founded by foreigners, also had their offices in the concessions, where they could comment on Chinese political events with relative freedom.[31] The foreign newspapers reflected the isolation of the foreign community from its Chinese surroundings. The papers covered political and social events of interest in the home countries and the concessions, and took most of their reporting on Chinese events from the Chinese press.

The foreigners lived on quiet residential lanes off the main commercial thoroughfares. Most made their living in trade and associated activities: shipping, inspection, finance, and export processing. A few worked for the utility companies that provided the concessions with water and electricity, or for the Belgian trolley company. Some foreigners settled permanently in Tianjin; they built elaborate homes and gardens, sent their children to foreign-run schools, and took home leave every five years. Many lived much more comfortably than they could have at home. One foreign resident recalled that "you could be a small clerk in one of the banks and keep a couple of polo ponies."[32]

But not all foreigners were established traders. Some arrived with no financial resources and would work as brokers or even at menial jobs until they could accumulate sufficient funds to start businesses of their own. In its treaty port years Tianjin was a city where fortunes could be made. Many of the buildings along Victoria Road were built by S. B. Talati, an Indian who arrived in Tianjin nearly destitute in the early twentieth century and began his business career running canteens for the foreign garrisons. He moved rapidly into real estate and accumulated an enormous fortune. Other immigrants, Jews from Russia, came to Tianjin after the October Revolution. They settled in a corner of the British concession called Xiao Bai Lou (Small White Building), became very active in the fur trade, and built their own synagogue and business club.[33]

Except for the Japanese concession, which was densely populated, the foreign areas were much more spacious than the old Chinese city and its neighboring districts. Wealthy Chinese officials and compradores were attracted to the concessions by the absence of crowding, as well as by the relative political stability of the foreign areas in a time of constant upheaval and civil war. Branch managers of Chinese firms, senior Chinese accountants, and office personnel also lived there. So did the sizable native population that fed, clothed, and waited on the foreigners and wealthy Chinese.

Continuing north along Victoria Road, the traveler noticed that it soon changed its name to Rue de France. The passage into the French concession was obvious not only because of the change in architecture—each concession was constructed in the style most popular in the home country—but also because of a sharp jog in the road. Each foreign power designed and built its own network of roads, and the width and direction of thoroughfares was not consistent across concession boundaries.

The proliferation of concessions in Tianjin gave the city a crazy-quilt look. On the east bank of the river, pink marble mansions lined the Via Matteo Ricci (one of them was an Italian lawn bowling club), while spires and minarets adorned the Russian concession. Each city within the city had its own sources of light and power and its own transport company and waterworks, as well as its own administration.

Nor were the foreigners united in their style of worship or their pursuit of missionary activities. The Russians built an Orthodox church on the east bank; the British imported a number of Protestant sects. The French were most vigorous in the propagation of Catholicism; they could claim more converts than any other foreign power in Tianjin. The French could also claim the highest number of international incidents caused by religious conflict. Our visitor, by now having traveled north through the French concession, could gaze upstream across the Hai River and barely glimpse the skeletal remains of the church at Wang Hai Lou. It had twice been burned by rioting Chinese crowds, during the Tianjin Massacre (1870) and the Boxer Rebellion (1900). In back of him (though blocked from view by the concession proper) loomed the triple domes of the new French cathedral at Lao Xi Kai. Attempts by the French to expand into this area, which was not part of their original concession, had sparked the general strike of 1916. In addition to their spiritual activities, various religious groups also founded hospitals and schools throughout the concessions and the native city.[34]

Turning left at the river and then left again one block, the traveler continued northwest along Rue du Chaylard and (beginning at the Japanese concession border) Asahi Road. This was also a commercial area, but unlike Victoria Road it catered to Chinese shoppers. It was developed during and after World War I by Chinese compradores and merchants, and extended north of the Japanese concession to the eastern boundary of the old city, where our earlier explorer had disembarked from his ship in 1816. Most of Tianjin's major department stores, including the famous Quan Ye Chang, were located in this quarter.[35]

When he got to the southeast corner of the old city, a traveler with any knowledge of local history stopped to survey the site where the city walls had once stood. In the summer of 1900 Tianjin had become a center of Boxer activity; Catholic and Protestant churches were burned. Several days later the foreign troops of eight nations arrived to lift "the siege of Tianjin." Fighting was fierce around the concessions, near the site of the East Station, and south of the walled city as far as the suburban village of Ba Li Tai. After a protracted battle the eight-nation expedition drove into the walled city through the south gate. Many Boxers died on and inside the city walls; much of the old city and the area north of it was destroyed. A provisional military government established by the foreigners then tore down the walls to ensure that no other anti-foreign force could ever take refuge there, and "the remains of the ruined walls and gateways were used for making roads and furnishing ballast for railway construction."[36] Only a lone archway at the east gate recalled the city's former splendor.

The old city never fully recovered from the events of 1900. Its commercial center was destroyed, and the former walled area had ceased to be the center of native political power when the offices of the imperial representatives had moved across the river in 1870. Several merchant guilds (Guangdong, Jiangsu, and Zhejiang) had their offices within the native city, and the area just north of the old city continued to flourish until the 1930's. But the big commercial powers were in the concessions and the new shopping area to the southeast. Dark and crowded, the old city contained no important industrial plants; they were scattered elsewhere in anarchic fashion throughout the greater Tianjin area.

Passing along the eastern border of the old city, the traveler soon crossed the Hai River and reached Dajing Road, a broad avenue that ran due northeast to the Central Station. The station was the terminus of the Beining Railroad (built in 1907) and the Jinpu (Tianjin-Pukou) Railroad (built in 1912). These two rail lines, as well as the Pinghan, Pingsui, and Zhengtai lines, which ran through Tianjin's two other railroad stations, linked Tianjin with a large area. The city's hinterland now expanded to include Hebei, Shanxi, Henan, northern Shandong, Shaanxi, Gansu, Qinghai, Xinjiang, Rehe, Chahar, Suiyuan, Ningxia, and the Northeast.[37]

Dajing Road, about two miles long, linked the new rail transport network with the old river network. The entire district surrounding it was the creation of Yuan Shikai, governor-general of Zhili province from 1903 to 1907. In a park at the south end of the street stood a complex of office buildings that held first the headquarters of the Zhili governor-general, later the Hebei provincial government, and finally the Tianjin municipal government.[38] In his years in Tianjin, Yuan sponsored many model factories and schools along Dajing Road. The city's first municipal park, the library, the mint, and the Public Security Bureau were located here as well. This concentration of official activities along Dajing Road stimulated commercial development, just as the government offices across the river had done a century before. The district abounded in restaurants, dry goods stores, shoe stores and hat shops, pharmacies, sauce and pickle shops, fresh- and dried-fruit warehouses, teashops, bookshops, and stands selling southern-style food. Some of the activity spilled back across the river and helped redevelop the northeast corner.[39]

By this time the guest might well be exhausted enough with foot travel to hail one of the many rickshaws that pulled foreigners and wealthy Chinese around Tianjin. He could ride in style back across the Jin Gang Bridge, along the northern edge of the old city, passing to the south of the Santiaoshi ironworking district and the millhands and home spinners of the Hebei district. Turning northwest, he arrived at the West Railroad Station, a cavernous yellow brick edifice built by the British. The pungent odor of fresh-milled grain came from the Chinese-owned flour mills clustered along the banks of the nearby Ziya River. Boats brought the unmilled grain right to the door of the factory.

Heading back down along the western edge of the old city, which was crowded with cotton yarn and cloth dealers, he could make a left turn where the west gate used to be. A right turn at the drum tower in the center of the old city would bring him down through Beimen Dajie, the gloomy street that was the old city's main north-south axis, which became narrower as the city grew more crowded and shops encroached on the thoroughfares. To the west and south of the old city lived many carpet weavers, as well as those who wove rayon and cotton by hand. The Xitou district to the west of the old city, undistinguished by any particular occupation, housed workers of every trade: handloom and carpet weavers, ironworkers, soybean packers, egg and peanut sorters, almond crushers, straw-braid plaiters, and people who sorted pig bristles and bird feathers for export.

Emerging at the southern edge of the old city, the traveler found himself in Tianjin's most densely populated area. One part of this district was nicknamed Sanbuguan (three who-cares?) because neither the Japanese, the French, nor the Chinese municipal government paid any attention to its development. It was crowded with cheap theaters, teahouses, vaudeville halls, drug shops, and flophouses. Although some of the residents were old Tianjiners, many were first-generation peasant immigrants who had come to make their fortunes by laboring in a handicraft workshop, selling secondhand goods, hustling for odd jobs, or finding work as entertainers or prostitutes.

Continuing south, the traveler passed the Japanese garrison at Haiguansi, eventually reaching the campus of Nankai University. Founded as a middle school in 1904, by 1930 it had become one of the distinguished universities of North China.[40]

By this time the foreign traveler was on the southern outskirts of the city. East, northeast, and northwest of him were many squalid pockets of crowded one-story working-class houses, interspersed with small handicraft workshops. To his west lived many of the rayon and carpet weavers. But the casual traveler might not stumble upon these neighborhoods, because except for the outlying districts where he had begun his tour and the Hebei district in the northern suburbs, Tianjin had no well-delineated industrial areas. Workers were scattered and squeezed into narrow alleys and tiny shantytowns, their workplaces often identical with the place they threw down a straw mat to sleep at night. Our tourist, taking refuge at one of the foreign clubs after his long journey, might reflect that he had seen not one city but many towns sprawled north to south: the neat government district to the northeast, the northern ironworking and textile area, the old city, the amusement quarters of Sanbuguan, the foreign concessions along the Hai River, and the new industrial districts. While it lacked architectural coherence, this chaotic urban layout had a historical logic, for Tianjin was a city built in waves—of foreigners, Chinese officials, warlords, and merchants.

CHAPTER TWO

Inconstant Industrialists

Underlying the spatial division of Tianjin was an urban economic structure fragmented into many parts. An analysis of this structure touches upon several questions that have long preoccupied historians of modern China. Architecture apart, in what ways was Tianjin a product of foreign forces? What role did the Chinese elite of Tianjin play in the city's development, and what factors encouraged or constrained their participation? More generally, how does an understanding of the growth of Tianjin help to confirm or challenge the usefulness of the categories "imperialism" and "feudalism," around which so much debate in the historical literature has been explicitly or implicitly organized?

INVESTORS AND POWER WIELDERS

Until 1949, Tianjin remained a city where trade came first. Much more capital was invested in commerce than in industry by every power-wielding group in the city. Tianjin's stature as one of the preeminent industrial cities of China notwithstanding, the development of modern industry, slowed by political instability, remained tentative and faltering. To understand why, and to establish the setting in which the working class grew, requires an examination of each ruling group that had a role in the development of Tianjin.

Foreigners

It was Tianjin as market and gateway to other markets that attracted foreign residents. During their 90 years in Tianjin, most of their efforts were devoted to expanding the port's foreign trade. This meant the development of all the supporting structures required by trade: customs inspection, shipping, insurance, finance, and a comfortable place for the traders to live.

Because some exports needed to be cleaned, sorted, and packed, several foreign firms opened export-processing factories. Usually no more than a warehouse with a machine or two, these factories represented almost the sum total of foreign investment in Tianjin industry. Not until the mid-1930's, when the Japanese began to buy and build spinning mills and other factories, did foreigners take a significant role in organizing modern industrial production.

In the first years of the treaty port, exports consisted of raw goods like "Dry Flowers, Medicines, Flint Steels, Black and Red Dates, Deer Horns, various fruits, nuts, seed, hair, fish bones, mushrooms, raisins, rhubarb, cotton, and salted cabbage."[1] Opium and cotton cloth dominated the import trade.[2]

From the end of the Sino-Japanese War (1895) to World War I, the scope of foreign activity in China greatly expanded. In Tianjin the net volume of foreign trade increased, in spite of reduced activity during the Boxer Rebellion and the last few years of the Qing dynasty.[3] Cotton yarn, cloth, sugar, kerosene, dyes, and opium were the major imports. During and after World War I, many foreign firms also began to import military hardware for warlord customers.[4]

After World War I, the pattern of imports began to change. Iron and steel, petroleum, machines, and machine parts became the predominant imports. Trading partners also changed: whereas the British had dominated the Tianjin trade prior to World War I, after the war the United States increased its share of the export trade, while Japan moved steadily toward preeminence in imports. The goods exported, however, were still mostly raw and semi-processed goods, such as cotton, sheep's wool, and eggs. The only significant exception to this pattern was the manufacture and export of carpets, which after World War I briefly became an important product on the foreign market.[5]

For most of the 1930's, Tianjin trade suffered from the effects of taxation and the worldwide Depression. New Chinese import taxes drove some trade out of Tianjin and into Japanese-sponsored smuggling zones in eastern Hebei. Foreign goods were dumped in Tianjin at artificially low prices, while the demand for Chinese goods decreased in the economically depressed West.[6] Yet despite its uneven economic fortunes between the two World Wars, the port of Tianjin was usually in second or third place among the treaty ports in volume of direct foreign trade. In the years just before the Japanese invasion of 1937, Tianjin handled about one-sixth the level of imports and one-third the level of exports of Shanghai.[7] But after the invasion trade was repeatedly affected by political upheavals, and after 1941 all trade outside the yen bloc was cut off. In 1945, exports to the United States resumed briefly, but civil war, inflation, and speculation brought trade to a virtual standstill by late 1948.[8]

From 1860 until 1949, foreigners controlled every stage of the passage of goods into and out of the port of Tianjin. The Imperial Maritime Customs Service, in charge of Tianjin's commerce after 1861, was managed by foreigners on behalf of the central government. Most of the revenues went to service foreign loans and, after 1900, the Boxer indemnity.[9] The vast majority of imported goods were carried in foreign bottoms; the British and later the Japanese owned most of the ships. With foreign ships came the need for shipyards that could repair and replace them, and by 1922 there were at least five in the vicinity of Tianjin, four of them foreign-owned. Foreigners also got into the business of unloading ships at Dagu and Tanggu, transferring the cargoes to barges for the journey to Tianjin.[10] Actual trading was carried on by the foreign-owned yanghang, which usually hired a Chinese compradore to act as agent with native merchants. The largest firms, such as Britain's Jardine, Matheson, and Japan's Mitsui and Mitsubishi, employed large Chinese and foreign staffs.[11]

An enterprising firm typically engaged in more than one type of trading activity. For instance, the American import firm of Robert Dollar Company (Da Lai Yanghang) started shipping pine to Shanghai and Tianjin in 1903. The company provided much of the wood used in Tianjin and Beijing, as well as in government-run railroads and mines. In 1923 the firm built a sawmill on the Hai River in Tianjin to saw wood for the North China market. Dollar also founded a wireless company, which attempted to monopolize the telegraph business. Other firms diversified their activities in like fashion, dealing in everything from buttons and bone powder to insurance and export inspection.[12] The activities of these firms were financed by the major foreign banks on or near "the Wall Street of North China." Foreign banks also lent money on behalf of their governments to the Qing government, and even issued paper currency. They served foreign nationals, very seldom dealing with Chinese merchants.[13]

If foreigners wished to live in the style to which they were accustomed in their home countries, they had to provide the facilities themselves. A

British firm initially took responsibility for supplying water from the Hai River to the British concession; in 1920 this function was taken over by the concession government, which dug wells to provide water. The rest of the city was served by the Tientsin Native City Water Works Company, founded by a German in 1902, which provided heavily filtered and chlorinated water from the Nanyun and Ziya rivers.

The British, French, and Japanese generated their own electricity, but power for everyone else was supplied by the Belgian Compagnie de Tramways et Eclairage de Tientsin. The same Belgian company also ran the streetcars, in 1930 employing 1,900 Chinese as drivers, ticket sellers, track repairmen, and factory workers. The trolley company was important not only because it provided light, transport, and employment, but also because it collected fares in copper. It played a crucial role in determining the local exchange rate of copper to silver, which in turn influenced the livelihood of most workers. The waterworks and trolley companies represented the largest early foreign investments in Tianjin, excluding the Kailuan mines.[14]

While foreign trade and its ancillary services grew steadily, the total foreign investment in Tianjin industry remained small. In Shanghai, foreign investment in industry provided a stimulus to industrial development in general, especially between 1895 and 1905. This was not true in Tianjin. Before 1914 there were only about 20 foreign-owned factories in the city. Most were small press-packing plants, owned by the trading firms, which cleaned wool for export.[15] Between World War I and the mid-1930's, foreigners continued to confine most of their industrial investment to export-processing. They owned several large egg factories, which sorted and sometimes froze eggs for export. Both foreign and Chinese firms were active in nut-sorting. Foreigners were active buyers in the carpet trade after World War I, but only occasionally supervised production themselves.

The only significant exceptions to this pattern of small-scale enterprise, little modern machinery, and processing for export were the Tianjin branch of the British and American Tobacco Company and the Japanese-owned Dong Ya tobacco plant. The Kailuan Mines, which were the major foreign investment in modern industry in North China, had corporate headquarters in Tianjin but the operations were in Tangshan.[16]

This investment pattern changed dramatically in the mid-1930's, when Japanese firms began to buy up ailing Chinese-owned cotton mills. By 1936, Japanese controlled most Tianjin mills, thus suddenly acquiring a dominant position in local industry. In 1937, Japanese enterprises accounted for just over half the total industrial capital invested in Tianjin. Native investment was a close second, with other foreign nationals investing only negligible amounts. But even with this influx of Japanese money into cotton spinning, foreign investment in Tianjin on the eve of World War II remained concentrated in finance and trade.[17]

Chinese Investors

Not all Tianjin investors were foreign; the local economy also had its native entrepreneurs. Most of them were members of the political elite, first Qing officials and later Republican warlords. Perhaps because of Tianjin's proximity to Beijing, the national capital until 1928, this official presence was uniquely strong in North China. Officials sponsored, built, and frequently managed many of Tianjin's industrial enterprises. The fact that Tianjin's modern industry took shape under bureaucratic aegis distinguished Tianjin from other major treaty ports and had significant implications for the course of the city's development.

Official involvement afforded Tianjin industry a modicum of protection, but also made it uniquely vulnerable. Tianjin factories were tied to the changing political fortunes of a shifting group of patrons. Enterprises could tumble with the so-called foreign affairs clique, vanish with Yuan Shikai, or lose their source of capital when a friendly local warlord investor lost his satrapy. The warlords in particular had only an ephemeral interest in industry, and were quite willing to put their money elsewhere when industrial investment seemed too risky. At the same time Chinese merchants, who under other circumstances might have become the core of a native capitalist class, never diverted a significant amount of their wealth from commerce to factory production.

Official Enterprises

After Tianjin became a treaty port, the Qing government deployed some of its most able officials to Tianjin to take charge of foreign affairs as well as local administration. For the first time in its history Tianjin became a nationally significant center of political activity.

Particularly after the 1870 appointment of Li Hongzhang as Governor-General of Zhili, the city also became a giant laboratory for experiments by the "foreign affairs clique" of the national government. In his quarter-century in Tianjin, Li supervised the building of Tianjin's infrastructure and sponsored industrial enterprises that were large and complex even by international standards. He sponsored the opening of the nearby Kaiping Mines, as well as a shipyard at Dagu, a telegraph bureau, a mint, and Tianjin's first railroad. Some of these were run exclusively by officials. Others, like the railroad and the telegraph bureau, had significant official involvement as well as merchant capital or participation.[18]

Li Hongzhang's main venture into manufacturing was the Tianjin Arsenal (Tianjin jiqi ju), which had been founded in 1866. He presided over its five expansions. Completely funded by the Qing government, the arsenal produced gunpowder, bullets, mines, machines, and even steel. One of its two divisions was located just south of the walled city at Haiguansi, about three miles due east of the city, on the other side of the Hai River. In its heyday it had 2,000 workers, some of them skilled craftsmen recruited from Guangdong and Shanghai. The demand for construction material and fuel generated by an enterprise of this size stimulated other self-strengthening projects. The arsenal was a major customer for the Kaiping coal mines, which were government-sponsored and privately run. It also needed cement, and the forerunner of one of North China's biggest companies, the Qixin Cement Company, was founded to help meet that need.[19]

The arsenal was the largest modern industrial enterprise in Tianjin before 1900, and had a concentration of workers and a sophistication of facilities that Tianjin was not to see again for many years. Whether it might eventually have helped stimulate the development of modern capitalist enterprise is a moot question. It was destroyed during the Boxer uprising in 1900. So complete was the arsenal's disappearance that most Tianjin residents born in the twentieth century have grown up not even knowing that Tianjin ever had such a large enterprise.[20]

Political instability, a recurrent phenomenon in the modern history of Tianjin, undermined both the official class and the institutions it had built. Yet despite their brief tenure, late Qing officials were directly responsible for the "Golden Age" of Tianjin's modern industry.[21] In the late nineteenth century Tianjin had an estimated 5,000 enterprise workers, a level that after the Boxer debacle was not to be realized again for several decades.

In the aftermath of the Boxer Rebellion, the Zhili provincial economy was a shambles. As the newly appointed Governor-General and Commissioner of Trade for the northern ports, Yuan Shikai moved effectively and ruthlessly to remedy this situation and to consolidate his power in the area. Under his administration the commercial economy of Tianjin began to recover, new municipal services appeared, and a modern police force and schools were founded.[22]

At the same time, Yuan appointed one of his subordinates, Zhou Xuexi, to head a new provincial Bureau of Industries. Zhou's avowed aim was to encourage local gentry and merchants to invest in industry. He sponsored a number of small model factories, training students from the countryside in the production of paper, iron, soap, textiles, glass, and toothpowder. Most of the factories, however, used handicraft methods and were intended to train apprentices in techniques appropriate to rural production, rather than restoring Tianjin to the scale of modern industrial production it had known before the Boxers.[23] Like Li Hongzhang's earlier enterprises, some of Zhou's factories were run by officials, whereas others were officially supervised and privately managed. But Zhou did not succeed in keeping merchants interested in industrial production, because he and Yuan were not willing to provide investment guarantees or share decision-making power. After Yuan left Tianjin in 1907, his economic reform program evaporated.[24]

Zhou became Finance Minister in several Republican cabinets and went on to help found, reorganize, or run most of the large enterprises in North China. His financial interests included the Luanzhou Mines, the Qixin Cement Company, several banks, and the Hua Xin Cotton Mills. His prominent quasi-official role in Tianjin industry—and his failure to enlist lasting merchant participation—are testimony to the strengths and weaknesses of an industrial sector sponsored by government officials.

Warlord Investments

In the years between the regime of Yuan Shikai and the Guomindang unification (1916–28), a dizzying succession of independent militarists or warlords occupied Tianjin, including Wu Peifu, Zhang Zuolin, Li Jinglin, and Feng Yuxiang.[25] Tianjin was also a favorite residence of warlords in defeat or retirement. Whether they were in or out of power, many of them chose Tianjin as a place to invest their considerable personal fortunes—the fruits of taxation in the territories they controlled.

These warlords invested most of their wealth not in industry, but in land and urban real estate. Several of them were among the city's biggest landlords. They were also its most active builders, constructing dwellings for rent as well as palatial retreats, in both Chinese and European style, for themselves and their families. Significant sums of warlord money went into gold, jewelry, pawnshops, native banks, foreign banks, grain shops, and of course the munitions trade.

Warlords first became interested in industry during World War I, when profits on industrial investment rose. Many warlords first invested in industries whose products went to the military, such as the manufacture of uniforms, dried food, and saddles. Those warlords who had official government positions used them to obtain tax exemptions and low railroad rates for their products. Soon, however, the warlords were attracted to two lucrative sectors that became the core of Tianjin's modern industry—cotton spinning and flour milling. Between 1914 and 1925, more than 40 percent of the new factories in Tianjin had warlords involved in their founding; they provided more than half the new capital invested. The flour milling industry had substantial warlord investment in six of 11 mills. The largest single investor in industry was Anhui warlord Ni Sichong, who put a total of eight million yuan (equivalent to approximately four million dollars in gold) into a cotton mill, a paint factory, and several flour mills. The money invested by this one man was almost twice the *total* amount invested in Tianjin industry between 1895 and 1914.[26]

Yet the political instability wrought by the incessant fighting between warlords undermined their own attempts to make money from industrial investment. By the early 1920's all industrial enterprises were affected by civil war. Heavy exactions levied by competing warlord governments discouraged trade and disrupted the market for industrial goods. Goods piled up, and even when there was an empty freight car available, merchants had to pay three to four times the prescribed price to get the military to move them.[27] These factors, combined with heavy taxation by the Guomindang after 1934 and the effects of the worldwide Depression, were among the causes of Tianjin's perpetual industrial crisis most frequently cited by contemporary analysts.

Warlords had financed a substantial part of Tianjin's only significant pre-1949 industrial boom. Then, having helped create the conditions under which industrial profits plummeted, they proceeded to switch their money out of industry and into more profitable (and time-honored) lines of investment.[28] Even at the height of their interest in industry, their financial commitment was only a fraction of the amount they invested in land and urban real estate. They needed steady profits to finance their quests for power; the instability caused by these quests for power made it impossible for industry to provide those profits.

Merchant Participation

Officials and warlords used their political power, however erratically, to develop Tianjin industry. The Chinese merchant community, which also accumulated large concentrations of wealth, might have been expected to provide another source of industrial investment. In fact, merchants were even less inclined than warlords to direct their money to industry. The majority preferred traditional avenues of investment, while the most enterprising tried to break into the foreign-controlled sector of international trade.

The oldest group of Tianjin merchants was known in local parlance as the "eight great families" (*ba da jia*). The term referred primarily to salt merchants, but also to others who had made fortunes dealing in land, grain, or shipping. Membership in this group changed over time, but all who belonged had substantial capital to invest. Salt merchants, for instance, could only reinvest a limited amount of their profits in the salt business since their dealings were limited by government-imposed quotas.

Like the warlords, Tianjin's wealthy merchants usually kept their money in land, native banks, pawnshops, private stores of gold and silver, and such items of conspicuous consumption as elaborate funerals, gambling, and fighting insects. A few families maintained private troupes of acrobats so they could perform, to the greater glory of their patrons, in the annual procession of the Heavenly Empress. Merchants also invested in commercial enterprises like cloth shops, jewelry stores, medicine shops, and breweries. In the twentieth century some of them also opened handicraft workshops that made military uniforms, towels, and other textile products. But they very rarely put money into factory production, unless it was an occasional project of the ubiquitous Zhou Xuexi or a minor investment in a flour mill. The only significant exception was the Bao Cheng Spinning Mill, which attracted capital from merchants involved in the yarn and cloth trade.[29]

A second group of Tianjin merchants were compradores, the Chinese employees of foreign trading firms.[30] The earliest Tianjin compradores were recruited from Ningbo and Guangzhou, where foreign firms had already been active for some time. Later, local people also joined the ranks of Tianjin compradores.[31] Compradores made commissions that might be as high as 20 percent of the value of a transaction, and by the late nineteenth century the most successful of them were rivaling the salt merchants for the status of richest people in town. Tianjin's four wealthiest compradores (at Jardine, Matheson, Butterfield and Swire, the Russo-Asiatic Bank, and the Hong Kong and Shanghai Banking Corporation) amassed fortunes as large as 20 million yuan.[32] Only one of the four, however, chose to invest in industry. Wu Maoding, the compradore for the Hong Kong and Shanghai Bank, had close ties with the "foreign affairs clique." Perhaps this official connection accounts for his early interest in industry. Prior to 1900 he was responsible for the founding of three of Tianjin's four private factories—a match factory, a tannery, and a woollen mill.[33]

Later compradores did not follow Wu's lead, choosing instead to put their money into real estate in the foreign concessions. During the warlord conflicts, only the concessions were regarded as really safe territory. The influx of wealthy Chinese into the area created a real estate boom that yielded speculative profits much higher than those from industrial ventures. Compradores were quick to capitalize on this situation. During World War I and the 1920's compradores, armed with experience and connections, opened their own import-export firms and did direct business with foreign companies. Their connections with foreign firms also aided them in establishing a number of small export-processing factories, the products of which were purchased by foreign trading firms.[34]

Compradores remained important in Tianjin economic life right up to 1949. They invested in commerce, lent money to native banks and merchants, and invested in pawnshops. But unlike their Shanghai brethren, Tianjin compradores after Wu Maoding never funded large-scale industrial production. One Chinese historian has argued that this was because Shanghai compradores built up their wealth gradually over a long period of time, while Tianjin compradores were parvenus (*baofahu*) who made and spent their money quickly.[35] Whether or not this is true, compradores were economically astute and adaptive enough to maintain their status through many political changes. Perhaps it was this very astuteness which led them to shun manufacturing ventures in an environment that rewarded trade and speculative activities rather than long-term industrial investment.

VANISHING OWNERS AND MELTING SPINDLES: THE CASE OF COTTON

The absence of a stable group of industrialists, a problem both caused and compounded by the political instability of North China, meant that local industry grew in erratic fits and starts. Nowhere is this more clear than in the case of Tianjin's largest mechanized industry, cotton spinning.[36] In its bid to become a cotton center of national stature, Tianjin had several advantages: a local class of moneyed investors, access to raw materials, and a large market. Changes in the political scene brought in new entrepreneurs and gave the mills at least three opportunities to flourish—during World War I, in the late 1930's, and immediately after the Allied victory in World War II. But in each case chronic warfare, as well as government policies that sometimes verged on the cannibalistic, ultimately made it impossible for the industry to prosper.

In the years after World War I, most of the Tianjin cotton mills were founded with the sponsorship of specific official or warlord cliques. Four of the mills were built at the southeastern edge of the concessions; two were north of the old city. Cao Kun, of the Fengtian warlord clique, was a major investor in the Heng Yuan Mill. The Yu Yuan Mill was dominated by the Anfu warlord clique. Its largest single stockholder was Ni Sichong (1.1 million yuan), and its original Board of Directors included Ni, Duan Qirui, and various high officials. Zhou Xuexi's Hua Xin Mill and the Yu Da Mill were other attractive targets for warlord investment.[37]

But after several years of profitable operation in the early 1920's, the mills fell victim to a number of problems. In 1922, and continuously from 1926 to 1929, a series of internecine warlord conflicts disrupted the transportation system so that cotton from the interior could not reach Tianjin, pushing raw cotton prices up. The cotton that did reach the market was heavily taxed by successive warlord governments, in spite of merchant and manufacturer protests. The perpetual state of civil war had indirect effects on the industry as well. Because of drought, war, and lack of government encouragement, cotton production fell steadily throughout Hebei after 1919. The impoverishment of a populace victimized by marauding armies limited the market for cotton goods. Finally, mills with warlord patronage like the Heng Yuan lost their financing when their sponsors suffered military or political reversals.[38]

The postwar resumption of foreign trade activity in the early 1920's further complicated the economic situation of the mills. When European merchants began once again to purchase Chinese raw cotton, the price received a further boost, making it more difficult for the local mills to obtain raw cotton.[39] At the same time imported cotton yarn and cloth found their way back onto the Chinese market, competing with a native product that was often inferior in quality. Shanghai yarn also crowded the local product off the Tianjin market. After 1926 each of the six mills began to show consistent losses, and by 1927 the national Chinese Cotton Millowners Association was complaining publicly that problems with transport, excessive taxation, and depressed demand for yarn caused by the years of civil war were combining to undermine the nascent industry.[40] The situation worsened after 1930, a year pinpointed by Chinese analysts as the transition from "chronic to acute crisis."[41] The cost of raw cotton continued to climb as the selling price of cotton yarn dropped, so that Tianjin mills lost 27 yuan on every bale of yarn they sold.[42]

Foreign competition put Chinese mills at a disadvantage. The products of Japanese cotton mills entered the Chinese market both legally through Tianjin and illegally through smuggling in eastern Hebei. Better capitalized than the Chinese mills, Japanese enterprises could afford to dump their wares at depressed prices in order to maintain and expand their share of the market. Japanese-owned mills on Chinese soil enjoyed similar advantages, as well as freedom from import duties. By spring 1934, Japanese and Shanghai yarn had taken over the Gaoyang handloom-weaving market. Finally, the Japanese invasion of Manchuria in 1931 denied an important market to Chinese mills, while Japanese mills sold their products there with ease.[43]

Domestic taxation imposed by the new Guomindang government compounded the problem. Because the consolidated tax *(tongshui)* did not differentiate between yarns of widely varying value, the Japanese, who specialized in higher-count (finer) yarns, paid almost the same amount in taxes as the Chinese producers of much cheaper, lower-count yarns. In addition, the revised 1934 tariff actually reduced the amount of duty levied on imported cotton piece goods, while duties rose on raw cotton and textile machinery needed by Chinese manufacturers. Local taxes on the cotton trade, so troublesome in the 1920's, continued to be a problem, especially after 1931 when the city had to raise revenue to meet new military expenses because of the Japanese threat.[44]

Tianjin mills were also technically inferior to foreign and foreign-owned mills. One writer estimated that for a factory of 10,000 spindles, a Chinese owner had to hire as many as 400 laborers, while a Japanese owner could make do with 120–50.[45] Managers could not afford to repair or replace outmoded equipment; the lack of funds could in turn be traced directly to the fact that most Chinese-owned mills were small joint-stock companies that had to pay annual dividends of about 10 percent on their bonds. Without sufficient funds to reinvest in their equipment, most went deeply into debt at high rates of interest in order to finance their expansion and to provide themselves with adequate circulating capital.[46]

Behind the dilapidated equipment and mounting debts was a management structure that, as economist H. D. Fong noted in 1932, was "polluted by ignorance, favoritism, and squeeze." Fong criticized the inefficiency of mills

established by inexperienced men who were attracted solely by the magnetism of huge profits during the War period. . . . The whole plant, worth millions of dollars, may be entrusted to a manager who knows nothing about spinning. The latter, usually the trusted appointee of the most influential stockholder, has frequently neither a grasp of the technical complexity of spinning and weaving, nor a knowledge of cost accounting, financing and marketing. Instead, he delegates his duties to the subordinates, and relies upon the good turn of luck for the mill's profits. In such a mill, the head of the spinning or weaving department, oftentimes a close friend or relative of the manager or the stockholder, considers his job as a source of squeeze, but delegates in turn his duties to one of the foremen who, although skilled in mechanics, lacks scientific training. Consequently, machinery is not well-kept, and is not running in an efficient order. Laborers are not well selected and trained, but recruited under the notorious contract system. The finished products deteriorate in quality, while their cost mounts higher and higher.[47]

By 1934 most of the Tianjin mills were near collapse.[48] At the same time, Tianjin quickly emerged as the key link in Japanese plans to establish "a great cotton center in North China." Japanese firms initially expanded their share in Tianjin textile manufacturing by purchasing mills that had been forced to close. Construction of new mills was under way as well, in the old cotton mill district southeast of the concessions. By early 1937 only three mills remained in Chinese hands: the Da Sheng, Heng Yuan, and Bei Yang.[49]

Four new mills were constructed in the first three years of Japanese rule. By the end of 1938 there were 462,000 spindles operating in Tianjin, an increase of 59 percent in 18 months.[50] Before the occupation, no mills in Tianjin had been able to spin yarn finer than 60-count; the Japanese installed machines that spun much finer yarn. Weaving capacity expanded from 2,500 to 7,800 looms. The market for Tianjin yarn and cloth widened as a result of North China's new stability. In 1938 four Tianjin mills (Kotai #6 and #7, Yu Feng, and Heng Yuan) were selling cloth principally in Hebei, but also in Shandong, Shanxi, Chahaer, Suiyuan, Henan, and central China. From 1937 to 1940 the Bei Yang Mill reported the most prosperous years since its founding. Optimistic government reports predicted an increase to 680,000 spindles by 1946.[51]

These sanguine projections, of course, were never realized. Although the period of expansion continued until 1940, by the later part of World War II the industry was in trouble. The growth of the Communist-controlled Liberated Areas surrounding Tianjin made it more difficult to obtain raw material, and available cotton was increasingly claimed by the Japanese Occupation government.[52] During the final years of the Japanese war effort, both Chinese and Japanese mills in Tianjin were forced to contribute iron to the military by melting down part of their equipment. The Bei Yang Mill "donated" more than a third of its spindle capacity, while most Japanese-owned mills met the same fate. The Yu Da Mill was converted into an alcohol factory. Only two Tianjin mills, the Yu Feng and the Shanghai, escaped the meltdown edict because of their connections within the Japanese government. At war's end four of the Japanese mills had stopped work, while four others operated at a fraction of their former capacity. Among the Chinese mills, the Bei Yang was closed and the Heng Yuan was operating at a reduced capacity. The city's total spindle capacity rose to about 506,000 in 1942, then declined because of iron "contributions" to about 407,400 by war's end. Of these, only about 28,000, as well as 1,000 looms, were actually in operation in 1945.[53]

Immediately after the Japanese surrender, the Executive Yuan of the Nationalist government organized the China Textile Industries Corporation to take over and run the mills that had belonged to the Japanese. A branch office was established at Tianjin in December 1945, and eventually the Corporation took control of seven cotton mills as well as a number of related establishments. Only the Heng Yuan and Bei Yang mills were returned to private control.[54] As an almost wholly government-owned industry during this period, the cotton mills escaped the worst of government pressure, and their machines were in no danger of being moved south or sold for scrap like those of many private factories. Cotton textile manufacturing dominated the city's industrial sector even more clearly than it had before the war. At the end of 1947, production of textiles accounted for 64 percent of the city's total industrial output.[55]

In spite of government patronage, however, the mills faced serious problems. The first of these was the damage suffered in the final years of the war. "When the various mills were taken over," the Corporation's annual report noted in 1946, "the machinery was mostly in great disrepair and the buildings were in a dilapidated state." The mills continued to be plagued by a lack of spare parts, a shortage of trained workers, and ineffective quality control.[56]

By mid-1948 the textile industry was forced to obtain about 80 percent of its raw cotton abroad, since the growth of the Liberated Areas had cut off access to Hebei cotton. Mills were also hindered by frequent power stoppages, which in one mill totaled more than 1,617 hours in 1947. Inflation was another pervasive problem. The total expenditures for Cotton Mill #4 (formerly the Shanghai Mill) for wages, manufacturing costs, and "business expenses" (*chang wu*) rose in 1927 from 992 million yuan in January to more than 17 billion yuan in December. After the conversion to "gold certificates" (*jinyuan quan*) in August 1948, it cost more than 900 "gold dollars" to produce one *jian* (181.44 kilograms) of yarn. Yet the official price ceiling set by the government was 707 "gold dollars," making it impossible, just as it had been in the early 1930's, for mills to sell their product at a profit.[57] Under these circumstances textile manufacturers, like most of the Tianjin population, were forced to speculate on the black market. Cloth, in particular, was used as a substitute for currency by many Tianjin residents to buy goods, pay rent, or lend and borrow money. The center for speculation in textiles was an alley off Haerbin Road, where 5,000–6,000 bolts of cloth changed hands every day. Since mills could sell 50 percent of their product as they pleased, much of it found its way to Haerbin Road.[58]

The final blow to the industry came when the government cut the city's supply of imported raw cotton from the United States from 668,000 piculs in 1947 to less than half that amount in 1948. By the end of 1948 the mills of Tianjin, the pride of the city's industrial sector for three decades, were operating only three days a week. At Liberation there was only enough cotton for ten days' spinning on hand in the city's storehouses.[59]

In the three decades from the founding of the cotton mills until 1949, three sets of investors with close ties to the political power structure of North China took over the Tianjin cotton mills. In each case, their interest in manufacturing was soon subordinated to the requirements of political survival. The cotton mills, like all Tianjin industry, became a resource to be milked for profits, taxed, dismantled, and ultimately abandoned as one ephemeral class of industrial patrons succeeded another.

CONCLUSION

Until 1949, trade dominated the Tianjin economy, and the foreigners dominated trade, since they could draw on financial and political resources far more substantial than those available to their Chinese counterparts. Chinese gained an independent foothold in trade only when, as during World War I, the foreign presence decreased.

Crudely put, undertakings that foreigners chose to spend their money on flourished, and those that they neglected foundered. Modern industry, except during a brief period in the late 1930's, fell into the latter category.

Tianjin's failure to attract foreign industrial investment that could rival Shanghai's can be partly explained by Tianjin's later opening as a treaty port, but other factors were important as well. Foreigners who came to North China were primarily interested in exporting raw materials from Tianjin's hinterland. The native products they purchased in Tianjin were all inexpensive and after processing could yield a high rate of profit. For- eigners had little incentive to invest capital in something that required elaborate facilities, when a warehouse with a baling machine or a few tables for sorting nuts was so lucrative. Continual political troubles in Tianjin's hinterland throughout the twentieth century slowed even this limited activity.

Furthermore, until the Chinese government regained tariff autonomy in 1929, it was financially advantageous for foreigners to import manufac- tured goods rather than producing them in Tianjin. They did invest in ex- tractive industries like the Kailuan Mines, but investment in factory in- dustry was constrained by some of the same factors that slowed Tianjin's development as a port: inadequate infrastructure and political instability.

For other parts of China, it has been argued that foreign control of fac- tory industry hindered the development of native manufactures. In the case of Tianjin, where there was little foreign industrial investment until the 1930's, the impact of imperialism was not manifested in direct compe- tition between local foreign and Chinese factories.[60] Yet the substantial for- eign presence in Tianjin influenced industry in a number of other ways. Foreign political intervention at the time of the Boxer Rebellion was re-

sponsible for the destruction of Tianjin's earliest large-scale factories. Foreign imports, bolstered by a favorable tax structure, undoubtedly hurt the
market for some Chinese goods.[61] It was only during World War I, when
the local market was briefly freed from foreign import competition, that
Tianjin manufacturing emerged.

In a trading pattern where manufactured goods were imported and agricultural and pastoral goods exported, the first industries to develop concentrated on the small-scale, labor-intensive processing of exports. When
Chinese entrepreneurs began to build larger factories after World War I,
they were dependent upon foreign sources for parts, machines, and sometimes raw material. Market fluctuations and price manipulations were
enough to push many a nascent factory under. To the extent also that foreigners developed a financial infrastructure that was capable of attracting
Chinese capital—for instance, when warlords made large deposits in foreign banks—it might be argued that foreigners diverted funds that might
otherwise have been invested in industry. Of course, the factors making
foreign banks safe and industrial investments risky were not all traceable
to foreigners. In sum, the effect of the foreign presence on Tianjin industry was substantial, but less direct than it was in regions of China where
foreigners controlled production.

Various groups of Chinese investors, official and private, also invested
in industry, but their efforts were ephemeral. Many of these investors were
tied to political elites whose tenure in power was short. Of all the Chinese
investors, warlords were the most involved in industrial production. Yet
their economic investment and their political style were ultimately at odds
with each other. They squeezed the banks that could have financed their
factories, taxed both industry and the consumer, and disrupted the raw
material supply and marketing of products with their wars. In the 1920's,
they were largely responsible for the troubles that made Tianjin's hinterland a much less satisfactory market than Shanghai's in the lower Yangzi.
Warlords were, at best, an inconstant friend to Tianjin industry.

Tianjin never developed an independent native capitalist class with an
interest in industry. Northern investors after Yuan Shikai had only a dim
appreciation of industrialization as a road to "wealth and power"; they
were more concerned with getting uniforms to their troops and money
into their own coffers. They were attracted to industry only as long as it
paid high dividends, and since they ran the factories in addition to funding
them, they often upped the dividends to compete with those offered by
commercial investments.

Nevertheless, industry never successfully competed with the older avenues of investment familiar to the political elite. Political instability helped

create an environment that consistently rewarded short-term speculative investment; manufacturing remained a high-risk enterprise. The result was a shortage of both fixed and circulating capital in industry, and a consequent vulnerability to financial crises. Undercapitalization was a persistent feature of the Tianjin industrial scene, and was cited by many contemporary analysts as the most important nonpolitical cause of the perpetual crisis in Tianjin industry.[62]

Throughout the treaty port period, plagued by political instability, ruled by a succession of masters, the Tianjin economy grew fitfully. Its hinterland remained unstable and only tenuously connected to the city throughout the Japanese occupation and the civil war period. The growth of the Liberated Areas in the 1940's only exacerbated the city's problems. The instability and fragmentation of the urban economy mirrored the instability and fragmentation of its ruling classes. In turn, the particular behavior of those ruling classes had important implications for the development of the working class.

Precisely because no group of Chinese investors stayed interested in industry for very long, none of them developed the kinds of managerial practices familiar to more experienced capitalists. Tianjin's large factories, superficially mechanized and "modern," were run with backward techniques of production and management in a system based on old-style connections. This affected the structure of hiring, the organization of work, and the methods used by inexperienced capitalists to impose factory discipline on equally inexperienced workers.

For foreigners and Chinese alike, interest in industry was subordinate to investment in other activities. Industry remained the occasional plaything of Tianjin's economically and politically powerful classes. A search for the working people of Tianjin must not be confined to the few mechanized factories, with their fickle and changing owners. It must also include the warehouses where exports were processed and the many handicraft workshops run by petty entrepreneurs who came to Tianjin from the Hebei countryside. It should not ignore the transport workers who hauled raw and finished goods to and from the factories. It must, in short, explore the varieties as well as the commonalities of work in a complex occupational structure, one shaped by the crisis-ridden and fragmented Tianjin economy.

CHAPTER THREE

Varieties of Work and Working Life

Like the city of Tianjin itself, local industry grew in a rapid and disorderly fashion in the twentieth century. Tianjin manufacturing did not develop in a neat historical progression from household to workshop to modern mill. Instead, all three types of production emerged simultaneously, with each of them sometimes helping to spur the others' growth.

This growth was most obvious in the modern manufacturing sector. Tianjin's six large cotton mills, six mechanized flour mills, four match factories, and two large cigarette plants were almost all built during and after World War I. Their raw red-brick structures transformed the skyline along the Hai River. Factory dormitories and clusters of hastily built housing began to create new working-class neighborhoods in outlying districts of the city. In the 1920's Tianjin bid fair to become North China's major manufacturing center.

Yet these modern factories by no means typified the Tianjin working environment. A large number of tiny workshops produced goods using handicraft or semi-mechanized methods. Iron tools and machine parts, carpets, figured cloth, and knitted hose were only a few of the products of these handicraft shops. The workshops were not remnants of an older artisanal sector; like the large factories, they were products of the 1920's economic boom.

In addition to the factory operatives and artisans employed in these establishments, some industries relied on casual laborers and outworkers. Many of these workers were women and children. Export-processing warehouses hired casual workers to sort eggs and wool or to crack walnuts. Match factories used sophisticated chemical processes to produce matchsticks, but employed female and child labor to glue the matchboxes (at home) and pack them by hand (in the workshop). Women outworkers were employed to spin wool for sale to carpet factories, make wreaths, weave mats, and sew military uniforms for the troops of each new warlord who arrived in Tianjin. Frequently the children of these women, or their younger siblings, worked alongside them for a minuscule piece rate.

Since these workers were hired on a casual or seasonal basis, they often were not counted as part of the working population in occupational surveys. But a significant percentage of Tianjin's "industrial" laborers were outworkers who never saw the inside of a large or mechanized factory. Like the artisans, their ranks were swelled by the growth of factory production.

Finally, Tianjin remained primarily a trading port, and large numbers of its workers were engaged in loading and unloading ships and hauling goods from one end of the expanding city to the other. The transport sector was the link between commerce and industry. Transport workers were divided into two groups: members of hereditary corporatist guilds dating from the early Qing dynasty, and a much larger number of rickshaw pullers and riverbank coolies who worked on an irregular basis.[1]

Workers, however broadly defined, constituted a small but increasing fraction of the Tianjin population: 3.4 percent in 1929, 11 percent in 1938, 13 percent in 1947. They were the second largest occupational group in the city; only the percentage of people employed in commerce was consistently greater (14 percent in 1938 and 16 percent in 1947). Transport workers constituted an additional 4–5 percent of the population, more if rickshaw pullers and itinerant coolies are included. The actual percentage of workers was even higher than these figures indicate, because those characterized as "not involved in production"—more than half the population—included many casual laborers as well as nonworking dependents (see Figure 1 and Table 1).

The Tianjin working class, then, included artisans, freight haulers, and casual laborers as well as factory hands. Most were newcomers to the city, but their employment niche varied with their gender, age, native place, and connections. They inhabited a diversity of living environments as well. Artisans usually left their families in the countryside and lived in their workshops, whereas factory workers frequently brought their families with them to find jobs in Tianjin as casual laborers.

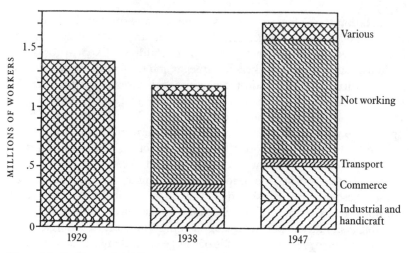

Fig. 1. Tianjin Occupational Structure, 1929–1947

Yet for all their diversity, the workers of Tianjin had much in common with one another. The development of Tianjin industry is not easily characterized by dichotomies like "preindustrial/industrial" or "traditional/modern." All the sectors of Tianjin industry were products of the treaty port era; none except transport had a long history in Tianjin. (For this reason, transport workers are treated separately in Chapter 5 below.) Workers never streamed out of outmoded workshops into more modern centers of production. Rather, as each sector grew, it drew workers from the nearby Hebei peasantry. To most peasant immigrants, all the work environments of Tianjin were new. Yet even the largest mills retained many features of the village environment. Just where a peasant ended up in this complex industrial structure had a great deal to do with village-based connections.

Furthermore, no matter what kind of workplace they entered, Tianjin workers found their employment precarious. Many came fleeing the economic and political uncertainties of their North China villages, but the city offered them scant refuge. Even the largest mills were vulnerable to sudden closings; for artisans and casual laborers, steady work was even more elusive. Life in any sector of the working class was life on the margin. It was always possible to tumble further down the social ladder: from factory worker to coolie, from millhand to prostitute. It was also possible to return to the villages of North China. Many workers did so on holidays, or when they married, fell ill, or lost their jobs—until natural disasters and

TABLE I
Tianjin Occupational Structure, 1929–1947

	1929		1938		1947	
Category	No. of workers	Pct. of total	No. of workers	Pct. of total	No. of workers	Pct. of total
Industrial and handicraft	47,519	3.4%	131,543	11.1%	229,833	13.4%
Commerce	—	—	166,598	14.0	283,311	16.5
Transport	—	—	60,839	5.1	65,118	3.8
Not working[a]	—	—	742,076	62.5	994,225	58.0
Other[b]	1,343,602	96.6	85,474	7.2	143,047	8.3
TOTAL	1,391,121	100.0%	1,186,530	100.0%	1,715,534	100.0%

SOURCES: 1929, *Chinese Economic Journal and Bulletin*, 20, No. 3 (March 1937); *Nankai Weekly Statistical Service*, 3, No. 17 (April 28, 1930), 81, 85–86. 1938, Tianjin tebie gongshu, *Tianjin tebie shi gongshu 27 nian xingzheng jiyao* (Government Office of the Special Municipality of Tianjin, administrative summary, 1938), Vol. II (Tianjin, 1938). 1947, Tianjin shi zhengfu tongjichu bian, *Tianjin shi zhuyao tongji ziliao shouce—dierhao: gongshang zhuanhao* (Handbook of major statistical materials for Tianjin—No. 2: special number on industry and commerce) (Tianjin: Tianjin shi zhengfu tongji chu bianyin, 1948), 1.
[a] Includes students, nonworking family members, criminals, welfare cases, and unemployed.
[b] Includes civil servants, professionals, and service workers.

war damaged the rural economy and cut it off from the cities. Although the working class as a whole was essential to Tianjin, individual workers were dispensable; they were short-term city dwellers by choice or necessity.

ARTISAN INDUSTRIES

The artisanal workshops of Tianjin were usually small, often employing fewer than 30 workers and almost always fewer than 100.[2] In these work-shops most tasks were performed without the use of power machinery; the level of capitalization per worker was low. More than 60 percent of Tianjin workers labored in this type of shop (see Table 2). Artisans, virtually all of them male, learned their trades by serving an apprenticeship in one of these shops. They came from the countryside, lived in their place of work (sometimes literally sleeping by their machines), and returned to their villages regularly, if infrequently.

In 1929, Tianjin's major artisanal industries were cotton and rayon weaving, cloth-bleaching, machine-making, carpet weaving, hosiery knit-ting, and ironworking. Together they accounted for less than 3 percent of the total investment in Tianjin industry, but they employed almost 20,000 people, or more than 40 percent of Tianjin workers (see Table 3).[3]

The artisanal sector of Tianjin industry did not have a long tradition. Most artisanal workshops were founded in the decade after World War I.[4]

TABLE 2
Amount of Investment per Worker in Yuan, 1929

Industry	Yuan per worker	Pct. all Tianjin workers
More than 1,000 yuan		
Flour milling	3,922	1.42%
Salt making (Tanggu)	3,854[a]	1.15
Soda making (Tanggu)	3,498[a]	1.21
Cotton spinning	1,250	35.35
Table oil/soy	1,243	.05
N = 18,618 workers		39.18%
500–999 yuan		
Match making	765	4.29%
Brewing and distilling	631	1.02
Soap making	599	.50
Hygienic cotton	525	.06
N = 2,793 workers		5.88%
400–499 yuan	0	0
300–399 yuan		
Cotton blanket weaving	304	.41%
N = 197 workers		.41%
200–299 yuan		
Aerated water	277	.15%
Mat weaving	250	.57
Gauze making	250	.17
Printing	217	.86
Cement and chinaware	208	.22
Paste making (1 worker)	200	.002
Painted cloth (3 workers)	200	.006
N = 940 workers		1.98%

Less than 200 yuan: mirror making (179), silk and cotton ribbon weaving (154), toilet articles (150), tanning (149), canned food (140), candle making (128), canvas weaving (115), buttons (111), oil (burning) (93), thread spools (80), rayon weaving (79), hatmaking (74), stationery (63), machinery (61), glassware (57), bleaching (57), miscellaneous (55), woollen yarn weaving (45), hosiery knitting (50), lampwick making (40), electroplating (38), dyeing and weaving (37), furring (35), towel weaving (35), intestines (34), battery making (33), cotton weaving (28), asbestos (27), coppersmith (26), wood and bamboo (19), braid weaving (17), carpet weaving (14), ironworks (10), bone and hornwork (4).[b]

N = 24,915 workers	52.43%[c]

SOURCES: Derived from Maxwell Stewart and Fu-an Fang, "A Statistical Study of Industry and Labor in China," *Chinese Economic Journal*, 7, No. 4 (Oct. 1930), 1085–87. Stewart and Fang's statistics are a corrected version of those collected by the Tianjin Bureau of Social Affairs (Tianjin shehui ju) in 1929 and printed, among other places, in Wu Ao, *Tianjin shi shehui ju tongji huikan* (A statistical issue of the Tianjin Bureau of Social Affairs) (Tianjin: Tianjin shehui ju, 1931), *passim*. The statistics collected by the Bureau were criticized by the Nankai University economist H. D. Fong for greatly underestimating the number of

Carpet weaving, for instance, did not become profitable until Western buyers were cut off from Near Eastern production during World War I. The industry showed steady growth throughout the 1920's.[5]

Artisanal industries frequently developed in conjunction with the more "modern" factory sector. Much of the handloom weaving done in small workshops, for instance, used cotton yarn spun in Tianjin's new mills.[6] Looms were made by local machine shops. The ironworking shops produced metal construction materials and tools for the construction of the treaty port. In each of these cases it was the new economic activity of treaty port Tianjin that created conditions for the development of handicraft industry.

Artisanal industries involved little capital investment, and were both responsive and vulnerable to economic fluctuations. When times were good, as they were in the mid-1920's, craftsmen founded new shops of their own, while established shopowners pooled their resources to open new branches. The most successful shopowners might even hope to become the owners of small factories. But Tianjin's unsettled political environment meant that times were frequently bad, although not all artisanal industries were equally affected.[7] In times of crisis, many shops closed outright. Others sent their craftsmen home but kept their unpaid apprentices. When master craftsmen in weaving, knitting, and carpets could no longer afford their own materials, they subcontracted work from larger establishments instead.[8] Although individual shops might close and whole branches of artisanal industry suffer, however, artisans as a group continued to make up roughly half the workforce until 1949.[9]

FACTORY INDUSTRIES

Tianjin's dualistic manufacturing sector also included a small number of large-scale modern factories. Almost 40 percent of all Tianjin workers were employed in enterprises capitalized at more than 1,000 yuan per worker (see Table 2). Cotton spinning, flour milling, match production, and cigarette manufacture were the most important of Tianjin's mecha-

carpet weavers and misestimating several other categories of handicraft workers. Fong, *Nankai Weekly Statistical Service*, 3, No. 42 (October 20, 1930), 201, 204.

NOTE: Percentages in the second column of figures do not total 100% because of rounding.

[a]Not included in the present study because of location in Tanggu, an hour's train ride from Tianjin.

[b]The actual amount of capital per worker may be slightly higher in some cases, since a total of 185 small workshops gave totals for number of workers, but not for capital investment.

[c]The number of handicraft workers in the smallest shops may have been even higher than 52%. Several industries (e.g. carpet weaving, hosiery knitting) were underestimated in this study, while others (e.g. shoemaking) were not included at all.

TABLE 3
Tianjin Occupational Structure, by Mechanized and Handicraft Sectors, 1929

Industry	No. of factories	Investment		Workers	
		Yuan	Pct. of total	No.	Pct. of total
Mechanized[a]					
Cotton spinning and weaving	6	20,990,000	67.2%	16,798	35.35%
Flour milling	5	2,655,000	8.5	677	1.42
Match making	4	1,560,000	4.9	2,040	4.29
SUBTOTAL	15	25,205,000	80.6%	19,515	41.06%
Handicraft[b]					
Cotton and rayon weaving	404/25	550,799	1.80%	8,575	18.00%
Bleaching	198/83	79,670	.26	1,404	2.95
Machinery	62/1	72,680	.23	1,197	2.51
Carpet weaving	161/8	69,867	.22	4,841	10.18
Hosiery knitting	78	64,662	.20	1,295	2.72
Ironworks	511/3	22,050	.07	2,207	4.64
SUBTOTAL	1,414/120	859,728	2.78%	19,519	41.00%
TOTAL[c]	2,186/185	31,226,944		47,519	

SOURCE: Derived from study by Stewart and Fang, cited in Table 2.

[a]Cigarette factories are not included in this survey.

[b]In column 1, figures on the left are for workshops that reported the amount of their investment; figures on the right represent nonreporting workshops.

[c]All industries were selected for line entries that had either >1,000 workers or >1 million yuan in investment. A saltworks and a soda factory were excluded from line entries (although not from the totals) because they were located in Tanggu.

nized industries. In 1929, the first three industries combined accounted for 80 percent of the city's industrial capital and slightly more than 40 percent of its workforce (see Table 3).

Of these industries, cotton spinning was by far the largest. By 1928, Tianjin's six cotton mills represented an investment of almost 21 million yuan and employed almost 17,000 people. The "Big Six" accounted for two-thirds of the industrial investment in the city, two-thirds of the motor power, and one-third of the manufacturing workforce. About four-fifths of the millhands were male adults, with the remainder of the workforce evenly divided between women and children. Women did not enter the Tianjin mills in large numbers until the Japanese occupation.[10]

Flour milling was the most intensely capitalized of all Tianjin industries, but employed far fewer people than the cotton mills. In 1932, the four mills operating had a combined capital of more than 2.5 million yuan and employed a total of about 600 people, virtually all of them male.[11] Match production, not nearly as well-capitalized as cotton or flour, was nevertheless a major employer. Together the two largest match factories employed 1,663 workers. Men made up almost nine-tenths of this workforce, with small numbers of women and children working in the plant itself. A far larger number of women and children were employed as outworkers and thus not counted in factory surveys.[12]

Most of the capital in the cotton, flour, and match factories came from Chinese investors. Cigarette manufacture was not included in the municipal surveys, perhaps because the two main cigarette factories were owned by foreigners. It was the only one of the four major factory industries that employed large numbers of women and girls from its inception.[13]

Most of these modern factories flourished briefly in the 1920's, then were decimated by renewed import competition, the burden of domestic taxation, warlord conflicts, and the world Depression. Their problems were aggravated by their inefficient managerial structure and low worker productivity. Of those modern plants which survived the stringent controls of eight years of Japanese occupation, many fell victim to inflation, extortion, and siege in the final hectic period of civil war that ended in 1949.[14]

ARTISANS AND FACTORY HANDS

The differences between the handicraft and the mechanized sectors in Tianjin at first glance seem far more striking than the similarities. Factory hands worked in plants with hundreds or even thousands of people, learned to operate large and dangerous machinery, and had to adapt to an impersonal system of factory discipline. Yet artisans and factory hands came from the same rural origins and used similar methods to find work. About three-quarters of each group were adult males. Children made up one-fifth of the factory workforce and 23 percent of the artisans. Until the cotton mills began to hire more women in the 1930's, the percentage of women in both factory and artisan sectors was small, perhaps as little as 5 and 2 percent, respectively, though women probably were undercounted.[15] Both factory workers and artisans frequently left their jobs; their ties to the villages were reinforced by marital arrangements, by regular trips home, and by the nature of hiring and the workplace in Tianjin itself.

Origins and Finding Work

Like Tianjin workers in almost every sector, artisans were recent migrants to the city from the villages of Hebei and Shandong. In hosiery knitting, carpet weaving, and handloom weaving, Tianjin natives were never more than 7 percent of the workforce, and usually they were 4 percent or less.[16]

While artisans came from dozens of rural counties, each industry seemed to draw clusters of workers from slightly different areas. A third of the carpet workers surveyed by Fong, for instance, came from Wuqing, Zaoqiang, and Shulu counties. Nangong and Wuqing natives together accounted for a quarter of all hosiery knitters. Ironworkers came from Jiaohe county.[17] The same counties that contributed large numbers of craftsmen to a particular industry almost always provided many of its apprentices. This clustering of workers from certain areas in certain industries often had its origin in local traditions of handicraft production. But it was most certainly perpetuated by the nature of the hiring process, which was personalistic in the extreme. Only 14 percent of carpet weavers and less than 9 percent of handloom weavers and hosiery knitters found work by going into a workshop and making application. The remainder were introduced into a place of work by friends, people from the same native place, relatives, or former co-apprentices. In most cases the introducers were themselves weavers or knitters. This means of finding work was used both by recent migrants from the countryside and by experienced craftsmen who left one Tianjin shop for another.[18] For apprentices, the hiring process depended even more heavily upon personal connections.

Like artisans, factory workers were overwhelmingly first-generation migrants to the city. In the three decades before Liberation, workers in the Tianjin cotton mills came mainly from five locations: the Tianjin suburbs, other villages in Hebei, Shandong, Henan, and (when new mills were being founded) Shanghai and its environs. Although skilled workers might be brought to a mill from other regions of China, ordinary operatives were natives of the Tianjin area or other parts of Hebei.[19]

Throughout the 1920's, these rural migrants were mostly men and boys. A government survey in 1929 reported that of 1,385,137 residents of the city proper counted in the census, 61 percent were male. In the central urban districts, men made up 60–69 percent of the total population. In suburban districts the figure ranged from 50 to 59 percent, indicating that there fewer families had been separated by migration. The census made a separate count of people who had left their home districts, presumably to seek work elsewhere; males made up almost 85 percent of this group.[20]

Local peasants found their way to the Tianjin cotton mills because they lived near the city and the city offered new sources of income. The economic status of these peasants varied. Some owned land and did not depend entirely upon their wages to support their families. Others were landless and the sole support of their households.[21] Peasants from outlying areas of Hebei or Shandong, on the other hand, came to Tianjin because of man-made and natural calamities: warlord conflicts, bandits, flood, and drought. These factors continued to push people into the city throughout the 1930's and 1940's, when many peasants fled to Tianjin as refugees from the violence of Japanese raids. Ji Kailin, a worker who came to Tianjin with his parents in 1943, described the deterioration of peasant life in his native Wen'an county under the Japanese:

> When it was harvest time, the Japanese would come around to speed up the harvest, and take the rice. It was called "public grain," a kind of tax. They took 50–60 percent of the harvest. . . . The people that grew the rice were not permitted to eat it. If [the Japanese] came on one of these expeditions and went into someone's house and saw that they had rice in the pot, they would burn the house down.

Because Ji's village had no permanent Japanese garrison, the CCP's Eighth Route Army was active there at night. The Japanese would send patrols to the village periodically to root out suspected Communist sympathizers. After the village headman was tortured and stabbed to death in one of these counterinsurgency sweeps, the villagers made it a practice to flee their homes as the Japanese approached.

After several years of occupation Ji's family decided to leave:

> We had enough to eat, but with this kind of unstable life you always had your heart in your mouth. First the old and the young left and went to the home of a relative, about fifteen li away. It had a Japanese garrison. At least in the garrison towns there weren't these mopping-up campaigns. . . . I lived there for several months. Then my whole family came to Tianjin one after another.
> There were more than 100 households in our village. Perhaps half the village left at that time.[22]

Ji's story is echoed by other Tianjin workers who grew up in Japanese-occupied rural areas.

The fact that so many factory workers came to Tianjin in the 1930's and 1940's as refugees with their families may be one reason for the relative underdevelopment of a contract labor system in Tianjin. Since the rural economy of occupied North China was in a state of collapse, there was no need to detach young rural residents from their families in order to move them off the land and into the city.[23] Like artisans, factory workers found jobs through a network of relatives, friends, and fellow villagers who provided them with introductions. In the cotton mills, management attempted repeatedly to replace this system of recruitment with a less personal, more "modern" set of hiring procedures (see Chapter 6 below). But in spite of these efforts, millhands continued to find work by depending on rural ties.

Apprentice and Child Labor

In all the artisanal industries, apprentices were an important part of the workforce. Smaller shops seemed to rely to the greatest degree on apprentice labor. Apprentices made up almost one-third of the workers in the carpet industry as a whole, but two-thirds of all handloom weavers and almost three-quarters of all hosiery knitters and button makers were apprentices. Virtually all those employed in making glass and weaving mats were apprentices. Workshops in the electroplating, soapmaking, tanning, ironworking, and machine-making industries all depended upon substantial percentages of apprentice labor.[24]

An apprentice needed not only an introducer but a guarantor. The introducer was usually a fellow-villager, relative, or friend. The guarantor had to be a person established in Tianjin who was willing to compensate the employer for board costs if the apprentice ran away, and to pay for medical expenses if the boy became sick or injured. Apprenticeship in most industries lasted slightly longer than three years, and was usually unpaid except for room, board, and (after a year of doing errands) job training. The terms of apprenticeship were sometimes formalized by an employers' association, if one existed. But even when the terms were unwritten, they varied little within or across industries.[25]

In artisanal industries elsewhere in the world, the institution of apprenticeship protected craftsmen by limiting entrance to a trade, and by preserving and transmitting trade secrets. When threatened by mechanized factory production, artisans frequently fought to defend this traditional organization of their crafts. In twentieth-century Tianjin, however, apprenticeship was less a means of protecting craftsman status than a disguised form of child labor. Apprentices were not guaranteed training in a skill. Many of the apprentices who worked long hours in Tianjin shops were unable to find employment as craftsmen when they completed their apprenticeships. Shopowners preferred to acquire a new batch of apprentices, who were cheaper and easier to control. Artisanal industries, subject to a variety of destabilizing forces, thus guaranteed little stability either to skilled craftsmen or to apprentices.[26]

Most apprentices were between the ages of fourteen and eighteen, but even skilled craftsmen in Tianjin shops were unusually young. A 1929 sample of more than 2,000 workers (not including apprentices) in small and medium-sized factories found their average age to be slightly older than twenty-four. In the three industries Fong studied, more than half the craftsmen were ages twenty-one to twenty-five.[27] This age structure resulted partly from the recent origins of the artisanal sector in Tianjin; it also reflected the fact that young men were the most likely group to migrate from the North China countryside.

Perhaps the most surprising way in which the factories resembled handicraft workshops was in the use of apprentice labor. In the early and mid-

1920's children made up more than a quarter of all cotton millhands, and in five of the six mills most of these children were paid a pittance or merely provided with room and board. Several mills had apprenticeship contracts similar to those in the handicraft sector. Overlapping with these formal apprenticeship arrangements was the practice of hiring child workers to perform unskilled tasks.[28] Although children could be paid less than adults, using the apprenticeship system to secure child labor for the mills was not wholly a product of economic logic. A 1926 survey noted that at the Bao Cheng Mill, apprentices were given food, clothing, and a subsidy, and went on to comment: "Hiring child workers is actually a loss for the factory, and each factory is unhappy with this system, but because their parents work in the factory and ask to carry them in, the factory has no way to refuse, and therefore accepts and uses them."[29] When the costs of food and a subsidy are calculated, apprentices might sometimes have cost more than both nonapprenticed child labor under fifteen and adult labor.[30] Yet family ties, the prevalence of apprenticeship in Tianjin handicraft industries, and the need to procure and rapidly train a docile labor force in a period of expansion all induced the mills in the 1920's to adopt an apprenticeship system, despite its economic disadvantages.

In the 1930's, however, the percentage of apprentices and other children in the mills declined. In 1929, children under sixteen were 14 percent of all millhands; by 1933 they were less than 3 percent. The large volume of "textile crisis" literature of the early 1930's does not mention apprentices at all. With an ample supply—even an oversupply—of trained adult labor on hand, perhaps children were no longer necessary. And in a period punctuated by frequent mill closings, management probably did not wish to have a group of resident children on hand to feed and house.[31]

Child labor came back into vogue when Japanese owners expanded the mills during the occupation. The increased demand for labor, the increased supply of refugees, and the desire of the Japanese millowners to secure a docile workforce all contributed to the rising employment of children. Children were drawn to the mills when their families came to the city as refugees; they were also recruited from outside Tianjin to come to the mills alone. They were divided into two groups: apprentices, who spent six months to two years learning a skill, and unskilled child laborers, who cleaned machines and carried loads. But the training process was often haphazard, and the distinction between child worker and apprentice was not always a clear one. Contemporary observers put the proportion of both categories of children in mills during the Japanese occupation at anywhere between one-third and two-thirds of the workforce.[32]

One female worker who was hired by a mill during the occupation was thirteen years old: "I came several times, but I was short, so I failed the test. . . . You had to be tall enough and weigh enough. If you came in the summer it wasn't easy to pass. We didn't wear very much. . . . In the winter you could wear a little more, the shoes were a little higher. You could look a little fatter and taller, and it was enough."[33]

Children labored in every department: boys in the departments where male adults predominated, girls in the women's departments. In the spinning mill they were most often put to work at piecing (*jietou*), joining ends of yarn together as it was wound onto bobbins. In the weaving mill they were assigned to heddling (*chuanzheng*), or threading the warp along a set of parallel cords in the loom. Both these jobs required excellent eyesight, dexterity, and concentration. A mill staff member in charge of training young workers comments that heddling "wasn't light work. When young children did it they would get so tired that they got lean and haggard."[34] Children also worked in the finishing department. Although their strength was inferior to that of adults, the mill management continued to use them because "they were cheap, they were young, they were pretty honest, and they didn't try to shirk the job."[35]

After 1945, mills under the aegis of the central government undertook to train young workers formally. Every government mill (seven of the ten in Tianjin) established a "training room" with a staff devoted to teaching young workers. Prospective trainees, once again, were required to have an introducer and a guarantor, and had to register with the labor department. After two or three months a group of trainees "graduated" and was turned over to the production group, and the next "class" was admitted. The move to more formal training of child workers was accompanied by an attempt to raise the social status of the millhands, since they were now government employees. They were frequently compared to students, and efforts were made to initiate a more select group of recruits into the mills.[36]

Children employed under a variety of arrangements, then, made up an important sector of the factory workforce, just as they did in the small workshops. And like adult handicraft workers, adult millhands tended to be young. A survey of 3,898 cotton mill workers in the late 1920's, 97 percent of them male, found that one-third were age sixteen to twenty, and another quarter were twenty-one to twenty-five years old. Only 15 percent of the workers were over thirty.[37]

Women in Tianjin Factories

One of the few ways in which the factory workforce differed from the artisan sector was in the participation of women. While artisans were almost always men, women worked as factory hands in the cigarette, match, and cotton industries. Their entrance into cotton spinning in the mid-1930's exhibited a distinct regional pattern, which differed from that of the industrial centers in the south.

In Shanghai, cotton was king and women cotton mill workers were his handmaidens. From at least the mid-1920's until Liberation, women were the majority of the workforce in the most important industry in China's largest industrial city. A 1932 survey found that 72.9 percent of Shanghai cotton mill workers were female, a percentage that rose still higher if female child workers were counted. The predominance of women in the Shanghai textile industry has led to an image in both popular and scholarly works of the woman cotton mill worker as quintessential victim and heroine of pre-Liberation industry.[38]

In North China, however, women entered the cotton mills later and in smaller numbers than their southern counterparts. In Tianjin, women were only 9.14 percent of the cotton mill workforce in 1929, or 13.24 percent if female children are included (see Table 4). It was not until the Japanese occupation, and the Japanese takeover of millownership, that the percentage of women rose to 39 percent, and in 1947 it was barely one-half.[39]

This regional difference in female workforce participation can be explained in a number of ways. In Shanghai many of the cotton mills were under Japanese management from the early 1920's on, whereas in Tianjin the cotton mill sector was almost completely Chinese-owned until the mid-1930's. It may be that the widespread use of female labor was a pattern imported by Japanese millowners from mills in Japan, and that Chinese millowners followed suit in Shanghai in order to keep labor costs competitive.[40]

A second factor was the role of women in the rural economy, since most millhands were peasant migrants to the city. Women in the rural areas near Shanghai participated in agricultural labor, as well as taking an active role in home handicraft production. In the north, on the other hand, women rarely worked in the fields, although they sometimes produced handicrafts at home. Southern women who had worked outside the physical confines of the house since childhood may have been more likely to enter a factory than northern women who had been confined at home.[41]

Another explanation given by foreign observers in North China was that women could not do factory work because their feet were bound more frequently in the north than in the south. In the 1920's, however, this custom was already on the wane throughout the country, and in 1929 only slightly more than a quarter of Tianjin women had bound feet. Furthermore,

TABLE 4
Women in Tianjin Cotton Mills, 1929 and 1938

Factory	1929		1938	
	No. of women in workforce	Pct. of workforce	No. of women in workforce	Pct. of workforce
Japanese-owned by 1938[a]				
Yu Yuan / Kotai #6	577	9.74%	3,380	40.17%
Hua Xin / Kotai #7	254	11.32	867	29.25
Bao Cheng / Tianjin	376	22.45	650	35.32
Yu Da	123	7.25	530	28.64
Yu Feng	—	—	1,897	36.38
Chinese-owned				
Heng Yuan	—	—	1,290	59.17
Bei Yang	213	10.44	850	49.79
TOTAL	1,543	9.14%	9,464	39.16%

SOURCES: 1929, Wu Ao, *Tianjin shi fangshaye diaocha baogao* (Report on an investigation of the Tianjin spinning industry), Tianjin: Tianjin shi shehui ju, 1931, 12, 39–41. 1938, Minami manshū tetsudō kabushiki kaisha (South Manchuria Railroad Co.), *Hokushina kōjō jittai chōsa hōkokusho: Tenshin no bu* (Report on the investigation of the actual condition of factories in North China: Tianjin), N.p., 1938, 92, 102, 111, 118, 128, 145, 150.
[a]In 1929 all these mills except Yu Da were still in Chinese hands.

women with bound feet in other parts of the country (e.g. the Jiangbei) worked in both field and factory. The actual distribution of footbinding throughout China, and its relationship to female confinement and women's work, is still poorly understood.[42]

The size and occupational structure of Tianjin may also have affected the percentage of women workers. Compared to those of Shanghai, Tianjin's industrial sector in general and the textile industry specifically were small. Millhands were in greater demand in Shanghai, and perhaps this was why the industry could accommodate more women workers. In Tianjin, where there were far fewer industrial jobs, they were filled by men, who were the primary wage earners in the family.[43]

Finally, the difference between Shanghai and Tianjin may have been merely chronological. The cotton mills in Shanghai dated from the mid-1890's, a full 20 years before the founding of their northern counterparts. Women entered the Shanghai mills in great numbers in the mid-1920's. Their entry can be partly attributed to management's search for cheap and tractable labor.[44] Similarly, Tianjin women began to appear in the mills in significant numbers in 1934, when the textile industry was both on the verge of economic collapse and wracked with the labor strife attendant upon mill closings. The decision to recruit women millhands may have been motivated by very similar management considerations in both cities—lowering the cost of labor, ridding the mills of powerful foremen, and ensuring labor peace. If so, then the Tianjin textile industry was merely tardy, not intrinsically different, in its use of female labor.

Marital Status of the Workforce

Many craftsmen over the age of twenty remained unmarried. About a third of the hosiery knitters and carpet weavers in this age group were married, while handloom weavers had a marriage rate of 61 percent. Fong attributed the high rate of bachelorhood to the low earning capacity of workers in these industries; many artisans simply did not earn enough to support a family.[45]

Even those craftsmen who managed to marry left their wives in the countryside, returning home several times a year. The districts with the most lopsided sex ratios in Tianjin—those with more than three men to every two women—were the same districts where toolmaking and the weaving of carpets, rayon, and cotton were carried on.[46] Whether married or not, craftsmen lived in the workshops that employed them. They had board fees deducted from their wages, or received both room and board free.[47] Like artisans, a significant proportion of adult factory workers remained unmarried. Only in the flour mills, where the workers were somewhat older than in other industries, did the proportion of married workers exceed one-half. Less than a third of the workers in the two largest match factories were married. In 1929, only 37 percent of adult male millhands were married, though the few adult women employed in the mills had a marriage rate of 62 percent. Marriage rates of male workers were probably low because of both the youthfulness of the workforce and the low pay, which forced many millhands to delay finding a bride until they could afford one.[48]

Women who entered the mill workforce after the mid-1930's were usually young and unmarried. If they married during the Japanese occupation they concealed the fact, because most mills had rules forbidding women employees to marry. Those who kept their marital status a secret were usually found out and fired as soon as they became visibly pregnant. Some attempted to prolong their tenure in the mills by binding their waists tightly to conceal the pregnancy.[49]

After the return of the Nationalists in 1945, married women joined the mill workforce in increasing numbers. This was apparently part of the postwar trend toward an older mill workforce, one partly composed of people who had begun work as children and were now of marriageable age. But, although maternity leave was provided in the national regulations of the China Textile Industries Corporation (see Chapter 6), interview data suggest that pregnant workers were still often forced to leave the mills, re-turning some time after the birth of their children.[50]

Pay and Turnover: The Inconstant Worker

Craftsmen were not an aristocracy of labor in Tianjin. In the late 1920's, the best-paid workmen were construction workers, tailors, and shoe-makers. Among men employed in manufacturing, however, there is little indication of a large wage spread between workers in "modern" and those in "less modern" industries. Factory hands in larger industries actually appeared to earn slightly more than workers in carpet weaving, hosiery knitting, and handloom weaving, although this may have been offset by their room and board costs.[51]

Nor is there evidence that craftsmen were more rooted in urban life than were factory workers. Most handicraft workers returned to their rural vil-lages for ten days or more at New Year's, during which time their contracts were renewed. If a workshop was in economic trouble, workers were laid off at one of the major festivals, and sometimes sent back to their native place with a travel allowance. Among the handicraft workers surveyed by Fong, three-quarters of the handloom weavers and more than half the car-pet and hosiery workers had been there three years or less, many workers having departed during business fluctuations.[52] Whether through their own choice or because of the instability of all Tianjin industry, artisans re-mained temporary sojourners in the city.

Tianjin factory hands left their jobs as frequently as artisans did. In the first decade of cotton mill operation, workers routinely moved in and out of the mills and between mills. In 1929, when the Yu Yuan Mill had been operating for 11 years, more than three-quarters of the workers had been there four years or less.[53] Workers left the mills for a variety of reasons. Among 3,968 millhands who left four factories investigated by Fong, al-most 40 percent either quit or were discharged because of "long absence." Another 13 percent left to return to their native place, 11 percent became sick or suffered an injury, and the rest left because of stealing, disobedience, fighting, bad work, or another job.[54] The high percentage who were sepa-rated because of "long absence," as distinct from "return to native place," may indicate that workers moved from job to job within Tianjin during this period. Fong also discovered that absentee rates were highest in February, during the Chinese New Year, when many workers returned to their villages to visit, and from June to August, when the oppressive heat kept workers out of the mills. As for the frequent return of workers to their native place, Fong commented that "this is due to the fact that most of the workers in

Tientsin are recruited from the neighboring districts and provinces. Whenever these workers have accumulated enough savings, they prefer to return home rather than stay away from their family members." [55] In this respect, it would appear that cotton mill workers were little different from their artisan counterparts.

The turnover rate was extraordinarily high during the Japanese occupation for several reasons. Difficult working conditions made it easy to fall ill. As economic conditions worsened, an increasing number of workers stole in order to make ends meet, and were fired when discovered (see Chapter 6). Many new Japanese mills were competing for the same labor pool, as were construction firms and warehouses that needed transport workers. Workers continued to return to their native village, where many had left their families, in years when the harvest was good. In periods when it looked as though the city might be attacked, some workers would leave, feeling that the villages were safer. Finally, the refusal of the mills to retain married or pregnant women contributed to high turnover. [56]

Turnover rates from the 1930's to the end of the Japanese occupation reflected both vulnerability (to illness, firings, and layoff), and a certain amount of leverage that enabled people to move around in order to improve their livelihood. The career of Chen Zhi, a male millhand, included eight moves between 1932 and 1945. He left his first mill job when the factory was sold, his second in order to be nearer his family, and his third when the employer tried to force him to work underwater stripping machines in a flooded workshop. After a brief stint in a fourth mill, he sought higher wages at a bicycle factory, an iron mill, and a machine shop, keeping the last job for a year even though it required him to walk 50 li a day to and from work. Later he returned to the fourth mill because his family lived nearby. Chen's experience typified that of many millhands. [57]

Some male workers adopted a strategy of seasonal employment, which kept them moving in and out of the mills:

During the season when the boats came in, there was a lot of work unloading cargo on the river. This was only for a short period of time. Maybe one day you would work for one hour and that boat would be finished. . . . You had to be strong or you couldn't do this work.

During the winter there was no work. During the "three frozen months" they would come back to the mills to work, because it was warm inside. They would make it through those three months until the boats came back, and then they would leave. [58]

Of course, turnover was not always a matter of worker choice. This was increasingly true during the final years of the occupation, when large-scale layoffs were common because of raw material shortages. At the very end of the Japanese period, hundreds of workers were fired and rehired several times in succession.[59]

In the postwar period, turnover decreased: "There was still some, but much less than in the Japanese period. People settled here, living in factory housing, and brought their families from the villages; . . . the percentage of young workers declined, and they didn't move around as much. . . . Women workers could stay in the mills after having children and after marriage."[60] This observation is consonant with our portrait of the labor force after World War II: it was an older group, an increasing proportion of the workers were female (and less likely to move, say, into transport), and it was not necessary to mount aggressive recruiting campaigns in order to staff the mills. But during most of the early period of modern industry in Tianjin, the factory workforce remained as transient and mobile as handicraft workers.

The Hierarchy of Jobs

Workers had very little choice about where they found a job. Their destinies were determined by the connections they brought with them from their native place in the countryside. Not all working-class jobs were regarded equally, however, either by investigators or by the workers themselves. Perceptions of the job hierarchy in Tianjin reflected concern about pay, working conditions, security, and sexual harassment.

Reports written by visitors to the cotton mills, for instance, often included meticulous descriptions of inadequate working conditions. Yet their predominant tone was one of approval of the progress wrought by modern machinery. T'ao Ling and Lydia Johnson, two YWCA industrial secretaries, conducted a study of female and child labor in Tianjin in 1927–28. Comparing the mills to the crowded, unsanitary handicraft workshops in which most women worked, they wrote: "These factories are housed in large, modern, well-lighted and airy buildings and are equipped with modern American machinery. That on which children work is made to accommodate their height. Overhead there is piping, with a fine steam spray which keeps the air moist; in the winter this steam keeps the workrooms fairly warm."[61]

In 1926 a British visitor from the Independent Labour Party, who had toured factories in Shanghai, Tianjin, and a number of other industrial centers, posed the question, "Are the workers better off in the modern factories than in the old handicraft industries?" He concluded that the answer was mixed. Large, modern factories were often "more hygienic" than small workshops. Wages were difficult to compare, because although modern factories paid more, handicraft workers were usually provided with room and board. Craftsmen's working hours were longer, but the working day "proceeds in a more leisurely and broken way than does work in a modern mill, where the worker is subsidiary to the machinery. It is not so monotonous or mechanical as mass production in a modern factory. . . . It is not so disciplined nor so driven."[62]

Investigators also distinguished between different types of factory work. YWCA secretary Johnson, who helped run one school for cotton mill girls and another for tobacco workers, observed in 1931:

> Two weeks ago, some twenty-five of the girls from another center, near the B.A.T. [British and American Tobacco] factory, came down on a Sunday afternoon to visit the Cotton Mill center. . . . The contrast between the two groups of workers was very marked—the tobacco workers, receiving a fairly good wage for these parts (about 50 cents mex [Mexican] per day) being neatly dressed and with much better general appearance than the cotton mill girls, who work 12 hours a day for a wage of from 25 cents to 40 cents per day.[63]

Investigating the attitudes of workers themselves is a trickier undertaking, since the only access to their perceptions is through contemporary interviews.[64] One clear consideration was economic: "In looking for work," Han Ruixiang explains, "the main thing people considered was the pay. The working environment—well, you couldn't consider that. The important thing was whether you could earn enough to live on. The best jobs were on the railroad, in the post office, and the customs—those were stable, secure jobs."[65] Compared to transport work or export processing, manufacturing work had fewer seasonal fluctuations. In a city where regular employment was hard to find, those who held a steady job considered themselves well off.[66]

Some regarded metalworking as superior to mill work. A millhand reported: "The machine industry was the best. For example, Santiaoshi. . . . At the beginning you suffered, but after you came out [became a craftsman], you were better off than in the cotton industry. Your status wasn't higher, but you were better off economically."[67] In addition, skilled metalworkers valued their relative control over the work process:

> People in other factories were even worse off than we were. Ours was skilled production. Mechanized manufacturing industries weren't skilled production. For example, the women workers in the textile mills. Most were child workers. Their production was set; their output was set. Every day—no matter whether you could take it today or not—the output was the same. They had a time-clock. When you came in and moved your ticket, the clock would mark it. When you got off work

you would pick up this ticket. It had printing on the top, and from the time shown, they would want so much from you. If you didn't have that much cloth, it wouldn't do. In our machine industry, you couldn't count the number of parts. The technological process wasn't stable. If today your blade was no good, or the material was no good, it all affected the output. So it couldn't be decided ahead of time.[68]

But carpet weaving, another skilled handicraft trade, seems to have ranked lower than cotton mill work, perhaps because it was less stable and required workers to meet high quotas.[69] Although pay might have been the main factor in evaluating a job, as Han Ruixiang asserts, factors such as stability and work pressure also figured in the evaluations.

Some strong young male workers alternated mill work with coolie work along the river to maximize their income. But men who had no fixed job and depended exclusively on temporary work in the transport sector were widely regarded as more unfortunate than those who could obtain a job in the mills. Perhaps even more worthy of pity were those who, during the Japanese occupation, had to work at two jobs in order to support a family: "If we worked the night shift at the mill, in the morning we had to go over to the new warehouse on the east bank and work. What was sleep? . . . We used to sneak naps in between jobs. After we got off work we would go back to work again. Round and round, in turns—that was the only way we could make a living."[70]

The job hierarchy looked different to women. Women had fewer employment possibilities than men, and the ones they had, including mill work, were not as lucrative. Aside from the cotton mills, women worked in several other large factories: the tobacco factories (notably the local subsidiary of the British and American Tobacco Company), the International Export Company, which processed eggs for export, and the match factories. They also worked in a number of small printing houses in the south city, printing trademarks and labels on presses powered by foot treadles.[71] In the 1940's women also began to move into carpet weaving. All these jobs offered steadier work than the casual labor market in which women played such a large role.

But extra-economic factors made factory work less desirable for women than outwork done in the home. The mills were regarded, especially by first-generation rural immigrants, as places where men and women mingled in a way that violated all accepted rules of social propriety. They were places where men and women unrelated by blood or even native-place ties spoke freely to one another in the course of a working day.[72] Such mixing was tolerable if the people involved were children, but when they reached adolescence the encounters became suspect. In workshops like the weaving mill, where women were rare, encounters were policed by the workers themselves: "I remember one time under the Japanese when a woman came to the weaving mill. She was bringing food to someone. Perhaps they got along well. They left together when he got off work. Some people followed them, jeering. Men and women weren't supposed to meet each other in those days."[73] In fear that such an encounter would take place without their knowledge or consent, parents sent their daughters to the mill reluctantly. "Eleven or twelve was all right," recalls Han Ruixiang. "The ones that were a little older, their families didn't want them to work in the factory."[74]

Behind this attitude lay not only a reluctance to part with traditional ways, but also the real possibility that a young woman would be sexually abused in the mill. Rape and sexual harassment were not uncommon occurrences (see Chapters 6 and 7). Women were assaulted both on the shop floor and on their way to and from work. For this reason, "the head of a household would see his daughter going off to work, and think, 'Well, this may be a means for us to live,' but at the same time he would be worried about his child. If you were good-looking in the old society, things might be difficult for you."[75]

The possibility that a woman worker might lose her virginity in the cotton mills clouded the marriage prospects even of those women who escaped actual assault. Women millhands had a difficult time "finding a mother-in-law"—that is, getting married. Even if a marriage was successfully arranged, "sometimes when the woman got married, the mother-in-law's household didn't trust her, looked down on her," recalls Zhang Chunfeng.[76] Victims were blamed for their own suffering, as indicated by a saying popular during the Japanese period: "Good men don't become soldiers, and good women don't go to work" (*Hao nan bu dang bing, hao nü bu gongzuo*). The disdain extended to the family of the girl, since "women workers had very low status. If people knew that the daughter of some family was working in the factory, they would look down on you."[77]

Just as women millhands were shunned because their chief qualification as brides, purity, was in doubt, so male cotton workers were regarded as deficient in their chief qualification, earning power. As much as possible, women workers "would look for someone from outside with higher status to marry." The ideal catch was difficult to find, however, and marriages between co-workers were not infrequent.[78]

In sum, the job hierarchy as perceived by workers themselves was complex, flexible, and somewhat idiosyncratic. It varied according to the general economic climate, the season, the sex and age of the workers, and their connections. Placing oneself in a favorable position in the hierarchy was one of the goals of working life.

CASUAL LABOR AND
THE WORKING-CLASS HOUSEHOLD

Tianjin was a city where many of the workers had no fixed occupation, but were specialists in *da ba cha*—local slang for doing whatever odd job was available. Many of these jobs, like coolie labor along the riverbank and sorting walnuts, were linked to the foreign trade of Tianjin, and varied with seasonal and economic cycles. Other jobs, performed at home, involved large numbers of women and children in the handicraft production of goods for export and for the interior.

The workers who constituted the casual labor force are even more elusive than the transport workers, since they lacked not only a fixed employer but also a fixed trade. Yet their lives can be partially reconstructed by examining the organization of working households. The explorations of the family, material life, and the margin of poverty that follow have three purposes: to follow home the laborers whose working lives we have already discussed, to locate and describe the casual laborers who are less conspicuous elsewhere, and to examine the experience of those who slipped out of the ranks of the working poor, through the "safety net" of partial employment as a casual laborer, and into the underclass of Tianjin.

Composition of the Household

Families were often separated during the course of migration to Tianjin. Parents or siblings remained on the land; sons or fathers moved to the city first. Urban household members frequently lived in groups different from the ones in which they had grown up. But in all the households surveyed in pre-Liberation Tianjin, kinship continued to be the basic organizing principle, the determinant of who lived with whom. Family ties guided and gave coherence to the complicated migration patterns of peasants entering and leaving the city. And during their sojourn in the city, no matter what its duration, the household unit, based on kinship ties, supported some members and deployed others in the search for work.[79]

A 1937 summary of surveys of urban and rural households in Shanghai, Beiping, Tianjin, and various provinces found that most rural households had more than five people in them, whereas urban households tended to have fewer than five.[80] The available data suggest that Tianjin households conformed to this pattern throughout the pre-Liberation period, hovering just below the five-person mark between 1930 and 1937 and surpassing it slightly after the war.[81] The few surveys that concentrated on workers and the poor found household sizes of under five, with one exception.[82]

If the working-class household reflected general population patterns in

Tianjin, then it was apt to have more men than women. From 1928 to 1947, men consistently outnumbered women in the urban population as a whole, accounting for 58–63 percent of the total.[83] Even the birth statistics seemed to favor males: of 14,746 births reported in 1936, 53 percent were male, while males accounted for 55 percent of the recorded births in 1947 and 54 percent of the recorded births in September 1948. When the 1936 births were analyzed by occupation of the father, male births outnumbered female in every category.[84] In Tianjin mortality statistics, on the other hand, women surpassed men. In 1936, women accounted for 50.2 percent of reported deaths (although they made up only 41 percent of the population). In 1947 they constituted 50.31 percent of the dead, in September 1948, 57 percent.[85]

The apparent propensity of females to be born in lesser numbers than males is probably explained by the practice of female infanticide; their higher death rate may well reflect the extreme economic vulnerability of women in the underclass. But the preponderance of men in the population as a whole cannot be explained by these factors alone. Among workers, at least, it was also the result of migration patterns in which males came to the city seeking work in greater numbers. Many men in artisanal industries, as noted earlier, lived at their workplace and had no family in the city. They, rather than household groups, may partly account for the imbalance in the sex ratio. Women in Tianjin moved in a world that was dominated numerically (as well as in other respects) by men.

Little else is known about the composition of working-class households. A survey of 132 households of handicraft workers in 1927–28 found that all heads of household (major earners) were male, most frequently men between the ages of twenty-one and forty. Very few daughters remained in their natal families after the age of sixteen; presumably they were married off around that age. Slightly more than half the household members were of working age, which the survey defined as between sixteen and fifty. Another 36 percent were children under sixteen.[86] These last percentages are misleading, however, for statistical and qualitative data alike indicate that virtually every member of a working-class household, no matter how young or old, contributed to the family income. A look at several working-class families illustrates the varying strategies they employed to keep themselves above the margin of subsistence.

The Household at Work

Most of the eight people in the family of Chen Guilan worked. In the late 1930's and early 1940's, her father and uncle bought and sold second-hand goods, a trade known in local slang as "shouting scrap" (*he polan*) because its practitioners walked the streets hawking their wares. Another uncle, who lived with the family occasionally, pulled a rickshaw. Guilan's mother took in sewing. Her brother was a street vendor. Her aunt worked at a series of odd jobs, while her grandmother cared for the youngest child.

Childhood did not last long in such a family. At the age of twelve, Guilan joined a group of girl cousins, led by an older female relative, and went each day to a warehouse in the British concession to crack walnuts. When this work stopped for the season, the group moved on to odd jobs in a cotton mill, peanut shelling, and picking over medicinal herbs (*mahuang*) for export. Most of the laborers in these jobs were women and girls. At the age of fourteen Guilan found more stable employment, weaving carpets in a small factory where she was paid by the foot (*chi*). But even with most members of the household working, the family remained close to the margin of subsistence. Family members saved their cornmeal to give to the uncle who was pulling a rickshaw, eating vegetables and beancurd dregs (*doufu zha*) as their daily fare.

When Guilan was sixteen she returned to her native village for a brief period, then came back to Tianjin with her family and settled in Xi Lou, a poor district where those with relatively stable employment lived side by side with casual laborers:

> In our courtyard were three men who shouted scrap, and one who sold celery, cabbage, and turnips. Some worked in cotton mills, some pulled rickshaws. One worked on the riverbank. They were all poor people.
> I was the only one in the courtyard who worked in a carpet factory. The women were all at home. None had a regular job. Some collected waste coal; some took in sewing. The boys, fourteen or fifteen years old, would collect scrap, or work at wedding and funeral processions, where they would carry the flags and make a few coppers. Sometimes seventeen- or eighteen-year-old boys would help out making tiles.[87]

Like the families in her courtyard, most of the families of her fellow workers at the carpet factory had no fixed occupation, but squeezed themselves into whatever economic niche they could construct, and diversified their sources of income by sending almost everyone out to work, or bringing in work to those who remained at home.

Chen Yihe, whose life as an ironworker is described in Chapter 4, was too young to work when his family first arrived in Tianjin, so he stayed at home with his sister-in-law. His mother and brother went out to work in the walnut warehouses, arranging their schedules and their routes to work so they would have a good chance of being hired anew each day:

> We lived in Hedong district . . . and they worked across the river in the British concession, cracking walnuts. . . . They earned twenty or thirty cents a day. Today there would be work, tomorrow there wouldn't be any.

They had to wake up at twelve midnight, because if you got there late they would have enough people and they wouldn't want you. They had to be at work at six in the morning. Why did they get up so early? Because they had to walk in circles to get there. At that time the lanes and streets all had bars. At a certain hour they would close them. They were afraid that poor people would rob them. So if you couldn't go through here, you might have to go to a place very far away before you could pass through. . . .

They paid by the catty. Women, men, anyone could do this kind of work. Nobody had a steady job.

Eventually Chen's brother became a clerk in a foreign firm, and Chen himself became an apprentice. With one of her sons bringing in an income of fifteen yuan a month and the other being fed and housed by an ironworking shop, Chen's mother was able to stop working.[88]

Even in families where one member or more worked in the cotton mills at a relatively stable job, other household members also took on odd jobs or performed tasks to lessen the household burden. While Zhang Wenqing and her brothers and sister worked in the Yu Yuan Cotton Mill, her father ran errands for foreigners. Her mother, who had bound feet and did not go out to work, made padded cotton jackets, pants, and shoes for the neighbors. In families where the male head of household worked in the cotton mills, the wives and children took in sewing for the single millhands in the neighborhood, went to the nearby suburbs to collect firewood and grass to use for fuel, and collected herbs for use in cooking. A 1929 investigation of 87 families whose male head of household worked in the Yu Yuan Mill found that wives, children, brothers, sisters, and parents of the major earner together contributed a fourth of the family's income.[89]

In spite of their difficult economic circumstances, working-class families made an effort to ensure future income by sending their sons to school whenever possible, even if they could only attend long enough to learn to read several hundred characters. Even those boys who received several years of education, however, often found themselves working as craftsmen or peddlers, rather than attaining the hoped-for jobs of clerk or scribe. Girls virtually never went to school.[90]

Mobility upward out of the working class was not possible for most working-class families. They concentrated their efforts on preventing a downward slide into the ranks of the marginal poor. With most members working, and perhaps one in school, a family could hope to maintain a spartan, often uncomfortable, but adequate standard of living.

MATERIAL LIFE

In spite of the flexibility and determination of working-class households in devising ways to maximize income, the average working-class family

TABLE 5
Household Expenses in Working-Class Families, 1927–1930

Category	(1) Weavers and sockmakers, 1929	(2) Handicraft workers, 1927–28	(3) Millhands, 1929	(4) Millhands, 1929–30
Number of households	199	132	12,687[a]	87
People per household	3.7	4.3		
Annual expenditure (yuan)	288.16	177.28	261	
Percent expenditure on:				
Food	56.2%	61.82%		63.8%
Clothing	7.3	6.95		6.7
Rent	16.1	14.05		7.1
Fuel	9.6	12.75		9.7
Miscellaneous	16.8	5.33		12.7

SOURCES: (1) Survey conducted in 1929 by the Nankai Committee on Social and Economic Research, reprinted in "Zhongguo laodong jieji shenghuofei zhi yanjiu" (Research into the living expenses of the Chinese laboring class), *Jingji yanjiu zhoukan*, No. 3 (March 17, 1930). (2) Feng Huanian Xiansheng jiniance, *Minguo shiliunian zhi shiqinian Tianjin shouyi gongren jiating shenghuo diaocha zhi fenxi* (An analysis of the investigation of the livelihood of Tianjin handicraft workers' households, 1927–28) (Tianjin: Li Rui, Hua Wenyu, Wu Daye yinzeng, 1932), 492, 503, 529. (3) Wu Ao, *Tianjin shi fangshaye diaocha baogao* (Report on an investigation of the Tianjin spinning industry) (Tianjin: Tianjin shi shehui ju, 1931), 51. (4) Fong, *Cotton Industry and Trade in China*, Vol. I (Tientsin: Chihli Press, 1932), 138.

[a] This study counted workers, not households.

spent almost all its earnings. Table 5 shows the average annual expenditures of several groups of workers surveyed in the late 1920's. In each group, more than half the family expenditures (sometimes almost two-thirds) went for food. Approximately another quarter went for shelter and fuel. Families minimized the amount of money they spent on clothing (about 7 percent of income) by stretching and patching and reusing their clothing until it literally fell apart, and then using the tatters for rags. Expenditures for miscellaneous goods, which ranged from cigarettes and wine to health care and education, were usually very low.

In the study of 132 handicraft workers conducted by Feng Huanian in 1927–28, the average annual income per household was 184.34 yuan. Of this, almost 98 percent was occupational income, with the rest coming from gifts to the family, loans, pawning goods, relief, and sales of personal property. If expenditures are compared to occupational income, each household had an average annual surplus of less than three yuan, or less than 2 percent of total occupational income. Even this scanty surplus may be an overstatement because, as Feng pointed out, working-class families made purchases in small, scattered quantities, and it was difficult for them to remember each purchase accurately. In the poorest of the households that Feng surveyed, there was a deficit of more than 11 percent between occupational income and expenditure. The income of working-class households, even if there were no unexpected expenses or period of unemployment, was just enough to maintain the simplest standard of material life.[91]

Shelter

Each time that Chen Guilan's family migrated to the city, they rented a room in a different district where poor and working people lived. No matter what neighborhood they chose, their accommodations were much the same. One-story houses, accessible through a maze of narrow lanes, were grouped around a small inner courtyard shared by three to ten families. Workers who had a bit of money to spare might manage to rent a house made of brick with a tile roof. The next most fortunate group lived in homes of unbaked clay, with a roof of sorghum stalks, coated inside and out with lime whitewash. The third and most common type of housing, while similar in construction, was covered only with a mud wash, which in the rainy season leaked incessantly. But the landlords, usually local real-estate dealers who lived in another district and sent agents to collect the rent each month, were not particularly interested in making repairs.[92] In one working-class district, wrote a reporter, the houses were so dilapidated that "pieces of mud fall down from the ceiling, and the reeds and wood frame threaten to collapse. It leaks when it rains, stinks when it is hot, and is freezing in the winter."[93]

Since houses faced in toward the courtyard, not much of their condition could be seen from the lane, and a local investigator found them deceptively prosperous-looking. But, he added,

as soon as you go into each courtyard and look, you realize that you have misjudged. The people who live here are mostly factory laborers; some have already lost their jobs, while others, even if they are not unemployed, cannot meet their expenses. . . . The entryway to every lane is crowded with women and children with haggard faces. There are many empty buildings. Clearly, although the rent is only one *yuan* per month, it is not easy to find tenants.[94]

Most families could afford only one room. The most common room size was 3⅓ meters long by 2⅔ meters wide by 2⅔ meters high. The rooms differed little from the housing workers had occupied in their native villages. Half the space or more was taken up by the *kang*, a hollow raised earthen platform that served simultaneously as bed, sitting room, and dining area. A stove off to one side of the kang was used for cooking and for heating the inside of the platform. A pot was built into the kang itself; its outside cover was even with the kang's surface. After they finished cooking, a family could put on the cover, place a mat on top, and use it as a seat.

At night the entire family slept on the kang, sometimes sharing a single quilt. Most rooms contained little else; water pails, table, stools, all were placed on the platform.[95]

Most rooms had one door and one window. With three or four people crowded into the room, the air was often stale. Some of the windows were made of glass, some of oiled paper, and some of paper with an inset of glass that let in a small amount of light. In summer a curtain of cloth or crude braided grass was hung in the doorway to keep insects out. It was also common to burn "reed incense" (*weizi xiang*) to ward off insects; this mingled with human sweat to replace coal fumes as the characteristic household odor of summer.[96]

In the stove that heated the kang, firewood and sorghum stalks were burned. Some houses also had another stove for heat and cooking, one that did not have a chimney. It required the use of coal briquets, which were made by mixing coal scraps, yellow dirt, and water, forming them into balls and slapping them onto the side of the house to dry. When lit they could burn for long periods, but if the fire in these stoves was not well tended and went out, it was very difficult to relight. The kang stove, on the other hand, could be extinguished and readily started up any time. Kerosene lamps, lit as rarely as possible to save fuel, completed the typical family's collection of household appliances.[97]

Food

An ongoing survey of the cost of living for Tianjin workers, which was begun in 1927 and continued until 1952, keyed its index to the cost of 24 foodstuffs frequently purchased by handicraft workers: Shanghai rice, United States flour, local flour, cornmeal, millet, mung beans, soybeans, bean sprouts, potatoes, beancurd, onions, garlic, two types of cabbage, spinach, chives, soy sauce, vinegar, sesame oil, salt, *mianjiang* (a sauce made from fermented steamed bread), and (on rare occasions) pork, beef, and mutton.[98]

The seeming profusion of foods, however, concealed a diet with little variation and (according to one contemporary observer) insufficient calories and protein. The workers surveyed by Feng Huanian spent about 62 percent of their income on food; 59 percent of that was spent on grain, another 17 percent on vegetables.[99] For breakfast, workers usually ate flat wheatcakes (*shaobing*), or plain deep-fried crullers (*youtiao*, known locally as *guozi*). Other possibilities, many of which could be bought from street vendors and eaten on the way to work, were beancurd soup, seasoned millet mush, boiled red sorghum (the lowest class of grain), or *gabacai* (soybean flour fried into a soft pancake, then mixed with oil, onion, cabbage, and spices). The noon meal was the day's most substantial repast; it might feature *bobo* (steamed cornmeal cakes), rice, eggplants, or green-bean soup in the summer, and noodles or roasted sweet potatoes in the winter. In the evening, steamed bread, bobo, or millet gruel made up the meal. Often several of these staples would be combined into a one-pot meal, recalls Chen Guilan: "We ate a lot of pickled vegetables and cornmeal cakes. Underneath we would put cabbage and boil it. It served as both food and drink." [100]

A working-class family ate meat several times a month at most; in a ten-month period in 1927–28, the 132 households Feng surveyed spent only an average of five strings of cash apiece on eggs. The other delicacies for which Tianjin was famous—melons, plum drink, and ice cream in summer, river crabs in winter, wild duck in spring and fall, and oil-fried locusts in season—were the sustenance of the upper classes, not the workers. When workers did buy meat, it was apt to be in the form of *yangdutang* (sheep-stomach soup), a stew made of the cooked entrails of sheep, which was cheap but often of dubious cleanliness.

Because many workers, especially those with large families, could not afford wheat flour or rice, they made do with cornmeal and other, cheaper grains. One ingenious device popular in working-class households was a mill, called *helemian*, which enabled workers to make noodles out of very coarse flour, such as sorghum or green-bean flour. Mixed with water to form a paste, the coarse flour was put inside a hollowed-out tube and forced through a copper sieve directly into a pot of boiling water. The mill converted grains that were too coarse to knead into useful foodstuffs. [101]

Most people could afford to buy enough food for only one day at a time. A typical purchase might be, for example, several stalks of onion, a bowl or two of beancurd, and several coppers' worth of condiments. "We would buy one or two coppers' worth of food, heat up the water, and pour it into the pot," says Chen Guilan. The only luxury items consumed by workers were cigarettes and small quantities of tea and cheap white liquor. [102]

Water was purchased daily from a water vendor who pushed a cart around working-class neighborhoods. He charged several coppers per purchase, depending upon the capacity of the buckets that household members carried on shoulder poles to fill with his water. Each family normally heated its own water, but itinerant peddlers also set up small stoves and sold hot water in small quantities on the street. Most families cooked at home; an exception was the rickshaw pullers, who had no set place or time to eat since they were always moving. They subsisted on wheat cakes, pickled vegetables, hot water, or (if business was good) noodles or steamed dumplings bought from a roadside stand. [103]

Clothing

"With what we earned, we had enough to eat, but not always enough to wear," recalls Chen Guilan. "My mother sometimes made clothes for me around the holidays. In the winter I wore a padded jacket and padded pants. It was cold! My mother made a pair of cotton padded shoes for me. We didn't buy anything." [104] Poor as her family was, there were some workers who were even worse off. Only half the women in the 132 handicraft households surveyed by Feng Huanian had a complete set of padded cotton clothes; children were equally ill-clad.

Clothing was made at home from Gaoyang homespun, local machine-woven cotton, raw cotton for padding, and occasionally a length of woollen goods. Workers preferred homespun clothing, which was dyed black or blue, because it was sturdy and did not show dirt. Most cotton mill workers surveyed by Wu Ao in the early 1930's had two sets of summer clothing, but some only had one, which they washed every ten days. Padded winter clothing was taken apart and washed once a year, as were the padded cotton quilts shared by family members. On their feet, workers wore padded cotton shoes in winter, canvas shoes in spring and fall, and often nothing in the summer. In their plain style of dress, noted Feng Huanian, Tianjin workers did not differ significantly from their counterparts in Beijing, but they were considerably more drab than Shanghai workers. [105]

Health, Public and Private

Unlike the concession areas, working-class neighborhoods had neither running water nor sewage disposal. Private toilets were unknown. At the end of the lane in Chen Guilan's neighborhood "there was a kind of reed shack open at the top that was the toilet. In the summer and winter there was no way to urinate, because we couldn't use it when it was raining or when a big wind was blowing. We didn't have raincoats or umbrellas. If we had to, we would wear a straw hat and just get wet. Most families used two buckets, one for urine and one for excrement, instead. Every morning we would pour lime on it." [106]

Once the buckets were full, it was standard practice just to heave them into the street. A visitor to Qian De Zhuang in 1936 observed with disgust that "the residents' garbage and waste water is just thrown anywhere. In the winter you can't smell it, but as soon as the spring air comes it starts to steam, giving off a strange fishy stench." [107]

The construction of public toilets did little to alleviate the problem. By 1948 Tianjin had 548 public toilets intended to serve almost 700,000 people who had no toilets at home, or one toilet for every 1,277 of these residents. About a dozen were run by the municipal health department,

while the remainder were constructed by "manure merchants" who profited by selling the manure they collected to nearby peasants to use as fertil-
izer. But the patrons of these public toilets were less than considerate of
those who came after them. A writer for the municipal government magazine complained:

> The people who come here . . . have never given a thought to public hygiene or
> public morals, and so they arbitrarily defecate outside the manure pit, and don't
> urinate in the urinal (*niaochi*), but instead just inside the door of the toilet. They
> have even started to aim (*sheji*) for places far outside the door, so that the surround-
> ing area is all rivers and lakes, and the people who come later simply have no way to
> set foot in the area. If it is summer, we can further imagine the frightful multitudes
> of flies, not to mention the pile after pile of manure maggots that have not yet be-
> come flies!

Women did not have the option of patronizing such establishments, since
public toilets were for men only.[108]

The lack of running water in working-class neighborhoods also meant
that anything more elaborate than a sponge bath was difficult to conduct at
home. While a few cotton mills provided bathhouses for their workers,
most places of work had no such facilities. Higher-paid workers went two
or three times a month to a public bathhouse, where they availed themselves of communal cement bathtubs filled with hot water, many with signs
above them admonishing drunks and old people to stay out. Poorer workers, however, did not bathe at all. In the summer they rinsed themselves in
a shallow place in the river, and in the winter they cleaned themselves with
damp towels. Of the handicraft workers surveyed by Feng, the average
family spent less than one cent (*fen*) per month per family on showers.[109]

For women workers, the advent of their menstrual period posed an additional set of hygiene problems, one often compounded by confusion
about what was happening to their bodies. Chen Guilan remembers:

> I was at work when I first got my period. I was fourteen. I went to the toilet in
> the factory. As soon as I squatted down I looked and thought, "Uh-oh. Why is
> there blood there?" I ran home. . . . I said to my grandmother, "It's awful! My
> rear end is bleeding!" My grandmother said, "Oh, you've got your period" (*Ni lai
> le shen shang le ba*). She fixed me a piece of cloth and made me a belt. . . . Then she
> put the cloth in it as a pad. After I used it I had to wash it. . . . In the villages they
> also used cloth. If we were in the factory and we had to change it, we would just
> steal a piece of cloth, or bring one ourselves. Then we would change it and throw
> the old piece down the toilet. We didn't have the means to pay a lot of attention to
> hygiene.[110]

The lack of sewage and water facilities was compounded in working-
class neighborhoods by pollution from nearby factories. In 1936 a resident
of Xi Guang Kai complained to the local newspaper that he and his neigh-

bors could not sleep at night because a nearby workshop was smelting copper and emitting nitric and hydrochloric acid fumes. Residents of the Hebei district in 1947 demanded that a military uniform factory build sewers near its dormitories so that workers would stop pouring their waste water into the street, where it had formed a greenish current more than one foot deep. The residents also requested that a local tannery stop piling up lime and scrap hides in one of the alleyways, and then dumping waste water where it would flow into the piles of hides and cause them to stink. (In this, as in most cases, the municipal government did little beyond ordering the factories and the neighborhood residents to clean up the area.) Even in areas where there were no nearby factories, the living conditions combined the harshness of village life with the squalor of urban dwelling, as in the Hebei district, where women spun yarn in their mud huts while "filth and smells abounded, and both courtyards and houses swarmed with children and pigs." [111]

Given the lack of adequate clothing or shelter from an often harsh climate, the poor diet, the lack of facilities for public or private hygiene, and the pollution, it is hardly surprising that the Tianjin population was ridden with disease. Each season had its particular scourge: in January it was tuberculosis and other respiratory problems, in February fevers and rashes, in March and April tuberculosis and typhoid, in May, June, and July fevers and rashes, in August and September tuberculosis, diarrhea, and digestive disorders, and in October through December tuberculosis once again. A 1936 study found that next to old age and strokes, the leading causes of death were tuberculosis, fevers, and rashes. February and July—the coldest and hottest months respectively—had the highest death rates. [112]

Just as each season had its most frequently fatal disease, so did each stage of life. Children under one year of age were most apt to succumb to diarrhea or enteritis. If they survived the first 12 months, their next five years of life were endangered by typhoid, typhus, dysentery, smallpox, diphtheria, measles, sores, fevers, rashes, convulsions, and digestive illnesses. As the variety of afflictions suggests, this was the age group with the highest mortality rate. After the age of sixteen, tuberculosis and other respiratory diseases were more frequent causes of death. This was especially true for workers in industry and transport, who were more likely to die of pulmonary and other types of tuberculosis than workers in agriculture or commerce (who more often fell victim to old age or strokes). [113]

If a worker had the misfortune to fall ill, and was not employed in one of the few large factories that provided some variety of clinic, he or she was apt to treat the illness with local medicinal herbs purchased from a traditional doctor. Few other options were available: the entire city of Tianjin in 1929 had only 74 Western-style doctors and 423 traditional doctors, serving a population of almost 1.4 million. Nor were these doctors evenly distributed. A 1948 article on the incidence of trachoma (which then afflicted 700,000 people in Tianjin), noted that one of the poorer districts had a single eye doctor serving more than a quarter of a million people, while a wealthier neighboring district had nine eye doctors for 86,000 people.[114]

Material life for the Tianjin working class was dirty, smoky, alternately freezing and steaming (with an interval of gritty spring winds), diseased, stinking, and above all, tiring. The contrast it made with the lives of Tianjin's rich was both obvious and overwhelming, as a writer on local customs observed in 1933:

> The rich pile up their property, eat luxurious and expensive food, and wear layer upon layer of expensive clothes. They live in imposing dwellings with spacious courtyards, in Western-style houses and huge mansions. When they travel they speed along in cars instead of on foot. Although those who have all this still regret that they don't have more, those who are onlookers stand in their dusty wake and have no hope of catching up.
>
> As for the toiling laborers and the poor peddlers, all day they exhaust themselves for very little return. Their lives: a bit of rice for a meal, a few pieces of fuel to cook it with, not enough clothes to cover their bodies, not enough food to fill them. They sometimes can't even find a hole in the city slums to house themselves. . . . The difference between these people and those who eat good grain every day and live in fine houses is like the difference between heaven and the abyss.[115]

THE MARGIN OF POVERTY

Our study thus far has depicted the lives of working-class households where everyone worked and at least one member was employed at a steady job. But in households where no one had a fixed occupation—where every member was a casual laborer, or unemployed—the contours of material life differed from those of the more fortunate members of the working class.

Struggling to exist on the margin of subsistence were the poor of Tianjin. They ate, dressed, sheltered themselves, and survived differently from the workers we have discussed thus far. Yet their experience is crucial to an understanding of the Tianjin working class, because Tianjin workers were frequently cast into the ranks of the poor by factory closings, illness, or other misfortune. At the same time the Tianjin poor, whether they were déclassé workers or refugees newly arrived from the countryside, were attempting to push upward into the ranks of the working class. This massive reserve army of labor no doubt helped to keep wages low, and also to shape an occupational structure in which few people had steady jobs. The life of this underclass was shared intermittently by many of the workers described earlier.

Paths to the Underclass

The first path to the Tianjin underclass, and the one involving the most precipitous downward slide, was to lose a working-class job because of seasonal or economic fluctuations. In government surveys the term "unemployed" was generally reserved for those who had been recently employed and had followed this path. Estimates of the size of this group varied from survey to survey and from era to era, ranging from 16.2 percent of the male population in 1928 to 40 percent of the total urban population in 1933. The most precise estimates were those made when some specific industry was in trouble, generating large numbers of unemployed people in a short period of time. Thus, in 1935, the Bureau of Social Affairs estimated that there were 10,000 unemployed people in the city, 4,000 of them cast into that category when two large textile mills closed down. In 1937 the carpet weavers and dyeworkers were said to be losing their jobs in large numbers. By 1941, the occupation government estimated that almost 17,000 men and 1,500 women were unemployed. In the postwar period unemployment figures, like all other figures, inflated rapidly, growing to 230,000 by the beginning of 1946. Two other 1946 surveys indicated that almost 100,000 industrial workers remained unemployed, while the remainder found casual jobs as rickshaw pullers, vendors, or other itinerant laborers. In the 20 years before Liberation, unemployment was consistently cited as a major social problem by the municipal authorities.[116]

A second path to the Tianjin underclass led in from the countryside, and was traversed by several large, and numberless small, waves of refugees in the 30 years before 1949. Several times in the 1920's, peasants were driven into the cities, fleeing civil war, famine, flood, and drought. A combination of these factors caused more than 30,000 people to seek shelter in Tianjin in the autumn of 1920. A foreign observer wrote:

> Great numbers of these famine stricken people are fleeing from their farms where there is nothing left, even the leaves and bark of the trees having been eaten in their dire need. They have taken their last cent to come to Tientsin. . . . Many have sold whatever remaining live stock they had for just enough to pay their railroad fare, while others, less fortunate, have pawned their clothes or sold their children for the price of a ticket and have swarmed into this city. There is now a camp on the outskirts of town where twenty thousand or more of these refugees are living in cave like houses which they have constructed from straw and mud.[117]

Municipal authorities and missionary groups scrambled to dispense food, clothing, and health care to these people, but the relief was insufficient and large numbers of them poured out of the refugee camp to beg in the streets of Tianjin each day. In desperation, the city government constructed a mud wall and a moat around the camp, fearing that if the number of refugees was not limited, none of them would get adequate care.[118]

The 1920 refugees were followed by other waves throughout the 1920's and 1930's. Israel Epstein remembers that during his boyhood in Tianjin, "the refugees would come in and they would die in the streets at night. If the winter wind blew up, they'd huddle in the doorways and you'd find them dead in the morning."[119] Of those who survived the winter, some returned to the countryside and some remained in Tianjin, joining the permanent ranks of the underclass.

In August 1939 a major flood caused by heavy rainfall and breached dikes turned 90 percent of the Tianjin population into refugees in their own hometown. In addition to inundating much of the city, the waters drowned 3,000 people in Hebei and rendered 600,000 homeless. Refugees poured into Tianjin in spite of the damage there, and events the following spring proved their choice a wise one: an estimated three million people in Hebei villages faced starvation when they were unable to plant their spring crops. Considering the alternative, life in the Tianjin underclass must have seemed less risky.[120] But the largest single influx of refugees came in the civil war period just before Liberation, moving into the city first from Hebei villages and later from the Northeast. By mid-1948 the number of refugees had reportedly reached 100,000.[121]

A third path to the underclass was one traveled exclusively by women. In 1928–29 the city government conducted a study of 50 destitute women who were taken in by the municipally sponsored Women's Relief Institute (Funü jiuji yuan). The study revealed that most of these women were concubines, child brides abused by their mothers-in-law, prostitutes who had been cruelly treated by brothel owners, or servants who found their living conditions intolerable. In short, they were women who were either victims of the family system that purported to offer them protection, or refugees from the narrow and often brutalizing range of work options available to them. These particular women were referred to the Relief Institute by the Women's Association, the Public Security Bureau, or the local court. For every one who came to the attention of the authorities, there were undoubtedly dozens of others who subsisted or died in marginal occupations.[122]

A fourth road to the underclass was followed by those who were born both poor and physically disabled. Some disabled people were able to carve out livelihoods for themselves. Nine hundred blind musicians and fortune tellers, for instance, petitioned the municipal government in 1936 to limit the hours of radio music broadcasts, because radios placed in store windows were drowning out their music and cutting into their income. But most disabled people were part of the permanent underclass that figured so prominently in government surveys of the poor.[123]

Government officials made valiant attempts to estimate the size of this underclass, but there are many indications that large numbers of people escaped their census-taking. Refugees were apparently counted in a separate category. Even with these omissions, however, the figures are impressive. A 1929–30 survey that included the disabled, those too old or too young to work, and widows and orphans with no source of support, as well as households where only one person was working and the resulting income was insufficient to support all household members, put the number at more than 95,000. In 1947, their number was estimated at 82,633. Enclaves of poor residents could be found in every district of Tianjin, yet many local citizens were unaware of the conditions under which their impoverished neighbors lived—so unaware, in fact, that discovery was a rude shock. A least one news reporter was so devastated by what he found in one district that he had no energy even to haggle over the price of a ride with the rickshaw puller who took him back to town.[124]

Daily Life in the Underclass

The poor of Tianjin were not always unemployed, but the employment they could find was marginal even by Tianjin standards. In 1935, for instance, a favored few residents of the Tie Dao Wai ("outside the railroad") area, which was known locally as Hell on Earth, worked at a local factory that made toilet paper out of grass. Even this job, which paid only 20 or 30 coppers a day, was hard to get. The usual range of occupations was cart puller, day laborer, junkseller, vendor, home spinner or weaver, beggar, and pickpocket. A government delegation that visited the Tu Fangzi district late one afternoon found that it was "almost time to beg for the evening meal, so many women and children . . . were getting ready to go out." The characteristic of these districts that was habitually commented upon by investigators, however, was that so many able-bodied people stayed home. One naive visitor reported the following incident in 1935:

> In another small room, we found two strong young men lying on a special bed which had bricks spread on the four sides and straw spread out in the middle. One saw us and sat up, and looked at us with a glazed stare. We asked why he didn't go out to work, and he said, "Where is there work?" He sighed, then said, "We want

work but there isn't any. When we beg no one will give because we are young. There's no way out but to starve to death!" When he finished talking he lay down again.[125]

The chasm that separated the poor from their more fortunate brothers and sisters in the working class was most obvious in the question of shelter. Where workers lived in brick, lime, or earthen dwellings, the underclass lived in *wopu*—huts constructed by setting up a wood frame and smearing mud and grass on it, or arranging a ramshackle lean-to of reed mats. The problems of dampness and leakage that afflicted working-class housing were compounded here. Nevertheless, many of the wopu, too, had landlords—but they collected their rent by the day rather than the month, and those who fell more than five days behind were evicted. To lighten this burden, sometimes two families shared one room.[126]

In 1947, an inquiring reporter in the Xi Guang Kai area found that one set of wopu had been built on top of a graveyard. Since the area was also a brackish swamp with a variable water table, many of the coffins became exposed, some in the water and some in the mud. Enterprising paupers had used them to build the frames for their wopu or to shore up their foundations. Strolling through the area, the reporter came to "the bank of a pool of stinking water," where he found "a coffin which is lined with rotten paper and grass on the inside. You can sit or lie, but not stand up. This is the home of a lame beggar." The unlucky tenant had been turned out of his wopu for failure to pay the rent; his remaining possessions, stored in the coffin while he went out to beg, consisted of a scrap of gunnysack and a spare bowl. "Since this is all he owns, he does not need doors or windows," mused the reporter, commenting that "the only good thing about the houses and wopu in this area is that when they collapse they will not kill anybody." He added that if the government would just declare that whoever took the coffins away could keep them, then they would be gone within the hour.[127]

The furnishings of the wopu were as stark as their exteriors. Few had kang; the furniture in one consisted of grass spread on the floor to form a bed, with half a brick covered with a tobacco sack serving as the pillow. Cooking was done over a pit in the ground, since most residents could not afford stoves; their fuel was wood chips and scraps of waste coal collected by the children. Some supplemented their diets of cornmeal and sorghum flour with wild plants; others collected the discarded outer leaves of cabbage, old turnips, or pieces of rotten pork sausage that had been thrown away along the riverbank.[128]

Like the food they ate, the clothing worn by the poor was scavenged from junkheaps. Most of the residents of one poor neighborhood in the Hebei district in 1935 had only one set of clothing, which they stuffed with cotton batting in the winter to ward off the cold. Of 71 households investigated in this district, not one reported any expenditures on clothing.[129]

Public health conditions in these districts were, if possible, even more wretched than those already described. One pauper neighborhood was located next to the city garbage dump; inventive residents sought to turn their location into a bonus by raising pigs for a living. In another district, a swampy area with poor drainage, people raised ducks. In the Xitou district an investigator visited more than 1,400 households and found a sick person in every one; residents, thinking he had come to distribute relief goods, lifted the grass or cotton curtains from their doorways as he walked by and called out the nature of their distress—widowhood, orphanhood, disease.[130]

Once a pauper's health was impaired, his or her life was frequently endangered because people had little money for doctors or medicine. Of 45 people who had recently fallen ill in one district in 1935, 38 had tried to treat themselves; only one had completely recovered. "Treatment" often consisted of spending precious coppers on incense to burn in front of shrines to Old Man Li (a sage of Jinghai county, near Tianjin) or Grandma Sun (a witch who was supposed to have magical healing powers).[131]

No amusement halls or brothels were found in the districts of the underclass ("these people have no money for bad habits," commented one reporter). Nor could they have spared their children from collecting scrap coal or junk to let them go to school, even if there had been public schools in the area. Even the heads of the local security units (*jiazhang*) were illiterate. In such a district, a girl was still regarded as a "money-losing product" (*pei qian huo*), since there was little possibility of her bringing enough income to the family to compensate for the food she ate.[132]

The extreme destitution of the Tianjin underclass meant that it frequently came to the attention of public and private charitable organizations. Aside from those run by the city, most were funded by private contributions from rich notables and merchants. Groups specialized in the salvation of women and former addicts, aided the ill and victims of disaster, and distributed clothes and hot gruel in winter to the needy.[133] While their efforts were laudable, and they undoubtedly made the difference between starvation and survival for many families, their impact on the underclass as a whole was minimal.

Artisans and factory hands shared similar origins, career patterns, and pay. Both differed from casual laborers primarily in the quality of the connections they could draw upon to find steady work. Transience and mobility characterized all three groups of workers. They were united as well in the precariousness of their material life. And they shared a disturbing proximity to the desperate poor of Tianjin, a group whose connections were insufficient to provide any employment at all. Awareness of life in the underclass must have loomed very large in the thinking of Tianjin workers as they struggled to find and keep a job.

CHAPTER FOUR

Flying Hammers, Walking Chisels: The Workers of Santiaoshi

Santiaoshi Avenue, a narrow street in the northern part of Tianjin, has a claim on working-class history that is out of all proportion to its modest length.[1] Recently demolished to make way for new housing, it was once the center of Tianjin's metalworking trades. Throughout the first 50 years of the twentieth century, tiny ironcasting and machine-building shops lined both sides of the street, totaling by conservative estimate about 75 establishments, and employing some 1,000 workers. These shops were run by small-scale capitalists, usually from peasant backgrounds, who hired a handful of workers and apprentices to manufacture small machines and machine parts. Mechanization came to the area slowly, and as late as the 1940's many of the shops had only a few lathes or a small furnace for casting iron.[2]

The industry of Santiaoshi offers a historically important contrast to industries like cotton textiles, where equipment and organization of production were transplanted (if not always successfully) from abroad. Santiaoshi continued the traditional Chinese organization of small-scale industry, one based on precapitalist forms of labor exploitation.[3] In the ironworking shops, owners and a small number of employees labored side by side. No clear distinction was made between work and leisure time. Apprentices in particular faced strictures on their nonworking time and behavior. They were not permitted to leave the factory, to let their hair grow long, to marry, or to put their hands behind their backs in the presence of the owner. They were required to wear mourning if a member of the owner's family died, to address his sons and daughters with terms of respect normally reserved for the older generation, to bow (*ketou*) to the owner at New Year's, and in some cases to join a religious sect of the owner's choosing. Many of these features of Santiaoshi life had their counterparts in the artisanal workshops of Europe and Russia. Seventeenth-century London apprentices were required to observe similar regulations. Masters doubled as shopkeepers in handicraft workshops in France under the Ancien Régime. And artisans in the nineteenth-century Russian Pale put in workdays as long as 18 hours in the same shops where they slept at night.[4]

Yet in spite of its continuity with earlier Chinese handicraft industry and its similarity to preindustrial European shops, Santiaoshi was a product of the treaty port period. In the first 50 years of the twentieth century, it grew from a swamp to a thriving industrial distict. Native entrepreneurs made important technical advances, which in turn enabled the shops in the district to increase in number and organizational complexity.

Perhaps because it *was* a new district whose owners and workers had come from the countryside, Santiaoshi exhibited few of the guild traditions that could be found in cities with older artisanal sectors. Tianjin machine-builders did not organize into guilds until the 1930's, and even then they did so on government initiative. Unlike craft guilds in 1920's Beijing, the Tianjin associations were not a jointly controlled organization of managers and workers. They had no religious function, worshiped no founder of the trade, and sponsored no annual theatrical performance. They offered no aid to a craftsman in distress and did not guarantee members a proper burial. No effective controls protected apprentices, who were little more than child laborers in disguise. No guild regulations protected craftsmen by mandating required skill levels and ensuring employment. Shopowners never organized effectively to ensure political protection for themselves, as they might have through a guild. And the workers of Santiaoshi had no well-developed urban artisanal tradition to defend, one that might have shaped worker militance when the district was threatened.[5] Nor did they give form to a new era of industrial class struggle. Owners and workers came from similar backgrounds and brought networks of rural relationships with them into the shops. Even as Santiaoshi industry grew larger and more complex, relationships on the shop floor changed very little. Class formation and class consciousness—of both capitalist and worker—did not develop as far or as fast as recent Chinese historiography has suggested.[6]

The tiny scale of Santiaoshi workshops was typical of Tianjin industry. A survey conducted throughout the city just after Liberation found more than 9,800 privately owned industrial enterprises, averaging 7.3 people per enterprise. Only 18 enterprises—including all the government-owned textile mills—employed more than 1,000 people apiece.[7] Yet, because workers in small-scale enterprises were less visible than those in large factories, their situation, and its contrast and continuity with that of modern industrial workers, has not been much discussed. By examining Santiaoshi first through the eyes of a shopowner, then from the vantage point of apprentices and craftsmen, we can explore the daily experience and the thinking of the district's emerging classes.

THREE STONE SLABS: DEVELOPMENT OF A DISTRICT

Just north of the old walled city is a triangular spit of land at the junction of the Nanyun and Beiyun rivers, bounded on the west by a short stretch of Hebei Avenue. It is said that when someone in Li Hongzhang's family died in the late nineteenth century, he built a road through the area and paved it with three rectangular slabs of stone to enable the funeral procession to pass in style. From this event came the name of the district: Santiaoshi, or "Three Stone Slabs"[8] (see Map 1, p. 14).

Although Santiaoshi was marshy and damp, it was too near the commercial center of nineteenth-century Tianjin to remain undeveloped. Docks lined the two rivers that bounded the district. From March to June and again from mid-July until the rivers froze, the two rivers were so crowded that ships had trouble passing one another. Traders disembarked to buy and sell along the length of Hebei Avenue. The commercial activity spilled over onto Santiaoshi Avenue, which crossed the district from west to east. Before the turn of the century the area had warehouses for wood, walnuts, almonds, fresh fruits, and medicines, as well as two dyeworks and a shop that cut wood for coffins.[9]

As early as the 1860's, each year during the agricultural slack season, groups of seven or eight peasants pushing handcarts and hauling their own bellows and stoves would come to Santiaoshi. Known as "traveling furnaces" (*xinglu*), they set up their equipment and began to make small parts for the boats docked nearby: "date-pit nails" with diamond-shaped heads, anchors, and wheel parts. Peasants bringing goods to market began to stop at Santiaoshi to have their tools and pots repaired. When it was time for spring plowing, the itinerant ironworkers would pack up and head back home. Home for most of them was Jiaohe county, a poor area about 360 li southwest of Tianjin. The craft of ironworking was well-developed there, and small groups of Jiaohe peasants had long traveled throughout the region repairing broken plowshares and worn-out pots.

The date when the first "traveling stove" settled in Tianjin is unclear. Sometime after 1860, however, a craftsman named Qin opened a small shop there. He and the two people who worked with him were so poor, it is said, that they shared a single jacket. But they had mastered a special skill: they knew how to make a kind of diecast pot (*yingmozi guo*) that was thin, light, and fuel-efficient. The pots produced by their shop, Qin Ji, were so popular that they soon drove out the thick, heavy Shanxi pots that had been common in the area.[10] By 1906 Qin Ji had 20 workers. Each spring they produced plowshares for the local peasants. As summertime approached they would switch to producing wheel rims, pots, hammers, and sewer pipes.[11]

Demand for construction goods from the British, who were expanding their concession, helped to stimulate an important technical advance in Santiaoshi: the development of an ironcasting technique (*fansha* or *zhutie*).[12] In 1900 Qin Ji was commissioned to make iron frames to support the new electrical lines being laid by the British. According to local folklore, Qin Ji invited a skilled craftsman who had worked at the Tianjin Arsenal (recently destroyed in the Boxer uprising) to help meet the delivery deadline. They paid him a high salary and plied him with good food and wine, but he was extremely secretive about his technique and would work only when no one else was around. When he was not working he would drape his work area with straw mats so that no one could inspect the goods. But he paid no attention to the manager's nephew, a lad of seventeen who frequented the factory in his spare time. Unbeknownst to the miserly craftsman, young Qin observed him closely, mastered his technique, and taught it to all the Qin Ji workers. From that time on, the ironcasting trade spread throughout Santiaoshi. Workers who had completed an apprenticeship at Qin Ji were in great demand as teachers.[13]

One of the most successful shops in Santiaoshi, Jin Ju Cheng Ironworks, was founded in 1897 by Ma Wenheng.[14] Ma had grown up in a peasant family just over the county line from Jiaohe. As a young man he studied business in a dry goods store in Bozhen. By the time he was twenty-four he had lost his job and returned home to live with his parents, who owned about 30 *mu* (about five acres) of land. For a while he earned a meager living tending an orchard for relatives, but he soon become convinced that there was no future for him on the farm. He mortgaged a piece of land for 500 strings (*diao*) of cash, and convinced his uncle and several relatives to put in 500 more. Bringing several cousins who knew how to work iron, they came to Tianjin's Quan Ye Chang area, set up their bellows and stove, built a wattle fence around the equipment, and began to make and repair tools.

After 1900, the Japanese extended their concession into the area. A wattle fence and a ramshackle shed did not meet the new building codes, so Ma and his relatives packed up their tools and moved northwest to Santiaoshi. From a local landlord they rented half a mu of land on the west end of the street. Then they built another wattle fence and constructed a simple shed where all the work was done. Inside the shed were piled rudimentary tools, mainly a cupola furnace (*huatielu*) that could heat about 100 catties (110 pounds) of iron, and bellows that took four people to pull. Ma relied on the skill of his workers to fashion dry molds of every shape.[15]

The account books prior to 1900 indicate that Jin Ju Cheng was producing mainly agricultural implements for the local market. The products were typical of the district: plowshares, pots, axles, anvils, weights, wire gauze, and medicine boxes for nearby pharmacies. This pattern gradually changed in the 11 years after the Boxer Rebellion. The account books for this period show frequent receipts of British money, mostly for stoves, and an increasing production of machine parts. Jin Ju Cheng also made iron weights to stabilize the cotton-hauling boats coming from the interior. This was the period when the fansha technique of ironcasting was introduced, and the scale of production expanded significantly.[16] Jin Ju Cheng's workforce also grew, from 12 long-term workers at the beginning of 1900 to 20 workers at the end of the year (possibly including temporary laborers and apprentices). In 1907 the shop employed 21 workers (five of these were temporary, eight were skilled, and eight were apprentices). By 1913 the number had grown to 39. Most were recruited from Ma's home village. The business showed steady growth throughout World War I. In 1916 the first piece of power machinery, a three-horsepower generator, was bought from a Japanese firm. In 1917 the owners were able to buy the land on which their shed stood, and in 1921 they constructed a solid, if not imposing, two-story factory building.

Meanwhile another trade, machine repair, was emerging in Santiaoshi alongside the ironcasting shops. In the earliest shops, founded at the turn of the century, each individual machine part was filed down by hand. But after 1900, the machine-repair business in Santiaoshi grew because of its geographical proximity to the local cotton trade. Santiaoshi warehouses had become a marketplace for the burgeoning trade in raw cotton between foreign firms and the interior. Traveling cotton merchants, who passed through Santiaoshi daily on their way to the warehouses, soon began to order gins and baling machines from local shops like Guo Tian Cheng, Chun Fa Tai, and Guo Tian Xiang.[17]

As the rural weaving industry developed, especially in the Gaoyang area, Santiaoshi shops learned to copy imported Japanese looms. One of the major importers of Japanese looms was a foreign firm called the Tamura Company. Tamura often had parts repaired and replaced by Guo Tian Cheng and other area shops. Around 1907, Tamura ordered a complete loom from Guo Tian Cheng. Since the shop had never made one before, Guo Erleng, one of the managers, went to Tamura's offices, examined a loom, came back to the shop, and began to replicate it. Over the next year the shop made many such looms for Tamura, being careful to attach the Tamura trademark to each one. At night they would move the looms in through the back door of the company, and in the morning Tamura would sell them through the front door as Japanese goods, turning a handsome profit. Impressed by the demand for their "imported" looms, the Guo Tian Cheng management soon started contacting Gaoyang merchants directly, telling them they could make looms that were identical to, but cheaper than, the Japanese models. A number of shops created similar niches for themselves in the expanding market. Business was so good that many firms opened on Santiaoshi Avenue or moved there from other parts of the city.[18]

As their machine-building business grew and assembly became a more complicated process, shops like Guo Tian Cheng could no longer produce the necessary parts themselves. In 1908, Guo Tian Cheng began to subcontract with Jin Ju Cheng Ironworks to cast whole sets of machine parts. The machine shops took charge of the final assembly.[19] The period during and immediately after World War I was a boom period for Tianjin industry in general, and the factories on Santiaoshi Avenue shared in the spreading prosperity. Small weaving and knitting workshops throughout the city ordered machines and parts from Santiaoshi. Although warlord conflicts led to work stoppages and periods of business loss, they were usually of short duration.[20] Between World War I and the Japanese invasion, at least 30 new factories were founded in Santiaoshi. Most of them fell into one of three categories. An existing shop might divide its capital to form a branch factory. A craftsman who had completed an apprenticeship at one of the shops might set up his own enterprise, maintaining close business ties with his former masters. Finally, an ironcasting shop might found its own machine shop, or vice versa.

The more successful ironcasting shops usually had a controlling interest in at least one machine-building shop. Accounts were kept separately, but since the managers were frequently close relatives, each shop could be assured of a reliable business associate.[21] In 1919, for instance, Jin Ju Cheng opened its own machine-building factory, Jin Ju Xing. Its main products were printing presses copied from the Japanese and sold through an agent in nearby Da Hutong (near the old northeast corner). The shop also made blades and Jacquard looms. Jin Ju Xing had a separate site and account books, but shared some management personnel with its parent plant.

The mid-1930's were a "Golden Age for the petty capitalists of Santiaoshi."[22] Among the machines and machine parts produced in Santiaoshi before the Japanese invasion were cotton gins, looms, Jacquard looms, cotton fluffers, noodle cutters, bicycle wheels, pots, stoves, wheels for cranes, diesel engines, lathes, flour milling machines, water pumps, steam pipes, water pipes, calendering machines, boilers, paper-making machines, oil presses, radiators, straw-hat-making machines, sock-knitting machines, printing presses, axle-making machines (*dazhou ji*), screws, nuts, plows, cart parts, and temple bells. The market for Santiaoshi's agricultural machines embraced every corner of Hebei, as well as parts of Shanxi, Shandong, Henan, and the Northeast (Manchuria). Santiaoshi's flour mills and dyeing, printing, and weaving machines went primarily to small factories in Tianjin, but also to many of the same outlying areas.[23]

This steady expansion of the district's repertoire of products was made possible partly by an incremental technical revolution. In the machining industry, hand-held files were gradually replaced by turning lathes. Since there was no electricity, the "turning" had to be done by hand. One person, usually an apprentice, turned a large iron wheel, transmitting power through a belt that moved the lathe, while a skilled laborer would do the actual machining. Nevertheless, in many shops hand-filing retained an important role. During and after World War I several machine-building shops began to experiment with *dian gunzi*, motors introduced by the foreigners. Many workers feared the new machines were dangerous, but their superior efficiency soon made them popular. Some shops rented motor generators from the electric company in the nearby Japanese concession, at a rate of six yuan per month, and powered the belts with 110-volt electricity. Shops that could not afford generators used boilers to produce steam to turn the belts. Shops that could not afford boilers continued turning lathes by hand, a practice that remained common well into the Japanese period.[24]

Meanwhile the ironcasting shops were undergoing a technical revolution of their own. From their earliest work with kilns they progressed to pouring (*dao guo*) and the use of dry rather than wet molds. The fansha technique gradually took hold. The power source of the shops changed as well, from hand-held bellows to hand-turned "wind gourds" (*feng hulu*) to electric fans hooked up to generators.[25] Equally important changes took place in the choice of raw materials. Scrap iron was replaced by iron from

Hubei, the Yangzi delta, and Anshan in the Northeast. Bar iron was whole-saled through hardware firms (*wujinye*), which bought iron from the mines and sold it to the factories. A Santiaoshi shop would usually buy exactly as much metal as was needed for a particular job, since it seldom had the extra capital to stockpile iron. Shops on good business terms with the hardware firms could buy on credit.

These improvements in technology and access to raw materials were important factors in the development of Santiaoshi. In at least one important respect, however, the traditional methods were not displaced. Except for De Li Xing, an unusually large machine shop, none of the shops had workers who specialized in the design or blueprinting of the machines they produced. Production depended on the traditional skills of the workers, and expansion of a shop's repertoire depended upon hiring skilled craftsmen who were experienced in the manufacture of another product. Perhaps for this reason, different shops specialized in single products for which they became well-known: De Li Xing in printing presses, and other shops in papermaking machines, looms, dyeing machines, or knitting frames.[26]

By the 1930's the most successful ironworking and machine-building shops were no longer simple one-room operations. Shops like Guo Tian Xiang and Jin Ju Cheng were divided into business and manufacturing departments. The business department typically consisted of an accountant, salesclerks, business apprentices, and one or more "runners" (*paojie*), whose job it was to solicit customers. In the manufacturing division there was sometimes a chief technician, and under him foremen, craftsmen, and apprentices. A manager, who was often also the sole investor, supervised both departments.[27] While these bigger shops might dominate the economic life of Santiaoshi, they were not entirely typical of the metalworking industry. In 1928 a Bureau of Social Affairs survey counted 514 ironworking shops in Tianjin, and was able to collect information about 511 of them. Numerically, they accounted for almost one-quarter of the total number of factories in Tianjin. But they had an average capital investment of only about 43 yuan per enterprise, and only 21 of them had electric power. Together they employed only 2,207 workers and apprentices—an average of 4.3 workers per enterprise.

The same survey found that the machine-building industry was slightly better capitalized and less dispersed. Sixty-two reporting factories (of 63 surveyed) had an average investment of 1,172 yuan. Shops in Santiaoshi and the surrounding area were usually capitalized at 1,000 yuan or less. They represented just .23 percent of the total capital invested in Tianjin

industry. Half of them used electric power. They employed 887 male workers and 310 male apprentices, a total of 1,197, or about 19 persons per
enterprise.[28]

In 1935 the Bureau of Social Affairs published another study of the
Tianjin ironcasting and machine-building industries. The survey showed
an industry still characterized by units of less than 30 people. Most shops
had some form of motor power, but in the vast majority of cases it was only
a one- or two-horsepower engine. Together they represented slightly more
than 1 percent of the total capital invested in Tianjin industry.[29]

Although many of the shopowners on Santiaoshi Avenue were related
by blood or native-place ties, their world was by no means free from ani-
mosity and competition. Ma Yunlong, nephew of the founder of Jin Ju
Cheng and manager of the shop from the 1920's until the 1950's, recalls
that "capitalists in Santiaoshi didn't work together. They competed both
openly and secretly." No guild organization attempted to prevent or regulate competition between member firms. Gift-giving and secret alliances
between shops were common features of business relationships.

Other shopowners were not the only actors with whom delicate alliances
had to be struck and maintained if a shop were to prosper. Small shopowners in Tianjin could not rely on the municipal government for legal or
physical protection; they had to negotiate, bully, or buy their way out of
conflicts. One source of trouble was the transport guilds, or *jiaohang*.
Ironcasting shops had to defer to the territorial ambitions of the jiaohang
and employ them to transport all their products. The shopowners chafed
under these restrictions. Ma remembers hearing from his father that
"there was once a large rumble between ironcasting workers and transport
guild workers. The ironcasters won the right to use their own transport,
and would only call in the guilds for minor errands, if the price was right.
But the guilds continued to be a problem, because they always tried to
charge high prices. When the two sides couldn't agree on the price there
would be a conflict." The guild that controlled transport for the Santiaoshi
area was run by someone known only as "Wang Four." Another famous
guild foreman in the area, named Cai, was unaffectionately known among
the ironcasters as *cai bangzi* (the rotten outer leaves of Chinese cabbage).
The bosses' boss, a shadowy and fearsome figure named Zhang Xiyuan,
would often travel through the area in a sedan chair. Ma explains that "we
were all polite to him, because we were afraid of him. He was tangled
up with all the local tyrants—Yuan Wenhui, Liu Guangkai, and Liu
Baozhen."[30]

In addition to the transport guilds, small shopowners like Ma Yunlong
had to contend with some unruly neighbors. The proximity of Jin Ju

Cheng to Santiaoshi's main assemblage of brothels, in Safe and Sound Lane (Ping An Li), caused the factory some trouble. The prostitutes, who Ma believes had been tricked into coming to the city or sold by their impoverished peasant families, served a mixed clientele. Many local workers went there, but problems arose when unwitting peasants decided to visit: "Those running the brothels were involved with the gangs. They had rumbles, or sometimes they would fight over prostitutes. People would come in from the villages, not knowing what was going on, and end up getting beaten." Those being beaten would flee into Jin Ju Cheng's factory yard, with their opponents in hot pursuit, causing frequent damage to Ma's equipment. He eventually built walls topped with barbed wire on two sides to keep such intruders out.[31]

A final scourge were the miscellaneous local "hoodlums" (*liumang*) who periodically made the lives of the shopowners miserable. "They would show up on the street and stand around looking threatening until people paid them off. They thought of various ways to extort our money," Ma recalls ruefully. Yet in spite of these problems, local owners preferred to reinvest their money in the district rather than acquiring village land or urban real estate, the traditional investments of the rich. In addition to Jin Ju Cheng and Jin Ju Xing, Ma himself was involved in the founding of a shop called Tong Yi Gong. He sent a group of craftsmen off to work at each new place in which he had an economic interest.[32]

When the Japanese occupied Tianjin in the summer of 1937 many workers, not knowing what to expect, left the city and fled to their native villages. By 1938 most of them had returned to a district which was bustling with new market demands created by the occupation. As the Japanese developed the local rubber industry, they needed iron molds; some Santiaoshi shops began to specialize in producing them. Others made stoves, wire-making machines, or crane parts required by the booming transport sector. Japanese attempts to improve cotton cultivation, and to construct mechanized plants for cotton processing throughout North China, expanded the market for Santiaoshi's cotton machines. New business flourished: 24 shops were founded in Santiaoshi during the occupation, some of them financed by merchants who had moved to Tianjin from the Northeast. Other northeastern merchants opened dyeworks in Tianjin, which in turn created a demand for dyeing machines produced by Santiaoshi machine shops.[33]

The bigger Santiaoshi shops signed exclusive contracts with Japanese firms (*yanghang*) for the manufacture of particular goods. Chen Wenbing, who came to Yong Mao Gong Ironworks as an apprentice in 1940, recalls that "Yong Mao Gong hung up a Sanyō Company sign. Sanyō Company was famous in Tianjin. We did work for them. As soon as it got to be winter we made stoves. In those days if you worked for the Japanese you would be in demand (*neng chidekai*). If you didn't have a Japanese sign your company couldn't get work or raw material." If a foreign firm wanted a job done and Yong Mao Gong could not handle it, it would subcontract out to smaller factories and deduct a commission ("take off a layer of skin").[34]

Under the direction of Japanese officials, in 1938 the metalworking trades organized a guild (Jiqi zhuzao hui) for the first time in the history of the district. If a large order had to be filled, the guild would act as agent for area shops and divide up the work among them. The bigger shops profited most from this arrangement.[35] The guild, however, was an arrangement imposed from above. It did little to regulate the trade internally or to negotiate with occupation authorities on behalf of the ironworking and machine-making shops.

After the beginning of the Pacific War, conditions in the district began a sharp decline. In 1942 the Japanese tightened their control over raw materials. Pig iron had to be bought from one of the Japanese firms. Special inspectors were sent to the various ironworks. If they found any bar iron, they would demand to see the required sales receipt from a foreign (Japanese) firm; failure to produce one might result in the arrest of the shop-owner. Nevertheless, small amounts of iron were sold on the black market at the southwest corner of the old city and on Second Street east of the river. The stalls of the dealers were called "iron nests" (*tie wozi*). They could not begin to supply the demand, and by 1944 many shops were reduced to buying broken lathes and melting them down to use as raw material. As usual, small firms suffered the most. But even firms like Jin Ju Cheng saw their marketing area shrink because the Japanese were unwilling to permit sales of looms and farm tools to areas where Communist organizers were active.[36] At Jin Ju Cheng, the workforce grew from 40 people before the occupation to 60 with the initial flush of new work, then dropped to 20 in the latter years of the war. Some workers left when conditions deteriorated. But the owners were embarrassed to lay anyone off, because all were relatives or fellow villagers, and letting them go involved a tremendous loss of face. Ma began to buy and hoard cornmeal, sometimes having his workers mill it themselves when there was no other work. Right before the Japanese surrender, even cornmeal was unavailable, and the remaining workers ate mixed grains (*zaliang*).

In spite of his skill at keeping the shop open in a deteriorating economic environment, Ma made one political blunder that almost cost him his shop. In 1942 Jin Ju Cheng sold six printing presses to a man from Shandong named Li. The deal was arranged through one of Ma's relatives. Because the Japanese were determined to prevent the export of any goods to Communist-held areas, nothing could leave Tianjin without a pass. Two guarantors, including one organization, were required before a pass would be issued. Ma went to the Public Security Bureau and presented himself as a guarantor. Interested both in making money and in opposing the Japanese, he did the same thing when Li returned to buy a second lot of five presses, although he was aware by this time that Li was affiliated with the Communists' Eighth Route Army. When the Japanese discovered that Li was from a Communist-controlled area, Ma suddenly found himself in serious trouble. He frantically wined and dined various Japanese officials, but was unable to prevent Japanese military police from smashing the machines in his shop. Eventually they forced him to sign a guarantee that he would no longer manufacture presses. Thereafter, his personal safety and the fate of his shop were precarious.[37]

As the situation in the district worsened, the only strategy for survival was to continue to manufacture goods for the Japanese. By the last years of the war, the occupation forces had stopped industrial construction and were concentrating their efforts on the manufacture of munitions. Chinese factories that did this work for them received preferential access to rationed supplies. Chen Yihe, who worked at the Chun Tai Machine Works from 1943 on, remembers that each person with a residence permit was normally permitted to purchase 15 catties (16.5 pounds) of grain.

> Maybe it would actually be soybean cake, or peanut cake. That's all they would let you eat. As for matches, each family was allowed one box per month. But if your factory was doing work for the Japanese, they'd give you better grain rations. Instead of a pack of cigarettes a month, you could get four packs, a carton of matches instead of a box. Of course, you had to pay money for these things, but at least they would give you ration cards for that quantity.[38]

In response to worsening conditions, some shopowners sought to strengthen their position by cultivating political relationships with the Japanese. To this day, local shopowners are remembered for the degree to which they collaborated. "We did what we had to do to survive during that period," Ma recalls.

> But in our hearts we hated the Japanese. We had to work for them in order to survive. But some people went further than that. Guo Dongbo [the owner of Guo Tian Xiang Machine Works] had no principles. He was the head of the machine guild under the Japanese. He became head of citizen's security (*baozhang*) for Santiaoshi Avenue. The Japanese used him. He even visited Japan.

Guo Dongbo was simple-minded. He would take his hat off and bow when he saw a Japanese. But when a Chinese came along he would puff out his chest (*tian duzi*). He wore a Japanese hat and carried a pistol. He forgot he was a Chinese.[39]

Guo Dongbo was not alone. Not only embattled Santiaoshi shopowners, but local toughs as well, survived by ingratiating themselves with the Japanese authorities and assuming petty posts in the district. Shops like Jin Ju Cheng were "squeezed" by extortionists on the one hand and a contracting market on the other.

The problems in Santiaoshi sharpened at the beginning of 1945, when the Japanese garrison command informed the heads of the guilds that factories would be assigned to manufacture a certain quota of artillery shells. Raw materials were supplied by the Japanese; payment was in rice, a rare grain on a market that in the late days of the war was dominated by cornmeal mixed with animal feed. On Santiaoshi Avenue alone more than 30 shops manufactured military goods; as the owners saw it, they had no choice. Even so, the number of Santiaoshi shops able to continue operation dwindled from 83 in 1937 to about 30 in 1945. It was with a feeling of great relief that Ma Yunlong and other shopowners greeted the Japanese surrender and the return of the Guomindang (GMD) in 1945.[40]

But restoration of GMD rule to Tianjin brought new troubles to the petty capitalists of Santiaoshi. For a brief period, business improved because of renewed economic contact with the villages. Then the government, concerned with the expanding area of Communist influence in North China, put strict controls on the "export" of tools and machines to the countryside, decreeing that they could be shipped only by train or steamer. But as the *Yishi bao*, a leading local newspaper, pointed out, trains did not reach much of the rural market, and places that steamers could go, such as Qingdao and Shanghai, had no need for the products of Santiaoshi. Bureaucratic regulation made the situation worse. In order to ship something from Santiaoshi to the northern suburb of Bei Can, a prospective buyer first had to obtain a permit from the Bei Can security bureau. He could then go to the Tianjin Smelting Guild (Yelian tongye gonghui), fill out a guarantee letter, secure three guarantors, send a letter with specification of the goods he wanted to the Garrison Materials Control Office (Jingbei bu wuzi guanzhi chu), and then get it stamped by the guild. After that it would take only one or two weeks to get his goods moved to Bei Can—unless any fighting flared up in the area, in which case he would get nothing. Those orders which did arrive sometimes contained only one-tenth of the goods requested. Shops also continued to have trouble buying pig iron and coke, and were forced to rely on scrap metal. The sources of coal in Suiyuan and Shandong were cut off by the fighting, and only a limited amount of expensive coal from the Kailuan mines remained available.[41]

A final problem facing Santiaoshi shopowners was the extortion practiced by various GMD officials. Their activities became so notorious in the district that their local appelation changed from Guomindang (National People's Party) to Guamindang (fleece-the-people party). For Ma Yunlong, the most unsettling element in this new situation was the feeling that, although the city was now controlled by a Chinese government, he had even less protection than he had had under the Japanese.

The first official representatives to visit the area were from the Investigation Bureau (Jicha chu). They threatened the owner of De Li Xing, accusing him of having manufactured products for the Japanese. Actually, De Li Xing had made not only machines, but also guns and gunpowder for the Japanese. But Ma could take scant comfort in the fact that *his* shop had not manufactured armaments; he was soon visited by an acquaintance at the Investigation Bureau who informed him that Jin Ju Cheng was next on their list. Ma tried to negotiate a cash gift with his acquaintance to head off the investigation, but the man's asking price was too high. Ma had no choice but to wait for the investigators to arrive. When they did, they accused Jin Ju Cheng of having made cannon for the Japanese, an unlikely feat since the shop had none of the requisite machinery. Undeterred by factual evidence, the investigators played on Ma's fears (he had, after all, manufactured machine parts for Japanese firms, like every other factory on the street). Through intermediaries, they extracted a large sum of money.

After the Investigation Bureau had concluded its work, Ma was visited in succession by agents from the military police corps (Xianbing dui), the army unified command (Juntong chu), and the public security bureau (Gongan ju). These last he found particularly despicable, since they had worked as police officers for the Japanese, then had changed uniforms after the war and continued working for the GMD. Each successive group repeated the accusation that Jin Ju Cheng had manufactured cannon. "No matter what you said to them about not having done work for the Japanese, they didn't listen, since what they were after was money. The only way to get rid of them was to pay them off."

For an entire year Ma was afraid to stay in the factory, for fear that one of these groups would arrest him. He knew that if he left the shop the police would not bother anyone else, since their targets were the owners and managers. He went through middlemen to deliver his bribes, fearful that if the officials confronted him personally they would demand even more. "For a whole year," he recalls with a grimace, "I didn't do anything useful. I spent a lot of money on bribes. There was no way to concentrate on business." Nor was his shop particularly unlucky; many factories faced the same problem. "When the police car would arrive in the afternoon, everyone who had to go hide would go hide, because we were never sure which one of us they would go after."

Jin Ju Cheng, like every other business in town, was also hurt by the worsening inflation. After the return of the Guomindang, Ma deposited his shop's earnings rather than buying goods with them immediately. Inflation soon made his savings worthless. The general economic decline affected the market demand for his products, and the shop was soon deep in debt. Ma was forced to draw on the same ingenuity that had kept him out of jail:

> I borrowed some money from a friend and used it to pay off some scattered debts. You had to conduct business like an art: if you had ten creditors, and they all came after you at once, it wouldn't go well with you! If you borrowed one big sum and used it to pay off several small debts, no one would be able to figure out that you were poor. If other people thought you were well-off, they would be happy to do business with you.

By 1948 even this debt-juggling strategy was ineffective. The shop simply did not have the money on hand to pay its debts, and there was so little work that it was only operating half-time. Ma had a conference with his long-term employees: should they close up or keep working? "It made me very sad. So many years, and now it was going to end. We decided to keep the shop but to let some people go. We kept a dozen or so who had the closest connections to us." The rest either went back to their home villages, drifted up to the Northeast to look for work there, or stayed in Tianjin "hanging around. This was the first time I had ever laid off such a big group of people." As a last resort, Ma took the few remaining assets in his shop and, like businessmen small and large throughout Tianjin, entered the world of speculation. He began by buying up confiscated goods that the GMD was auctioning off. "They would sell five things for the price of eight and keep the price of three as their profit. Everyone involved in this took a cut." Ma too bought, sold, and took his cut. He and his few remaining workers did a small amount of ironcasting, when there was work.[42]

By mid-1948, the *Yishi bao* found that of 80 ironworking factories it surveyed, 30 had closed and more than 20 others had stopped work. The rest were using material they had purchased previously and only "lighting the furnace" every week or so. "Santiaoshi Avenue, in the Hebei district where the factories were concentrated, used to be full of the noise of jangling and pounding until you wished yourself deaf," a reporter wrote. "But now Santiaoshi is still and silent, and workers with sad faces sleep beside the cold furnaces." Meanwhile the rural market was in desperate need of iron tools. An owner who visited his native village in early 1948 found that there were very few pots in the villages. "Two or three households share one," he told a reporter, "and whoever breaks it is in trouble." He estimated that filling this demand alone would take three to five years.[43] Nor was the machine industry in better shape. A forum sponsored by a local industrial magazine in mid-1948 found that only about 20–30 percent of the city's machine works could manage to stay open, while the rest found it more profitable to strip their machines and sell the parts.[44]

Even factories that were much better capitalized than those on Santiaoshi Avenue were ruined by the strictures on shipping their products. In July 1948 the Tianjin Iron and Steel Mill (Tianjin gangtie chang), originally constructed by the Japanese, could not meet its payroll. Neither the banks nor the parent company in Beijing could help out. The manager, in a lament that might have been echoed by the proprietors of every Santiaoshi shop, declared, "Running a factory these days is like carrying a corpse on your back. You can't put it down, you can't stop, you're exhausted from rushing around, and there is no end in sight. The future is unimaginable!"[45] In a state of virtual paralysis, Santiaoshi awaited the Communist forces.

The economic fortunes of Santiaoshi typify the course of development of handicraft and semi-mechanized shops in many trades throughout the city. Founded during a boom period by small entrepreneurs, these shops showed a great deal of flexibility in responding to new market demands. They grew rapidly until the Japanese occupation. The entrepreneurial spirit of the petty capitalists of Santiaoshi was manifest. These shopowners had made their lives in the district and they intended to stay there, not to make a quick fortune and return to their home villages. In Santiaoshi a small native capitalist class was beginning to grow—one partially dependent upon foreign customers, it is true, but rooted in the area and in a specific craft. Unlike many of their more powerful brethren downtown, they maintained a stable interest in a single enterprise over many years.

Yet crucial elements of Santiaoshi life were not governed by the rules of entrepreneurship, but by the need to survive in a city full of predators. These ranged from the transport guilds, who at least performed a service, through local toughs to petty government officials. Santiaoshi factory owners knew how to use money and personal connections to handle these relationships, but they lacked the power, the organization, and the money to command the constant protection of a powerful patron. Certainly none of Tianjin's governments found it in their interest to play that role. The absence of a guild organization that could effectively represent the economic interests of the members was a product both of the district's short history and of Tianjin's unstable political environment. Santiaoshi shops could muster little resistance when a succession of municipal administrations moved to exploit them. Small shops had even less control over local economic fluctuations, which were exacerbated by political struggles in the region. The political vulnerability of Santiaoshi shops, combined with their weak capitalization and their dependence upon precarious raw material supplies, drove them to near-collapse in the final decade before Liberation. It was in this environment that Santiaoshi workers struggled to make a living.

THE WORKERS OF SANTIAOSHI

Social Origins

The social origins of workers and owners in Santiaoshi were intertwined and frequently identical. A post-Liberation study of 107 Santiaoshi shopowners found that 41 of them were from Jiaohe county, 13 were from Tianjin, and 11 were from Wuqiao.[46] Apprentices showed a similar pattern. The account books for Guo Tian Xiang Machine Works record 98 apprentices who entered the factory from January 1925 to March 1933. The largest single group of apprentices, more than one-fifth the total number, came from Wuqiao county, as did the owner, Guo Dongbo. Although Guo Tian Xiang was a machine-building factory rather than an ironworks, the second largest group came from the traditional home of the ironcasters, Jiaohe. Ninety-seven percent were from Hebei, while 3 percent came from Shandong. Only four were natives of Tianjin city.[47]

A second sample, of 73 ironcasters, comprises men who worked after Liberation in a single factory, the Machine Casting Factory (Jixie zhuzao chang). Before Liberation, they had been distributed among at least 16 small ironworks.[48] Almost 80 percent (58 workers) came from Jiaohe county. The second largest group (five workers) came from Fucheng, Ma Yunlong's home county, which bordered Jiaohe. The number of factories represented does not permit us to conclude that workers from particular counties were routed into particular factories. But it appear that most ironcasting workers were from Jiaohe, whereas machine-builders came from more diverse locations, including Wuqiao, Jiaohe, Ningjian, and Dacheng counties.[49]

Of the 73 ironcasters surveyed, 67 percent were classified after Liberation as having come from poor peasant families. But middle peasants constituted a sizable group (23 percent), and it was not necessarily the poorest peasant families or even the poorest counties that sent the most sons to become metalworkers. Interviews with former workers indicate that for many peasants, the Japanese invasion might have been at least as important a factor as rural poverty in the decision to leave.

No comparative statistics survive on the class position of owners and workers in their native villages, and so it is difficult to tell whether owners typically came from wealthier peasant families than did workers. But this is doubtful, since many Santiaoshi capitalists had first come to Tianjin as apprentices or workers themselves. Of 32 Santiaoshi shopowners surveyed after Liberation, 17 had begun their careers either as handicraft iron-workers or as apprentices. Many of the rest had worked in closely related trades.[50]

It was not mere geographical proximity to Tianjin that drew young male peasants to the shops of Santiaoshi. In general, counties from southeast Hebei (Jiaohe, Wuqiao), rather than those from the immediate suburban area, contributed the most workers. A particular tradition of peasant iron-working in that part of the province fostered this pattern, and the practice of introducing relatives and fellow villagers into the shops reinforced it.

The hundreds of interviews collected from 1958 to 1972 and stored in the Santiaoshi History Museum Archives point to several reasons for leaving the land. One was economic hardship in the villages. Gao Hongren's story is typical: "In 1942 the harvest was no good in my home, Yin county. Add to that that we had very little land. So life at the time was very hard. Sometimes for three or five days we had nothing to cook (*jiebukai guo*). We couldn't manage. So I went through the introduction of a *tongxiang* [person from the same area] to enter the Zheng Cheng Ironworks as an apprentice."[51] Few reminiscences were collected from workers who arrived in Tianjin before 1937. But it is clear that the chaos accompanying the Japanese invasion aggravated rural difficulties, displaced many peasants, and increased the suffering of those who remained. Liu Bingwen, a worker who came to Tianjin in 1940, recalls that "when the Japanese occupied Jiaohe county, there were several battles with them."

They burned 70 percent of our village. Our house was burned by the Japanese. My grandfather was killed by an artillery shell. After they came everyone in the village fled. Life didn't settle down in our village until after the Japanese surrender. It was worse than in the cities—the countryside was a mess. The guerrillas were fighting them. Life for the common people was very unstable.[52]

Even in years that were free from invasion or natural disaster, Tianjin looked attractive to peasants from Jiaohe. One Santiaoshi worker explained that "coming to the city to learn a skill had long since become a habit with people from our area. Generally families with two or three sons would have one come to the city to learn a skill."[53] Migrating to Santiaoshi did not necessarily mean that a peasant boy intended to stay there. It was a means of maximizing income for the worker, as well as his family back in the village, to whom he could eventually hope to send remittances. It also diversified a peasant household's sources of income; if the crops failed, someone in the family would still be earning money. As Liu Bingwen sees it, "We people from the countryside all had this way of thinking: if this place had work, we'd do it. If it had no work we would leave. When there was farm work to do, we'd go home to do it. When there wasn't any, if we couldn't support ourselves there, we'd come out again."[54] In short, the answer to the classic question, "Were peasants pushed out of the countryside by difficulties there or pulled to the cities by the promise of a better life?" seems to be "both" in the case of Santiaoshi—especially since a peasant in search of work might make several such migrations back and forth for different reasons during his working life.

Santiaoshi workers came to the city with parents or (more commonly) alone. They came fleeing bad harvests, invasion, and flood. They came hoping to learn a remunerative skill. But no matter what their reasons for making the journey, a crucial factor which enabled them to settle in Tianjin was a connection with someone already established there. Some had relatives who were willing to house them until they could support themselves. Others were introduced by relatives who were already craftsmen. Boys who had no relatives in Santiaoshi sought introductions from fellow villagers. Frequently, an apprentice was related to the shopowner who took him in or to the chief foreman of the shop; native-place ties between owner and craftsman were even more common.

Connections between a particular rural area and a particular type of work were reinforced by this system. Ma Yunlong recalls:

> Every Spring Festival when my father came home, relatives and friends would come to the house and turn over their kids to him to take back to Tianjin "to find a rice bowl." He took several back every year. Of 100 households in my village, 60 eventually sent people to Tianjin to do ironwork.
> Some of my relatives and fellow villagers who learned how to cast iron in my father's factory later went on to open their own in Tianjin, Jinan, and the Northeast. There were Jiaohe people everywhere, clear up to Korea. Local people [in the cities] didn't want to do this kind of work because it was hard and dirty.[55]

Although owners and foremen frequently went back to the countryside at New Year's and brought boys back with them to work, factories in Santiaoshi apparently never made a systematic effort to recruit apprentices. As Chen Yihe explains it, "At that time you didn't need to go to the villages, didn't need to recruit people. If you opened a small business and gave free board, plenty of people would come to work."[56]

Terms of Apprenticeship

Those who found their way to Santiaoshi shops as apprentices were exclusively male and typically sixteen or seventeen years of age.[57] They usually had little or no previous urban work experience and few skills. To obtain a job, a boy commonly needed an introducer and a guarantor, unless he was already personally known to the owner. Sometimes, as in the case of Chen Wenbing, the introducer was a relative who already worked in the shop. Sometimes, as with Chen Yihe, it was a relative who merely knew a fellow villager who worked in the district. The guarantors were usually local businessmen, also men with some connection, however distant, to the aspiring worker.

Even in cases where there was an oral agreement with no written pledge, it was understood that if the apprentice stole anything or ran away, the guarantor would pay the factory owner for the food he had eaten during his training. If the apprentice died, the guarantor was responsible for burying him and for notifying the family. Since this could be a significant burden, no one volunteered to guarantee a stranger. "There wasn't anything in it for the guarantor," remembers Chen Yihe. "But they all were relatives or friends. It was a matter of human feelings (*renqing guanxi*). If I didn't know you or understand you, I wouldn't guarantee you."[58]

One of the features of almost every Santiaoshi oral history collected since Liberation is a rendition of the "body-selling contract" (*maishenqi*) signed with a thumbprint by the would-be apprentice. The accounts of the contract terms are graphic, colorful, and generally in verse form, for example:

Fei tie zou zan	Flying hammers, walking chisels,
Dasi wu yuan.	Bashed to death and none to blame
Tou jing tiao he	Kill yourself in well or river
yu ben hao wu guan.	Won't be our shop bears the shame.
Xuetu buman taopao	If you flee before you're finished
Baoren pei fan.	Guarantor must pay the claim.[59]

In fact, the language of the few printed apprenticeship contracts that survive is considerably more prosaic, and it appears that both the term "body-selling contract" and the poetic jingles are products of political campaigns in the 1950's. In a typical contract signed in 1935, Wang Mobin, a boy from the Tianjin suburbs, entered the Guangda Factory. In signing his name, he agreed to serve an apprenticeship of three years, to remain in the factory unless he received permission to leave, and to study diligently. If he left without completing his term, he was to pay the owner for the food he had eaten. The owner agreed to pay the apprentice a nominal amount of pocket money. The remainder of the contract enumerated the responsibilities of the guarantor (see Appendix). The terms of apprenticeship were virtually identical to those mandated by the craft guilds in other Chinese cities.[60]

In a few ironworking shops the signing of an apprenticeship contract was a ceremonial occasion that underscored the obligation of the apprentice to the shop that was taking him in. Wang Weizhen, who entered an ironworks in 1913, recalled that after he completed a trial period the owner called him and six or seven other boys into the room.

> He explained the contract and said clearly that if you signed, you had to keep working and couldn't leave as you pleased. If you agreed, he asked the middleman to fill in the contract. Then within ten days he would pick a good day to conduct the ceremony. The child and the middleman would sign the contract. If the child's home was nearby, his father would come too.
>
> We would also lay out a table of offerings, and burn incense and ketou to the gods (*lao junye*). The apprentice would ketou to the foreman, the middleman, and the craftsmen, and last of all would call out (*rangrang*) to his senior fellow apprentices.

After this the apprentice would spend a few dollars and invite guests for a meal. If he could not afford to do so, the factory management would advance him the money and deduct it from his New Year's bonus. His graduation to the rank of craftsman would be marked by a similar rite of passage: "You would invite guests again, craftsmen, relatives, friends, and people in the same trade. You would thank them and ketou to them, and then you could discard the contract."[61] However, the available evidence suggests that such ceremonies were rare. The agreement to begin an apprenticeship was usually concluded with considerably less fanfare, reflecting the weakness of guild traditions in Santiaoshi.

All the printed contract forms that survive are from machine shops, and variations may have existed between the machine-building and ironworking trades. In the machine industry, the owner was anxious to ensure that he got his money's worth from the boys he trained. One former owner has suggested that the technique of machining was complicated, and that anyone who mastered it would be in demand. He explained that the owners feared that once apprentices had learned the trade, they would immediately go elsewhere to work for pay. Therefore they used the apprenticeship contract to ensure themselves a cheap source of labor for a certain length of time.[62]

The ironworkers were a more transient group than the machine makers, and the terms of apprenticeship in ironworking were not as strict. In the casting industry, one old worker recalls, a four-year apprenticeship was standard, but the introducer and guarantor were not responsible if the boy fled. "If you were caught you would be beaten—if you weren't caught that was the end of the matter. There were lots of people around who wanted to learn these skills. Also, in the ironcasting trade people moved around from shop to shop a lot. Sometimes if you went looking for the person who had recommended an apprentice for the job, you couldn't find him." [63]

In both machine and ironcasting shops, written contracts apparently came into common use only just before the Japanese invasion. The impulse for their adoption came not from Santiaoshi owners who wanted to codify restrictions on their apprentices, but from the municipal Bureau of Social Affairs (Shehui ju), which wanted to prevent abuse of child workers and to avoid labor conflicts. The Bureau turned its attention to apprenticeship contracts because, as a national labor publication reported in 1935, "in Tianjin all the factories, aside from a dozen or so companies, use apprentices. Their wages are low, they are easy to manage, and there are many advantages to having them in the factory. The number of apprentices in a factory often exceeds the number of hired workers." The article went on to note that while their duties varied from factory to factory, apprentices in the machine and metals trades did the heaviest work. [64]

By mid-1936 the Bureau of Social Affairs had developed a standard apprenticeship contract, printed up several hundred of them, and given them out to large and small factories to use as a model. [65] The model contract specified that the factory was obligated to teach the apprentice a skill and to assume responsibility for expenses. Factory owners were not to permit apprentices to handle explosive or poisonous materials, operate dangerous machinery, or work near high-voltage electrical lines. For their part, apprentices were exhorted to respect all factory regulations, not to terminate the apprenticeship, and not to take holidays (except as decreed by management) unless they agreed to make up the work time. The factory was free to terminate the contract if the apprentice broke the factory rules, was absent from work for more than three days, stole, or disobeyed one of the people responsible for his training. The apprentice in turn could terminate the contract if the factory did not fulfill its obligations, harmed his health or character, or was otherwise cruel to him. The factory was not to prevent the apprentice from engaging in business after the completion of his apprenticeship. Finally, children under thirteen were not permitted to become apprentices. Any disputes were to be referred to the Bureau of Social Affairs for arbitration. [66]

Like most labor regulations issued by government agencies in this period, this one was not widely observed. In February 1937 *Yishi bao* reported that few factories had begun to use the model contract. The Bureau of Social Affairs was planning to have all factories complete a form describing their terms of apprenticeship and then to order improvements.[67] This effort at reform was cut short by the occupation, but printed contracts distributed by the Japanese-organized guilds later came into common use. Significantly, they did not say anything about the right of an apprentice to terminate his contract. The ironworking and machining trades showed little inclination to regulate themselves, and government attempts to compensate for the lack of guild regulation were hampered by frequent changes in municipal administration.

Life as an Apprentice

Chen Yihe began his apprenticeship at the Yalun Machine Factory, a shop with four lathes and about 30 people, in 1939. He was eleven years old.

I was the smallest of the apprentices. They had no motor power, so two people would turn a lathe by hand. You would turn a big wheel to move the line shaft and the line shaft would move the lathe. One of the older apprentices and I turned the wheel.

We got up every day before dawn. You had to oil all the machines, oil the line shaft, then set the table and cook for the craftsmen. After they ate we would clear the table and start to turn the wheel. We would stop at noon, wash our hands, and set the table for the craftsmen to eat.[68]

Mealtimes provided scant diversion. In the 1920's, workers in the more prosperous shops ate steamed bread and had two meals of meat each month. But standard fare under the Japanese and during the subsequent civil war was cornmeal cakes (*wotou*) and vegetables pickled by the factory. A brief meal in the yard or in the workshop itself, and then "after dinner we would wipe the table and the two of us would go back and turn the wheel."[69] This daily routine went on all year, with seasonal variations; the workday ended at seven or eight P.M. in the heat of summer, but was extended to midnight in the winter. "In the ninth lunar month the weather would get cold, and then people could take a longer workday. Each year on the ninth day of the ninth month, at the beginning of winter, the owner would put out some money and we would have a meal with meat in it. There was a rhyme at that time that went: *Jiu yue jiu, chi dun rou, heitian baitian lian zhou zuo* (Double nine, eat some meat, Nighttime daytime on our feet)."[70] Skillful or clumsy, smart or dull-witted, the apprentice worked an even longer day than the skilled craftsman. He not only prepared the tools for the day's work and cooked the food for the craftsmen, he was also expected to draw water so the craftsmen could wash after work, to spread the bedding, and to perform miscellaneous tasks. In some shops it was well past midnight when the apprentices crawled into the low-ceilinged loft above the workshop to sleep for a few hours on a straw mat.

Extreme fatigue induced by long hours of labor is the memory most frequently mentioned by former Santiaoshi apprentices. The archives at the Santiaoshi Historical Museum abound with descriptions of apprentices who crawled under large casting pots and slept for three days, burrowed into boxes of dirt and slept, dozed off while taking a bath in an iron pot, or fell asleep while squatting on the toilet.[71] Fatigue, of course, led to accidents. An apprentice sleepily starting work in the predawn winter darkness could easily be spattered with molten iron as it hit tools that had frozen overnight. One of Chen Wenbing's fellow apprentices, injured in this way, soon lost the sight of one eye. He was fired and sent back to his native village.[72] The machining industry was equally hazardous, and it was all too common for an apprentice to crush his hand in a lathe, be whipped into the air by a machine belt, or have his leg broken by an axle.[73]

Fire was a frequent occurrence in the rickety handicraft workshops and crowded back alleys of Tianjin, and here too the burden of disaster seemed to fall most heavily on the young apprentices. In November 1936 a fire at the Shuang Ju Gong Ironworks destoyed the entire factory, causing losses of tens of thousands of yuan. The cause was a faulty generator. It was not until the flames were extinguished that police discovered two apprentices were missing. Under the loft where the apprentices slept (directly over the kitchen where the explosion had taken place), they dug through the rubble and found two charred corpses. Wang Changxing, 16, of Jiaohe county, and Wang Laichi, 16, of Xian county, had come to the factory less than three months before.[74]

The efforts of the Bureau of Social Affairs to clean up conditions in the metalworking trades, like its efforts to regulate apprenticeship, seem to have had little effect. A 1934 inspection resulted in warnings to several Santiaoshi shops. The inspector noted that the work area in Guo Tian Cheng "needs repair to avoid danger." The Quan Sheng De Ironworks was found to be "very small, and because business is not good they do not have the wherewithal to repair the whole factory building." The inspector felt that the machine room should be repaired immediately to avoid accidents. The Chun Tai Ironworks was described as "very dilapidated and lacking in light." De Li Xing, Guo Tian Cheng, and Quan Sheng De were given verbal admonitions by the Bureau to clean up their work areas, but no sanctions were imposed.[75]

These conditions—onerous labor, long days, and inadequate safety precautions—typified all the handicraft and semi-mechanized industries in Tianjin. Located in cramped, ramshackle quarters, small workshops frequently collapsed on their workers after heavy rains. Roof beams in one dyeworks, dried out by the fire under the dyepots, gave way one day in 1937 and buried the workers. In spite of the Bureau of Social Affairs admonition that apprentices were not to handle dangerous substances, seven apprentices in a woodworking shop near Santiaoshi were injured and one was killed when a container of alcohol they were using to treat unpainted furniture exploded.[76]

Owners and workers shared these uncomfortable and dangerous work environments, but even the smallest factories had certain stratifications. At the top, of course, was the owner. Since he was there to supervise production, and sometimes to participate in it, the apprentices learned to watch him carefully. Chen Wenbing remembers that the owner at Yong Mao Gong Ironworks "understood the trade" (*bijiao neihang*). "Sometimes we'd be doing a piece of work and make a mistake. The first time you did something wrong he wouldn't say anything, or the second time, but the third time he would ask what you were doing, or hit you."[77] The relationship of apprentices to skilled craftsmen was more complex. Craftsmen might try to protect an apprentice from the owner or foreman, or they might become irritated and hit the boy themselves. The ideal relationship of teacher and student, which a stronger guild tradition would have encouraged and which the Bureau of Social Affairs hoped to foster, seems never to have materialized. As a writer observed in 1928, "Because in Tianjin and the surrounding area the new-style small machine factories are flourishing, most apprentices do their apprenticeship in a factory, and don't have a so-called master (*yeshi*). Therefore there is not a close relationship between the teacher and the apprentices. Both of them are working for the factory owner, and the only difference is that they collect different wages."[78]

For the apprentice there was little respite from the closed world of the factory. Except at New Year's, he was not permitted to return home, and in any case, for those from distant rural counties the journey would have been prohibitively expensive. Liu Bingwen explains that "when we were apprentices we hardly ever went out of the factory. We were working 15, 16 hours a day, and on the streets the Japanese were often seizing people for forced labor, so we didn't dare go out. There was no bathhouse. We washed in a basin. On holidays the owner would give us some money to go take a shower. We cut our own hair. We had no shears, so we used knives."[79] Unless they had relatives or friends in nearby factories, apprentices had little contact with any workplace outside their own.

Although the work was hard in Santiaoshi, there is no reason to suspect that apprenticeship conditions were atypically harsh; rather they should be taken as an indication of the dismal situation in handicraft and semi-mechanized shops throughout the city—and, historically, in almost all early industrial enterprises. The gradual introduction of machinery increased work hazards, but did little to ameliorate the intensity of labor or the length of the working day.

After a year, new apprentices would come to the shop, and then a senior apprentice could stop turning the wheel that powered the lathe and start working on the machines. By then, he had seen enough of the work to quickly pick up the necessary techniques. For the remainder of his apprenticeship, he was no longer the lowest-ranking person in the shop. Between apprentices, as between apprentices and owners, a hierarchy existed: "If I came a day earlier than you I had the right to hit you."[80] On the other hand, there was a certain solidarity among the apprentices fostered by the fact that "we were all poor children. We tried to help each other out. If I saw that you were sick, I'd take some money—or borrow some money if I didn't have any—and buy some hot water for you to drink."[81]

Further details about relationships within the shops have been obscured by politically motivated post-Liberation accounts bent on dividing these tiny enterprises along class lines. The more complicated portrait that emerges from interviews, however, is one of relationships ranging from mutual assistance through neglect to cruelty. The length of the working day, which exhausted everyone, tended to brutalize relationships between apprentices, workers, and owners. Beyond that, connections of blood or native place, or the individual predilections of a foreman or a boss, might make life as an apprentice either miserable, tolerable, or (more commonly) some mixture of the two.

It can be argued that there were economic advantages for the owners in the extensive use of apprentice labor. Apprentices could be had for the price of their food and a few dollars each month or on holidays. They performed arduous tasks that had to be done but required little skill. They were young and easy to manage. Perhaps for these reasons, some employers hired many more apprentices than craftsmen. In Chen Yihe's factory there were 30 apprentices and only eight workers; in other factories the ratio might be as high as 40 to one. This high percentage of apprentice labor seems to have been typical of industries in distress. In Beijing in the 1920's, carpet-weaving shops that were pressed by foreign competition hired an average of almost three apprentices per worker, while in healthier industries the proportion was reversed.[82]

Many apprentices, once they finished their training, found themselves unemployed, a situation also typical of the troubled carpet-weaving industry in Beijing. It was easy for the factory to maintain a few skilled craftsmen and use a new cohort of unpaid child laborers to do the bulk of the work rather than retain and pay the people who had learned the trade there. Completing an apprenticeship did not guarantee a place in the industry as a craftsman. In several ways this was an abuse of the apprenticeship system. It permitted unpaid children to do the work of adults, failed to protect or control entry into the trade, and ultimately led to a degree of unemployment among skilled craftsmen that was advantageous only to the shopowners. If the Santiaoshi district had had a longer history or a stronger guild organization, such practices might well have provoked the organized ire of the craftsmen.[83]

Yet the persistence of the apprenticeship system until Liberation cannot be explained by cost-effectiveness alone. Apprentices, after all, had to be fed and clothed. They were not as skillful as experienced workers and, if the descriptions of their age and general frailty are accurate, they were certainly not as productive. Accidents in which they were involved, whether they resulted in damage to property or to persons, were potentially costly. If there was really such a surplus of labor in Tianjin, why were the owners not better off hiring skilled people at a low wage dictated by the market?

The answer probably lies partly in the traditional organization of a trade based on "connections." Santiaoshi workshops, which had begun as small bands of relatives or neighbors engaging in itinerant metalwork, maintained themselves throughout the pre-Liberation period by relying on connections—between owners, between owners and their native villages, and by extension between owners and their apprentices. Many owners felt no paternalistic obligation to take good care of their young charges, and often had only a distant relationship to them. Nevertheless, the apprenticeship system, with its use of guarantors and introducers, made the procurement of labor a far cry from the impersonality of a "free" labor market. It gave the owner a stable source of labor, one that was accountable to him through connections that might be much older than his shop. It made the recruitment of labor an extension of relationships already familiar to everyone involved: relative, neighbor, friend of friend.

For the apprentice, the arrangement provided a certain security that might be crucial to households in economic trouble. Although apprentices could make no financial contribution to their families, by leaving home they removed a burden. Those who succeeded in finding a job after completing their apprenticeship could look forward to a future as a skilled laborer who could contribute to the household. In a trade where few of the workers were literate, where skills were transmitted orally and by observation, serving an apprenticeship was the only way to learn. And while apprentices were often miserable because of their working and living conditions, most of them stayed where they were. As Chen Wenbing reflects, "It was very hard, but what else could I do? Aside from my relative who had gotten me this job, I didn't know anyone else. There was nowhere I could go. I didn't know any other trades. He had told me that life was hard in Santiaoshi, but there was no way to live at home, so I came. Anyway you could keep body and soul together; you could scrape by." [84]

Life as a Craftsman

In many ways, the life of a skilled worker in Santiaoshi did not differ significantly from that of an apprentice. Like the apprentices, workers lived in the factory, sleeping in flea- and lice-infested bedding either in a jerry-built loft or in the workshop itself. Like apprentices, they spent 330 to 360 days a year in "cramped and ill-lit workspaces, with a stuffy atmosphere, coal fumes everywhere, messy, with dust flying about," and often had "a prisoner's unkempt hair and a mourner's unwashed face, as though they had lost their health." [85] Workers might eat slightly better food than apprentices, but if the factory fell on hard times (as most did during the occupation and the civil war), everyone was apt to be fed cornmeal or even coarser grains. Workers could go to sleep earlier and rise later than the apprentices, but 11- and 12-hour days were the norm in the industry, and the work was hard and dirty. [86]

But there were two aspects of life as a craftsman which were quite different from that of an apprentice: craftsmen were paid wages, and they could move from job to job. Since they paid no room fees while they lived in the factory, their economic status improved noticeably once they finished their apprenticeships. As Liu Bingwen put it, when he was an apprentice he "didn't even have two sets of clothes. I was like a beggar. After we became craftsmen we could mail a little money home. . . . My apprenticeship was finished. I had a skill. I got paid six dollars. Some people made eight." [87]

The income of a skilled craftsman in Santiaoshi was not sufficient to bring a wife and children to the city. [88] Virtually without exception, workers who married found wives from their home villages and visited them once a year, continuing to live in the factories after their marriage. As Chen Wenbing explained, "We [he and Liu Bingwen] both married after Liberation, because here you couldn't find a girlfriend. We were from outside Tianjin with low wages and couldn't support a family. The people at Yong Mao Gong were mostly from the countryside. Some were married, some weren't. All of them got married at the appropriate time. But they went to the countryside to get married." [89]

If craftsmen had brought their wives to the city, the family would have had to rent a room even if the workman himself remained in the factory.

The woman would either have remained in the house or perhaps would have sought low-paying temporary day labor in one of the export-processing companies. In contrast, a wife who remained on the land could farm and contribute to the household of the craftsman's parents, while the worker could send them a monthly subsidy.

This arrangement also helped to cushion the family unit against sudden unemployment. Although some highly skilled craftsmen, or those with close family connections to an owner, might remain at a single shop for many years, a much larger pool of men moved from job to job. Between the time they completed their apprenticeships in the early 1940's and Liberation in 1949, Chen Yihe, Chen Wenbing, and Liu Bingwen each worked at two different shops. Sometimes they changed jobs seeking better wages; sometimes they were laid off when a factory closed or cut back its operations. All three men went home to their native villages at New Year's, and Chen Wenbing and Liu both returned home to live and help their parents with farmwork between jobs. If they had had dependents in the city these frequent job changes might have meant economic disaster; as it was they were minor events in the normal course of a worker's life.

The Mental Universe of the Santiaoshi Worker

The fact that most craftsmen still called the countryside home and returned there regularly, as well as the instability of life in Santiaoshi, kept them from thinking of themselves as urban dwellers. Unlike apprentices, they were not confined to the factory, but their involvement in urban life was limited to an occasional day off, when they would visit a bathhouse, go to the bird market, listen to storytellers, see a local opera, or seek satisfaction in the local red-light district. In the 1920's, nearby Pu Le Street offered restaurants, shoe stores, a theater where popular forms of opera were performed, and many brothels. The entertainment in the area catered to officials and warlords, but workers could find amusement there as well. After most of the street was destroyed by fire, nearby Xin Le Street replaced it as the amusement quarter. A movie theater and two restaurants, as well as a teahouse where local drumsinging was performed, graced the area. Ma Yunlong and other shopowners issued two tickets per month to each worker for the local bathhouse.[90]

Normally, though, workers spent their waking and sleeping hours in the factory and did not seek any involvement outside the workplace. Although they earned their livelihood in the city, their aspirations remained focused on their home villages. "Life in Tianjin was better than in the villages," commented Ma Yunlong. "You got what you worked for in the city. You could go back to the village, buy some land, and be rich."[91] Their involvement with their home villages, as well as the demands of a long working day, kept them from forming lasting connections to urban institutions of any kind. They also apparently had few ties, through kinship or native place, to other sectors of the working class. Perhaps this isolation was reinforced by their common places of origin and their concentration in one urban district. Santiaoshi workers remained enclosed in the narrow world of the workshop.

Neither religion nor secret societies of any variety made many inroads into the world of Santiaoshi. Chen Wenbing recalls that a few workers at Yong Mao Gong Ironworks were Catholic or Protestant. Some workers observed Buddhist rituals. They had heard of the Yi Guan Dao, a popular religious sect (see Chapter 6), but they thought of it as a Japanese organization; no one joined.[92] In Chen Yihe's factory the Yi Guan Dao gained some popularity, because "under the Japanese there was that kind of current in society. People in the Yi Guan Dao got protection (*renshen baohu*). Several people in our factory joined. They made offerings to the Eight Immortals." But the attitude of the majority is summed up in his comment: "No matter what poor people believed in, it didn't work. Only believing in having enough to eat was real."[93]

When they felt that the owner was interfering with their acquisition of enough to eat, Santiaoshi workers took action. But it was not the type of highly visible and self-conscious action glorified in post-Liberation factory histories. For apprentices, the most common form of protest was to flee the shop. Chen Wenbing remembers that "if an apprentice didn't want to keep working there, first he would get someone to arrange another job for him, then at night he would run away." Those who got caught would be beaten, but since many left the city and returned to their native villages, they were seldom caught.[94]

For craftsmen, the tiny scale of most factories and the perpetual instability of employment militated against strikes. Owners frequently worked alongside the craftsmen and slept in the shop at night. Chen Wenbing puts it succinctly, "We didn't have strikes. If you struck they would fire you." For this reason protest was confined to slowdowns, known in local slang as "soaking mushrooms." In Chen Yihe's factory one foreman would get up even before the workers in the morning, and after he called everyone to get up and work, he would go back to sleep. The exhausted workers devised a simple means of dealing with the situation: "When he wasn't around we wouldn't work very hard."[95]

A craftsman who was secure in his position could be more blatant about his protest and gamble that he had enough leverage to get what he wanted: "If you weren't satisfied you just didn't work. The foreman and the capitalist could tell. They'd come after you. You'd just say, 'I'm not making very much money.' Some they fired. Some they gave more money to."[96] Ma Yunlong, knowing that there were always other village boys eager for a job in Tianjin, would say to disaffected workers, "Three-legged frogs are hard to find, but there are plenty of two-legged men around." His most skilled workers, secure in their knowledge that skilled craftsmen could usually get work in the district, would counter, "If you won't provide for the old man, then some other place will!" (*Zhe bu yang ye, hai you yang ye chu!*) Apprentices, of course, had no bargaining leverage.[97]

Another form of dealing with an intolerable work situation was to steal a bit of raw material for resale on the black market, or to destroy or hide tools to slow down the work process.[98] But workers did not push such methods very far. Unlike the cotton mills, where the economic consequences of pilferage to the factory were not immediately obvious because the factories were so large, the tiny ironworks and machine shops were usually close enough to economic difficulty that the connection between theft and business losses was visible to everyone. And, as Chen Yihe comments, "Whoever came into that factory was seeking a living there. No one wanted it to close."[99]

After the Japanese surrender the Communist Party enjoyed a brief period of open work in Tianjin. This was followed by several years of active underground organizing when the GMD reestablished control. But no special effort was made to organize in Santiaoshi, which was under the "urban residents" (*shimin*) wing of the Tianjin party committee rather than the "industrial work" section.

At the same time the reconstituted Bureau of Social Affairs made an effort to organize all Tianjin workers into government-sponsored unions. Ironically, it was this effort by the GMD government that led to Santiaoshi's only recorded large-scale labor struggle. The conflict began in the spring of 1947, when workers were making 50,000 yuan per month but three bushels (one *dan*) of millet cost 30,000–40,000 yuan. Workers at the De He Ironworks put forward demands for a raise; several of them were fired. These activists continued trying to organize the union from the outside, and made contact with the city union director, Wang Shouge. More than 130 workers signed up to join a union, and in June they conducted a two-week slowdown when the owner opposed their efforts. After a series of conflicts with the factory owner and the Military Law Bureau (Junfa chu), the Bureau of Social Affairs stepped in to mediate. By the end of the year the workers had successfully founded their union planning committee, and their wages had been raised, but the campaign's leaders had all been fired or had left.[100]

This slowdown was the product of a time of extraordinary political and economic chaos, even for Tianjin. The details of its development are not clear, and the main activists have never been located or interviewed about their role in the struggle. But it stands out as a unique event in the history of the district; in no way does it typify the experience of most Santiaoshi workers or reflect their degree of formal organization. Like most of the workers in Tianjin's small handicraft or semi-mechanized factories, Santiaoshi workers did not stray far from traditional ties to native place and family. Getting and keeping a job in Santiaoshi, or coping with intervals when jobs were unavailable, depended upon those traditional ties rather than upon new ones forged in the workplace.

Conclusion

The lack of any associational activity in Santiaoshi is striking. Unbroken by any religious or political movement, life in the district appears to have had a certain ahistorical quality; the district in 1948 was bigger and more economically troubled than it had been in 1927, but it was not really different. Workers continued to enter, work, and leave intermittently, never settling down long enough to make Santiaoshi one of the city's residential working-class neighborhoods.

The quiescence of Tianjin's ironworkers and machine makers was a product of the district's short and troubled history. Relationships between owners and workers in Santiaoshi exhibited many "classic" preindustrial features. The persistence of an apprentice system with clearly defined obligations on both sides was one instance of this. The persistence of blood ties and native-place connections as the determining factor in the hiring process was another. Unity of working and living environments was a third. Even between Ma Yunlong and his skilled workers, who had the freedom to leave and the skills to support themselves, the weight of traditional ties cemented owner and laborers together. These ties, and the shopowner's direct participation in production and residence at the factory, may well have tended to mute conflict and to enforce a solidarity that encompassed everyone in the shop rather than expressing itself along class lines.

Yet paradoxically, class conflict (or the lack thereof) in the shops was also shaped by the weakness of other traditions. Santiaoshi was a new district run by entrepreneurs who were themselves strangers to the city. They did not rely on guild organizations to protect or regulate themselves. In other cities, guilds sometimes became embroiled in conflicts with the government, or withheld products of their shops in order to obtain better terms.[101] Santiaoshi guilds were not founded until the late 1930's; they

acted as agents *for* the government rather than representing shops in dealings with the municipal administration. Guild weakness denied the metalworking trades a powerful tool for survival in a predatory city.

This weakened industry in turn denied to workers protections and
privileges, and perhaps a craft consciousness, that they would have enjoyed under a strong guild system. Santiaoshi craftsmen never joined
guilds as individual members. They had no experience of an urban artisanal tradition, legitimized by guild regulations and religious practice, that
might have been theirs to defend. In this respect they differed from their
Beijing brothers, and from their counterparts in Europe as well. In nineteenth-century Marseille, for instance, working-class protest was dominated by artisans, who had more information, organizing experience, and
commitment than other sectors of the working class, and who were free
from the worst material want. None of these conditions obtained in Tianjin. When their livelihood was threatened, Santiaoshi craftsmen did not
play the militant role of their European brothers; instead, they left the district.[102] Ultimately, in a district and a city that experienced recurrent damage from economic pressure and political exploitation, neither owners nor
workers had much room to maneuver for better working conditions. The
goal of both groups was survival, and outside threats to their survival
pushed them together rather than apart.

Santiaoshi symbolizes many of the factors militating against the formation of a Tianjin working class: the lack of a clear division of labor, a pre-
requisite for the emergence of clearly articulated classes; continuing ties of
both owners and workers to the countryside; a weak artisanal tradition;
and economic and political instability in the larger urban environment. Although labor relations were not harmonious, the factors that united owners
and workers in Santiaoshi, and in many of Tianjin's smaller factories, were
still more compelling than those which divided them. Workplace relations
in Santiaoshi—like those in handicraft industries throughout the city—
show the interaction of an aspiring capitalist class and a nascent working
class, neither of which was fully formed.

CHAPTER FIVE

Winning the Turf:
The Transport Workers

The transport workers and the guilds that controlled them, with a history of more than 200 years, were among the oldest and most important participants in the making of the Tianjin working class. Tianjin lived by trade: it was the meeting point of five rivers, an important juncture on the Grand Canal, the loading point for sea shipment of goods from North and Northwest China, the entry point for foreign imports and Shanghai goods, and the major northern station of two railroad lines. Goods that entered, left, or moved within the city were transported by a human corps that may have numbered one-tenth of the urban population—far more than the number engaged in industrial manufacture.

Transport workers were of several types—freight haulers who worked for highly organized corporatist guilds, rickshaw pullers and three-wheeled cart (*sanlunche*) drivers who rented their vehicles on a daily basis,[1] and casual laborers who picked up odd jobs unloading cargo along the river. Of these groups, the guild workers had the longest history. They were also the most numerous, the most contentious, and the only group about whom enough information survives to permit a partial reconstruction of their story.[2]

This study limits itself to those transport workers who were primarily engaged in the manual movement of goods, whether on the docks, at the railroad stations, or in the warehouses and factories of the city. It also makes passing mention of those transport workers who, though not members of the guilds, also used their physical strength to transport goods: the rickshaw pullers and sanlunche pedalers. Those who operated motor-driven machinery, like trolley drivers and employees of the railroad lines, are excluded, because the organization of their work was completely different from that of the "traditional" sector, and (in the case of the railroad workers) their intercity mobility meant that they were tied to a regionally based, more militant sector of the working class, one that deserves a study of its own.

The transport guilds were among the most feared and despised organizations in pre-Liberation Tianjin. Jealously guarding territories within which only one guild could move goods, they "maintained these monopolies through threats and thuggery against businessmen, bribes and favors for the authorities, and guile accompanied by occasional savagery."[3] A Tianjin folk rhyme placed them with others at the bottom of the social order:

Che Chuan Dian Jiao Ya	Carter, Boatman, Innkeeper, Transport worker, Broker—
Wu zui ye gai sha.	Even if innocent, they deserve to be killed.[4]

The guild bosses kept as much as 80 percent of the fees paid to transport coolies. Their power over the coolies was enhanced by their membership in the Qing Bang, or Green Gang, an organization that counted both bosses and workers among its members. Violence and the threat of violence were a way of life in the transport industry, used by the bosses against their rivals, their clients, and their workers, and by the workers against one another. This well-established transport culture of territoriality and violence meant that a worker had to form vertical alliances with powerful bosses in order to survive. Like the craftsmen of Santiaoshi, transport workers depended on "preindustrial" patron-client bonds. But compared to the Santiaoshi ironworkers, they were involved with larger, more mobile, and less familial workplace organizations—the transport guilds.[5]

FORMATION OF THE TRANSPORT GUILDS

The transport guilds were a byproduct of the development of Tianjin as a commercial center. The three main factors in the growth of Tianjin were also the three reasons for the development of the guilds: convenience of transportation, proximity to the capital, and the nearby location of areas rich in cotton and other *tu chan*, or local products.[6]

In the late Ming and early Qing periods, government officials frequently passed through Tianjin on their way to and from the capital. The task of carrying their sedan chairs and transporting their luggage was performed by the local poor, known simply as "bearers" (*fuzi*). At the same time, commercial traffic with South China was growing under the sponsorship of resident southern merchants, who imported goods from Guangdong (*Guang huo*), as well as sugar and paper, to Tianjin. The people who transported these goods were active in the old city area and around Needle Market Street (Zhen Shi Jie). A third group of workers specialized in the transport of grain and salt, mostly along the east bank of the Hai River (the Hedong district).

By the early eighteenth century, these three groups of workers had gradually become organized into a guild system, in which groups of workers received government permission to monopolize transport in a particular area. Official notices were pasted up in each sector, delimiting its boundaries and naming the authorized transport agent. From the Kangxi to the Xianfeng reigns (1662–1861), the Qing government issued "dragon tickets" (*long piao*) or other notices of official approval to the transport guilds. Under the Guangxu emperor (1875–1908), successive magistrates issued 11 orders supporting the special privileges of the guilds.

The actual process of guild formation is unclear in many respects. Some sources suggest that the guilds first carved out territories (*di duan*) for themselves, and later won government approval as a sign of solicitude for the welfare of the coolies, or as a reward for services rendered.[7] Other sources describe the emergence of two parallel guild systems: a government-sponsored one with offices by each city gate, which was set up to handle official traffic but later transported goods for merchants as well, and a group of private guilds along the river. The government system, which was known as the Four Gates Transport Guild (Si Kou Jiaohang) because of its location, was later farmed out to private operators, and the two systems merged.

The guild system was a source of tax revenue as well as a means of regulating transport. The Four Gates system was divided into constituent taxpaying guilds. Tax collection apparently was delegated to local merchants. In the tradition of tax-farmers everywhere in China, they hiked the tax rates and took a cut for themselves, and were thoroughly hated by the transport guilds. This particular system of taxation endured until 1936.[8]

From the beginnings of the guild system in the late Ming until the opening of Tianjin as a treaty port in 1860, the means of transport and the mode of labor organization were simple. Goods were moved by shoulder pole and by hand-pushed cart. Each sector had a "labor boss" (*fuzi tou*); there was no city-wide guild organization. The labor boss would use the "shouting method" to send people out to work—that is, he would assign tasks by calling out the names of the coolies, in a strict rotation. No matter who went out on a job, the income would be turned in to the boss and divided equally among all the workers. The guilds were divided into those which moved goods from ships into warehouses—"fresh goods" in local trade talk—and those which moved "ripe goods" from warehouses to other locations.[9]

With the opening of Tianjin to foreign trade, the scale of sea shipping was greatly expanded, and a new docking area was constructed along the riverside frontage of the concession areas. Peasants, displaced by the building of the concessions, obtained permission from the foreigners to operate transport guilds.[10] They worked along both banks of the Hai River, loading and unloading steamboats. Horse-drawn carts and later a small number of motor vehicles were introduced, although human muscle power was still used extensively. The method of labor organization was modified: workers drew lots, in the form of bamboo slips placed in a tube, to determine the order in which they would go out to work. As before, everyone got a turn before a new rotation began. Guilds ranged in size from one or two coolies, with a boss supervising, to several hundred people arranged in an elaborate hierarchy.

A similar process of peasant displacement and guild formation took place when the first three Tianjin railroad stations were built between 1888 and 1911. Displaced peasants were issued "dragon tickets" and given permission to load and unload goods for a living. Each village in the vicinity of the railroad stations chose a boss (*tou mu*); most guilds were named after the villages.[11] In the first 50 years of the twentieth century, the number of guilds and transport workers continued to increase, but the structure of the industry changed very little. Guilds specialized in work along the river, at the railroad station, or within the city.

Two types of docks lined the five rivers that converged in Tianjin: those slightly upstream, which handled shipments by junk (*minchuan*) from the interior, and those along the Hai River in the concession areas, which served steamships. The three largest steamship docks, built in the twentieth century, belonged to the British firms of Butterfield and Swire and Jardine, Matheson, and to the Chinese-owned China Merchants' Steam Navigation Company. Both junk and steamship docks flourished in the twentieth century. "From about the 10th of March to near the 20th of November," wrote a foreign visitor in 1900, "the transferring of cargoes is the most conspicuous form of work one sees."

The rivers are crowded with river boats as well as with many tugs and lighters. The boat-crowded river-ways extend throughout the native city in even a more congested form than in the native settlements, and give a total length of crowded riverway of ten to twelve miles. Thousands of coolies fill the passage ways along the Bund, carrying articles of commerce to and from these boats.[12]

During the busy season, the docks were open and operating 50 workdays a month (with day and night shifts each counting as a "day"); in the slack season, they ran 20 days per month.[13]

Before the Japanese occupation, the two British docks hired people by the month, providing room and board in addition to a monthly wage. The Chinese dock hired workers on a daily basis. During the occupation all three docks were controlled by Japanese firms, reverting to their original ownership after the war. But no matter who was running the docks, or what type of wage system they constructed, the actual hiring was in the hands of the transport guild bosses, who worked on contract from the various dockowners. When a boat arrived, workers would come looking for the guild boss to receive their job assignments; when there was no boat, they would look elsewhere for jobs as day laborers. If work was slow or there was a surplus of labor, the dockowners limited the number of trips each coolie could make between boat and dock. But if there were many boats to be unloaded and a shortage of coolies, or if it was dark or raining, the transport guilds would negotiate for higher fees and the right to carry unlimited loads. Only when every guild member was employed would the foreman hire temporary laborers to fill the gap.[14]

Just before Liberation, Tianjin had 84 separate docks, seven of them large steamship docks, with 4,229 dockworkers. The dockside guilds were responsible only for loading and unloading ships; for transport within the city, they turned the goods over to a separate group of freight guilds.[15]

By the 1940's most merchandise coming to Tianjin from the interior arrived by rail.[16] At Liberation there were an estimated 2,419 workers engaged in loading and unloading goods at the city's four railroad stations. They were divided into yellowcaps, who loaded the freight cars under the supervision of guild foremen, and redcaps, who handled passenger luggage. Redcaps had slightly more independence of operation than the other railroad coolies.[17] A large railroad warehouse complex at the East Station (the site of "Gate #6," a post-Liberation opera about transport workers) employed an additional thousand workers.[18]

The third and most common type of transport guild was engaged in hauling freight around the city. Whether goods arrived by ship or train, once unloaded they were moved by the freight guilds. Warehouses could not hire coolies at random to move goods for them, but had to use the transport guild that controlled their district. If a warehouse had an altercation with the local guild, it could not choose to give its business to another guild as it pleased. In spite of government attempts to regulate the freight charges, powerful freight guilds charged merchants exorbitant fees. Warehouse owners resented these restrictions, but they received in return a guarantee of safe handling. The freight guilds were required to pay for any missing goods when the shipment was delivered, and so they very seldom lost the goods they transported or engaged in systematic theft.[19]

Some freight-hauling guilds specialized in loading and unloading goods for specific factories, on a subcontracting basis.[20] Still other guilds, in addition to providing transport services, acted as general labor subcontractors. A large sawmill opened by an American firm in 1923, for instance, was staffed exclusively by temporary workers hired through a transport guild foreman. Wages were paid to the foreman, who distributed them to the workers.[21]

Just before Liberation, Tianjin had 227 separate transport guilds in Tianjin, and 3,032 bosses. A total of 60,000–70,000 people made their living in the transport industry.[22] Whether they worked on the docks, at the railroad stations, or in the commercial and industrial districts of the city, the organization of these guilds was fixed by tradition. They were run by a hereditary corps of bosses, commonly referred to as "those with slips" (*zai qian de*), who directed and profited from the labor of the coolies. The guilds as a whole had a well-developed code of behavior, one shaped by their connections with nineteenth-century urban ruffians (*hunhunr*) and twentieth-century membership in the Qing Bang, or Green Gang.

ANATOMY OF A TRANSPORT GUILD

Those with Slips

The "slips" held by the guild bosses were simultaneously licenses to engage in the transport business, and shares in a specific transport guild. The origin of these slips is obscure, but they were apparently related to the government grant of monopoly rights over a certain territory. Some of these rights dated from the Kangxi period (1662–1722). The slips could be inherited, pawned, or sold to others who had slips.[23]

The slips were jealously guarded, since they were a guarantee of livelihood for a man and his descendants. Those with "live" or "red" slips were not required to participate directly in the physical labor of moving goods, although they were frequently involved in supervising labor and keeping accounts. "Dead" or "black" slips were given to people who had been injured in fights over guild turf, and to the dependents of guild members killed in such fights. They were entitled to a share of the guild profits even if they did not participate at all in transport work. A third group, drawn from among those with "red" slips, formed a dare-to-die corps in the event of territorial struggles; presumably they became members of the "black" group if injured. Those with slips had job security, and were entitled to drive out those without slips as they pleased.[24]

All those with slips were considered guild bosses, but among bosses there were a number of lesser distinctions. The larger guilds had a chief boss (*zongtou*) who presided over lower-level bosses. The latter, in turn, took charge of hiring workers, maintaining vehicles, and keeping accounts. Under them were the "street-standers" (*zhanjie*), who patrolled and supervised workers, and also checked to make sure that merchants were not transporting their goods privately.

Some of Tianjin's major guilds were divided into branch organizations that could directly organize work themselves, but they had to give half their income to the main guild. Others were actually amalgamations of smaller guilds, with each one claiming a share of the income depending upon its size. The smaller guilds had a simpler, but similar, organizational structure. On the docks, where foreign and Chinese firms contracted out to the guilds for a supply of coolie labor, guild bosses served as chief contractors, subcontractors, and foremen.[25]

The bosses of the largest transport guilds often invested the substantial incomes that they earned from transport in a number of other economic ventures. During the occupation, the main boss for the three steamship docks received payments of more than 2,000 yuan a month. This small fortune, and others like it, were channeled into real estate, cloth shops, paper factories, bathhouses, jewelry shops, warehouses, native banks, hotels, theaters, brothels, and a lifestyle of conspicuous consumption which included entertainment by dancing girls and prostitutes.[26]

Those at the very top of the industry were indistinguishable in their personal lifestyle from the commercial elite of the city. They hobnobbed with the political elite as well. The daily life of smaller bosses, in contrast, was not all that different from that of the coolies they hired—those without slips.

Those Without Slips

Workers enjoyed none of the hereditary rights or income guaranteed to the bosses. Coolies were hired to perform two tasks: pulling or driving the carts, and loading, unloading, and weighing the goods.[27] Very little is known about the social origins of these workers.[28] Unlike artisans and factory hands, many of them were Tianjin natives.[29] All the workers were male. More than half of them were between the ages of twenty-five and forty-five; this was apparently one industry in which the need for adult muscle-power and stamina precluded the use of child labor.[30] Most transport workers were illiterate.[31] The vast majority were married, and the little data available indicate that their families usually resided with them in the city, in contrast to the living arrangements of many factory and handicraft workers.[32] Despite indications that transport workers were older and more settled in their family arrangements than other sectors of the working class, they had a reputation as social drifters. A 1942 report commented that many dockworkers were people who had committed "evil deeds" and fled their place of origin, and who continued to change jobs periodically.[33]

It is extremely difficult to estimate actual rates of turnover for the transport industry, because workers might be employed by the same guild for years but move around from job to job as they were subcontracted out by the guild. For instance, the 1941 survey that found rates of turnover as high as 75 percent among dockworkers is written from the point of view of the North China Transportation Company, not the guilds. Since workers may have stayed with the same guild while they hauled freight for a number of different companies, this may not be an accurate indicator of turnover.[34]

Most transport workers had originally worked at other urban occupations (factory worker, merchant, vendor, soldier), and had taken up transport work after losing their jobs. Workers in the transport guilds were near the bottom of the occupational hierarchy—only slightly above the rickshaw pullers and coolies hired on a casual basis, who had even less job security.[35]

Guild workers paid for their relative security of employment. Workers commonly received less than a third of the total transport fee paid by the customer. The rest was skimmed off directly by "those with slips," or appropriated indirectly through required payments for the vehicles or the horses (which also belonged to the bosses). After these charges were paid, there were still miscellaneous fees such as "whip money," "grease money" (for oiling the cart), and a "cart-bottom payment" charged by the police. In some cases, the actual income of a worker was less than 10 percent of the transport fee.[36] This high rate of exploitation was another factor helping to keep transport workers at the bottom of the job hierarchy.[37]

Hauling freight in pre-Liberation Tianjin was onerous and dangerous work. The coolies who worked along the docks were graphically described by a reporter in 1936:

> There are lots of people there, but you seldom see them talking, just hear people catching their breath, faces covered with sweat and mud, green veins protruding. Their necks have been rubbed so raw by the loads they balance that the skin no longer hurts or itches. The flesh ripples on their upper arms, showing endless strength. The flesh on their chests is purple. Some have a bush of black hair on their chests. If you look closely, their chests are also jumping, as though the heart wanted to jump right out. Their blood probably circulates very quickly!

Carrying piles of wood, rice, and flour down the gangplank to the river-bank, a coolie had to watch his balance, or he might fall into the river. Under the weight of the loads he carried, "his body looked like a bow, with head and feet only a foot or so apart."[38] Accidents among the transport workers were often fatal: "There was a warehouse right near the Gordon Hall. . . a little north, towards the French Concession. . . . They used to take the stuff down to the river to load on barges. I remember one time the flour wasn't well stacked and it collapsed on the workers and a number of them were crushed to death."[39]

For freight haulers in the city proper, the situation was complicated by the chaotic traffic situation. A foreign observer wrote after one harrowing trip across the city:

> There is a net-work of tram lines throughout the city, and while distances yearly become greater, the trams are both a means of simplifying life, and also make transportation more hazardous. These combined with every kind of motor vehicle of the latest lines are subject to definite speed laws, but as the laws in each concession differ as to the rate of speed a given vehicle may travel per hour, speed laws are constantly violated both by the trams which plunge head-long through the streets, and by the motors which dodge promiscuously through the crowded thorough fares. . . . With rickshaws and other human drawn carts, the hub-bub of the city would fluster the most clever Fifth Avenue traffic officer![40]

Guild members working in this hazardous environment had the security of knowing that their fellow workers would look after them and their families in the event of an accident.

The same was not true of coolies hired on a casual basis. The newspapers in the 1930's and 1940's abounded with stories of casual workers who had been crushed to death while loading goods along the riverbank. In one such case a seventeen-year-old temporary dockworker was crushed by a heavy plank of wood and lay on the ground bleeding to death for half an hour while the local "responsible people" ignored him. He was finally found by the police.[41]

Rickshaw coolies faced the same traffic hazards as guild freight haulers, and had a few more problems besides. Because they pulled their own vehicles without benefit of any draft animals, they were, according to one foreign observer, "exposed to great heat, cold and wet. They get terribly hot running and consequently suffer much from chills in cold weather. The pulling also affects their hearts and it is said that they die soon after the age of 50."[42]

In addition, though all freight haulers might run afoul of the traffic regulations, it was the rickshaw pullers, unprotected by any guild organization, who were most likely to be abused by the police. "Rickshaw pullers depend on running the roads for their livelihood, but the roads are full of their deadly enemies," wrote a reporter in 1935.

It is easy on a crowded street to violate some rule of the road, and then these "iron-faced heartless heroes of the road" [the police] will hit you on the head with a club, or take your seat cushion and throw it to the side of the road like a discus to try their skill and show their true heroic qualities, or play a melodious and tasteful symphony with their hands on your face.

In addition, police frequently extorted "nameless taxes" from passing rickshaw pullers.[43]

Transport workers, like artisans and factory hands, lived at the edge of subsistence.[44] A reporter described them in 1947:

Some are regular workers, some are short-term workers, and punishment and hardships are their lot. They are the people we often see pulling carts on the street, who work like draft animals and pass each day with draft animals. What passes into their stomachs is the cold wind, black-meal cakes, and endless insults. What flows out are blood, sweat, and tears, and the labor power that is squeezed out through the utmost exertion. But the reward they receive does not reach 10 or 20 percent of that taken by "those with slips."[45]

To widen their margin of subsistence, transport guild workers frequently stole some of the goods they moved—a type of theft that should be distinguished from the larger-scale extortion practiced by their employers. They also took what leisure moments they could, gambling on the docks between jobs, or gathering at the guild offices to drink hot tea, play the *sanxian* (a three-stringed instrument), tell stories, and sing opera.[46]

Territory

The territories within which a guild could transport goods were fixed by government decree, begun by Qing officials and continued by every government until Liberation. The smallest guild might have jurisdiction over several buildings or several lanes; the largest guilds controlled entire train stations or major dock areas and operated their own warehouses.

Aside from simple geographical divisions of territory, there were a number of other conventions for dividing up the work. One guild might take exclusive responsibility for all the goods moved by a large commercial firm or a factory. Or it might take a large enterprise like the Kailuan Mines and divide it by area, subcontracting the work. Two or three guilds might share the business provided by a large enterprise, each taking a certain number of days per month.[47]

Certain guilds were limited to transport of certain goods (produce, hardware, skin and fur, grains) or to certain stages of the transport process ("fresh" and "ripe" goods). Finally, some guilds reached agreements where they pooled their resources, with each guild taking a set percentage of the fee.

By these methods, all transport in Tianjin was controlled by the guilds. The system had some advantages for merchants. It allowed for a very fine-tuned response to transport needs, and provided a system of responsibility based on quasi-personal relationships. But no matter how elaborate the territorial divisions, they were never adequate to prevent conflicts between guilds, and between guilds and their customers. When these conflicts arose, they were routinely settled by violence. The form which that violence took was shaped by two urban traditions which profoundly influenced the transport guilds: those of the hunhunr and the Qing Bang.

URBAN TRADITIONS

Hunhunr: The "Dark Drifters"

"Tianjin has many local scoundrels," complained an unofficial gazetteer in 1884, "more than any other province."

There are rascally vagabonds who wait for the market days, who live together and eat in a large group called the "mess group" (*guo huo*), and call themselves *hunhunr* or *hun xingzi*. They are elements who have no fear of death, who control the market, harass the merchants, form cliques and collect in crowds, and take any pretext to create a quarrel and fight over land in Tianjin. This is called "staging a rumble" (*da chunjia*). . . . They do as they like and rely on brute force, harming the local inhabitants, and that is not the worst of it. If they are brought up on charges, they are capable of bearing great punishment, several hundred strokes of the rod, and they won't let out the slightest sound. Their mouths don't beg for forgiveness, their faces don't change expression.[48]

The hunhunr, groups of urban hoodlums, were the scourge of official Tianjin throughout much of the nineteenth century. Tradition holds that they were originally a branch sect of the Elder Brother Society who gradually forgot their roots. The hunhunr bands were made up of young male loafers, as well as some workers who had lost their jobs. Their group activities centered around a rented room where they ate and drank together, and where they also stored caches of weapons, such as short spears, broadswords, and axe-handles, in preparation for fighting. They were conspicuous for their unconventional mode of dress: dark pants and jacket with a blue pouch at the waist, brightly colored shoes, and a wig worn on top of the queue, sometimes adorned with a jasmine flower or two. Their way of walking was also unusual: they would step forward with the left foot and drag the right foot behind them as though it were wounded.[49]

Hunhunr supported themselves and their bands through a variety of lucrative activities. They ran gambling dens, with some members of the band running the games and some acting as bouncers. They inserted themselves as middlemen between peasants bringing produce from the countryside and urban peddlers, collecting a commission from both groups for their services. They did the same for the local fishermen. Combining offers of service with threats of retaliation to those who refused to buy, they moved in on the grain warehouses along the river. As minor moneymaking ventures, they ran small ferryboats, carried sedan chairs for weddings and funerals, and counterfeited coins of low-quality brass adulterated with sand. Finally, they operated transport guilds.

The hunhunr achieved local notoriety not so much through these economic ventures as through the methods they used to muscle in on one another's moneymaking. All these methods were based on one principle: heroic stoicism in the face of danger or pain. If a hunhunr cried out in pain during a fight, his opponent was to stop fighting immediately, and the weakling was kicked out of the band. If someone rushed him with a knife, he was to bare his chest; if attacked with an axe-handle, he was required to run at it head first, to prove that he was fearless. Anyone who violated these dicta became a laughingstock among the other hunhunr.

Thus, if one band of hunhunr decided that they wanted a share of the profits from a gambling den, they chose one of their members to go to the den and create a disturbance. When the bouncers came running, he was to lie down and demand that they beat him, which they usually did (being careful not to kill him, since that might attract official attention and force the closing of the den). If the instigator endured the beating without crying out, he was ceremoniously covered with a red quilt by the den management and carried home to nurse his injuries. The management was then obliged to send him a string or two of cash every day for as long as the gambling den operated. In Tianjin slang, this practice was referred to as "No beating, no acquaintance" (*bu da, bu xiang shi*).

A more grisly method of extortion was to enter the den and cut a chunk of flesh from one's own leg to use instead of money as a stake in the game. If the dealer took the chunk of flesh without flinching, there was a stalemate. An experienced owner would come rushing over at the outset and, making solicitous noises, rub salt powder in the wound. If the man who had mutilated himself persisted in talking and laughing as though nothing had happened, he was entitled to collect a daily subsidy by virtue of his demonstration of true grit.

Similar methods, all featuring heroic posturing, were used to move in on the grain shops and the transport guilds. One Tianjin legend holds that during the Xianfeng reign (1851–61), a hunhunr who wanted to run the Four Gates Transport Guild challenged all comers to jump into a pot of boiling oil to vie for control of the turf. When there were no takers, he ordered one of his relatives to jump in. The man was fried to a crisp instantly, but his relatives gained permanent control over the territory.[50]

The hunhunr were also responsible for developing the group rumble into a high art. This remained the characteristic form of struggle between transport guilds until Liberation. A rumble might be precipitated by conflicts over any of the economic ventures described above. Time and place were agreed upon in advance, and the night before the fight all the men involved (who might number in the hundreds) had a good meal. For the most serious fights, volunteers drew death lots. It was agreed that if they were not killed in combat themselves, they would surrender to the police and take responsibility for any deaths that occurred on the opposing side. On the appointed day the bands marched in order, leaders first, and attacked their opponents with fists and knives until there were deaths or injuries. At that point someone would step out and declare an end to the fight. The county magistrate would then arrest and interrogate the preselected holders of "death lots," in a government hall crowded with hunhunr who had come to make sure their brothers did not cry out under torture.[51]

Hunhunr who survived until middle age went into semi-retirement, opening small brothels, theaters, entertainment houses (*laoziguan*), or pawnshops, or else becoming usurers. Others served as petty police officials or messengers at the *yamen* (government office), abandoning the outer trappings of their ruffian youth. Those who had accumulated small fortunes might engage in some public works, such as the support of firefighting societies, or the organization of religious parades. Significantly, these were the same types of charitable activities performed by the transport guild bosses at this time. In this, as in other activities, there was a great deal of overlap between the two groups.

In spite of these good works, however, the troublemaking ways of the hunhunr, and particularly their penchant for street fighting, kept them in constant conflict with the municipal authorities. This conflict was ultimately responsible for their decline. After the Tianjin Massacre in 1870, Zeng Guofan was sent by the Qing court to Tianjin to negotiate with the French. Since 18 foreign nationals had been killed in the incident, the French were demanding that the culprits be caught and punished. Zeng took this opportunity to execute a number of hunhunr who were in prison for fighting, apparently with little regard to their actual involvement in the incident. Years later, Li Hongzhang and Yuan Shikai served as governors-general of Zhili. Yuan in particular detested the hunhunr and beheaded a number of them, and their influence waned during his term of office in the first decade of the twentieth century.[52]

The hunhunr left no particular organizational legacy to twentieth-century transport workers. What they bequeathed was a set of attitudes that centered on respect for those who were most able to perform difficult physical feats and withstand punishment silently. The hunhunr outlook on life was summarized by one observer in the maxim, "Today there is wine, today we will get drunk." [53] It remained to a later arrival in Tianjin, the Qing Bang or Green Gang, to enshrine these attitudes in organizational form.

Qing Bang: The Green Gang

The decline of the hunhunr corresponded with the rise of the Qing Bang in Tianjin, and the membership of the two groups apparently overlapped. The Qing Bang had been founded in the early eighteenth century as a mutual protection society among sailors involved in grain transport along the Grand Canal.[54] When transport of grain along the Canal ceased in 1901,

the members of the Green Band saw their society and its historic past threatened with extinction. They therefore reorientated themselves and enlarged the organization of the *pang*, while maintaining the name, the flags, the insignia of the boats, and all the rules. Admission was no longer restricted to cereal transporters and the association's influence spread throughout the North and South, while the number of members suddenly increased.[55]

A substantial part of the new membership apparently came from among dockworkers in the treaty ports, and (in Tianjin, at least) from among the ranks of the hunhunr.[56]

In the first five decades of the twentieth century, the Tianjin membership expanded to include not only dockworkers, but rickshaw pullers, small merchants, laborers, handicraft workers, restaurant employees, and the managers of brothels, teahouses, and entertainment halls. In short, it encompassed virtually all the social strata that had been involved with the hunhunr, as well as the entire transport industry.

The influence of the Qing Bang, however, was not limited to the lower reaches of society. In the early years of the Republic, both the son of Yuan Shikai and some of Yuan's chief enemies joined the Qing Bang in hopes of bending it to their own political purposes. From the early 1920's until the Japanese invasion, virtually every warlord or Guomindang official who ruled Tianjin (Li Jinglin, Zhang Zongcheng, Zhu Yupu, Li Dasen) was a member of the gang. It won adherents among gentry, peasants, workers, merchants, military personnel, and police.[57] Individual gang leaders like Bai Yunsheng amassed large personal fortunes through speculative activities, and lived in great luxury in the concessions.[58]

Tianjin gang leaders never reached the social heights attained by their

Shanghai counterparts, however. "There was nobody in Tianjin who had
the kind of control that Du Yuesheng and Wang Xiaolai and those people
had in Shanghai," recalls Israel Epstein.

> In Shanghai, the same people who ran the gangs had banks and had the opium
> trade, and were highly respectable and honored citizens who were written up in
> the papers for having founded hospitals. You didn't have anything quite like that in
> Tianjin; they were smaller and more fragmented. I couldn't tell you who . . . the
> czars were in Tianjin, but in Shanghai it was very obvious.[59]

Although hierarchically organized in groups of elders and disciples, the
Qing Bang was far from a unified organization. Struggles between gang
factions, as well as struggles in which gang members served as hired thugs,
rocked the city at every social stratum, and they ranged from high-level
political assassinations to local squabbles between guild bosses or mill
foremen.[60]

The gangs continued to operate, albeit less conspicuously, throughout
the occupation. In the early 1940's the occupation government expressed
its concern that some gang members, operating from a base in the French
concession, were acting as spies for the Chongqing (Guomindang) government. But others worked closely with the Japanese, collecting intelligence,
recruiting laborers to be sent to Japan, and supplying women to the occupation troops.[61]

During the 1920's and 1930's, and again after the occupation, the presence of the Qing Bang in the transport industry was particularly noticeable. The bosses of the major guilds were also elders in the Qing Bang:
men like Yuan Wenhui, descendant of one of the oldest guild families; Ba
Yanqing, boss of the Hebei Avenue Guild, head of the city-wide transport
union, a member of the Guomindang Party Committee and of the Hong
Bang as well; Zhai Chunhe, boss of the Chun He Guild and the adopted
son of Yuan Wenhui; and Ma Wenyuan, nicknamed the "Third Gentleman" (*San Ye*), also a member of the Guomindang Party Committee, who
was later immortalized as one of the villains in the post-Liberation drama
"Gate #6."[62]

Kenneth Lieberthal argues that the transport guilds "functioned as
front organizations for secret-society leaders to control the Tientsin transport industry." The transport guilds "provided a convenient organizational structure through which to manage transport. . . . The secret societies (through the coolie associations) thus set the price structure in
transport, provided the necessary labor, and guaranteed the safe shipment
of goods."[63] Lieberthal's formulation implies that the Qing Bang operated
as an autonomous unit that made independent decisions about the transport industry, and then executed those decisions through the guilds. Yet

no surviving historical evidence indicates that the Qing Bang functioned as a separate organization with priorities of its own. It seems more accurate to say that the master-disciple relationship of the Qing Bang reinforced alliances between the transport bosses, virtually all of whom were gang members. It probably also enabled them to forge alliances with government officials and other members of the Tianjin ruling elite. The Qing Bang acted as the mortar that held the structure of the transport guilds together, and cemented them into the larger structure of urban society.[64]

For ordinary transport workers in twentieth-century Tianjin, membership in the Qing Bang became a requisite for employment. One had to be not only a member, but usually the disciple of a particular elder, to get a job on the docks. Even the rickshaw pullers, who were not organized into guilds, found that the garage owners who rented vehicles to them would not rent to a non-gang member.[65] Gang membership, under the tutelage of someone who was at once a transport boss and a gang elder, strengthened the hierarchical relationship between boss and worker, bestowing obligations on each. Disciples were expected to present gifts to their elder/boss on holidays. Elders were expected to protect their disciples if they were attacked by others. A ceremony in which disciples were accepted by the elder, known as "opening the mountain door" (*kai shan men*), underscored the solemnity of these ties. Conducted in a so-called "incense hall" (*xiang tang*), which could be in a home or a public place, it featured candles, incense, and wooden signs. A special gang member who knew the ceremonies was called in to officiate.[66]

Gang membership provided workers with a modicum of material security:

> The gangs were half guilds, half protection rackets, half philanthropic societies—that is, if you behaved . . . . People joined as a form of insurance, not only against getting beat up, but if they were ill . . . the gang would put out a little bit of money. There was a certain amount of protection in this thing. This is the way they held on to their people, both terror and small handouts.[67]

More important, gang membership offered the security of alliances with a network of other workers and bosses, who were bound by notions of heroic behavior and mutual loyalty to support one another.[68] Alliances were crucial to survival and to the accumulation of power in the industry; those who were best at making alliances were most successful.[69] For a transport boss, alliances with more powerful bosses enlarged his scope of economic activity and minimized the possibility of conflict. For a transport worker, as Lieberthal observed,

> life in the city approached the Hobbesian world of a war of all against all, since the municipal government's power did not reach down far enough to protect people in

this social stratum. Living in this relatively anarchic environment, the potential secret-society member encountered violence as a way of life. On the margin of subsistence, with no recourse to police protection and unable to sustain missing more than a few days' work, he fully understood the aphorism that "might makes right." He had to establish *kuan-hsi* [connections] with the strongest power in his area in order to survive. The secret society's value in this context lay in its ability to offer a potential member security.[70]

But although the transport worker shared Qing Bang membership with an estimated 250,000 transport, factory, and handicraft workers in Tianjin,[71] gang membership apparently did not equip him with an expanded notion of membership in the working class. The world of the transport worker remained very limited. Lieberthal notes that "a former Tientsin dock worker could describe the city's geography only in terms of the various turf boundaries when he was interviewed many years later in Hong Kong."[72] Gang membership provided the transport worker with a job and a set of alliances within his own transport guild, but it did not broaden his view of the municipal landscape to include members beyond that guild. The violent struggles between guilds that punctuated Tianjin life until 1949 were not at all alleviated by the fact that combatants on all sides were members of the Qing Bang.

VIOLENCE

Guild vs. Guild: Rumbles over Turf

Life in the transport trade was imbued with violence. Indeed, the boundaries of a transport worker's world were literally defined by violence, for although each guild had its inherited territory, sanctioned by government decree, infractions were frequent. A guild member caught poaching on another's territory had to confess his mistake, and his boss had to apologize as well, or bloodshed would ensue.[73]

Given the spirit of braggadocio which characterized guild behavior, such an apology was usually not forthcoming. When "the fight for business gives rise to grudges" between guilds, commented a local publication in 1884, "they mobilize and brandish their fists and carry weapons, and neither will back down. They call this 'struggling for the market.'"[74] At the turn of the century, struggles over territory between the guilds reportedly led to several deaths almost every day.[75]

Rumbles over turf in the twentieth century showed little of the stylized flair of those between hunhunr gangs, but they were no less bloody. In July 1935, for example, *Yishi bao* reported that the Tong Yi Guild, which moved nightsoil for all the manure-processing factories in the Xi Ying Men district of town, had been involved in a fight with another guild. On the morning of July 23, when several Tong Yi workers were preparing to load nightsoil onto a boat, more than ten men appeared with knives, clubs, and axes. The Tong Yi group fled with these men in pursuit; one Tong Yi worker was caught and killed and another seriously wounded. When police investigated the incident, they learned from the Tong Yi boss that another guild, the Hui Le, was probably responsible. The Hui Le and the Tong Yi had been fighting over territory since 1923, and had been involved in numerous lawsuits and street fights. On the basis of this testimony, police arrested four bosses of the Hui Le, who admitted their guilt and were remanded to the county court.[76]

This type of straightforward conflict over disputed territory was common until Liberation in every sector of the industry—on the docks as well as between freight haulers. While it might start as a conflict between bosses, it inevitably expanded to include transport workers as well.[77]

Another type of territorial conflict between guilds occurred when merchants tried to switch their business from one guild to another. In the Hebei district, for example, there was a transport boss named Li Chunming, and a guild run by three other bosses, the Zhang brothers. In November 1935, one of the Zhang brothers was unloading goods at a warehouse in Santiaoshi and got into a quarrel with a transport worker named Wang. As a result of their scuffling, some goods fell and seriously injured a passing pedestrian. Li Chunming helped negotiate a settlement in which Zhang and Wang would each pay part of the injured man's medical expenses. The warehouse owner, fearful that he would also be held liable for the injured man's expenses, decided to sever all connections with Zhang and Wang, and to hire Li Chunming to move goods for him instead. Furious, Zhang accused Li of setting out to ruin his business, and led his brothers to smash Li's office. All parties involved were hauled off to the local police station, where the Zhang brothers accused Li of conspiring to monopolize the market. The case was sent to court.[78]

Trying to unravel the accusations and counteraccusations in the aftermath of one of these incidents must have been well-nigh impossible for the courts. In a typical case in the Hou Jia Hou area, for example, two transport bosses named Xing and Chen moved meat for local butcher shops. Chen was caught stealing meat from a load he was moving; he was fired and the business was turned over to Xing. The next day Chen brought a crowd of people to Xing's house. An argument ensued in which Chen received a stab wound in the head. Xing told the police that Chen had inflicted the wound on himself for purposes of blackmail, a common practice in such conflicts; the courts were asked to determine the truth.[79]

If a boss thought himself powerful enough, he would not hesitate to try to extort money from other transport bosses. Cai Yugui, aged 25, an up-start boss in Santiaoshi, demanded in 1926 that Hao Fengming, boss of a guild with 70 people, pay him several dollars a year as a sign of "filial re-spect." When Hao refused, Cai hit him on the head four times with an axe, then insisted, somewhat improbably, that Hao had inflicted the wounds on himself. This case, like the others, was sent to court.[80]

Sometimes it was impossible to sort out in the melee which guilds were involved in a particular fight. A report of a fight in District 2 in March 1948 said only that five workers had been waiting to pick up day labor jobs at a warehouse when they saw a mob of 20 or 30 workers coming toward them, carrying a gunnysack full of weapons. The mob charged into a local restaurant where one of the waiting laborers was eating, pulled him out, and began to beat him. When the others attempted to flee, they were pur-sued and stabbed. Police arrived in time to catch only one of the assailants, and the newspaper report was silent about the cause of this organized act of violence, or the identity of the perpetrators.[81]

Occasionally, the conflicts took the form of gangland-style executions. Zhang Jinming, a powerful transport boss who was known locally as the "Second Gentleman," was kidnapped from a melon patch he owned in July 1948. His body was found several days later in a sorghum field in the suburbs. Zhang's son could only tell the police that his father "had a lot of enemies."[82]

Guilds vs. Merchants

Guild bosses did not hesitate to use the same repertoire of extortion and intimidation on their own customers. If a merchant did not want to use the services of a particular guild and preferred to move his own goods, he was still obliged to pay the guild a fee, known variously as the "street-crossing fee" or the "passing-the-shoulders fee."[83] Failure to pay the fee could be dangerous. When two peasants from Xian county brought their boats to Tianjin loaded with cabbage in March 1936, they were greeted at the dock by a local transport boss who informed them that no matter where they docked, they would have to pay a transport fee. After they refused, he re-turned with a club-wielding gang, which rushed the boats and seriously injured one of the peasants. When the guild boss was subsequently ar-rested, he justified his actions by saying that the peasants owed him a transport fee.[84]

Not only naive peasants from the countryside, but well-established owners of local factories as well, lived in fear of the guilds. The Rui Sheng Xiang Dyeworks, a factory founded in the mid-1920's that employed more than 20 people, found itself in economic trouble in 1935. The owner tried to negotiate with the local guild for a reduction in the "passing-the-shoulders fee." The transport boss at first refused and verbally insulted the factory owner. Finally the two parties reached an arrangement where the factory paid an annual fee of 75 yuan to the guild, and was free to move its own goods. This agreement lasted for several months, until a rival guild from another district arrived one day and unloaded a large shipment of goods. When the local guild boss got wind of this, he sent a mob of 50 people to the factory, where they beat workers and staff and smashed everything they could find. The manager and workers fled. Police arrested more than ten of the mob. When the factory owner returned to inspect the damage, a dozen more guild members showed up and blockaded the factory; police returned and arrested several of them. A dozen employees of the dyeworks were injured in the assault, some of them seriously. As late as 1947, reports appeared in the local press that groups of transport bosses, and their workers, were beating and terrorizing factory owners in an effort to acquire more business.[85] A local merchant appealed to the municipal government for protection:

> As for the transport guilds in Tianjin today: do they represent feudal power or not? What contribution do they make to society? Who is it that protects them, and causes them to exploit those countrymen who sell their strength to work as beasts of burden? . . . Aren't they the same as mountain bandits and wilderness thieves, who establish themselves on a mountain, declare themselves chiefs and, with their henchmen in tow, tell passersby that they must "leave some money behind to buy their way"? These evil transport guilds, with their fat heads and big ears! When they open their mouths it's "We won the turf"; when they close their mouths it's "Our ancestors leaped into a pot of oil." Mr. Mayor, can't you eliminate this pest from the city of Tianjin? No matter what kind of organization they have, they cannot be permitted to be this insolent.[86]

Most guild bosses, because they owned vehicles operated by human or animal power, stubbornly opposed the efforts of some merchants to introduce motor vehicles. When the in-house transport guild for one of Tianjin's largest match factories kept raising its fees, the factory management became dissatisfied and bought several trucks. The guild boss then sent out some of his hired toughs to hinder the work, and also threatened to kill the general manager of the factory. Eventually the factory had to turn control of transport back to the guild.[87]

Workers vs. Guild Bosses, One Another, and Society

Post-Liberation accounts have stressed the brutality of guild bosses toward their workers, and there are numerous cases of bosses using the strong-arm tactics described above on recalcitrant workers in their own employ.[88] Yet violence was not the exclusive prerogative of the bosses. The pre-Liberation press offers ample evidence that whereas workers were willing to take up cudgels for their bosses, they were also capable of taking up cudgels against them.

The 1935 case of transport worker Su Zhenbao is typical of a worker-boss conflict. Laid off by a foreman named Yu for a trivial offense, Su went to Yu's house with a wooden club and assaulted him. Two of Yu's nephews, as well as Su's brother, jumped into the fray, and Su bit a large chunk out of Yu's hand.[89] Yu was luckier than Yang Derun, one of Tianjin's most famous transport guild bosses. One of Yang's workers, angry at being cheated out of his fair share of pay, got into an argument with Yang and stabbed him six times in the head and once in the chest. After his arrest, the worker testified that Yang exploited his workers, distributing money only once a week, and that his workers frequently could not cover their expenses.[90] Another boss, who made what his employees regarded as excessive deductions from their pay, was assaulted by a group of them and beaten.[91]

But violence within the guilds did not always cross class lines. Fights between two transport workers in which one was beaten or stabbed were just as common as those which pitted boss against worker.[92] Worse, transport workers were apt to bring their penchant for fighting into their off-hour activities. One such instance involved five brothers in the Lu family (named, respectively, Eldest, Two, Three, Four, and Five), who worked together in a transport guild in Santiaoshi. To celebrate the Dragon Boat Festival in 1936, Five and a friend went to see a movie, but were thrown out by the usher for neglecting to buy tickets. They got into a fight with the theater management and were fined a dollar by the police. The following day, Five returned with his four brothers to smash the theater. Fearing that this was not the end of the matter, the theater manager went to Santiaoshi to ask the local guild bosses to intercede. He was intercepted by the Lu family and their friends, and beaten. A member of the Lu gang named Wang Zhanyuan was then stabbed six times in the head and back by fellow gang members, who went to the police claiming that the theater manager had done it. Following a police investigation, the Lu brothers were all arrested.[93]

Violence, both individual and collective, was the language of negotiation in the transport industry. Because they frequently resorted to a range of violent activities, transport bosses and their workers were among the most feared and despised people in Tianjin. They also attracted a great deal of government attention, and successive attempts to regulate their activities occupied every government, from the officials of the imperial Qing dynasty to the Communists.

THE GOVERNMENT AND THE GUILDS

By the late nineteenth century the relationship between the government and the guilds was already set. The former promulgated regulations; the latter followed them when it strengthened their own position and ignored them when it did not. A local publication described the situation: "The local government has already clearly defined the boundaries and drawn up regulations. It is not permitted to mix, to cross boundaries, or to have disagreements. Furthermore, now all those who have goods to be moved or luggage to be carried must hire according to sector, determine the mileage, and then reach a verbal agreement about the number of carriers." The system did not operate smoothly, however: "When they encounter people from other parts and lonely travelers, they frequently make numerous demands of them. This is going a bit too far in taking advantage of strangers. . . . Recklessly careening about in a continuous stream on the road, they are indeed unreasonable and detestable."[94]

The efforts of Yuan Shikai in the last years of the Qing to put an end to local hunhunr conflicts may have temporarily decreased the number of street fights, but it left the structure of the transport guilds intact. The guilds operated uninterrupted during the years of the early Republic and warlord rule. After the Guomindang government was established in Tianjin in 1928, an effort was made to organize some of the transport workers into unions. But government organizers soon found that the freight haulers, while "very oppressed, were scattered and hard to organize," and lamented that their fighting spirit was usually directed into private altercations rather than union activities. On closer inspection, several of the branches of the municipal union appear to have been transport guilds that joined the union *en masse*, with their leadership structure intact and the bosses serving as union "secretaries."[95] By the mid-1930's, the city's Bureau of Social Affairs had established a municipal transport union. Ba Yanqing, a prominent local guild boss, was installed as its director. With several tens of thousands of transport workers in the city, and frequent street brawls over territory filling the local press, the union asked the city to redefine the territorial boundaries and end the fighting.[96]

A curious tug of war between the municipal agencies and the guilds ensued. The city government in early 1936 ordered the Bureau of Social Affairs to do something about the guilds; the Bureau in turn asked the transport union to conduct an investigation; after a month of bureaucratic buck-passing, in mid-April the city began to unveil its plan for guild reform. The Four Gates system was to be abolished; it was no longer to be a tax-collecting unit or an excuse for guilds to monopolize particular areas.

This represented a partial victory for the guilds, since they had opposed the transport tax for decades.[97]

Several weeks later the second stage of the plan was announced in a joint communiqué by three government bureaus: Social Affairs, Public Security, and Finance. They issued an order announcing that henceforth merchants had the freedom to decide who was going to move their merchandise, and that the guilds were no longer permitted to charge "street-crossing fees." The Public Security Bureau was to set rates for moving merchandise, and any guild found extorting fees in excess of the set rates was to be punished.[98]

This directive virtually eliminated the basis of guild power, and the guild bosses reacted immediately. Putting aside their territorial wars, they united in a petition to the city government to withdraw the directive. The petition expounded at great length on the poverty and vulnerability of the coolies, who "have no knowledge of industry or commerce, and can only use their labor as beasts of burden, to make use of the wages of their blood and sweat to support themselves." If implemented, the guild bosses maintained, the order would throw thousands of men out of work and make beggars of them and their families. The transport union took up the appeal on behalf of the guilds, and implored the mayor to "think of another appropriate method of reform" to ensure the livelihood of the coolies. The guilds demonstrated their sincerity by abruptly ceasing all fights over turf.[99]

No more was heard of reform efforts until August, when a much-modified reform plan was put into effect. The guilds were permitted to maintain their monopoly rights on transport. All 103 guilds registered with the Bureau of Social Affairs in the following months. The bosses were called together by the Bureau in November and enjoined from blackmailing, tricking customers, invading territory, or fighting. They were warned that they would lose their rights to operate if they violated these provisions. Although some territorial conflicts were reported in early 1937, their number did seem to decrease, and in any event local conflicts were soon overshadowed by the Japanese invasion.[100]

In this case the government had attempted to abolish the guild system, but apparently enough political pressure was brought to bear to dissuade government officials from this course of action. One can only speculate about the nature of this pressure and the role of high-level party supporters like Ba Yanqing, or the shared Qing Bang membership of the political elite and the guild bosses, in deflecting government action against the guilds.

The occupation government, which should have been less susceptible to local political pressure, also proved unable to dislodge the guilds. In July 1938, a year after the occupation, it made one attempt to do so. The Railroad Bureau, complaining that there were many transport guilds and that their "moral quality was not uniform," tried to turn the work of loading goods over to the International Transport Company, a government organization. Once again the guilds complained. Railroad transport workers, they said, were displaced peasants who had traditionally been permitted to move goods on the railroad. After a great deal of protest, the government finally agreed to let the guilds retain their rights, only asking that they work under the nominal supervision of the International Transport Company.[101]

New guild regulations were issued by the municipal government later in 1938. Guilds were once again required to register. This time the boss had to guarantee the good character of his workers, and obtain two guarantors for himself. The rental, sale, or transfer of guild rights was no longer permitted. The new regulation set fees for transport and forbid the bosses to use coercive methods against the merchants. Further, under the new regulations each guild boss was ordered to keep detailed accounts of the wages he owed his employees, and was not to withhold wages.

These elaborate provisions proved largely cosmetic. They did nothing to threaten guild control, and no evidence indicates that the wage or price provisions were enforced. Beneath the façade of government regulations, guild bosses Yuan Wenhui and Ba Yanqing, supported by the occupation government, presided over an industry that operated much as it always had. The only noticeable difference was that the guilds now sent presents to the Japanese transport companies rather than to Chinese government officials.[102]

A similar flurry of governmental regulations, with similar results, marked the postwar regulation of the guilds. There was another registration drive. The politically agile Ba Yanqing remained at the head of the municipal union. The city created a municipal transport office that was intended to supplant the guilds but ended up being forced out of business by them. The bosses were encouraged to distribute higher wages to their workers, to no noticeable effect.[103]

The real threat to guild power between the end of the war and Liberation came not from the municipal government, but from two other organizations. One was the Black Flag Brigade, a group even more mysterious than the Qing Bang, which according to one contemporary account "burned and murdered and stole" in Tianjin in the years before Liberation. By force of arms the Black Flag Brigade managed to appropriate the right to transport large shipments of goods, and when the guilds interfered it "took up knives" against them. Here was an organization that could outmaneuver the guilds at their own game.

The second organization to threaten the guilds was the Customs Clearing Office (Baoguan hang), which acted as a broker between the guilds and the owners of goods, setting artificially high prices and fleecing both parties in the process. Extortion was certainly not an unusual practice among government departments during this period, and even the powerful transport guilds were unable to stop it.[104]

The guilds survived these threats just as they had survived previous government attempts to remove them—by bribing, intimidating, and maneuvering their way through the difficult years until Liberation. They had the capacity to paralyze the economy, and they used that threat to good advantage. They survived because they were experts at giving and receiving patronage, and patronage was the coin of the realm in pre-Liberation Tianjin. Throughout their long history the guild bosses bought off those above them, threatened those who were equal to them (other guilds and merchants), and maintained control over those below them by providing protection and security. So well-entrenched were they in the Tianjin urban scene that it took several years and a major campaign to dislodge them after 1949.[105]

Because their methods were so successful, the traditional guild structure was preserved virtually intact throughout Tianjin's development as a treaty port. By participating in the guild structure and submitting to the bosses, transport workers obtained work that was physically punishing but secure. They also received protection in the most violent of Tianjin's industries. The dual need for work and protection ensured the continuing strength of vertical alliances. Even as the modern city of Tianjin took shape around it, the oldest urban sector of the Tianjin working class—the transport workers—remained enmeshed in a traditional structure and a set of loyalties that effectively precluded its participation in the making of a class-conscious labor force. The need to obtain protection, however, was not limited to the transport workers. Similar patterns of cross-class loyalties, and similar types of violence in defense of those loyalties, prevailed in the "modern" Tianjin cotton mills as well.

Sea of Wheels and Belts:
The Cotton Mill Workers

The Tianjin cotton mills, from their founding after World War I until 1949, were contested terrain. Their power-driven machinery and sprawling physical plant gave them the appearance of unambiguous monuments to industrial progress. But the shop floor was the site of a complex and multifaceted struggle, in which a weak, inexperienced, and transient capitalist class attempted to impose industrial discipline on changing groups of workers.[1] Millowners and millhands each tried to shape five aspects of working life to their own advantage: recruitment, work time, nonworking time, protection, and livelihood. In all these arenas, foremen played a pivotal role, maximizing their autonomy from the owners while binding workers to them with ties of individual loyalty. Workers, for their part, made active adaptations to their new environment, drawing on pre-factory, extra-factory, and eventually in-factory ties to make their new situation bearable.[2]

RECRUITMENT: THE STRUGGLE AT
THE FACTORY GATE

No matter which group of owners was in control of the mills, one of their primary concerns was to ensure a stable supply of inexpensive and docile labor. In a new industrial environment like Tianjin, workers had to be recruited from the countryside. Millowners first depended upon fore-men in this recruiting process. Later they tried to circumscribe the fore-men's role because of the corruption and inefficiencies produced by the foremen-dominated system. The owners' desire to limit the power of the foremen and reduce the intractability of the workers led in the 1930's to the recruitment of women.

Workers had their own agenda in the recruitment process—to find and keep the best job possible. Their dependence upon pre-factory connec-tions to locate work buttressed the position of the foremen. But vertical alliances in the cotton mills were not as strong as those in Santiaoshi or as compelling as those in the transport industry. Once employed in the mills, workers sometimes chose to leave. In spite of economic need and vertical bonds, they were not always willing to conform to the demands of indus-trial time.

Factory Hiring Practices

The struggle for control of the workplace began even before millhands entered the factory gates, in the procedures for recruiting and hiring work-ers. In spite of repeated attempts to alter this process over a 30-year pe-riod, factory owners had less control over hiring, and thus over their work-ers, than they would have liked.

Because mechanized spinning was new to North China, when the mills first opened in the late teens and early 1920's, no local pool of skilled labor existed. Some millowners sent agents to Shanghai and Henan to procure skilled labor, while others recruited and trained apprentices and adult workers from the villages around Tianjin. "Some workers," observed H. D. Fong in 1932, "were sent back by the mill to their native districts, where they could better persuade fellow countrymen to join the mill in Tientsin." Workers recruited by these mills were given travel allowances, and, in the case of apprentices, free room and board as well. In this early period, aggressive recruiting strategies built up the mill workforce to a total of 16,898 by 1929, more than three-quarters of them adult males.[3]

During the years of the world Depression, however, these aggressive re-cruiting strategies became unnecessary. With more workers seeking jobs than there were spaces available, mills began to stiffen requirements for new workers. Applicants had to be of a certain height and weight, have a good temperament, secure a guarantor who was not employed in the mills, and have no previous history of criminal activity or trouble-making in other mills. Job tests were also instituted.[4]

Parallel to the growth of formal requirements, however, was an informal introduction system that resembled the one prevailing in the handicraft workshops. In a period of labor surplus like the early 1930's, an aspiring worker could not hope to enter the mills unless he had a connection with someone already working there. This relationship might be with a relative or fellow villager who was employed by the mills, or it might be with the foreman himself. Foremen were responsible for recommending new workers to the management. The combination of formal and informal requirements regulated access to the mills, and foremen played a key role in mediating between the two systems.[5]

Factory owners initially found this method of hiring advantageous, because it relieved them of a major management responsibility. As in the new industries of eighteenth-century Britain, their central problem was to procure and train a labor force. The use of foremen as intermediaries in Tianjin constituted an indirect form of labor procurement and training that released them from part of this task.[6] But they eventually discovered that it conceded too much power to the foremen. When the Heng Yuan Mill was taken over by a trust company in 1934, one of the new management's first acts was to fire all the workers and announce its intention to abolish the "foreman system" (*gongtouzhi*). Henceforth workers were to be recruited directly by the factory. Part of the reason for the firings was to eliminate the tiny fiefdoms commanded by local foremen, and to assign an experienced worker to supervise each shift and test subordinates.

A group of 20 foremen objected strenuously to these measures, and demanded a government investigation. This investigation found that under the foreman system, the mill had employed almost three times as many people as should have been required to run a plant that size. Perhaps the new management had suspected that when workers were hired by foremen concerned with building their own power, the resulting system might not be very efficient. This mill, like others, then began to hire both southern and local women workers (a development discussed later in this chapter). Although the search for docile and inexpensive labor was undoubtedly one of their motives, the millowners also hoped to establish a more formal hiring process, over which they would have greater control.[7]

As Japanese companies bought up most of the Tianjin mills in 1936, they intensified attempts to rationalize hiring procedures and to take control away from the foremen. Often this involved firing most of the original foremen and workers.[8] After the Japanese invasion, the rapid expansion of the industry led to a labor shortage, and all the recruiting methods used by the Japanese attempted to circumvent the foreman system.

The first method used by the Japanese mills was to set up recruiting stations in neighborhoods on the outskirts of Tianjin, where recent peasant migrants tended to gather. In He Jia Kou, Dong Lou, Qian De

Zhuang, and Xuan Lou, a family would be commissioned by the factory to recruit workers. The family would locate people from villages in the area and introduce them to the factory, receiving a commission of two dollars per head if the worker remained at the mill for 15 days or more. These recruiting families did not support themselves exclusively by this work; sometimes a member of the family already worked in the factory.

The Japanese mills also employed full-time recruiters who sought laborers in Tianjin. The factory issued these recruiters a set of photographs showing the mill's facilities. A recruiter would then rent a room in a hotel (two favorite spots were the Hebei Cultural Hotel in the north of the city and the Shanghai Hotel in the amusement quarter) and hang up a sign announcing the establishment of a "recruiting station." People from out of town would sign up, and the recruiter would send them to the factory in groups of four or five. His commission was the same as that paid to the recruiting families. In addition, the mills sent agents to Qingdao and Jinan to entice experienced workers to leave textile mills there. This was accomplished by sneaking into the workers' dormitories and promising higher pay to millhands who would come to Tianjin. This type of recruiting was also common in Tianjin itself, where raids on other mills were not unknown in a period of labor shortage.

Finally, the Japanese mills recruited every morning at eight o'clock at the factory gate. If the factory needed 20 workers that day, the personnel department would call 20 people over, measure and weigh them, and quiz them about their previous work experience and age. In all these cases, the people doing the recruiting were employees of the personnel office, not foremen with a role in supervising production.[9]

While these efforts may have succeeded in limiting the foreman's role, the system of "connections" as a whole was impervious to Japanese attempts to rationalize it away. Hiring by connection built upon native-place ties and provided patronage for the millhands, at a price. As a former millhand described the system:

The recruiting foreman was usually a foreman or a staff person in the factory. He would have relationships in the factory. . . . If he introduced a lot of people into the factory, it had advantages for him. . . . For instance, there was one foreman named Zheng from Tangshan. He introduced a lot of people from Tangshan into the mill. After he introduced them, of course they attached themselves to him. For instance, he could protect them. If an honest person were bullied, he would speak up for him. At New Year's and on festivals people would send him presents. They were a kind of power base for him in the factory.[10]

It was not unheard of during the occupation, although it was certainly not condoned by the millowners, for a foreman to charge several months' wages to provide an introduction.[11] Even more common was the practice of sending a present to the foreman with a request for work. "If you didn't send enough," remembers one worker, "they would take the present but ignore the request."[12]

The system survived because it had advantages not only for the foremen, but for the workers. In addition to protection, a powerful foreman could provide access to cleaner, lighter jobs in the mills. The elaborate recruiting procedures established by Japanese millowners became a method of last resort for those who had no connections.[13]

When the Guomindang government returned to Tianjin in 1945, and its wholly owned subsidiary corporation took over most of Tianjin's mills, another attempt was made to formalize the recruiting process. But the most reliable method of finding work in the mills was still recourse to connections. A staff member in the personnel office described the system as follows: "It wasn't like the Japanese period when they would post notices and you would come sign up. It was all a matter of who knew whose children. It was harder to get into the factory than it had been under the Japanese. You had to know somebody."[14] Once again, the foreman controlled access to the mill gate.

Recruitment procedures in the cotton mills had both formal and informal aspects throughout the 30 years before Liberation. In periods when the industry was expanding (the early 1920's and the late 1930's), formal procedures were developed to attract workers to the mills. In periods when the industry needed fewer workers, formal procedures were developed to keep them out. In both cases, however, it is difficult to say whether a high percentage of workers ever entered the factory by going through formal channels at all.

The informal procedures were a constant. They supplemented the formal ones in boom times and supplanted them when work was hard to find. In good times and bad, millowners sought to maximize the effectiveness of their formal requirements, while workers and foremen relied on connections to obtain what they wanted—a job in the mills for the former, and power on the shop floor for the latter. The result was a hiring system which resembled that of the smallest handicraft workshops in the centrality of personal connections.

Recruitment of Women: The Case of Heng Yuan

The hiring of women millhands in the mid-1930's was an outgrowth of the struggle to recruit a cheap and tractable labor force, and to circumscribe the power of the foremen. The partial feminization of the mill workforce in Tianjin came almost 15 years later than it did in the older Shanghai cotton industry. In Shanghai, millowners altered the sexual division of labor in the early and mid-1920's to rid their workplaces of politically militant males.[15] Tianjin millhands were less politically active—or at least their militant activities were easier to suppress (see Chapter 8)—and no parallel move took place there until 1935.

The first mill to hire large numbers of women operatives was the Heng Yuan. The management, which had previously refused to employ any women at all, explained the change in hiring policy by stating that women were "richer in patience than men." But an additional consideration was a desire to break the power of local foremen. By the end of October 1935 the mill was ready to hire 1,000 new workers, all female. Women were recruited from Shanghai by labor contractors to become spinners. The Bureau of Social Affairs, disturbed at the factory's decision to recruit people from the south while the local unemployment rate was rising, urged the Heng Yuan management to hire locally except for skilled foremen. Perhaps in response to this pressure, the mill agreed to hire local women workers as well. According to a local newspaper report, "poor women from all over the city heard this news and rushed to respond."[16]

Initially women from Xi Yao Wa, one of the city's poorest districts, were hired to polish the machines and sort raw cotton at wages of 25 and 20 cents a day, respectively. A few days later, the mill hired 30 women workers out of a pool of 600 applicants. Those selected were between the ages of sixteen and twenty-four, had natural feet, and either had had experience in other mills or were eager to learn. Women were required to give their age, place of birth, family circumstances, previous mill experience, and marital status, and to provide a guarantor. Then they were given a test. Successful applicants were to receive five weeks of training in carding, drawing, roving, spinning, and reeling.[17]

Local women did not adjust easily to the rigors of factory life. The Heng Yuan management had promised that each woman would be supplied with food, housing, clothes, and bedding by the factory, would live in heated dormitories equipped with iron beds, and would pay no more than three yuan of their wages per month for all these services. But this seemingly idyllic arrangement lasted no more than a week. On December 14, a news report stated that some of the women wanted to stop working because the factory was providing nothing to eat but steamed bread, millet, and vegetables cooked in a large cauldron. They were also dissatisfied with the dormitory facilities, and complained of inadequate heat. When one of the women tried to leave and was stopped by the guard at the gate, a quarrel ensued. She offered to pay the factory for her room and board, as stipulated in the hiring agreement, and left. The next day ten more women followed suit. Some of their families refused to repay the factory, and when a group of them went to the factory and got into a fight with the guards, the police intervened. They decreed that the families of the poorest women did not have to repay the board fees. By December 14, a week after the hirings, only ten of the 30 women workers were left in the factory.[18]

If the factory management had any second thoughts about the docility of women workers, they did not put them on paper. But they did state publicly that they were not sure they wanted to hire any more *local* women. On December 16 a group of 40 women workers arrived from Shanghai; they were joined by a second group a week later.[19]

In mid-January 1936, with 400 southern women working at the mill, the management launched its second attempt at local recruiting. This time they decided to hire only women between the ages of sixteen and twenty who had no previous work experience. Two weeks later the mill workforce had grown to 500 women. At a press conference, representatives of management announced their intention to make the lives of these women "homelike" (*jiatinghua*). Before reopening the mill, they pointed out, they had renovated the dormitories, the dining hall, the hospital, and the lighting, as well as the production equipment. They planned to hire men to run the generator, repair the machines, guard the plant, and do the weaving, but all other operations were to be performed by women. However, since Tianjin women were "difficult to recruit," the management intended to pay special attention to treating them well and "protecting" them. Reporters who attended the press conference were given a tour of clean dormitories that housed 12 workers per room, were shown the factory bathhouse where workers showered twice a week, and were told of plans to play radio music in the dining hall and show movies every week.[20]

Recruiting of southern workers continued along with the local hiring efforts. In March, 500 more women workers arrived by train from Shanghai. But the importation of southern workers did not go as smoothly as the management had hoped. In February an inexperienced worker had caused a boiler explosion; the local newspaper pointedly criticized the factory's refusal to rehire experienced local workers to tend the boiler. In March a worker lost a hand in the cotton cleaning department. The press blamed those who had hired the southerners, noting that most of the new workers from Shanghai were not experienced, and that workers had been injuring hands and feet daily.[21] The factory's troubles with the southerners did not end there. By early April, nine Shanghai women petitioned the local Bureau of Social Affairs to be paid their wages and permitted to return to Shanghai. After a week in Tianjin and two days of work, they had decided that they were "unaccustomed to the place and could not work" (*shuitu bu fu, bu neng gongzuo).* The head of the Heng Yuan personnel department protested that if the mill management had to pay to send the workers back to Shanghai, they would soon be overwhelmed with similar requests which they could not afford to meet. Finally it was agreed that the Shanghai labor recruiters should pay for the return journey, and plans were made to send the women home on the first available boat.[22]

In spite of these troubles with local and imported millhands, by mid-April the Heng Yuan workforce had expanded to 1,400 people, nine-tenths of them women. A month later the management prepared to hire a new group of women workers, ignoring protests from former male workers at the mill who had been promised first chance at the jobs in a layoff agreement with the previous management. This conflict continued into the summer, with 200 of the old workers occupying factory dormitories in lieu of back pay. After several of them were arrested, they were finally forced out at the end of August, and their representatives had to sign an agreement that they would never bother the factory again. Newspaper reports of these events repeatedly refer to "the workers and their families." All workers under the old management at the Heng Yuan were male; a workforce of married men whose families resided with them was being replaced by women who, even if married, lived in dormitories without their families.[23]

Ultimately, the hiring of women workers from Shanghai was not successful. By mid-August, 300 of 700 women had gone back to Shanghai because they were not satisfied with their wages or treatment, and it was estimated that most of the rest would leave when their initial contracts were up. In late 1936 the management, perhaps rethinking their approach to acquiring a cheap and quiet labor force, announced their intention to hire child workers for a work/study program.[24]

The transition to female labor in the Tianjin cotton mills was not a smooth process. Even in a period of depression and unemployment, many women were dissatisfied enough to leave the mills almost as soon as they arrived. Women from Shanghai undoubtedly found the physical and cultural environment of Tianjin difficult to adjust to. A news report in early 1937 observed that they often left the mill after hours wearing "luxurious clothes, curled hair, high heels, and coats with leather collars, looking like young ladies of the leisure class. They use their wages to buy clothes and to make themselves up."[25] This kind of conspicuous display was probably regarded with a mixture of envy and disapproval by the more conservative local workers, and it is not surprising that Shanghai women soon longed for their more cosmopolitan native city.

A more perplexing question is why local workers, whom every economic factor indicates were desperate for work, quit the mills so readily.

TABLE 6
Wage Rates in the Yu Yuan Mill, 1929
(yuan per month)

Job[a]	Men	Women	Job[a]	Men	Women
Electrician	23.53		Carding (S)	13.20	11.30
Mechanic/smith	21.55		Drawing-in (S)	13.20	9.95
Carpenter	18.00		Finishing (W)	13.17	
Mixing (S)	17.60		Coolies	13.03	
Weaving (W)	17.10		Baling (S)	12.93	
Roving (S)	15.87	14.83	Reeling (S)	12.80	9.93
Sizing (W)	15.72		Warp Winding (W)	12.72	
Slubbing (S)	13.93	12.18	Winding (W)	12.23	10.43
Spinning (S)	13.72	11.58	Warping (W)	12.08	9.48
Scutching (S)	13.53		ALL	15.33	11.35

SOURCE: Derived from H. D. Fong, *Cotton Industry and Trade in China*, Vol. I (Tientsin: Chihli Press, 1932), 134.

   NOTE: Fong himself comes up with a different job hierarchy based upon examination of the same workers, but using only their daily wages on the first and last day of the six-month period, rather than their actual earnings for the entire six months (*ibid.*, 128–29). For a comparable set of wage statistics collected several months later, see Wu Ao, *Tianjin shi fangshaye diaocha baogao* (Report on an investigation of the Tianjin spinning industry) (Tianjin: Tianjin shi shehui ju, 1931), 59–65. For a detailed analysis of wages in three Tianjin mills from 1926–29, which does not, however, give such a thorough breakdown by job, see Liu Xinquan, "Huabei shachang gongren gongzi tongji" (Statistics on the wages of cotton mill workers in North China), *Shehui kexue zazhi*, 6, No. 1, (March 1935), 148–56.
   [a](S) = spinning; (W) = weaving.

Perhaps their situation was similar to that of American silk workers a century earlier. In Nantucket in the 1830's, many women and children applied for work in a silk filature, but interest dropped off after a month. The money they could earn was not enough to offset their distaste for industrial discipline.[26] The local women who left the Heng Yuan Mill had families who backed them up in their quarrel with the mill guards. Presumably these same families could also provide them with a place to live while they sought other manufacturing jobs, took in outwork, or awaited an arranged marriage. Meager as family resources might have been, they gave women workers a modicum of leverage in finding a tolerable work situation.

   Whatever the problems of transition to female labor, women continued to enter the mills, changing the sexual division of labor as they did so. In the spinning mill, cotton was cleaned (mixing, scutching), carded, combined into a uniform thread (drawing), pulled into a finer strand (roving), spun, and reeled. In the weaving mill, the warp thread was set, starched (sizing), and prepared for weaving (reeding). The cloth was then woven, finished, and packed.[27] In the late 1920's, women had accounted for more than half the workforce only in the warping department. The only other significant concentrations of women workers had been in reeling (41.05

percent) and roving (32.19 percent).[28] But by the late 1930's, virtually all spinners, reelers, warpers, and reeders were women.[29]

In the weaving departments, women and girls were found in the preparation workshop (where yarn was prepared for weaving), but generally not in the weaving mill itself. Women also worked in the finishing department, where cloth was inspected for flaws. But although an increasing number of operations came to be regarded as appropriate women's work, cleaning, carding, drawing, repair, and maintenance work remained the province of men. The sexual division of labor did not change as rapidly or as thoroughly as it did in the Shanghai mills, where by the 1940's only technicians' jobs were reserved exclusively for male millhands.[30]

The use of female labor, in addition to undermining the power of the foremen, saved the millowners money. As early as 1929, men not only were concentrated in the highest-paying jobs, they also were paid more than women for the same tasks. Women in only two departments, slubbing and roving, made more than the lowest-paid men in the mill (see Table 6).

Comparative wage data, collected both before and after the entrance of

TABLE 7
Average Wage per Day of Workers in the Big Six, 1929
(yuan)

Category	Wage	Category	Wage
Men	.47	Boys	.32
Women	.39	Girls	.33
ALL	.46	ALL	.32

SOURCE: Wu Ao, *Tianjin shi fangshaye*, 44–48.

TABLE 8
Average Wage per Day of Workers in Four Mills, 1938
(yuan)

Mill	Spinning		Weaving	
	Men	Women	Men	Women
Gong Da #6	.40	.36	.40	.35
Gong Da #7	.47	.41	.43	.33
Tianjin	.466	.403	.372	.423
Yu Da	.496[a]	.424[b]		

SOURCE: Minami manshū, 92, 103, 112, 119.
[a]Figure for all men workers in mill.
[b]Figure for all women workers in mill.

women into the mills in large numbers, confirm that men earned more than women (see Tables 7 and 8). A wage differential for the postoccupation period is more difficult to establish, because government-owned mills in 1945–49 classified workers according to grade rather than sex, and no information survives about comparative grade levels of men and women. But interview data confirm that both before and after the Japanese surrender, women were ranked one to two grades lower than men, and therefore were paid less.[31]

The struggle over recruitment was never conclusively settled. Millowners in the 1930's did succeed in temporarily limiting the foreman's power, and when they began to hire women they altered the structure of the workforce and lowered its cost. But they never brought hiring securely under their control; foremen continued to be the linchpin and the beneficiary of the recruitment process. Nor, despite the desperation of many in the Tianjin working class, did millowners ever enjoy a completely captive labor market in which to recruit. Each new group of workers had to make its own peace with the demands of a manufacturing job, and some chose to leave rather than conform. For those who stayed, the shop floor became the site of a struggle over how work time was to be spent.

WORK TIME: THE STRUGGLE ON THE SHOP FLOOR

Like factories everywhere in the world in the early stages of industrialization, the Tianjin cotton mills presented workers with a series of new demands. The logic of mechanized production required them to work fixed shifts and to keep pace with machines, in an environment where the temperature and the speed of work were adjusted to the needs of cotton thread rather than human beings.

The shop floor, however, was not the site simply of "neutral and inevitable technological change,"[32] but of struggle. Three codes of order, those of owners, foremen, and workers, competed for control. The owners set the terms of work time: the length of the workday, the organization of production, the system of pay, and the rules of behavior. They enforced industrial discipline, like their British counterparts a century earlier, with an ad hoc assortment of carrot and stick methods: piecework rates and bonuses for good attendance on the one hand; fines, searches, beatings, sexual abuse, and dismissal on the other.[33]

But though they made the rules, the owners could not always enforce them. Their attempts to manipulate systems of payment were frequently thwarted by the larger chaos of the Tianjin economy. Their agents on the shop floor, the foremen, were responsible for maintaining work discipline, but their abusive methods resulted in a situation that was the antithesis of rational industrial order. And the workers, sometimes behind the backs of the foremen and sometimes with their apparent cooperation, learned to make the workday shorter and more tolerable for themselves by "soaking mushrooms."

The Working Day

"The whistle blows on a winter morning," wrote a Tianjin cotton mill worker to the local newspaper in 1935, "and the workers who have been waiting outside the gate come in, half-asleep, yawning and coughing. Here are children of seven and eight and old people, men and women." In order to be there an hour before his shift began, as required, this worker had risen before dawn and walked ten li (about three miles).[34] Since workers had no watches, those who lived within hearing of the mill depended upon the sound of the factory whistle to wake them up: "They blew the whistle three times. Once at five, once at five-thirty, once at five-forty-five. . . . At the first whistle my mother would call me to wake up; at the second I would start out."[35]

Workers had no money for transportation, and the process of getting to and from work on foot was time-consuming. It became more complicated when the city was occupied by the Japanese in 1937. Every worker had to carry a pass and present it at military checkpoints. Workers who came from suburban villages were obliged to carry a "citizen's card" (*liangmin zheng*) giving their residential district, occupation, age, and sex. Without this documentation they were apt to be accused of being provocateurs sent in from rural districts controlled by the Eighth Route Army.[36]

Even after travel became less hazardous with the war's end, workers were often tardy, both because of the distances involved and because of their resistance to the requirements of industrial time. In November 1947, Cotton Mill #4 issued an announcement warning employees that they would be docked one-tenth of their pay if they were ten minutes late and would not be permitted to enter after that. This rule was apparently unenforceable, for it was followed three weeks later by a modified, "winter" version, which fined rather than denied entry to nearby workers who were up to half an hour late. Workers who lived across the Hai River could arrive one-and-a-half hours late without being denied entry.[37]

Once inside the mill, workers faced a day of ten to twelve hours, spent, if a worker was conscientious, in perpetual motion:

The factory is like a sea of machines, belts, wheels, wheels, belts. . . . Especially in the weaving and spinning departments, people move in a light fog [because of water sprayed from showerheads to keep the humidity high]. They let their bodies sink into the sea of wheels and belts, some walking back and forth, some motionless, some watching the waste cotton on the machines, or piecing, their ten fingers moving ceaselessly.

The people and machines are one body; the machines move, and the people follow their motions. While the machines move, people don't dare to stop their aching arms and fingers, don't dare to stop their exhausted feet.[38]

By the time the millhand finished work, stood in line to be searched for stolen goods on the way out, and walked home, he or she would have no energy for anything but sleep. Even single workers who lived in factory housing and traveled only a few yards to work were no exception, wrote a reporter after visiting a factory dormitory in 1937: "Although the factory provides swings, ping-pong tables, and other forms of amusement, only a few workers have the heart for amusement when they get off work. . . . They eat, then sleep."[39]

At the end of a set period of time, usually a week, the day and night shifts in the mills rotated. Depending upon the schedule of the particular mill, one shift of workers might then have 36 hours off rather than the usual 12. With the exception of this break, the mills ran seven days a week, and everyone had a turn at night work. "The people working night shift think only of sleep," wrote a cotton mill worker in 1935, "but if the thread breaks while they're sleeping, the boss will curse them, or worse, fire them. The worst time is from two to five A.M." Because workers routinely had their schedules turned upside down, they were always tired. This was especially true of child workers, who found it difficult to sleep during the daylight hours.[40]

Holidays were more frequent during the two periods of Guomindang rule (1928–37 and 1945–49) than during the occupation, because they included the anniversaries of the founding of the Republic, National Day, Sun Yatsen's birthday and the anniversary of his death, and various other holidays commemorating the 1911 Revolution. Unlike the workshops of Santiaoshi, the cotton mills observed these occasions as well as the Spring, Dragon Boat, and Mid-Autumn Festivals. From 1945 to 1949, the government mills also had Sundays off.[41]

Nevertheless, millhands spent virtually all their waking lives in activities related to their work: getting to and from the mills, performing repetitive and exacting tasks during their shifts, and rotating their off-hour chores to conform to the rotations in their work schedules. The requirements of the working day, and the struggle of the workers to bend those requirements, dominated the organization of working-class life.

Space, Heat, Dust, and Speed

Although the cotton mills were larger than the workshops of Santiaoshi, they were often just as cramped and uncomfortable. A 1929 inspection of the reeling department of the Yu Yuan Mill found that it was "upstairs, and accessible only by narrow stairways. There are two elevators, which are for moving yarn, and four wooden stairways, two of which are circular, and the other two very steep. If there were ever a fire it would be a disaster."[42] Machines in some departments were spaced too close together for adults to work there comfortably: "In the spinning department of the Hua Xin mill, 63% of the workers are piecers, and half of these are children. The spindles are three feet off the ground, with very little space between them. Adults have to bend over in order to piece, so that it is easier for children to do this work."[43] This workshop was noisier than the others in the spinning department, but quiet compared to the weaving mill, where the noise made by power-driven shuttles reached deafening levels.

Spinning workshops had to be kept warm and moist to keep the thread from breaking. This kept the workers warm in winter; a 1947 survey of six government mills found that the temperature in January ranged from 50 to 77 degrees Fahrenheit. It also made them uncomfortable in the summer, with workshop temperatures in July and August rising into the 80's and 90's. A further source of discomfort was the humidity, which was seldom under 50 percent and in summertime often as high as 80 percent.[44] Ventilation facilities were nonexistent. "When it was hot," recalls Zhang Chunfeng, "on the average they had to carry out a dozen workers a day. . . . They would carry them to the doorway to get some air. Then they would go back to work."[45]

Depending upon the workshop, a millhand might be plagued by floating cotton dust in the cleaning room,[46] or made uncomfortable by excessive moisture in the reeling room. The thread was moistened after spinning and before reeling to increase its tensile strength and make it easier to reel. The 1929 inspectors commented that in the room where this operation was performed the millhands had to "work on a wet floor, no matter whether winter or summer. It is very hot in summer, and causes accidents. In winter people get wet coming into the factory and freeze going out. Workers up to about the age of seventeen can't make enough at this to support themselves, while those who are older get back pains from it."[47]

The heat, humidity, and dust left workers dirty at the end of a shift. "All the workers worked and lived in the same clothes," remembers a foreigner who lived in Tianjin in the 1920's, "so you could always tell the cotton mill workers because they were covered with lint. They had summer clothes and winter clothes and that's what they wore all summer or winter, whether they were working or not."[48] Most of the mills provided showerhouses for the millhands. In a typical mill, the bathhouse used by male workers featured a communal tub in which the water was changed twice a day. The women's shower at the same mill was described by the inspectors as dark and smelly, and with a floor so encrusted with dirt that the writer wondered how people could bear to step on it after they removed their shoes and socks. Not surprisingly, very few women made use of the facility.[49]

Millhands were allowed a short meal break at mid-shift. Those who lived in the single workers' dorms commonly banded together in groups of several dozen, rented one of the dormitory kitchens, and hired a cook. For breakfast and dinner they usually ate steamed bread and rice gruel, pickled vegetables, bean sprouts, and cabbage. At noon they had a more elaborate meal of rice, noodles with sauce, or steamed dumplings (*baozi*). On days when they switched shifts they ate meat. A second group of people ordered their food from area restaurants for delivery to the factory, and ate much the same fare. These two groups spent almost half their monthly salaries (7.00 or 7.50 yuan in 1929) on food.

Workers who lived at home came to work carrying crullers (*youtiao*) or wheat cakes (*dabing*), then had their mid-shift meal sent in by a family member. The 1929 investigation observed that they paid only 3.50–7.00 yuan for a month's food, and also ate rice and white flour. A fourth group of people purchased their food piecemeal from street vendors, who sometimes came into the factory to sell snacks. Workers on night shift bought their food on their way to work because they were not permitted to leave the workroom during their half-hour dinner break.[50]

At mealtime, the group kitchens and restaurants would deliver directly to the factory dining hall, a room furnished with long tables and benches. Workers with families went to the factory gate to collect their food. In most mills "next to the dining room a public kitchen was maintained together with a water pot, where the workers might steam their rice or bread and get hot water for drinking or washing."[51] Some workers ate in the dining hall, some at their machines. Especially for those who were paid by the piece, time away from the machines was money lost. Government and private reports frequently noted that workers were driven by economic considerations to eat at their machines and consume food covered with cotton dust.[52]

The food supply for mill workers worsened considerably in the middle and later years of the Japanese occupation. Rice and white flour were reserved for the military forces and forbidden to the general population. Cornmeal, sweet potatoes, soybeans, sorghum flour, and beancake (*doubing*) were standard fare.[53] Workers on night shift, remembers Zhang Wenqing,

had no set time for eating. We would bring a little beancake, put it in a small sack that we had sewn into our pockets, soak it, put a little salt on it, put it back in our pockets, and eat it while we worked. When we finished eating, there was no hot water, so we drank cold water. On the night shift there were people farting all over the place and it stank, because we weren't digesting our food properly.[54]

Space, heat, dust, and mealtime breaks are measurable aspects of working life, but pressure on the workers to complete a certain quota or merely to keep up with the machines is not. The stress of keeping pace with a tireless machine was a feature of working-class experience unique to the modern sector. Those who worked for piece wages, inspectors observed in 1929, seldom stopped to rest. The women did not appear to be in good health, and problems such as aching legs and backs were common. Children were given quotas equal to those of adults.[55]

The conditions under which millhands labored and the lack of variation in their diet combined to make them susceptible to a variety of ailments. Cough and eyestrain, the two most common complaints for which treatment was sought, were probably either caused or aggravated by dust and the exacting demands of operating precision machinery.[56] Other ailments, while not direct products of the working situation, reflected the inadequacy of basic living conditions. Child workers were often bowlegged, the result of inadequate nutrition. Older workers were prone to arthritis. Inspections of the dormitories frequently found that the rooms were small and crowded, inadequately ventilated, and conducive to the spread of disease. As late as 1946, a cholera epidemic killed many cotton mill workers, prompting the government mills to administer preventive injections the following year.[57]

Constant danger was involved in working with power-driven machinery for long hours at high speed. From 1923 to 1928 there were 46 major injuries to workers at the Yu Yuan Mill. More than a quarter of the patients seen by the Yu Yuan and Hua Xin clinics in 1928–29 required surgery as a result of industrial accidents. The occupational hazards varied by workshop. In the cotton cleaning department, rapidly rotating blades were the main problem, while in the weaving mill a shuttle could fly off a loom with enough force to kill a nearby worker. The latter hazard could have been prevented by protective wire mesh between looms and around machine belts, but such safety devices were not employed in the Tianjin mills.[58]

The mills provided rudimentary health facilities for workers. As early as 1929 every mill in Tianjin had a clinic, "which in its simplest form was composed of one or two rooms for visiting patients, with a small stock of medicine." The practice was continued during the occupation. Yet mill-hands feared to seek treatment for potentially serious ailments because they might be sent home or, worse, fired.[59]

Pay

Manipulating the system of pay was one method by which management could extract speedy and productive labor from workers. In the late 1920's, both time and piece wage systems were in use in the Tianjin mills.[60] Cleaners, carders, balers, mechanics, smiths, carpenters, electricians, sizers, finishers, and coolies were paid by the day. Rovers, spinners, reelers, bundlers, warp and filling winders, warpers, drawers, and weavers were paid on a time-plus-piece system under which "a time rate was fixed, but a standard was also set for a day's work, above which a piece rate was given in addition to the time rate."[61] Of the jobs paid by time, all but one were held exclusively by men; of the jobs paid by piece, all but two were held by workers of both sexes. Women were thus virtually all paid piece wages, while men might be paid by either time or piece.

In addition to the base wage, workers might also receive bonuses. Bonuses equivalent to one or two days' pay were routinely paid to mill-hands who worked continuously for two weeks. This practice reflected management attempts to assure themselves of a stable workforce with a low rate of absenteeism.[62] Bonuses for good work and discipline were also issued at the discretion of the foremen. It was standard practice for the mills to pay bonuses either in cash or in kind on traditional holidays, and conflicts over the size of these holiday bonuses often lay behind labor disputes.[63]

But if the wage system reflected the imposition of industrial time, in periods of political instability it also mirrored the weakness of the capitalist class. At several points in their short history, the mills were trapped in an economy forced back to the barter stage by inflation. In the latter part of the Japanese occupation and again from about 1946 until Liberation, a portion of cotton mill wages was routinely paid in kind. Though it is not clear what percentage of the wage was in cash and what percentage was in goods, workers frequently complained that the grain issued as pay under the Japanese was the lowest-quality cornmeal, sweet potatoes, sorghum, or soybeans, and that it was frequently moldy or adulterated with dirt, stones, and glass slivers.[64] Workers sometimes did not receive the full amount they were owed, as a former child worker remembers:

One time I was standing in line. The wind was blowing very hard. When you got there they would push you to pick up your grain quickly. I took it home. I was happy because it was light, and I thought I was getting strong enough to carry things. When I got to the gate my father met me. My mother made tea for me and had me sit on the kang when I got home. When we weighed it we found that it was 28 catties of soybeans. They were supposed to give you 40 catties. They had poured some of it out and given me 28 catties. And a third of that was dirt.[65]

Toward the end of the Japanese period, as inflation gradually became a problem, "the size of the bags of grain we were paid in kept shrinking," recalls Zhang Wenqing. "The price didn't go up, but the bags shrank."[66]

The inflation of the late Japanese period, however, was minuscule compared to that which afflicted the Guomindang regime. Since most cotton mill workers labored in government-owned mills, they were more directly influenced by government policies intended to offset inflation than other sectors of the working class, but this was often no protection. Immediately after the Japanese surrender, workers were paid in currency, sometimes with a supplement of cloth or cornmeal. The practice of issuing wages in kind became more elaborate as the inflation got worse. In 1947, Cotton Mill #4 distributed cloth on every payday. In addition, workers were issued wheat tickets, with which they could buy flour at a relatively low set price, and have the amount deducted from their pay.[67]

But in spite of these measures, and the attempt to tie wages to a frequently updated cost-of-living index, inflation made any amount of pay pitifully inadequate. A notice issued by Cotton Mill #4 in November 1947 explained that since there was a shortage of paper currency, payment would henceforth only be issued in 10,000 yuan notes. Those workers whose wages were less than 10,000 yuan were to have payments for two pay periods combined. The set price at which the factory sold wheat flour during this period was 79,700 yuan for half a bag. A post-Liberation Chinese researcher has calculated that in September 1948, the average monthly wage of a worker in a government-owned mill could purchase 347 catties of cornmeal; by October the same worker could only afford to buy 50 catties. Speculation on staple items aggravated the problem. Workers were paid on a scale adjusted to official prices, but goods on the black market were much more expensive.[68]

Toward the end of the Guomindang period, workers strategized to cope with a situation in which "prices would go up several times a day."

Suppose you were paid every two weeks, and your wages were worth 100 catties of cornmeal. If you were paid in the morning the best thing to do was at noon, when your family came to bring you lunch, to give them the money to go to a grain shop quickly and buy it. At that time perhaps you could buy 80 catties. If you waited until afternoon it wouldn't be worth so much.[69]

"At the end," comments a third worker, "half a month's wage was enough to buy a head of cabbage." [70]

By paying wages in kind, millowners tried to protect themselves against inflation, and perhaps provide a welfare service to their workers as well. This type of paternalistic practice was not unique to China. It was common in eighteenth-century England, for instance, for management to purchase grain wholesale and sell it at cost or less in times of harvest failure. [71] But in Tianjin the efforts of millowners were dwarfed, and their attempts to use pay systems to control the workforce rendered futile, when the entire economy entered an inflationary spiral.

WORK DISCIPLINE, FORMAL AND INFORMAL

Unlike the shops of Santiaoshi, where work discipline might be harsh but was seldom codified in writing, the cotton mills kept meticulous contemporary records of their factory rules, backed up by a system of financial punishments and rewards. While many of these were never successfully enforced, they point to discipline problems as perceived by the management and are therefore a useful, if partial, guide to life on the shop floor.

Workers in the Heng Yuan Mill were threatened with fines or dismissal if they incited other people to impair the work of the factory; leaked work-related secrets; violated rules and order and did not respect the directions of the staff; talked, joked, laughed, sang, argued, fought, or were remiss in their work; acted indecently toward women; left their place without permission during work time and impaired the work of others; left the premises without securing permission from the staff; took materials or tools from the factory without securing permission from the staff, or brought useless materials into the factory; smoked in the factory or played with matches and other explosive material; read newspapers, magazines, or novels in the factory; carried material and parts out of the factory; or committed other types of improper actions. [72]

Workers were expected to submit to searches on their way into the factory (to ensure that they carried no matches or cigarettes), and on their way out (to make sure that they were not stealing yarn, cloth, or tools). These searches were most commonly cited as a feature of working life during the Japanese period, but they were standard practice as early as 1929, when one factory provided boxes near the exits where workers were exhorted to deposit anything they might have taken. Those who did not do so and were caught with the goods were charged with theft. [73] As late as 1947, one of the government-owned mills issued a notice warning that

A fire in a mill in Yingkou was caused by an ash from an employee's cigarette. It caused a great deal of damage. Therefore this factory is once again stating the rule that smoking is forbidden in the factory and that workers are not permitted to bring in cigarettes. If the guards at the door discover any, the offenders will be dealt with severely.[74]

In addition to submitting to searches, workers were expected to meet any visiting relatives or friends "in an appointed place." Visitors were not to be "permitted to rush into the factory." Unlike the handicraft workshops, the factory had clearly delineated boundaries and access was tightly controlled. A bonus was promised to any worker who caught others stealing, whose work was especially good, or who "exerted all effort to save the factory from fire and other unusual circumstances."[75]

High-ranking managers promulgated these regulations, but played only an intermittent role in enforcing them. During the Japanese occupation the top executives in each mill were Japanese. "Their method of management was as follows," explains Han Ruixiang, a former worker in the personnel department of a Japanese mill. "When work began, they would go to each workshop, and if they saw something wrong they would call the foreman. . . . He would take care of it directly. Hit someone, or punish them, or fire them."[76] Except for one inspection tour in the morning and one in the afternoon, workshop directors did not visit the workshop. Their immediate subordinates also spent a great deal of time away from the shop floor. Workers were expected to bow to the managers on their periodic tours, when they were often accompanied by translators. In general, however, the Japanese were rather distant overseers. Workers hated them and gave them derogatory nicknames, but, in the main, they avoided them.[77]

Much more flexibility and interaction characterized the relationship of workers with foremen, partly because the foremen themselves had an ambivalent relationship with the Japanese managers. Foremen, too, might be cursed or beaten by the Japanese. They were usually obsequious in the presence of the managers, but whether they chose to abuse the workers or to protect them was a product of individual character and political inclination. Foremen were often brutal disciplinarians. The accounts of those who came to the mills as children are filled with memories of violence, usually blows directed at them by foremen for working inefficiently or breaking rules they did not understand:

As soon as I entered the factory I was hit. I don't know why. Foremen always hit people then. . . . There were a lot of children in our workshop. We were all about ten years old. . . . I don't know why, but the more he was there, the harder it was for me to get hold of the heddle right. [The heddle was one of the sets of parallel cords on a frame that was used to guide warp threads in a loom. It had to be threaded by hand.] The more afraid you got, the less you could get hold of it; the less you could get hold of it, the more mistakes you made. I would get slapped. I didn't dare look up.[78]

Former child workers recall being hit for going to the lavatory without waiting for a pass, for playing or sleeping on the job, and for many other infractions.[79]

But the power of the foremen was not limited to disciplinary action. As in industrializing America and late-nineteenth-century Russia, they controlled work assignments as well.[80] In order to win favored treatment, it was customary to send presents to the foremen on holidays or special occasions. When a specific foreman had helped a worker to secure a job, unwritten rules regulated a worker's future obligations to him or her:

> After you went to work, if he had a baby, or got married, or his parents had a birthday, or his baby completed its first month of life, each time you had to go call on him and give him presents. If he didn't have a baby or get married, at New Year's and other festivals, the foreman would sell big bottles of soy sauce. It was worth fifty cents but he sold it to us for a dollar fifty. Everyone had to buy it.[81]

As times became harder in the final years of the Guomindang government, it seemed to workers that the frequency of these demands increased, until finally "every month they used up part of our wages."[82] The burden of economic obligation to the foreman, unquestioned in more stable times, became intolerable in an era of rapid inflation.

Another side to relationships with the foremen combined elements of work discipline, brutality, and barter. That was the demand made on women workers for sexual favors. To be sure, it was not only foremen but also male fellow workers who subjected women to sexual harassment. Zhang Wenqing, who began work at age thirteen during the occupation, recalls that "some of the girls would walk to work together. Some of the boys would also travel in groups, and jump out at the girls and scare us. You couldn't walk by yourself."[83] Nor was this behavior limited to children or to the wartime period. As early as 1929 a factory manager complained to a municipal investigator that in winter, when it was still dark at the time the night shift let out, workers were seizing the opportunity to "take liberties with women workers," liberties which he described enigmatically as "carrying women on their backs and running every which way" (*beifu nugong luan pao*), or smearing the women's faces with "black ash oil" (*hei huiyou*). The management responded by installing lights on the road outside the mill, and sometimes provided escorts home for women workers.[84]

Nevertheless, while male workers might harass women and girls on their way to and from work, it was the foremen who had the power in the workshop to insult women workers and frequently to rape them. Sexual abuse was used as a means of disciplining errant workers:

Sometimes if you made a mistake, he would insult you. You wouldn't dare say anything. But if you came back so angry you were crying, everyone would know. Once a Japanese called one of the women into a small room, and we didn't know why she had gone. Later she came out, and the Japanese person left. When we were resting, I went to another corner with her, and she cried. I said, "Look, we work together, don't be afraid." She told me. When she finished telling me, the next day she didn't come back to work.[85]

As a punishment for stealing:

I remember under the Japanese there was someone named Zhao Shumei. She was in the finishing department. She had no father. She had an older brother and four younger brothers. They depended on her brother, who worked in the dining hall, and on her in the finishing department. They were all very honest, but they couldn't make ends meet, and in the end she stole. She was arrested and taken to the Japanese military police. She was raped. She was held there for two days. Everyone sympathized with her, but there was nothing we could do.[86]

As punishment for being sick: "If a woman was sick and didn't go to work, he would go to inspect and find out why she hadn't come to work. She would be alone in her room in the dormitory because everyone else was at work, and he would take this opportunity to take liberties with her."[87] And for refusing sexual advances: "A Japanese took a fancy to her. He wanted her. She didn't submit, and so he beat her. Right in the workshop he would find reasons to beat her. In the end she had to give in. She still kept coming to work. Sometimes he went to her house."[88]

Sexual barter was often a woman's only currency to guarantee her continued employment in the mill: "This happened under the Guomindang, too. Even more. There were people who played up to the foremen, and people that the foremen took a fancy to. If you didn't go along, he would always pick on you. Some people couldn't take it and had to leave. There were some the foreman fired if they didn't consent. It was a common thing."[89] The reluctance of household heads to let their daughters go to work in the mills, the prevailing conservatism on this issue in spite of pressing economic need, and the common observation that women mill-hands had a difficult time finding a spouse were all, in part, consequences of this vulnerability of women workers to sexual abuse.

Militarization of the Workplace

The political situation in the world outside the mill gates frequently impinged upon daily work routines. In the Tianjin mills, the maintenance of discipline on the shop floor was not solely the responsibility of foremen and managers. Factories employed their own guards. In addition, police or military personnel were frequently called upon to maintain order. Sometimes they were summoned by the management as a response to specific worker disturbances, as when warlord troops were used to break up worker demonstrations in the mid-1920's. During the occupation, military personnel in the mills were a reminder that textile production was important to the Japanese war effort. And in the postwar period, their presence expressed the government's determination to prevent Communist organizers from winning adherents among the workers.

Workers who were in no way political activists, including many who never participated in any organized activity at all, were affected daily by the militarization of the workplace:

> Under the Japanese there was a garrison. They weren't actually military people, but demobilized military people. They organized a garrison, and underneath it a Chinese security patrol.
> Under the Nationalists, the police from the public security bureau lived in the factory. There was a patrol and under them several security guards. Almost like the Japanese garrison.[90]

The military presence became more pronounced in the late 1940's as the civil war widened: "In the factory, as it got closer to Liberation, control got tighter. Our factory had several strikes. Every time the Guomindang sent troops with machine guns to face the workers."[91] Nor was the policing limited to full-time security staff: "Even the head of personnel had a gun. He collaborated with the Nationalist Southern Investigative District, a special agent organization. They organized some secret activities, listened to what kinds of rumors there were inside. On the surface he was the head of personnel, but actually he was doing this kind of thing."[92]

By 1948, with the city under martial law, military personnel often searched millhands on their way to and from work and on the shop floor, subjecting them to a degree of surveillance that had not been achieved even under occupation by a foreign power.[93] The immediate effect of police and military presence in the mills was to reinforce the power of the mill management. Yet workers, denied an environment in which open resistance was possible, structured indirect forms of protest that shaped the workday to their own needs. One of these was "soaking mushrooms."

Soaking Mushrooms

"Soaking mushrooms," a slang term for a work slowdown, was a survival strategy generated spontaneously on the shop floor. It required a high degree of coordination between workers, as well as collaboration with foremen, but it seldom demanded formal organization.

When a government investigator visited the Yu Yuan Mill in 1929, the management complained to him about several bad habits that impaired the efficiency of the workforce. Most of these habits (visiting brothels, gambling, taking liberties with women workers, stealing) were not directly related to the requirements of work time, with one significant exception. Workers responded to what they regarded as the excessive speed of machine production by secretly smearing oil on the machine belts. This caused the machines to turn more slowly, which meant that the thread would break less frequently and the work would be easier. It also meant that the output of yarn was reduced. In order to prevent the oil from penetrating the machine belts, the management put a heavy coat of rosin on each one, a costly and time-consuming procedure. Some workers retaliated by cutting the machine belts with knives so that they could rest while the machines were being repaired.[94]

For workers being paid by the piece, such simple sabotage would only have resulted in a cut in wages, so they adopted other methods:

The rovers, whose output is measured by means of a hank meter, are noted for hank stealing through meter manipulation. The mill, at last, has to guard the meter with an iron fence which is locked. The weavers, again, may manipulate the gear in such a way as to give greater distance between the wefts. In that way, the texture of the cloth woven is loosened, but the length is increased without additional effort on the part of the weaver. The mill, consequently, suffers from the inferior quality of its output, and not infrequently it is unable to sell 110 pieces of its cloth at an equivalent price for 100 pieces.[95]

These practices continued during the Japanese occupation.[96]

A more passive mode of seeking a degree of control over the working environment, and one that carried fewer risks of discovery, was simply not to work unless a foreman was around to watch. "People catch naps a great deal at night, and there is also a lot of gambling going on, especially throwing dice," noted the government investigator in 1929. Workers would relax by sneaking off to the lavatories, where, as one worker observed, "even though it stinks a bit, still you're free to talk and joke there. If you have a cigarette you can sneak a few puffs. But if you are discovered you may be cursed, fined, or fired." This strategy of escape, however, did not work in the reeling, preparation, or weaving departments, where the pressure of payment by the piece kept workers at the machines.[97]

Even for pieceworkers, the strategy of "soaking mushrooms" seems to have become endemic during the occupation. Virtually every interview with a veteran of the Japanese mills includes a version of a typical workday like the following:

> We had a rule. Right after we came to work we had to work very hard. Watch six looms. If four of them stopped, you would get kicked. So that first hour after we arrived at work was very busy. Nobody goofed off. We got all the machines moving.
>
> At about eight, after two hours of work, the foreman would go off to take a rest. The Japanese manager went off to the lounge (*keting*). He went to have a smoke and drink some water. Then we could take it easy. Some of the machines stopped. We would lie down on the floor and rest for a while. Some people went to the bathroom. In the workshop, maybe half the machines stopped.
>
> At about eleven we would figure that they had about finished resting. We would work hard again for two hours. . . .
>
> Sometimes a person would play up to them. He would say, "As soon as you left, they didn't work so hard." So they changed their methods. One would pretend to leave when in fact he hadn't left. He would come back in less than half an hour, and when he saw that the machines were stopped he would start hitting and pushing people.
>
> What were we supposed to do? We were fifteen or sixteen years old. We were tired. We couldn't take it. So we set up a lookout system. The person next to the door kept an eye out. When he saw the foreman coming, he would wave a piece of cloth. They kept such strict control over us that we had to think of a way to rest a bit more.[98]

The story was similar in every workshop. Only the signals used to warn people of the foreman's approach would vary. In the spinning mill it was "a yarn tube thrown into the workshop by a worker near the door. When it hit the ground, everyone would know that someone was coming and would get down to work fast."[99] In the finishing department it was a person watching in the doorway who "would put up her hands when the Japanese were coming, and everyone would run back to work."[100]

Child workers even transformed the shop floor into a playground, although the consequences could be disastrous:

> We were kids and we used to play. Even when the machines were running, we would play. We would take some thread and roll it up into two balls, tie them together with a piece of string, and play with them.
>
> Once they got hung up in the machine belt and they were making a lot of noise. All my machines had stopped. A Japanese person saw it. He hit me and dragged me off to the office. It just so happened that the Japanese who was *his* supervisor was in the office. They hit me. They said that I was deliberately making trouble. Then they took me off to the guard's room at the door. They would grab me every two or three hours and beat me once. They made me kneel there for a day and a night.[101]

"Soaking mushrooms" appears not to have been so extensively practiced in the postwar period. Whether this was because working conditions improved, or because supervision tightened, or because these forms of labor protest were replaced by more active ones is unclear. Another unresolved issue is the role of Chinese foremen in protecting or joining workers who "soaked mushrooms" behind the backs of Japanese management. But the degree of cooperation that workers developed to slow down the pace of work served them well in other shop floor activities, like stealing to maintain a minimum livelihood.

The Struggle over Nonworking Time

If the handicraft workshops of Tianjin were a closed and narrow world, the cotton mills were planned communities complete with a full range of welfare services. The Yu Yuan Mill, for example, was lauded in government and academic surveys for its dormitories, dining hall, clinic, schools for workers and their children, consumers' cooperative, bathhouse, athletic field, and martial arts society, as well as its paid maternity leave, disability benefits, funeral subsidy, and the bonus paid workers so they could purchase melons in the summer.[102] Equally impressive lists of benefits crowded the reports on the government mills after World War II. The Yu Yuan's successor provided all the previously listed benefits, as well as drama and music troupes, a child-care center, and English classes.[103]

This provision of services was not unique to China. In eighteenth-century England, it was common in the early years of industrialization for the employer to provide worker housing, if factories were built in new areas. Medical assistance, death grants, and company stores were also standard. In nineteenth-century Moscow, factory owners sponsored cooperatives that sold food and supplies.[104] Millowners had to provide an infrastructure where none existed. In Tianjin's years of rapid expansion, housing must have been in short supply, particularly in the suburban districts where the mills were built.

But company housing, in Tianjin as in England, had another purpose as well. It was an attempt to extend the imposition of factory discipline, of regular industrial work habits, to nonworking time. Had they been able to, the Tianjin millowners would have made of the factory a closed environment, serviced by company institutions and secured by company guards. But workers voted with their feet, resisting the attempt to turn housing into a "tool of discipline."[105]

During the Japanese period the Kotai #6 Mill built a 500-room dormitory complex called New Virtue Lane. Not many workers chose to live there. Their reluctance was partly attributable to frequent job changes, but other reasons were important as well. Many workers did not want management to be able to locate them after working hours. A member of the personnel department at that time explains: "Life was too hard and sometimes people were forced to take a little something from the mill. If it was discovered by the factory, they would come looking for you. So people didn't want to live in the factory even if they were new buildings. The dormitories were 50–60 percent empty. Workers also wanted to avoid being traced to their homes if they did not show up at work. When staff from the personnel department went out to investigate truant workers, they would find that "eight out of ten households didn't live at the address they had given."[106]

Given this reluctance to be accountable to the factory outside working hours (and sometimes during working hours), only single workers who had come to Tianjin by themselves and had no connections or local family lived in the dormitories. Dormitory residents accounted for only about one-fifth or one-quarter of all workers. Most of these single workers during the Japanese period were young enough to be classified as child workers. Recruited by mill personnel who had shown them pictures of recreation facilities, they arrived to find rooms that held eight to 40 people, had iron bunkbeds or "dead" earthen sleeping platforms (called "dead" because they had no stove underneath and could not be heated), and were alternately freezing and mosquito-ridden.[107]

Most important, these dormitories were locked, replicating the closed world of the handicraft workshops with its captive apprentices. Except during holidays, resident workers were not permitted to venture outside the mill gates. Dormitory residents were issued special coveralls which identified them, and their work cards were marked with a double red stripe or some other simple indicator. People from a single workshop lived together. When their shift ended, they would return to the dormitory to eat. Some were actually issued their breakfast and dinner—two pieces of steamed bread per meal—as they passed the checkpoint between the workshop and the dormitory. "If you were sick you got nothing to eat and just had to lie there hungry," remembers one worker. Death in the dormitories from untreated illnesses was not unknown.[108] "When we worked night shift we would often play during the day," another recalls of his childhood in the mills, "but we still couldn't go outside the courtyard. We would play marbles."[109]

Resident workers could hope for only occasional relief from the sequestered world of workshop, dormitory, and courtyard, and even then certain procedures had to be followed: "If you lived in the dormitories and wanted to go out you had to have a guarantor. You couldn't go out when you pleased. Every year or so I wanted to go home to have a look. A person from the same room guaranteed me." [110] Regular workers who lived at home were not normally permitted to visit the dormitories, which were guarded. If family members of millhands came to Tianjin, they were often refused entry to the dormitories as well.

As with the apprentices at Santiaoshi, flight was a frequent response to life in the dormitories. Cheng Changli remembers two recruits from Qingdao, aged eleven and fourteen, who climbed over the factory wall and fled. One was caught and beaten. "When people left," he says, "they left their bedding behind. About every other month the factory would fill up a cart with quilts and mattresses and take them to the south city to sell." [111]

With the end of the war came widespread factory shutdowns, and when the mills reopened in early 1946, the role of the dormitories as an instrument of workplace control began to change. More families moved into factory housing, and conditions in the single workers' dormitories became more relaxed. The reasons for this change are not clear. Perhaps the temporary stability of 1946 encouraged more workers to bring their families to the city. People who had come to the mills as children of twelve or thirteen were now of marriageable age and less likely to be living in a single workers' dormitory. The workforce as a whole was apparently older, although no statistical data are available on this point. [112]

Millowners also tried to regulate the off-hour behavior of workers who never lived in the factory compound. Many mills, for instance, issued special rules at holiday time forbidding staff members to accept bribes and enjoining workers from gambling. [113] Yet except for those who had no local resources, workers were fairly successful in maintaining control over their nonworking time. Whenever possible they lived with kin who could reinforce the connections they had brought with them to the city, rather than entering the world of industrial regularity that the millowners sought to provide.

Patronage and the Struggle for Protection

In the struggle over the workday, owners set the terms, foremen enforced them, and workers adapted. But the struggle for patronage and protection in the mills was one that, in a sense, took place on the workers' own turf. The millhands drew on ties with relatives and fellow villagers, forged cross-class alliances with foremen and gang elders, and formed fictive kinship bonds with laborers from the same workshop. These networks gave a coherence and continuity to factory life that helped workers to survive in a conflict-ridden, often violent environment. [114] Gang membership, paradoxically, became the source of both violence and protection from violence.

Workers usually came into the mills not as isolated individuals, but as members of geographical and family networks, which channeled them into a specific mill or workshop and offered them some protection once they were there. Ji Kailin recalls:

There were many people from Wen'an county in our factory. Maybe one-fifth. Not all from my village—the whole county. The people in our village were introduced by a man named Liu [a low-level foreman in the mill]. Some of the people from my county were in contact with one another, some weren't. But once you found out that someone was from Wen'an, your relations were closer. We would help each other out. Some became sworn brothers. . . . Workers from one locality had a small-group mentality. Some places even had native-place associations.[115]

Yet workers in a single cotton mill, unlike those in the Santiaoshi iron-works, were not from a single native place. The size of the mill workforce, the lack of linkage to a particular local handicraft tradition like metalwork-ing, and the prevalence of refugee labor ensured that each mill contained two or more geographical networks. When they interacted, the encounter was often hostile, as Ji points out:

At lunch my family would bring me food. I put it down and went to wash my hands, and when I came back I couldn't eat it, because it was full of sand. A worker from Tangshan named Zheng had put it in. He had been recruited by the foreman named Zheng [also from Tangshan and possibly a relative] that I mentioned before. I asked him why he had done it. He didn't talk reason, he just came at me and hit me. I was very angry at the time, and picked up a piece of metal and hit him in the arm.

After that he told foreman Zheng, who came to my house looking for me. I hid. He stood in my house cursing, and then people talked to him, and the thing died down, because he had no justification.

Those people from Tangshan had pretty close relations. If someone bullied one of them, they would help one another out.[116]

Interwoven with the geographical networks were the family networks found in the mills. Given the role of connections in obtaining a mill job, it is not surprising that groups of relatives tended to cluster in a particular mill. Even before the Japanese occupation, siblings followed one another. The story of Zhang Jiagui in 1931 is typical: "When we came to Tianjin [from the northern suburbs] we rented a small room. . . . My brother in-troduced me into the mill, so I didn't need a guarantor. My younger sister was in the spinning room. We all came at about the same time. There were four or five of us at work: my two younger sisters, two older brothers."[117] This pattern continued when families of refugees came to the city during the occupation. Ji Kailin entered a mill in 1943, with his sister-in-law and his wife. (He was ten years old at the time, and his wife was a child bride who lived with his family; he did not formally marry until seven years later.) Gao Fengqi and his younger sister entered a mill together in 1940. Zhang Chunfeng describes her entry into the Kotai #6 Mill in 1940 in the following manner:

My older sister worked in the old Yu Yuan, the predecessor of the Japanese Kotai #6 Mill. At the age of twelve she started work in the spooling department. . . . I had three older brothers in this factory. The oldest sister at age seventeen got a woman's disease (*funü bing*) and died. At that time my second sister was in the spinning department. She was already seventeen. She found a mother-in-law, and as soon as she got married she couldn't work anymore. So I took her place.[118]

Once inside the mills, relatives protected one another, going to and from work together and helping family members deal with foremen and bullies among their fellow workers. By continuing to rely upon these connections, a worker might improve his or her place in the mill hierarchy, change mills, or even move outside the textile industry.

In addition to the connections workers brought with them, they created new connections in the mills as a response to the working situation. Labor historians have traditionally looked to these new modes of association as a measure of working-class consciousness, because they are based upon common experience as workers rather than upon place of origin or position in the family. Yet in Tianjin these new connections were not discontinuous with the old. Forms of association within the mills built upon older ties, and were both strengthened and limited by them.

Forming associations for the purpose of mutual protection was an important survival strategy. Such an association might draw on blood or native-place ties, but was not limited to them. These associations were usually sex-segregated and often secret. Brotherhoods and gang membership for men, sisterhoods and religious groups for women, were the most common forms. Members, not always mill workers, frequently pledged allegiance to an outside figure, either human or divine. Among millhands in Tianjin, "swearing brotherhood was very, very common," recalls Han Ruixiang.

There were many sworn brothers (*meng xiongdi*) in the factory. The smallest group had three people, the largest 108. There were also groups of 72. Under the Japanese we formed a group of seven, under the Nationalists a group of 28.

What was the purpose? We would help one another out in case of trouble, keep an eye on one another. There was no oppression or bullying among members. They were people who had frequent contact with one another. They had the same viewpoint. They had sympathy.

Those who decided to swear brotherhood were not necessarily from the same native place. "They were usually from one workshop. They worked together." Groups were sometimes formed spontaneously, but their organization was strictly hierarchical: "A man who organized a lot of people was called a big brother. If he saw a lot of people who got along well, he would say, 'We can get together.' Sometimes a group of people would invite a big brother to be the head of their alliance."

The hierarchy was reflected in the formal ceremony where brotherhood was sworn:

> They would all get together, and invite the big brother who was heading the alliance. Perhaps he was a member of the older generation. Or at least he was an elder brother. After he arrived they would sit down, and each person would say what his birthday was, and they would line up in order of age. All 28 of them. I was No. 28, the youngest. After we lined up, the person organizing the alliance would formally announce who the elder brother was. Everyone would bow to him. Then they would drink together.

While such a group had no formal activities, it did provide a basic organizational unit that might be employed in an activity like stealing, and so it was regarded with suspicion by the Japanese. "They weren't happy with this, because it wasn't advantageous to them. No matter how you put it, it wasn't advantageous, because if something went wrong the people in the group would cover up for one another." [119]

Swearing allegiance with a particular group of men was not necessarily a permanent commitment. Perhaps reflecting the high rate of turnover in the mills, workers formed and re-formed groups as the need arose: "I swore brotherhood once under the Japanese. Then I swore brotherhood twice under the Nationalists. Sometimes you would be in a group with the same people. There was duplication. The last group of 28 would have a few of the group before in it, and this group would too." [120]

The factory history of the Yu Yuan Mill indicates that groups of sworn brothers were consciously used to foster labor protest in two periods— during the 1926 strike, and in 1947–48. In both cases, Communist organizers reportedly persuaded groups of "brothers" to join a labor union *en masse,* or else organized new groups of sworn brothers to undertake small-scale labor struggles. Brotherhoods, however, did not always engage in political activity. In 1929 the municipal survey noted that sworn brothers went to plays together, drank together, and visited one another when there was a wedding or a funeral. These groups were part mutual protection society, part mutual aid society, and part social clique. [121]

Seeking more substantial protection than an independent group of workers could provide, sworn brotherhoods would sometimes affiliate themselves with one of the gangs active in Tianjin—either the Qing Bang or the Hong Bang. While these gangs had their main base of power in Tianjin in the transport industry, they could be found in so many other areas of endeavor that one Chinese sociologist, Li Shiyu, has called pre-Liberation Tianjin a "Qing Bang world" (*Qing Bang shijie*). Both these gangs, but especially the Qing Bang, had interests in the bath houses, the hotels, the gambling and opium dens, and the brothels of Tianjin. Most foremen in large factories were members of the Qing Bang from the 1920's until Liberation.[122] Maintaining good relations with a foreman was the surest path to advancement in the mills, and gang membership was an effective way to cement good relations:

In the Qing Bang when you acknowledged someone as your master he was your elder (*lao tou*). Even if you were older than he was, he was still your elder, a generation above you. In the Hong Bang they called him "Big Brother." As soon as you mentioned your elder's name, or said that you were so-and-so's disciple, people would look at you in a new way and wouldn't dare mess with you. As though your social status had risen. It served the purpose of protection.[123]

While the "elder" of a millhand might not be his direct supervisor in the mill, swearing allegiance to him served much the same purpose as obtaining the patronage of a powerful foreman by other means, because he could be called upon to intercede with the supervisor if necessary.

Gang membership differed from other modes of patronage in the mills, in that the hierarchical structure of the gangs extended well beyond the mill gates, into the power structure of Tianjin. Although the connections are shadowy, it is clear that members of the Tianjin elite, and the underworld shadow elite as well, belonged to the gangs and built their power base partly by relying upon the membership of cotton mill workers and staff. Han Ruixiang's account is instructive in tracing one gang network:

Who were these elders? As far as I knew, some of them were scholars. Like the Qing Bang elder Zhang Xinzhi was the head of the Guomindang newspaper office. They were all outside the factory. There weren't any who worked. Another group were Guomindang party hacks. . . . Some were local landlords and tyrants . . . these kinds of elders were not scholars. There was a lot of fighting among them. They were also in charge of the transport guilds, and the docks.

I joined the Hong Bang. My elder was Jiang Bore. You needed an introduction. It was all men; women didn't join. Most of the Hong Bang people were from the south. I was introduced to Big Brother Jiang. He was a president of a university in the Flower Park. It was said that the students at that university were not upright students (*zhengpai de xuesheng*).

These people had connections with people who were big bureaucrats at that time. There was someone in the Hong Bang named Zhao who worked in Cotton Mill #4. He knew Dong Kecheng at Cotton Mill #2. Dong Kecheng worked in the same workshop as my younger brother. He used to come around to my house and he got to know me. He asked me, "Where are you from?" I said, "I'm from Shandong." "There aren't very many Shandong people in Tianjin. Do you have any *laoxiang* [fellow natives] here? How did you come to Tianjin? Come get to know a few more people!"

I got to know Zhao Zhongming, who worked in Cotton Mill #4. Then they had me meet Big Brother Jiang. . . . The object of joining a gang was to get out of the mill, to do something where we could have power and money. . . . Our elder was a southerner. I don't know if there were other Hong Bang factions in Tianjin or not. There were one or two hundred of us under Jiang.

A powerful elder with many disciples and influence outside the mills could be a great deal of help to a millhand in trouble. "If you had a wedding in your family and needed something, if you had a funeral, he would take care of everything." [124] He could also protect a hapless worker from dangers outside the mill walls. One worker joined the Qing Bang to avoid being seized as a corvée laborer:

I joined the Qing Bang under the Japanese, in about 1944. Why did I join? I didn't know what it was all about. They told me if I joined I wouldn't be bullied. At that time I had left Gong Da Cotton Mill and gone to a small factory, a private one. I was working with someone there. He said that the Japanese were seizing people to go to work as laborers everywhere. He said that if I didn't join, the Japanese would seize me and take me away. So I went to see one of the elders. We burned incense. The disciples bowed to him. They wanted five dollars. [125]

In addition to this initiation fee, an elder expected presents on festivals, birthdays, and other special occasions, much as the foremen did. But the protection and patronage he provided were apparently worth the price to the millhands, for an estimated 80–90 percent of the male workers in the Tianjin mills joined either the Qing Bang or the Hong Bang in the 1940's: "You *had* to join. There was an elder here and one there. Whoever didn't belong to one belonged to the other. It was under the Japanese, too, but there were even more [members] under the Nationalists. It was also for the sake of being able to eat. To be tricked and bullied a little less." [126]

Of the two gangs, the Qing Bang had many more adherents. [127] Each of them owed allegiance to an elder, but the elders were not arranged in a hierarchy with clear lines of deference. Factions merged and split, and sometimes conflicts between factions were played out in the textile mills. As in the transport guilds, it was often the interests of foremen, not workers, that were involved. Yet workers were drawn into the conflicts and the ensuing violence: "As for the influence of these conflicts on the factory, aside from the armed struggles outside . . . there would be a fight where someone was not killed, but wounded. The other side then wounded one of their own men, put him there, and said that the other side had done it. These were all people from inside the factory. But the leader wasn't from the factory." [128] This violence sometimes reached the shop floor. One woman who was not a member of any gang retains vivid memories of gang-related violence and its influence on factory life:

In our factory there were several gangs. Qing Bang, Hong Bang. They divided up territory. . . . There was always fighting going on here. As soon as a fight broke out they would stop the machines and insult one another. . . . The heads of the factions each had some power, and they would use workers who were afraid of being bullied. . . . They wouldn't come out themselves. People were fighting their own class brothers.[129]

Gang violence could also take the form of prolonged vendettas, involving elders and members of chains of allegiances that extended far beyond the factory gates. In 1948, for instance, the Tianjin newspaper *Yishi bao* reported that since the beginning of 1947, there had been a series of attacks on foremen (*zu zhang*) in Mill #2, all of them staged in the immediate vicinity of the factory. Two foremen, Wu Bolin and Pan Changqing, had been successively wounded by more than 20 people. "This," commented the newspaper, "is an organized activity."[130]

Han Ruixiang was working in Cotton Mill #2 at the time, and explains the origins of the attacks as follows:

In 1948 in our factory there was a conflict between two Qing Bang factions. It was this way: At Spring Festival the factory director would buy a lot of fruit— apples and snacks—to make offerings. There would be an offering at every machine. After they burned incense, everyone wanted the fruit. Of course the big foremen got them—the little foremen couldn't.

Because of this question of fruit offerings, the two Qing Bang factions got into a conflict. . . . Pan Changqing wanted the fruit offerings to be given to him. The foreman who was in charge of the whole weaving mill, Wu Bolin, told him, "You'd better wise up," and took the fruit away. Later Pan told his elder. This business gradually got bigger and bigger.

As the disciples of the foremen in the factory and their elders outside the factory became involved, the adherents of one faction began to attack the followers of the other:

In the East Building, Old Three Sun [Sun Buquan], who was in the Gua Jia Si faction of the Qing Bang—he was the one with the four dragons on his arm—took an axe and cut up Bian Ruzi. Usually they didn't kill them, only wounded them. Cut them in the leg. . . . The elder of Bian Ruzi had connections with officials. They brought charges, and it went to court.

The method they used was this: They would wound one of their own people and say that the other side had done it. The person who was wounded couldn't know in advance. Otherwise it might be discovered. . . . They were all in the factory; they were all low-level foremen with a bit of power (*xiao gebo ger de xiao batou*). . . . The attackers drew lots.

Two men [from the same faction] walked together to the banks of the river and one used a knife to stab the other, and then ran. . . . After they wounded him they said the other side had done it. The upshot of the whole thing was that a mediator appeared. He was also a Qing Bang elder—Zhang Xinzhi from the newspaper office. Everyone sat down to drink and eat together and that was the end of it. Meanwhile the man who had been stabbed was in the hospital. . . . This kind of thing was very frequent.[131]

According to subsequent reports in the local newspaper, however, this was not the end of the matter. Shortly after the February stabbing of Bian Ruzi, it was discovered that the attack had been ordered by Yan Laide, aged fifty-eight, who was head of the Gua Jia Si faction of the Qing Bang.

Sun Buquan, who had done the stabbing, was a disciple of Yan. Sun's younger brother Sun Buhai, aged twenty-one, and Zhang Xuejin, also twenty-one, both coolies in the area and members of the same faction, wounded themselves with knives and accused Wu Bolin, head of the weaving mill, of having stabbed them. When the truth came out during an investigation they were detained, along with Yan, Sun Buquan, and three other disciples who all worked in the transport industry.[132]

At some point during these conflicts, the paper went on to report, "there was again a suspicious collection of sanlunche outside the factory. When they were searched, a collection of murder weapons was confiscated before anything could happen." Perhaps alarmed by the entrance of the notoriously violent transport workers into the conflict, the factory appealed to the military police for protection. The management noted that Yan, a member of the Qing Bang, had several dozen "claws and fangs" (accomplices) under him, and that further violence was likely.[133] As predicted, trouble flared up again, at the end of July. This time a complaint was brought by the foremen against the factory director, Peng Xuezhou. The foremen accused Peng of corruption, exploiting the workers, managing a Shandong mill for the Japanese military during the war, and collaborating with outsiders to threaten the safety of the foremen.

This last accusation illustrates the conjunction of blood relations, geographical networks, and gang affiliations in the cotton mills. At the beginning of July, the local Qing Bang elder who had been arrested in conjunction with the February incident, Yan Laide, was released by the military police. Factory Director Peng, who was from Hunan, had meanwhile brought many of his *tongxiang* and relatives into the factory, including a nephew, Peng Shoujian, and another relative, Hu Shijian, who were both technicians. They were also apparently disciples of Yan Laide, for on July 21 they accompanied him on a visit through the factory, "strolling and talking."

The foremen, who remembered all too clearly that Yan had masterminded the February assaults on one of their own, were furious about this and complained to the union, which during this period was dominated by the foremen. The union took the matter up with Factory Director Peng, who promised to fire his relatives if the allegation against Yan proved to be true. But when an investigative committee produced proof that Yan had in fact come to the factory, Peng pleaded illness and stopped coming to work. At this point a group of foremen and workers "got sick of waiting" and called in the manager of the plant, demanding that the two relatives be fired. The conclusion of the article is ambiguous, but it suggests that the offenders were given a stiff warning rather than sacked.[134]

As the preceding account makes clear, the fact that workers joined the gangs for protection and patronage by no means made the gangs into worker's organizations. On the contrary, the price a millhand paid for protection was to be drawn into conflicts, and sometimes injured, in the service of foremen or figures outside the factory to whom a cotton mill worker was just another expendable pawn. Gang allegiances persisted despite their evident drawbacks because millworkers needed protection, and group membership was the most reliable way to obtain it. Like the traditional groups on which millhands depended—those based on kinship and native-place ties—the gangs included members from different class backgrounds who might normally have been expected to oppose one another. Rather than squaring off against the foremen, as post-Liberation factory histories describe, apparently workers *and* their foremen just as often squared off against workers and foremen allied to a rival elder. Much of the violence in the mills, subsequently labelled "class struggle," might be more accurately characterized as gang warfare.

Women's Groups: Sisterhoods and Religious Beliefs

Although work may have placed women and men in the same department, their respective social networks tended to keep them apart. Women remained aloof from gang membership and the conflicts it generated. When women banded together for mutual protection, they did so in groups of sworn sisters (*jiebai zimei*). These groups might begin informally with women in the same workshop: "If several people got along together, they would look out for one another. If there was some problem, if I was sick, you would help me out with my work."[135] Later the relationship might be formalized:

We were together most of the time. We all got along. They would swear sisterhood with a group of five or seven. It was always an odd number. Eleven. No even numbers. Generally, sworn sisters didn't have any political objective. We were together: big sister, second sister, third sister, fourth sister. We got along. We would share hard times and good.[136]

Virtually no information survives about the nature or function of these groups of women. A 1929 government report suggests that they were not as strong as the brotherhoods formed by male mill workers, that women had less opportunity than men to gather socially outside the factory, and that women's groups frequently broke up because of quarrels.[137] The composition of the groups reflected divisions in the workforce. Women who lived at home did not swear sisterhood with those who resided in factory dormitories, because the latter did not remain in the mills very long before fleeing. Post-Liberation factory histories suggest that the sisterhoods were frequently turned to political ends, resisting insults by foremen during the Japanese period or forming strike action groups in the postwar period. But since their organization was apparently less formalized than that of the men, and since they never affiliated themselves with larger, more visible organizations like the gangs, they remain mysterious.[138]

Another source of protection sought out by women workers was a deity. The evidence of religious beliefs among millhands is scattered and ambiguous. One worker states that most millhands held some form of Buddhist beliefs, while another adds that it was usually the women who joined religious groups like the Long Hua Hui or the Yi Guan Dao.[139] The Yi Guan Dao, which flourished in occupied areas during the anti-Japanese war, purported to trace its origins to White Lotus sects as far back as the Song dynasty. An eclectic blend of Confucian thought, Daoist cosmology, Buddhist scriptures, and various superstitious practices, the Yi Guan Dao took as its central deity a Heavenly Mother (Wusheng Laomu) who was the creator of the earth. At the end of each era, she dispatched a messenger to earth to reorder the world. Members believed that the Heavenly Mother would save them and their relatives in the event of a great calamity.

The sect began to grow in Tianjin in the 1930's. Its leader, Zhang Tianran, who many adherents believed was the herald of a new era, was from Jining in Shandong, but lived in Tianjin and Beijing intermittently from 1934 until his death in 1947. Organized in temples (*tan*), believers congregated several times a month, or conducted rituals of incense burning and bowing at home. Members were expected to pay entrance fees and to finance the printing of religious texts.[140] The Yi Guan Dao had some following in the factories, especially among women workers. Zhang Wenqing remembers that millhands usually "followed their families. If the parents joined, the kids joined."[141] A similar sect, the Long Hua Hui, also had some followers among the millhands, to whom it taught secret phrases that were supposed to protect the one who recited them:

Zao chu men	Out at morn
Wan chu men	Out at night
Chu men jiu you jiejiu shen	Spirit saves you from all fright.
Si da tian huang gei ni yin lu	Four great emperors guide you onward
Ba da jin gang hu ni shen.	Eight great warriors lend their might.[142]

Tantalizing as these hints are, they remain mysterious indicators of what may have been a substantial amount of religious activity in the mills. Sect membership may well have constituted an important component of mill life, but the stigma attached to it after 1949 has obscured its extent and its form. Membership seems to have been more widespread in the cotton mills, where women workers were present, than in all-male Santiaoshi. But the implications of this pattern remain elusive.

THE STRUGGLE OVER LIVELIHOOD

Workers in the Tianjin cotton mills were always paid a wage that kept them uncomfortably close to the margin of subsistence. As the Tianjin economy grew more unstable in the 1940's, the struggle over livelihood became a defensive struggle for survival. The authority of the owners was buttressed by outside military power, and so open forms of labor conflict were rare. Instead, workers acquired what they regarded as a tolerable living wage by stealing from the mill. Whether intended as a form of protest [143] or merely as a hastily devised means of scraping by, stealing involved a high degree of organization among workers, as well as manipulation of cross-class alliances.

Large and well-organized stealing rings operated in every mill. In 1929 the Yu Yuan management told visitors that the theft of yarn was a major problem. Boxes placed near the mill exits, with signs posted near them encouraging workers to deposit pilfered goods, were to no avail. Nor did the guards who were responsible for searching workers at the gate prove to be of much use, since they were often in league with the thieves and neglected to search them thoroughly—in return for a payoff. On the main street of Xiao Liu Zhuang, the suburban district where the Yu Yuan Mill was located, many people specialized in buying the stolen yarn for resale. [144]

Driven by a worsening economic situation, workers during the Japanese occupation enlarged the scope of their thievery. Individual workers hid cloth in their socks and thread in their lunchboxes. Groups of workers threw goods over the wall for pickup by outside collaborators. Leather machine belts and lead, tools, and raw materials found their way out of the factory. [145] Considerable organization was required to sustain thefts of such scope and variety:

> We stole whatever we produced (*gan ma tou ma*). Spinners stole yarn; weavers stole cloth. We were all of one mind at that time. Men and women . . . worked together. When the thread came down, and the Japanese weren't watching, . . . we would pull the thread off and hide it in our clothes. People like me with this kind of build [tall and thin] could stuff in ten catties. In the weaving mill, everyone took the warping thread and hid it in their clothes . . . in the winter. . . . Then we would put on our outer garments.

The men brought the goods to the women. The women just had on a pair of underpants and an undershirt, but they never tried to take advantage of us. . . . When it was almost quitting time, at about four in the afternoon, we would start to put it on. . . . We called it "bringing the goods up" (*shang huo*). Actually, it was stealing.[146]

Supervisory personnel at all but the highest levels were participants in this activity: "The foremen were in on it too. The Japanese were in the minority. They couldn't keep an eye on so many people."[147]

Once the thread was safely concealed, the next hurdle was the guards at the gate. If they did their jobs as they were supposed to, the searches were thorough, time-consuming, and humiliating. "When we got off work we had to line up to be searched. Pull out our pockets, pull off our shoes," recalls one worker. Another remembers having to "unbutton your buttons and open your pants." The procedure added one more irritating episode to an exhausting day of work: "If you got off work at six, it was after eight by the time you got home."[148]

A guard who was paid off in advance, however, would let a worker who was literally stuffed to the earlobes with pilfered yarn go by. The Japanese management was quick to recognize this problem. They erected a partition that reached from the roof to the shoulder level of the workers, so that the guards could not see who they were searching. But this ingenious preventive measure was in vain:

They interfered with the collaboration between us and the searchers. . . . But we also had a way of dealing with them. If I had contact with you, and you knew that I was going to go by your station and that you were supposed to let me go, I would put some kind of a signal on my socks or shoes, so that you would look and know it was me. That was one way. There were quite a few.[149]

For a would-be thief to be successful, and have the chance to repeat his or her act, suitable expressions of gratitude to all collaborators were required: "People on the outside sold what we stole. If I stole ten catties, lots of people took a cut. Two catties went to the searcher. You let me go, I give you two catties. I also had to buy off the foremen—one or two catties. I only kept 30 or 40 percent of it. . . . I gave it to the people on the outside to sell." The buyers of stolen yarn were also well-organized: "They sold it to the countryside. . . . I would ask him if he wanted yarn. If he did, I would say, "I'll bring it to you at twelve tomorrow." I would bring it to his house or to a prearranged place. Out of ten catties, two were his profit. . . . He would pay me on delivery. I would take it and go off to buy grain. I had to eat. I had to scrape by."[150]

Millhands did not get rich from stealing; theft was just a means of "scraping by." And even though, at a remove of almost 40 years, the erstwhile thieves retell their stories with some relish, it is also clear that the risks were enormous.

> The Japanese were smart. Sometimes they would stand there and direct you to another searcher [one with whom no arrangement had been made]. . . . They had to arrest some people or the Japanese would get after them. . . . The men did more stealing than the women. They would take you to the guard room and hang you up and beat you. . . . Or they would send you off to do corvée labor (*laoyi*). Of ten who were sent, ten would die. . . .
> A woman in the warping room stole some thread. . . . They beat her outside, naked, in the winter. They made her stand out there for a long time. When they finished beating her, they fired her. . . . That was the form of struggle at that time. . . . Anyway, we figured no matter what we did, we would die.[151]

The fact that workers were willing to keep stealing in the face of such brutal punishment is a testimony to their desperation. They did whatever they could to avoid the guards: "We used to do some of it in the bathroom. People used to hide yarn and cloth in the nightsoil containers and take them out with the nightsoil."[152] Or they would contrive to make off with a whole shipment of cloth: "Whole carts of merchandise. It was all arranged. . . . You had to arrange it with the officials, too. They had special agents out. You had to buy them off. That was for stealing a whole shipment at once. One person couldn't do that alone. Several people had to pool their efforts."[153]

After the Japanese surrender, it appears that the scale of theft was reduced, partly because the economic situation improved and partly because the mills were no longer under foreign control. Workers "felt that this was ours, we couldn't steal it."[154] As inflation began once again to erode the standard of living, pilferage resumed, but never again returned to the same grand scale. Nor were the punishments so draconian. A 1947 announcement to the workers at Cotton Mill #4 warned: "Today a worker in the reeling room, Hu Yufa, was caught stealing a bobbin of yarn. This is against factory rules. He was fired and his wages were confiscated. This is the first case of theft this year. After this, if there are any cases of employees stealing company property, they will without exception be fined."[155] Ironically, petty police agents out for personal gain rather than mill officials posed the biggest threat to workers who stole during this period.

> Outside the factory were police and special agents on the road. They could search and arrest people as they pleased. They were all in it for money. If you paid them off, you could take anything and it wouldn't matter. So most people who were stealing would carry a little money.
> This was especially common in 1948. There would be four or five of them outside the gate, leaning against the wall. It was all for extortion. Some police did this

too. They would take off their uniforms, change into plainclothes, and wait there. If they found that you had something on you, you had to give them money for sure or they would arrest you. Lots of people were arrested.[156]

Just as Ma Yunlong spent much of his time dodging government extortionists in Santiaoshi after the war, so cotton mill workers tried to avoid the plainclothesmen outside the mill gate. In both cases law enforcement officials made money by combining blackmail and protection. The days when Chinese inside and outside the mills had formed a "united front" of thieves to outwit the Japanese were over.

The dynamic of struggle in the Tianjin cotton mills was not one of monolithic exploitation and unified resistance. Millowners, foremen, and workers, as well as numerous factions that crossed class lines, tried to impose order on a new working environment. In each of the struggles described above, the outcome was inconclusive. Owners never got a stable workforce selected on merit; nor could they regulate worker behavior as they wished. Foremen as a group made out rather well, but the position of an individual foreman was always precarious. And workers, vulnerable to the factory world in obvious ways, were never fully transformed into an industrial proletariat. They made alliances with fellow workers, but also continued to rely upon vertical bonds with foremen. And their ties to members of their own class were conditioned as much by kinship and native place as by common experience in the mills. They continued to draw resources from the old world of the village, and to replicate some of the relationships of the preindustrial workplace, even as they displayed considerable ingenuity in coping with the new demands of industrial work in the mills.

CHAPTER SEVEN

Drumsongs and the Devil's Market: Patterns of Working-Class Life

Most Tianjin workers were veterans of a major migration to the city, where many of them found that stable work was hard to come by. Yet even though they moved from village to city and from job to job in the course of their working lives, theirs was not in any sense a rootless existence. Marginality and economic insecurity made it absolutely necessary that they preserve ties with kin and fellow villagers. This continuity of rural networks, reinforced by workers' experiences on the job, also influenced the way they spent their nonworking time. Leisure activities, holiday customs, and rites of passage not only continued rural practices, but provided the occasion for workers to renew the relationships they had brought to the city.

Of course, workers did not remain untouched by the city in which they lived. In search of protection, they enlarged their network of connections in ways that were unavailable and unnecessary in their home villages. When they went to the amusement halls of Sanbuguan, they heard the songs and stories of counties other than their own. And they did not remain unscathed by their battle for survival; conflicts erupted regularly in vendettas, in crimes of passion and revenge. But these signs of strain should not be confused with cultural breakdown. Working-class life was full of disorder, not anomie; community bonds and standards of conduct were not attenuated, but reinforced.

MARKETS AND AMUSEMENTS

Though workers never had much money to spend, visits to the lively markets that crowded the city landscape were an important part of working-class life. Food had to be purchased daily, a chore that often necessitated a trip to the local money shop as well as the market. Many laborers who could not find steady work elsewhere entered the marketplace as itinerant vendors of secondhand goods. Workers who lacked even the money to buy an inexpensive vaudeville ticket could spend their free time in the marketplace "watching the show" (*kan renao*) or engaging in one of the streetside gambling games run by local hustlers.

Aside from the old city and the concession areas, the main vegetable markets of Tianjin were located to the north and east of the old city, and in the southeastern cotton mill district of Xiao Liu Zhuang. Another vegetable market shared space with a cloth market to the southwest of the old city, where peddlers began hawking silk and satin remnants at six A.M. each day. Nearby was a fish market where most of the peddlers used scales that were one or two ounces short, prompting customers to bring their own scales and engage in frequent shouting matches with the vendors. A 1936 visitor to this market chuckled at the old women who became so engrossed in these arguments that they neglected to keep an eye on their baskets and wallets, which were promptly lightened for them by swarms of pickpockets.[1]

Most vegetable markets also featured stalls vending Tianjin's famous street foods: steamed breads with sweet or meat filling, wheat cakes (known variously as *shaobing*, *huoshao*, or *ganlao*), crullers, meat dumplings (*jiaozi*, or *bianshi* in Tianjin dialect), fried shredded soybean cake (*gabacai*), wheatcakes stuffed with beef, mutton, or pork, and *you jianbao*, cold steamed dumplings refried in oil. Stalls in the market areas near factories and along the riverbanks did a thriving business in these foods, as well as eggs, hot wine, peanuts, and spicy pickled cabbage.[2]

The city's most riotous market for secondhand goods, which supplied many of the other markets, was held before dawn each day near Xi Guang Kai. Known locally as the Devil's Market, it was the gathering place for itinerant dealers who "shouted scrap," as well as an unloading point for stolen goods. The merchandise for sale on a typical morning in 1936 included a pair of cotton-padded pants with its resident batch of lice, scrap iron and copper, old books, foreign clocks, and shoes with the dirt collected by their previous owner still on them. Antique merchants and junk dealers bought and sold feverishly, then packed up to move on to other markets, and by nine A.M. each day the area was deserted.

Some wares from the Devil's Market were sold throughout the city by "scrap shouters" who made the rounds of every lane, at the same time buying old goods and rags for the next day's market. Other items from the market appeared later in the day in the antique market near the southwest corner of the old city. There old gramophones and imperial coins were tossed carelessly on shelves next to scrap iron, copper, records, newspapers and used books (sold by the catty), and wooden furniture. This market was different from the others, noted a local guidebook wryly, because one could see the original owners of the goods, "sloppily dressed, furtively talking business with the stall owners, signaling their prices in their sleeves, to avoid letting outsiders hear." One reason for this furtiveness was suggested by the same author: "People come to this market looking for goods that have been stolen from them. If it is a wallet, it will have changed appearance. Although the original object is still the same, the money inside has disappeared without a trace."[3]

Most markets closed well before dusk, but the night market in the former Austrian concession opened for business along the river after dark. It cost five *mao* per day to rent a place and a lantern. Vendors sold socks, handkerchiefs, cosmetics, plum drink, deep-fried peanuts, silk, satin, hides, and wicker chairs.

Financial transactions in these markets were complicated by a dual currency system that squeezed different groups of workers in different ways. Laborers in factories and larger establishments were paid in silver dollars or fractions thereof, whereas rickshaw pullers and casual laborers were paid in copper cash. Stores that sold daily-use items demanded copper cash in payment, so workers paid in silver had to change their wages for copper at small money shops throughout the city. Money shops a few hundred feet apart set different exchange rates, and national and international economic fluctuations also influenced the rate of exchange.

The rate fluctuated seasonally as well. The value of copper on the market was highest around the Chinese New Year, when business was brisk and copper was in demand to buy daily-use goods. From February to July, when business was slow and copper was in less demand, its value fell. Another, smaller rise in value took place at about the time of the Mid-Autumn Festival, when farm products entered the market and copper was needed to purchase them. A dip in value from October to November was generally followed by another rise as the next New Year approached. Workers paid in silver thus found that their salaries were worth least precisely at the time when their expenses were greatest.[4]

In response, workers patronized pawnshops, despite interest rates as high as 15 percent and a pawn period of only three months. Business was brisk just before the Spring Festival, when people needed cash to meet their end-of-year debts. Many of the customers were factory workers, freight haulers, and rickshaw pullers. The poorest of these would pawn their goods at dawn and reclaim them in the evening with the day's earnings. In 1947 Tianjin had 44 pawnshops, more than 1,000 small-scale pawnshops called *xiaoyadian*, and more than 100 secondhand stores. The profusion of these establishments in Tianjin was indirect testimony to the need of poor people for short-term credit, whatever the price.[5]

Marginal finances did not dissuade workers from gambling at stalls in the markets. In one popular game, a kind of lottery called *yaohui*, a pair of dice was thrown into a globe with wooden slots in it. When the globe was shaken, the numerals on the dice showed through the slots; players bet on which numbers would appear. Another game was a variation on bowling that cost one copper a turn. A skillful bowler could win 200 pieces of candy. A third game, which was especially favored by carpet weavers, featured betting on dice: "Several people could get together a few mao, squat by the booth, and if the dice came up 18, they would win a pair of very nice teacups and see the pitiful face of the booth-owner as he took a loss. This amused everyone for a while."[6]

The most popular area for working-class entertainment in Tianjin was Sanbuguan ("three who-cares"), a large lot at the end of Hua An Avenue in the south city. Whereas workers generally could not afford to go to opera performances, movies, or dance halls, they turned out on holidays or during rare moments of leisure to visit Sanbuguan. Most of the crowds on the district's street during the New Year season, wrote a reporter in 1935, wore "loose and unfashionable clothing, brand-new hats, and semi-modern shoes. They are all factory workers, apprentices, and coolies." The entertainments they enjoyed, he continued, were very different from those sought out by members of the upper classes.[7] The Sanbuguan lot was lined with stalls on all sides. Those on the south end sold old clothing to coolies and rickshaw pullers; those on the north featured lampshades, socks, and old pairs of spectacles. Nearby, itinerant barbers arrived carrying tents and small stoves and proceeded to ply their trade. A few stalls down, scribes wrote letters on behalf of the illiterate.

The streetside doctors of Tianjin were among the city's most skilled hustlers. They frequently dressed in short jackets and long gowns, affecting the garb of upper-class gentlemen. Some sold medicines that, it was alleged, would help the patient give up opium or heroin. Some claimed to cure venereal disease. Often three of them would set up their carts in a row, with each man loudly denouncing the other two as quacks. At one 1936 market, a medicine seller named Yang Baoting, dressed in a suit of old Western-style clothes, proved particularly adept at captivating customers. Wearing a white paper armband imprinted with the words Director, Illness Prevention Hospital, he beat on a copper drum and called out, "Take my medicine and you'll never be sick again! Cures everything! The medicine arrives and the illness departs! If everyone in the country ate a little we could have a strong nation right away!" Competing with Yang were the practitioners of various martial arts, who used their performances as an opportunity to sell medicines. They demanded that their audiences throw money on the ground before they began a performance, and at frequent intervals increased the required amount.

Other health practitioners were more specialized: pedicurists trimmed the feet of tired laborers, and a guidebook recorded that "every three steps there is a stall specially devoted to pulling teeth."[8] One streetcorner dentist in 1936 employed a model of a full set of teeth, run by batteries, which opened and closed on command. He told his working-class customers that its movements came in response to his telepathic orders. He also claimed that those who took his medicine could "cut new teeth, get rid of bad teeth, and grow good teeth." Cures for deafness and mental disorders were offered at neighboring stalls. A medication commonly purchased by coolies was "cow embryo pellets" (*niutai wan*), very popular because they were said to increase physical strength. The pellets contained cow placenta, or sometimes ground-up ants, which were supposed to contain a kind of *yi suan* (literally "ant acid").[9]

Also at the northern end of Sanbuguan were an open-air teahouse, a place where people played chess, and a "wrestling show" where two dummies were manipulated by one man. Some stalls featured peepshows in wooden boxes. For a copper, the customer was permitted to view eight pictures of foreign scenes or illustrations of popular Chinese stories, while the peepshow owner sang an accompaniment or gave a running commentary. Some peepholes showed cuts from Charlie Chaplin movies during the day, and switched to more salacious material (*rou gan de pianzi*) at night.

In the 1920's and 1930's, Tianjin, along with Beijing, was a major national center of folk entertaiment (*quyi*). New performers launched their careers and famous ones returned to play at the Yanle and Shenping tea gardens in the south city. Other artists performed in the open air at Sanbuguan, Qian De Zhuang, and other working-class districts.[10]

The main entertainments in Sanbuguan took place in the large reed-mat sheds that occupied most of the lot and served as theaters and vaudeville houses. Their thatched roofs leaked badly when it rained, earning them the nickname "*yulai, san!*"—"When it rains, scatter!"—a pun on the Chinese word for umbrella, *yusan*. Inside the sheds were long rows of wooden benches; several plank benches on a high frame made the stage. For a few coppers, local workers could enjoy a wide variety of performing arts.

The most popular form of entertainment in Sanbuguan was *bengbeng xi*. *Bengbeng* was a corruption of *ban bian*, or half-cast, so called because it featured several roles from a dramatic piece, rather than a full-cast performance.[11] Each *bengbeng* hut in Sanbuguan had red-and-gold announcements pasted up outside, listing the day's featured performances. The price of admission for men was one copper a set; women could pay five coppers and listen for half a day. The admission fee was not collected at the door, however. Instead, after each piece the cast would bang the drums to signal that it was time to pay, and then send people around to collect money from everyone in the audience. Money was collected at ten-minute intervals, because "everyone who goes can only stay for a short time, so there is a lot of coming and going."

Some sheds ran a special morning show to cater to workers who labored on the night shift. The afternoon show drew more passers-by, and the laborers returned at night. Prosperous *bengbeng* sheds took in as much as 2,000 coppers a day. The shed owner kept about a fifth of the proceeds; the remainder went to the performers. But actors rarely made a living wage, and often had to supplement their income by working as casual laborers.[12]

Another form of entertainment was drumsinging, or *dagu*. The *dagu* was a drum as high as a man's chest, set in a frame, which was played with a single drumstick. To one side, another performer played a stringed instrument. Singers, many of them female, sang versified stories and accompanied themselves on these instruments. Drumsinging had numerous regional variations. Some, like the Shandong *li hua pian*, involved finger cymbals. Beijing drumsongs retold traditional stories taken from old Manchu ballads. The female performers in Sanbuguan were frequently young women who were taken from local brothels by underworld characters and "turned out" as performers. Once they became professional singers, they no longer worked as prostitutes.[13]

Related to drumsinging, but with less elaborate musical accompaniment, was storytelling (*pingshu*), which was performed in these reed shacks and in teahouses throughout Tianjin. The storyteller, an old man, would recite a classical tale full of wondrous feats in a rapid rhyming singsong, punctuating his recitation with an occasional beat of drum or gong. "The eyes of the audience follow all the movements of his actions," wrote a reporter who saw one of these men perform. "When he speaks happily and with force, drops of spittle always fly onto the faces of the audience, but they don't feel them."[14]

Other types of entertainment, some of them particular to Tianjin, were performed in the reed shacks and in teahouses called *laoziguan,* where prostitutes doubled as stage entertainers. The prostitutes sang in groups of five or six, accompanied by two or three male performers who beat out the rhythm. Their repertoire consisted of "current tunes" (*shidiao*), a type of bawdy song also known as a "brothel tune." The *laoziguan* were places of entertainment in themselves as well as recruiting grounds for brothel patrons.[15]

Another form of theatrical entertainment found in the reed shacks was the crosstalk (*xiangsheng*), performed by three to five people. Generally two of them did most of the talking, one acting as a foil for the other, while the rest of the performers occasionally interjected jokes or songs. The crosstalks were full of sexual innuendo, and thus, according to one guidebook, "most sex-mad lower-class customers are happy to listen for hours." Money was collected after each crosstalk.[16]

The vaudeville houses (*za shua chang*) featured variety shows that combined theatrical performances with acrobatics, conjuring, and juggling. One performer would spin a top (*men hulu*) by skillfully manipulating a string at its base. Another would balance a jar on his forehead, while a third kicked a tuft of feathers tied to a string of coins, never letting it touch the ground. Other performers juggled plates or forked tools as tall as a man. A musician would perform the "ten not-idles," in which he sang and used both hands and feet to play different musical instruments. Next to him a magician pulled goldfish bowls out of silk carpets. The revue was completed by people performing various martial arts.[17]

Amusement areas similar to Sanbuguan were found adjacent to most working-class districts. Near the Central Station, where workers from the railroad and the Hua Xin Cotton Mill gathered after work, was a smaller replica of Sanbuguan called the Xiaoying Market. Smoke from the train station covered all the buildings with a black haze. Inside the market "the sweet sound of women singing, the clamor of gongs and drums," lured the millhand coming off his shift. The market was divided into sections for opera and acrobatics, and over on the west side were people selling "blood-red donkey meat, pitch-black sheep's stomach, and snow-white bean flour sausage" (*jianfen*).[18] Qian De Zhuang and the Hedong district each had similar gathering places.

Some forms of local theater, opera, and vaudeville were popular with workers because they were similar to the entertainment in their native villages. Homesick peasants from Henan could listen to songs sung in the *zhuizi* style. People from Shandong could hear the pear blossom drumsongs (*li hua pian*), which had begun in the countryside as simple songs performed in the agricultural slack season, with the rhythm beaten out on two pieces of a broken plowshare. *Leting* drumsong, from Leting county in east Hebei, had also begun as a way for part-time folk artists to pick up some extra money during the slack season. Workers from Beiping particularly fancied songs in the tambourine drumsong (*danxian*) style, performed by male singers who accompanied themselves on tambourines.[19] And the overwhelming majority of workers, former peasants from Hebei villages, were entertained by *bengbeng xi*.

By the end of the Republican period, one reporter commented that these various folk performing arts were being transformed by their sojourn in the city, perhaps heralding the development of new urban cultural forms.[20] In Tianjin, Beijing drumsinging and many other genres moved "away from extended stories performed to simple music, in open-air stages, towards a repertoire of shorter stories, sung to more elaborate music, presented ultimately in teahouse theaters which made a specialty of offering these performances for the price of a glass of tea." New forms of drumsong, like *erhuang*, were developed by folk performers in 1920's Tianjin. The repertoire of the drumsingers, however, emphasized themes that would have been familiar to peasant immigrants. Some pieces celebrated the exploits of well-known figures from the famous novels *Three Kingdoms*, *Water Margin*, and *Dream of the Red Chamber*. Others, set in the countryside, promoted filial piety. New pieces developed by Liu Baoquan, the "king of the drumsingers" who spent much of his career in Tianjin, "implied approval of a way of life that is guided by the highest principles of mutual personal obligation."[21]

Other forms of local entertainment, like the "current tunes" (*shidiao*), were created by Tianjin workers in their urban environment, using dialect and expressions peculiar to Tianjin. Unlike the drumsongs, they were brief, no more than 60 lines long. One type of current tune, the "gable-leaning tune," was created by shoemakers who leaned against the workshop gables as they cobbled and sang. The gable tunes were popular with other craftsmen and transport workers. Another type, the "mandarin duck tune," was devoted to love and sexual relations. In the nineteenth century these tunes were performed by the hunhunr for their own amusement; in the twentieth century they were sung in low-class brothels. Rickshaw tunes were sung by the pullers as they sat awaiting fares.

Some of the current tunes were picked up, refined, and performed by local artists. Others were popularized in south city brothels. The subjects of the songs included the events of each season of the year, a man's grief for his dead wife, a bachelor's longing for a spouse, a stepmother's cruel treatment of her stepchild, and a prostitute's sorrow at her sad lot. Some also dealt with comic themes. Tianjin workers in the older sectors of the working class, such as transport, were particularly fond of these songs. In the reed sheds of Sanbuguan, aficionados of all types mingled and heard performances from other counties and provinces. The variety of folk performance made the south city famous, not only among local workers, but among some of the wealthy residents as well.[22]

Even in their moments of leisure, workers could not leave the grim world in which they labored behind them. Soldiers, officials, and local ruffians frequently extorted money from vendors, and roughed up anyone who got in their way. Even famous performing artists usually had to seek patronage from a Qing Bang boss before they were allowed to perform. And street hoodlums made the lives of all who visited the south city less secure.[23]

In spite of the special admission price offered women in the opera houses of Sanbuguan, the patrons of these amusement areas were virtually all male. Large numbers of unmarried men, or men who had left their wives in the villages, sought entertainment there. Although local women sometimes worked outside the home, it was still considered highly inappropriate for them, especially if they were unmarried, to frequent the vaudeville or storytelling houses. When women came to Sanbuguan, it was usually not as consumers of working-class culture. Rather, they performed in the teahouses and worked in a trade that flourished in a city with many more men than women—prostitution.[24]

SEX, VIOLENCE, AND VULNERABILITY

The Class Structure of Prostitution in Tianjin

Long before the development of an industrial working class in Tianjin, prostitutes served the merchant community and the soldiers who were stationed in the city. In 1884 the main red-light district was outside the north gate of the city, just off to one side of the largest marketing area. Brothels were divided into high-class establishments, called "big shops," and less expensive places. The procedures for greeting a guest were prescribed by tradition:

Whenever a guest arrives, a male servant welcomes him, asks him to have a seat, and then lifts up the screen and calls loudly, "Receive the guest!" As soon as he sees the fabled beauty enter the room in a leisurely fashion, her hair ornaments moving as she passes by, his eyes are riveted upon her. He may pick a prostitute, and she will open the cigarette box for him and prepare some tea. This is called "having a seat," and costs half the price of spending a night. If for some reason the guest says that she doesn't meet his fancy, and leaves, it is called "hitting the chaff lamp" [*da kang deng*].[25]

Life in the brothels was far from peaceful. Customers who were displeased by an insufficiently attentive reception, those who could not find a prostitute who matched their preconceived notions of beauty, and those who were just plain out for extortion frequently created incidents. The situation was further complicated by the local hunhunr, who demanded payments from clients and would promptly instigate a brawl if they were not paid off, all in the name of protecting a particular prostitute. "So the love nest," intoned one nineteenth-century writer, "sometimes becomes an armed camp." [26]

Even at this early period the city had several other red-light districts that catered to specific populations. In the Purple Bamboo Grove district of the concession area were women from Guangdong, who entertained wealthy merchants from the south as well as foreign traders. In the twentieth century they were joined by prostitutes from Russia, Korea, and Japan, who served the foreign population. And outside the west gate of the city were the forerunners of prostitute communities that would later attract the male working-class population: "local prostitutes, who mostly live in low rooms with mud walls and lounge in the doorways soliciting customers." Unlike the cultured, elaborately coiffed ladies of the north city, they were "charming women of middle age, incarnations of hell, and it is rather hard for them to attract people"—or so one writer said. [27]

By the late 1920's the class structure of Tianjin had grown considerably more complicated, and so had the market for sexual services. Prostitution in the Republican period was legal but regulated, and so in 1929 the Bureau of Social Affairs undertook the task of registering and classifying all prostitutes within the city limits. The women were divided into five grades and a number of subcategories, the largest single group being third-grade prostitutes. A lower third-grade prostitute earned from one to four mao a day, while one of the fifth grade made from seven *fen* to three mao. (A woman millhand, in comparison, could expect to make about four mao a day.) [28]

Of 2,910 women in 571 brothels covered by the survey, almost one-third were from Tianjin proper. Another third were from villages throughout Hebei, while the rest were natives of Beiping, Shandong, and a number of other places. According to the survey, almost 60 percent of them had been forced into prostitution, while another 30 percent had chosen it. The remainder had been sold, rented, or tricked. More than 40 percent of the working prostitutes covered by this survey were married. [29]

The paths by which these women arrived at this trade are unclear, since no record survives in their own words. The conventional wisdom among their working-class neighbors is that they were tricked or kidnapped from their homes and sold into the brothels. [30] Given the limited job options for

women, undoubtedly economic need played a larger role than is acknowledged retrospectively. From the viewpoint of municipal and academic investigators, millhands and prostitutes were employed in occupations that
required separate analytical frameworks. From the point of view of the
women themselves, however, both factory work and prostitution provided
jobs in an unstable urban environment where employment was hard to
come by. Which type of work a woman did had a great deal to do with luck
and connections, and very little to do with personal choice. In any case,
neither the motivations of the women nor many details about the organization of the sexual service industry were recorded by contemporary observers. Instead they offered dire warnings about the danger of visiting the
brothels.

The worst ire of these observers was reserved for brothels of the third
class and below, those in Qian De Zhuang, Sanbuguan, the southwest corner, and other working-class amusement areas. A 1936 survey of cotton
mill workers noted that the entire clientele of the "Lao Ma Tang" (old
mother halls) in some districts comprised cotton mill workers. Prostitutes
in these establishments, the survey said, were extremely polite and attentive to the male millhands, leading them to waste their hard-earned money
on sexual favors and often to contract diseases that they had no money to
treat.[31] An unofficial gazetteer warned in 1931:

[Third-class brothels] are more poisonous than those of the first or second class.
Lower still are the local prostitutes who live in filthy places. They are either loath-
some-looking or already old. Laborers congregate there. For three mao they are
permitted to spend the night. Further, there are those who entertain several patrons in one day, and therefore have the worst cases of venereal disease. People who
come in contact with them immediately contract syphilis, injure their health, and
kill themselves. . . . Further, there is a kind of secret prostitute who is especially
dangerous. Those in this group do not have a fixed address. They come from other
places, and use the cover of prostitution to practice their tricks. People who fall
into their clutches at minimum will lose their money, and in more serious cases
their lives may be in danger. New arrivals in Tianjin, please be kind enough to
avoid this pitfall.[32]

Prostitute as temptress, seducer, despoiler, and perhaps extortionist—
these were the images presented in the prescriptive social literature of the
time. For some working-class residents of Tianjin, the popular image was
slightly different, compounded of about equal parts of shame, revulsion,
fascination, and humor, all obscured by a moral code that decreed it improper to discuss the subject. Chen Guilan inadvertently violated this
proscription when she first saw prostitutes, as a young girl in Sanbuguan:

When I was nine, I went with an older person from our courtyard to a restaurant to buy some of their leftover food. At the southwest corner was a brothel.

When I got home I said to my grandmother, "Grandma, there's someone over there who is very rich. In his doorway many people are getting married. They are all wearing dresses and makeup." . . . They were dragging men into the building. My grandmother said, "Don't talk about that!" And my mother said, "Don't talk!" At that time, if they said not to talk, you didn't talk.

Afterward I heard my grandmother say, "She must have gone past Zhao Jia brothel." Later I understood.

The only subsequent reference to prostitution in the Chen household stemmed from a comic misunderstanding by her younger brother: "Qian De Zhuang was called 'sticky fish nest' (*nian yu wo*) because of the brothels. People just in from the countryside thought they actually sold fish there. My younger brother . . . asked my uncle, 'Can we go buy some sticky fish?' My uncle thought that it was very funny." Although Guilan learned not to discuss the subject, silence did not stifle her curiosity: "I knew it was a bad place. The people there were dirty. They had dirty diseases. But even though I knew this, when I was small I liked to look. I liked to see the 'small wives' [prostitutes] wearing such beautiful clothes. In those days, what poor people could afford to wear such multicolored clothes?"[33]

Tianjin prostitution differed in its extent and elaboration from the organization of the sexual service market in the countryside. It was not a matter of one or two "broken shoes" (as prostitutes were called) in a village, but of a complex trade organized along class lines, catering to a highly segmented market. Working-class men patronized the lower grade of brothel. They did not normally encounter prostitutes who served the upper classes, women who moved in a different world. Prostitutes who worked out of the big hotels downtown, for instance, protested vehemently in 1947 when the government tried to move them into brothels in the south city area. They had no desire to pay fees to brothels or to submit to their rules; they objected to the thin walls and inferior living conditions found in the south city. Organizing themselves, the women elected one of their number to make their case to the municipal government and the press. But most Tianjin prostitutes remained hostage to an urban occupational structure that gave them few options for survival.[34]

The Logic of Working-Class Crime

Tianjiners, commented the author of a survey of local customs in 1933, were a distressingly litigious people. As the density of the population increased in the first 30 years of the twentieth century, so did the number of disputes among local citizens. Most civil cases concerned debts, the division of property, divorce, and family quarrels, but about as many criminal cases as civil suits were brought to court.[35]

Of 16,469 crimes recorded in 1929, almost 10,000 fell in the category "causing harm," a general term that apparently applied to personal assaults as well as damage to property. Another 3,083 cases involved burglary or theft, and 1,210 were cases of injury to marriage and the family. Twenty murders were committed in the city that year.[36]

A disproportionate number of these crimes were committed by members of the working class. Of 5,802 criminals whose cases were processed by the local courts in 1930, 40 percent were workers—a percentage far higher than their proportion of the total urban population (about 6.8 percent). In that year workers committed 52 percent of all the thefts, 53 percent of the offenses related to gambling, 24 percent of all the drug-related crimes, and 48 percent of the cases of assault on persons and property. In contrast, employees in the commercial sector were responsible for only slightly more than a fifth of all crimes, while the unemployed, whose economic desperation one might suspect would drive them to frequent criminal acts, committed slightly more than a quarter.[37]

Although the newspapers are an incomplete guide to worker motivation, since they tended to report the most lurid and sensational crimes, they do give a rough index of the kinds of violence which Tianjin workers regularly perpetrated. The crimes involving workers that were reported in the *Yishi bao* and several other publications in the mid-1930's and late 1940's fall into three main categories: crimes of economic desperation, crimes of passion, and crimes of frustration and revenge. Each type was a response to specifically urban conditions, showing more clearly than other working-class behavior the stresses of urban life.

Crimes of economic desperation were the sort of offenses that could be expected from any group who lived as close to economic disaster as did Tianjin workers. Whenever a major factory laid off workers, industrial pundits routinely warned that a new crime wave could be expected to follow. When two textile mills closed down in 1935, leaving 4,000 millhands idle, a visiting ILO correspondent noted that "just a few days after the closure, two cases of robbery were committed by the unemployed workers employed formerly in these two factories." Readers of a Chinese-language ILO publication were similarly cautioned in 1937 that former dyeworkers and carpet weavers could easily become thieves, if something was not done to provide them with a livelihood. And, in fact, most inhabitants of the Hebei #3 Jail in Tianjin in the early 1930's were paupers and workers who had committed acts of theft.[38]

Yet surprisingly little was said of these economic crimes in the daily newspaper, perhaps because they did not offer much in the way of variety, perhaps because theft cases were handled by the military garrison headquarters rather than the local court (*difang fayuan*), and were thus less public. The only time that economically desperate workers seemed to merit journalistic coverage was when their troubles drove them to attempt suicide. A case was reported in 1936 of a young widow who worked with her mother in the Bei Yang Cotton Mill. When the widow contracted an illness and couldn't work but lacked the money for treatment, she tried to stab herself with scissors but was saved by her mother.[39]

Crimes of passion made much better copy, and are interesting for the insight they provide into working-class mores. These crimes reflected both the increased economic activity of women outside the home and the vulnerability that frequently resulted.

In a 1947 case a woman named Cao Dezhi was charged with conspiring with Wu Shuzhong, a sanlunche pedaler, to poison Cao's husband Wang (also a sanlunche driver). Cao had been married to Wang for five years, wrote the reporter, but she often went running off to Wu's house and returned late. Her husband had no proof that anything was amiss, but in an eerie premonition of his own death he told his brother, "After I die, don't weep, but watch what happens and see if my corpse has anything strange about it." Soon thereafter he ate steamed bread and mutton meatballs prepared by his wife, and died almost immediately. Cao told the neighbors that he had died of tuberculosis, and less than three days later she and her brother went to arrange her marriage to Wu. The neighbors, when interviewed, volunteered their opinion that Wu was a "scoundrel" who had had "warm relations" with Cao before her husband's untimely death.[40]

Frequently, adultery led to violence. Du Kai, a twenty-five-year-old rickshaw puller in Xi Guang Kai, was married to a woman named Zhou. When Du's friend Meng began an affair with Zhou, Du was furious at first, but reconsidered his position when his wife convinced him to let Meng pay all the household expenses in return for her services. This arrangement worked for a while, but when Du, in a fit of jealousy, ordered Meng out of the house, Meng cursed him. Du subsequently stabbed Meng 13 times with a vegetable knife as he lay sleeping. When the case came to court, Du was sentenced to five years in prison, and the vegetable knife was confiscated.[41]

The sexual vulnerability of women workers was not confined to the workplace. In 1935, one Chen Guoxing, a worker at the British and American Tobacco factory, abducted a fellow worker, a girl named Liu Yuzhen who was not yet sixteen. Chen already had a wife, but this did not deter him from keeping Liu in a hotel room in the Japanese concession for three days. When her parents lodged a complaint against him, he informed the police that he had been having sexual relations with Liu for four months, had taken her to the Japanese concession more than 20 times, and that in fact it was she who was pursuing him, in spite of his protests that he was already married. In court, Chen and his lawyer centered their defense around the argument that Liu was "willing." "If you weren't happy," Chen asked her in court, "why did it happen more than 20 times?" Liu did not answer him, and the conclusion of the case is not recorded.[42]

In an audacious case of abduction in 1947, a cotton mill worker named Zhang Zhijiu "harbored evil intentions" toward a fourteen-year-old mill-hand, Yu Shuyuan. He arranged to meet her in a market area to eat one night, then took her to a movie. When the movie was over he announced that it was too late for her to go home, took her to a hotel, and raped her twice. The next day she was afraid to return home, but after two days of absence her mother went to the factory, took her home, found out what had happened, and forbade her to go out. Zhang eventually found her when she went out to do an errand ten days later, and convinced her to go to his aunt's house in a suburban district. When Yu's father, an iron-worker, came in search of her, Zhang's relatives hid the girl in an inner room, but her father found the house, smashed the lock on the door, and "father and daughter rushed into each other's arms." Zhang, his aunt, and his uncle were subsequently arrested.[43]

In another case, a slightly more sophisticated woman cotton mill worker was more successful at protecting her virtue. Xue Shuping and Li Shiying, two women workers from Shandong, lived together near the cotton mills on the southeast end of town. (This was a fairly uncommon housing arrangement; single workers normally lived with families or in the factory dormitories.) One afternoon Xue's boyfriend came to visit, and when Xue went out to buy peanuts, he grabbed Li and tried to rape her. When Li registered a complaint with the local police, they arrested both the boyfriend and Xue on suspicion of attempted rape (why, they reasoned, had Xue gone out so suddenly, if not to give her boyfriend a chance to make advances to her roommate?) and sent them both off for further questioning.[44] For each of the cases in which action was successfully brought against the perpetrator, however, many undoubtedly went unreported. The stigma attached to women who lost their virginity would injure their marriage prospects, and so it was in their interest (and the interest of their families) to bear assault in silence.

Many crimes of frustration and revenge, the third type of common offense, grew out of grudges that smoldered in confined working environments and finally burst forth into violence. Occasionally the violence was directed by owner against worker, or vice versa. In 1936, for instance, the manager of a weaving factory in Xi Guang Kai was arrested because he had accused one of his women outworkers of stealing and had had her beaten when she protested, causing her to have a miscarriage. When he was ordered by the local Investigation Office to pay her medical expenses, he and his wife compounded the crime by stabbing the woman in the head and seriously wounding her. In a more conventional case recorded in 1941, the manager of an electrical appliances factory was stabbed by a disgruntled former employee as he rode to work in his rickshaw. The manager was wounded; the rickshaw puller, in trying to prevent the assault, was killed; the worker was arrested.[45]

But violence also erupted between workers who nursed petty quarrels into full-blown confrontations. In 1935 the *Yishi bao* published accounts of two such cases. In the first, two workers in a sporting goods factory, named Huang and Li, were long-term enemies. When Huang was laid off, Li was pleased and spread rumors about him. Huang concluded that Li was responsible for his firing and stabbed him repeatedly with the ubiquitous vegetable knife, this time one from the factory kitchen. Huang was arrested. In the second case, two workers in a match factory who habitually cursed each other finally came to blows, and one stabbed the other with a foot-long knife that he had bought for the occasion and concealed under his bed. One worker ended up in the hospital, near death, the other in the local jail.[46]

Personal vendettas frequently grew into full-scale rumbles involving crowds of workers; this mode of settling disputes was apparently not confined to the transport industry or the cotton mills. Workers drew on whatever networks they had developed to protect themselves in such conflicts. One 1936 case involved a flour mill worker named Ma who got into a fight with a transport worker named Yang Yaba ("Deaf-and-dumb Yang") over how to load flour on a boat. When the foreman and Ma's fellow workers broke up the fight, Ma's ire turned against them. He returned the following day with his parents, a blind uncle, and 30 friends, all of them armed. They smashed the glass in the workers' rest area and injured several workers before the police arrived and arrested four of the attackers and some of the wounded.[47]

Rumbles could become riots directed not against individuals, but against an institution and its property. In a 1947 case a worker from a military grain factory got into a fight with the military police over a ticket on a public bus. When he was detained by the police, several dozen of his fellow workers took the bus to the bus company to report that he had never returned. Some of them were detained as well, and the stage was set for a full-scale feud between the bus company and the workers. The next day, a worker from the same factory had his foot crushed by a bus in the middle of the road. With that, a mob of more than 100 workers went to the bus yard, beat up the drivers and ticket sellers, smashed four buses, and dragged three bus workers off with them. Military police broke up the riot, and in spite of a similar incident a week later, the bus company and the management of the grain factory concluded a peace treaty shortly thereafter.[48]

Sudden violence also marred leisure activities. One afternoon in February 1948, a male worker in a uniform factory brought four women into a theater to watch a movie. Like the transport worker in a similar case described in Chapter 5, he was summarily ejected for neglecting to buy a ticket. He returned the next day with about 70 fellow workers and vandalized the theater, pausing only to beat up the parents of the manager, who was absent. He and his friends then proceeded to escort the manager's parents past a local police station. When the father called out "Save us!" a number of policemen came running out. A worker stepped forward to grab a policeman's gun and it went off, wounding the worker in the chest. He died that night.[49]

Working-class violence, at work and on the streets, was usually directed against members of the same class. Workers in the city remained relatively isolated from other urban classes. On the streets as in the workplaces, those most vulnerable to individual acts of violence were workers who could not draw upon protective alliances with family, friends, and patrons. Yet workers who did have access to such networks used them not only for protection, but to perpetrate violent acts against others more vulnerable than themselves. Individual acts of revenge then took on the forms of group violence so familiar to laborers from their workplace experience.

RHYTHMS AND PASSAGES

Poverty, in Tianjin as elsewhere, was never an impediment to ritual or celebration. Drawn into work situations that were in many respects new, Tianjin workers clung to the folk customs that they had practiced in the North China villages. The agricultural calendar no longer dictated their working lives, but its festivals continued to mark the passing of each year for them. And with whatever financial means they could muster, they delivered their babies, arranged their children's marriages, and buried their dead as they had done before coming to Tianjin. Workers used all these occasions to reaffirm existing ties with family and fellow villagers, and to strengthen new ties with foremen and sworn brothers.

Rhythms: Holidays

Many workers returned to their home villages at New Year and renewed their rural ties directly. Others stayed in Tianjin, but reproduced rural customs and reaffirmed rural networks in the city.

The lunar new year or Spring Festival, which fell in January or February of each year, was preceded by a month of feverish preparations. On the eighth day of the twelfth lunar month, Tianjin residents prepared a gruel of mixed grains and dried fruits, called *labazhou*, and friends and relatives ate it together. This was also the day for preparation of *labacu*, a crock of vinegar in which cloves of garlic were placed; after three weeks of soaking, the vinegar would be ready to eat with steamed dumplings on New Year's day. Because this was a very busy season, it was called *yaoming de laba*, literally "the eighth day of the last month that-will-be-the-death-of-me."[50]

For another reason as well, the twelfth lunar month was a time of intensified pressure on working-class families. Traditionally, debts had to be collected before the Spring Festival began, and during the last few weeks of the year creditors came to the homes of those who owed them money. The head of the debtor household sometimes fled, leaving them to press his wife for payment, curse his children, and refuse to leave until satisfied.[51]

At about this time, special New Year's markets opened near each gate of the old city and in other districts throughout Tianjin. They sold such traditional New Year's goods as couplets printed on long vertical strips of red paper, to be pasted on each side of the door of every home (*duilian*), red paper cut-outs of pigs or the God of Wealth to be pasted on the windows (*diaoqianr*), scenes from plays and stories printed in garish colors on thin paper to decorate the inside of people's homes (*nianhua*), tops, lanterns, firecrackers, fireworks, incense, fragrant candles, and images of the kitchen god. These were the same trappings used to observe the Spring Festival in the countryside. Workers believed that if they did not have a few candles, incense, and images to greet the New Year, they would be even poorer the following year, and so they scrimped to buy these goods.

On the twenty-third day of the twelfth lunar month, every family performed the annual sacrifice to the kitchen god. Candy and melons were sacrificed to the god; grass and water were provided for the mount that he would ride to heaven. His picture was then burned, sending him on his way, along with hopes that the sweetmeats would induce him to give a good report about the family once he reached his destination.

Preparations reached their high point in the last few days before the New Year. Since local customs demanded that a cooking fire must not be lit for several days after the New Year, all steamed bread and other staple goods had to be made or bought beforehand. On New Year's eve (*chu xi*), it was the custom for the family to stay awake until past midnight. In the house of Chen Guilan, the family would prepare steamed dumplings (*jiaozi*) in the afternoon, and then play cards until midnight:

At midnight we offered sacrifices. It was like this both in Tianjin and in the countryside. . . . We had an incense burner. On the table we would spread out red paper, and burn incense. When one stick of incense was almost burned down we would start the next one. . . . Then we would eat jiaozi. We would sacrifice the jiaozi to the Buddha; then we would all eat them.

We didn't believe in religion. The Buddha? It was just a piece of paper with a painting of an old man on it, who represented the spirits.

Before we could eat the jiaozi the daughter-in-law and son had to bow (*ketou*) to the elders. . . . After that the children were supposed to bow to the grandparents and parents.[52]

Throughout the night of New Year's eve, people set off firecrackers in the streets. The next morning they arose early, ate jiaozi once again, dressed in their best outfits, and went out for the first of several days' calls on relatives and friends. This was one village custom, preserved intact in the city, that helped renew rural ties:

People in the villages attach a great deal of importance to the New Year and the festivals. The custom of paying a New Year's call is very widespread. You ketou to the older generation, and make a bow with your hands clasped when you meet people. . . .

This custom was preserved after we came here. . . . We would go pay New Year's calls on fellow-townsmen and relatives. . . . Some would also send presents. . . . At first we would ketou, but later we would just make a motion as though we were going to, and people would tell us, "Don't bother. Forget it!". . . The important thing was to go to the person's house and express your feeling (*linghui gan-qing*). If you didn't go, it didn't look good.[53]

During the first five days of the new year, it was forbidden to handle raw rice or flour. The significance of this taboo was twofold: scattered grains of raw rice represented disorder, while previously prepared foods had already been made orderly, signifying harmony in the coming year; and every family should appear rich enough to be eating last year's food. After the second day it was permissible to use raw flour, but not raw rice. Women were supposed to be released from their habitual cooking chores by this custom. The family spent its leisure time at home, talking and gambling.

Foods were prescribed for the holiday season. On the first day people of every class ate jiaozi, which symbolized renewal. Because New Year's day marked the beginning of a five-month period during which creditors could not press for the collection of debts, the dumplings were often called "life-saving jiaozi." On the second day the traditional food was noodles, on the third day a kind of large dumpling called *hezi*, on the fourth day ordinary food, and on the fifth day jiaozi once again. Also on the fifth day, red paper flowers that had decorated the houses were taken down and thrown into the street. It was considered bad luck to pick them up, but auspicious to stamp or spit on them.

Although many people had returned to work by the second or third day of the New Year, the holiday season extended until the fifteenth day of the first month. This was called the Lantern Festival, or the "small New Year's." Once again a ketou was called for, and the members of each household hung lanterns and ate sweet dumplings (*yuanxiao*) made of glutinous rice and boiled in water.

Ten days after the end of the New Year's festivities, on the twenty-fifth day of the month, the ritual of "filling the storehouse" (*tian cang*) was performed. Several days before the ritual, people drew a circle with ashes or lime on the floors of their houses, and a similar one outside. Inside the circles they placed money and grain, wrapped in the red paper cut-outs that had been pasted on the window during New Year's. The money and goods were then covered with bricks. At daybreak on the twenty-fifth, the celebrants set off firecrackers, then removed the bricks to see whether the characters on the coins were facing up or down. Up signified good luck; down meant an ordinary year. They then inspected the grain to see how much of it had stuck to the bricks, in order to predict the harvest. While this latter procedure had less significance in the city than it had to working peasants in the villages, it was still valued as a general indicator of the family's fortunes for the coming year. It was traditional to eat noodles on the twenty-fifth, but aside from preparing the food, women were forbidden to work on that day, for it was feared that their sewing needles would put out the eyes of the god of the storehouse.

Some New Year's taboos, like one against haircuts, were in force for the first month of the year. On the second day of the second month, upon arising, people took a broom, tapped the edge of the kang where they had slept, and intoned, "Second month, second day / strike the kang / scorpion, centipede / now begone" (*Er yue er / qiao kang yan / xiezi wugong / bujianmian*). With that, they spread a trail of ashes from their rooms to the edge of the nearest body of water; this symbolized the exit of the slothful dragon of winter and the holiday season, and the entry of a diligent, rich dragon that would bring both money and (in the villages) rain for the spring seedlings. After this ritual, people cut their hair.

Traditional foods for this day included pancakes, *menzi* (a kind of bean jelly cut in diamond shapes and deep-fried, which symbolized the scales of the bad, lazy dragon), and a salad of bean noodles and bean sprouts, which represented the dragon's whiskers. Women spent the day cooking and gambling, but once again were not supposed to do any needlework, for fear of damaging the eyes of the new dragon.

The third day of the third month was the Pure Brightness Festival (*Qingming jie*), which was celebrated in Tianjin, as elsewhere in China, by sweeping the graves of ancestors and offering them sacrifices. It was followed by the birthday of the Buddha on the eighth day of the fourth month, when most temples had celebrations that were widely attended by urban residents. Images of the city gods were taken out of their temples and paraded through the streets. The twenty-eighth day of the fourth month was the birthday of the Medicine King, a Taoist spirit who originally had been a doctor during the Warring States period (475–221 B.C.). This was celebrated with processions in the Hedong district, the suburban village of Yang Liu Qing, and the area west of the city.

The fifth day of the fifth month was the Dragon Boat Festival. Most residents spread mugwort and willow on their doors, in the belief that they would help to ward off the five poisonous creatures: scorpions, vipers, centipedes, lizards, and toads. Small children wore silk embroidered bags with pepper and other spices in them, and red orpiment or flowers of sulphur (*xionghuang*) was smeared on the crowns of their heads, their ears, and their bottoms, to combat poisonous insects. Paper cut-outs of the insects were pasted on the walls. Everyone ate *zongzi*, rice dumplings shaped like a pointed cylinder filled with dates or meat and steamed in bamboo leaves. It was customary to send *zongzi* to the daughters of the family, even after they had married and moved away.

The "dragon boats" for which the festival was named were boats with a dragon figurehead that were raced on the waterways as part of the festivities; many urban residents turned out to watch.

The sixth month was relatively uneventful, with the exception of the sixth day, which was set aside for airing clothes. On the seventh day of the seventh month, young women prayed to the "weaving girl" (a constellation with a romantic legend attached to it) for a mate.

The fifteenth day of the month was the Ghost Festival, when families conducted a ceremony of remembrance at the graves of the newly dead. "River lanterns" were launched along the rivers. These were small model boats made of wood and paper by the rich households of Tianjin; poorer households substituted half a hollowed-out watermelon. Candles were placed inside, along with snacks to feed the hungry spirits of the dead.[54]

The Mid-Autumn Festival fell on the fifteenth day of the eighth month. Married women returned to their parents' homes for this holiday. Families gathered in their courtyards to admire the full moon, to eat moon cakes, and to sacrifice cakes and fruits to the moon. Paper cut-outs depicted the rabbit in the moon and the legendary beauty Chang E flying to the moon. A ketou was required of the younger people in many homes. From the

Mid-Autumn Festival until the New Year season, only two minor holidays occurred: the Double Nine (ninth day of the ninth month), when some people went to the countryside to climb to the highest point in the vicinity and eat glutinous rice-flour cakes; and the first day of the tenth month, when people burned paper replicas of winter garments to send them off to the spirits of the dead.

Most of the holidays in the lunar calendar cycle were derived from the rhythms of rural life, and even in the city people preserved many of the original practices that characterized the village celebrations. As in the villages, festivals were also times when creditors appeared and expenses strained the family budget. In the cities, these tensions were exacerbated at holiday time by layoffs, disputes over bonuses, and shutdowns (see Chapter 8).

Passages: Marriage

By the time Chen Guilan came of marriageable age, she had lived in Tianjin with her family more than seven years and had worked at a number of jobs. But like many rural immigrants, her parents relied on village relationships in making matches for their children. Just as men went back to their villages to find a bride, so families sometimes sent their young women back to the villages for marriage, or at least tried to locate a spouse for them through family and native-place networks.

The marriage of Chen Guilan to Xing Minzhi was arranged by Guilan's uncle during one of the extended return visits the Chen family made to their home village. Her uncle's wife came from the same village as the prospective groom. Guilan's family was satisfied with the match because the Xing household was better off economically than their own. The Xing family was satisfied because Chen Guilan was a great beauty. The two young people, of course, never saw each other before the wedding. The matchmaker did the talking:

The introducer would say to the man's family, "This girl is good. She works well, does this and that well, she's good-looking and she never goes out the door" (*da men bu chu, er men bu lai*). When the introducer went to the woman's family, she would say, "He's a good boy, very honest." Then she would explain the family's circumstances—how many people in the household, and so forth.[55]

Guilan was nineteen when she married; she had worked in the city for seven years. Yet the matchmaker still invoked rural values on what characterized a good bride—a willingness to work hard and a secluded upbringing. Though her future in-laws must have known of her jobs in the city, they accepted these verities of an earlier era as assurances that she had been brought up properly and would make a good addition to their household.

The day before the wedding, Guilan rode a cart from her parents' home to that of her future mother-in-law. (One common way of referring to the marriage of a woman was "to take a mother-in-law," an expression that aptly emphasized the central nature of this relationship in the life of the young bride.) Her hair was combed into a bun, and she wore new red clothes and "dragon and phoenix flowers" in her hair. When she reached her new home, she remembers,

> I sat on the kang. The next day at four in the morning we got up and bowed to heaven and earth. Eight older people were there, and several small boys at the side who carried lighted lanterns. Then we moved from one room to another one.
>
> After the ceremony we ate jiaozi. I couldn't eat; I was too anxious. Everyone who got married in those days cried. You didn't know what the family was like, or the man you were marrying. You didn't know what their household was like. I was afraid of being treated badly, like my cousin was.

After her marriage, she continued to sit on the kang for three days, and on the fourth day she returned to her parents' home for a short visit. Then she began her life as a daughter-in-law. Her first task was to make a pair of pants for her husband's mother, to whom she was expected to defer in all matters. Later,

> after the twentieth day, my family sent a big cart to take me back home. Before I left, I had to ketou to my mother-in-law and the older members of the family. Just me, not my husband. I asked my mother-in-law, "Mother, how many days should I stay?" She would tell you. If she said ten days, you couldn't come back on the eleventh day, or she would be unhappy.[56]

Fortunately, Guilan's mother-in-law was an unusually enlightened woman, and Guilan's relationship with her was relatively good.

Even though they no longer lived in the countryside, working-class families in Tianjin did their best to preserve the forms of a rural wedding, adjusted according to their means. The bride and groom were usually several years older than their counterparts in wealthier families because the families had to save longer to meet the wedding expenses. Customs observed by some families included the exchange of a marriage proposal on which were written the dates and times of birth of both parties; the employment of a diviner to determine whether the match was suitable; the presentation of gifts to the household of the bride by the family of the groom; and the marriage procession in a sedan chair or the equivalent. A number of superstitious practices were associated with the arrival of the bride: she was supposed to step over a saddle on her way into the house, since the word for "saddle" was a homonym for "peace"; she was required to carry a copper mirror at her waist to ward off demons. After her arrival the couple ate "son and grandson dumplings" and "long life noodles."[57]

But even for families in dire economic straits, the absolutely irreducible requirement for a wedding was a sedan chair. Shops specialized in the rental of chairs and other wedding paraphernalia, such as lanterns, flags, gongs, and parasols.[58] Since the rental of the chair could be prohibitively expensive, some working-class families devised an ingenious solution: "A *lingjiao* (sedan chair) cost ten *yuan* and a *ganjiao* cost five. We got a *ganjiao*. That means that another person had already finished using it. After they finished we would get it. That was why it was called *ganjiao* ('catching a sedan chair'). . . . The first person to ride in the chair would pay a higher price."[59]

The wedding often occasioned considerable financial hardship for the family of the groom. Zhang Jiagui, a male cotton mill worker who married in the early 1940's, also "caught a sedan chair." Nevertheless, he recalls, "It was hard to put on a wedding in those days. My mother borrowed from everywhere." Some families with sons chose to arrange a match years in advance and take the future daughter-in-law into her new home to grow up. In that case the wedding festivities were much less elaborate.[60]

Birth Customs

From the point of view of the groom's family, the primary purpose of marriage was to ensure the production of heirs. If a daughter-in-law failed to produce a child in the first two or three years of marriage, her in-laws frequently expressed doubts about her, and both mother-in-law and daughter-in-law began to beseech the spirits to grant their request for a child.[61]

One method of seeking fertility was to eat "bumping eggs," which were placed in the bath water of a newborn child when it was washed on the third day. After the midwife had finished the ceremonial bath, she fished out two eggs that had knocked against each other and gave them to the woman who wished to become pregnant. The woman was supposed to sit on a hole in the room with her back to the door while she ate the eggs.

A second method was to go to the Temple of the Heavenly Empress (see Chapter 1) and beseech her for a child. Next to the image of the goddess in the temple were a number of tiny earthen figures of babies. After the woman burned incense and prayed, she was to take one of these figures home with her and conceal it under the mat on the kang. After three days she was to take it out, dress it up, and offer it food three times a day. If she subsequently did give birth to a child, the earthen figure was treated as the elder brother, and the actual child became the second in line.

A third method of seeking a child was practiced by the mother-in-law. On New Year's eve at midnight, without letting anyone know, she was to pick up a brick or any other object she found in the shadows, bring it back to the house and conceal it, taking pains not to let her daughter-in-law see it. Later, if a child was born, he or she was given the name of that object as a baby name.

A final inducement to fertility was also the responsibility of the mother-in-law. On New Year's eve, when preparing the jiaozi, she was to secretly put a date and a chestnut in the filling. She was not allowed to make any distinguishing mark on the dumplings that had the special filling, and when people in the family ate them that night they were not permitted to pick and choose. But if the daughter-in-law happened to get the dumplings with the date and chestnut, that meant that she would definitely have a child in the coming year, because the homonyms for "date" and "chestnut" meant "to have a child soon" (*zao li zi*).

A pregnant woman had to be extremely careful not to violate certain taboos. She was not to eavesdrop on other people's conversations or to pass salt or ginger to anyone else. Violations of these rules were said to lead to a difficult delivery. A woman who changed the arrangement of anything in her room, worked too hard, moved anything heavy, or ate foods with strong flavors could expect to miscarry. Anyone who entered a construction site while pregnant, or saw a dead person being laid into the coffin, risked giving birth to a child with a harelip (*san pian zui*). If two pregnant women used the same string in the beautifying procedure of removing facial hair, it was believed that their children would go crazy and die. Finally, a pregnant woman was enjoined from sitting on the bed of a nursing mother, for fear that she would steal the mother's milk.

As the delivery date approached, numerous methods were used to predict whether the child would be a boy or a girl. If the expectant mother, when walking, strode with her right foot first, craved hot food, or had a flat shape to her stomach, the baby would be a girl. If she strode with her left foot, wanted sour food, or had a pointy stomach, it would be a boy. Women were reminded at every stage of the pregnancy that a boy was the preferred offspring. The birthing room was called a "happiness room" if the child born there was male; the birthplace of a girl was simply called the "birth room," and was shunned as a dirty place.

Babies in working-class families were invariably delivered by midwives or by female relatives. Some women, like Chen Guilan, went back to their native villages to give birth.[62] The birth day was marked by an exchange of presents between the family and close relatives. The first of several celebrations was held on the third day after the birth, when the baby was washed by the midwife in the presence of relatives. The midwife was supposed to lightly press a set of metal scales against the child's body, saying that she was pressing with the weight of 1,000 catties in the hope that this would help the child to bear heavy burdens later in life. She also mimed using a lock to seal the child's mouth, so that in future it would speak and act carefully. Then, when the bath was completed, she coaxed those present to throw some coins into the bath water, saying that the more money people threw, the greater the child's ability and wealth would be. The coins were kept by the midwife.

After the bathing day, the child was not shown to strangers for twelve days, for fear of illness. Family celebrations were held after the baby had lived for a month (*man yue*), after which the mother was allowed to resume a normal routine. A similar party was held 100 days after the birth. At such parties, large strips of red paper were hung on the walls, inscribed with such phrases as "many sons and grandsons."[63]

Funerals

Funeral processions in Tianjin were elaborate public affairs, provided that the relatives of the deceased were rich enough to finance them. The city supported more than 180 shops that specialized in providing goods for funerals (some supplied wedding goods as well). A full-scale funeral procession required fans, signs, banners, portable pavilions, memorial arches, flags, gongs, parasols, tables, benches, red and white staffs (red for virgins, white for everybody else), and life-sized figures of children.

Although most poor people could not hope to afford this regalia and had to be satisfied with a procession consisting of a sedan chair and a cheap coffin, the funerals of the rich were very much a part of working-class life in Tianjin. Many poor people made their living from the funeral business by acting as hired mourners. The young boys in Chen Guilan's courtyard did this to pick up a few extra coppers; adults also participated as pallbearers. The latter were organized by the beggars' guild, which had a citywide monopoly on the pallbearer business.[64]

No matter what their income, relatives provided the deceased with a clean set of burial clothes and a hat. Then they put on mourning clothes, sent out death notices to relatives and friends, and if possible hired Buddhist or Daoist priests to read the scriptures. On the third day after the death, the spirit of the deceased was said to return to pick up traveling expenses for the journey to the other world. That evening the family gathered to cry by the coffin. Later, an auspicious day was selected for the laying-in ceremony, at which the family offered sacrifices and prostrated themselves before placing the corpse in the coffin. In working-class families, the coffin was often placed in the courtyard, since housing conditions were cramped. On a fixed day after the death (most frequently the seventh, ninth, eleventh, or thirteenth day), the funeral procession set out for the burial place. After the burial the family burned paper money and goods at the grave. On their return home the family members were supposed to place a piece of candy in their mouths and jump over a fire to cleanse themselves of contact with the dead before entering the house. Sacrifices were performed at set intervals after the person's death.[65]

Funerals, like weddings, could be a ruinous expense. Families went into debt to buy burial clothes and to rent a burial plot for deceased parents; to do otherwise would violate the codes of filial piety and invite bad luck and the scathing judgment of the neighbors. In some cases the expense of a funeral was partially offset by gifts of goods or money received by the family of the dead person.[66]

Most of the rhythms and passages of working-class life reflected the peasant origins of those who labored in Tianjin. "Peasants," commented Ji Kailin, "all have a kind of provincialism. It is very strong, especially among the older people. They don't want to die in a strange land. Accent, and the way of speaking, are not changed lightly. The thinking of peasants is also not very easy to change."[67] The patterns of life outside the workplace in Tianjin confirm what the organization of work itself has already suggested: much of peasant culture was preserved, and some peasant ties were renewed, by the way workers spent their nonworking time in Tianjin. Yet the city was not merely an overgrown urban village. Neighborhoods threw people from different rural districts together. Markets and amusement places gave male workers a new set of gathering places. Workers became dependent on markets, vulnerable to currency fluctuations, and beholden to pawnshops in ways that differed from rural patterns. Working-class culture in Tianjin drew upon rural resources and began to transform them in the urban environment.

This transformation of familiar rural forms was most obvious in the markets and amusement places of Tianjin, where a new lower-class urbanized culture was beginning to take shape. The markets became places of entertainment in themselves, with a scale and variety unknown to rural dwellers. Amusements were popular precisely because they drew upon rural entertainment forms. But they grew more sophisticated and more suited to an urban audience that flocked to see them not on occasional rural holidays, but at frequent short intervals of escape from the rigors of the workplace. Many of the entertainers came from the same background as their audience, the workers and casual laborers of Tianjin. The lives of the entertainers, like the lives of their working-class customers, were economically precarious and subject to bullying from those more powerful than they. Entertainers too were workers, performing for other workers in a distinctly urban milieu.

The activities of workers outside work time frequently mirrored two themes of the workplace: vulnerability and violence. When male workers visited Tianjin prostitutes, for instance, they were buying the services of people who, like their own sisters and daughters, came from rural, working-class, or casual labor backgrounds. The difference was that prostitutes, disadvantaged by their gender as well as their background, were unable to make alliances that would enable them to find more respected or lucrative work. Tianjin's occupational structure gave women very few opportunities for steady employment. In 1929 the Bureau of Social Affairs counted almost twice as many prostitutes as female millhands in the city.[68] Prostitutes were among the most vulnerable workers in Tianjin. They were frequently sold into prostitution by families whose survival strategies would not allow them to support another female member. They could count on little in the way of protection. They provided a form of labor that was uniquely visible, but they were also emblematic of a sector of the female working class that was much less visible—that of concubines, servants, and slaves, the providers of domestic and sexual services.

Like vulnerability, the violence of the workplace also found its echo in the larger urban environment. Institutionalized violence in the transport guilds and mills was organized around finding a patron and protecting his turf so that he could in turn continue to provide protection to individual workers. Much of the individual, "private" violence recounted in this chapter was probably understood by workers as a cautionary tale about the fate of those who lost patronage. Those unfortunate, unprotected workers could easily be driven to crimes of economic desperation, have their (female) virtue impugned, or become vulnerable to revenge by their workplace enemies. Institutionalized violence remained such a persistent feature of working-class life precisely because it buttressed the power of patrons who could protect workers against both economic vulnerability and individual violence.

The rhythms and passages of working-class life offer a final clue to the emergence of an urban working-class culture. Most of the festival observances and rites of passage practiced in Tianjin conformed closely to rural customs. But they also provided an occasion for cementing new relationships in an urban setting. The major holidays, too, were a time when working-class discontent took visible and organized form in the workplace, as workers fought for the right and the means to observe the festivals as rural custom dictated. Rural traditions, as well as urban relationships and workplace pressures, helped structure the forms of working-class protest.

CHAPTER EIGHT

The Shaping of Working-Class Protest

To those who have measured working-class consciousness by looking at the formation of unions and the frequency of strikes, Tianjin has always seemed a rather quiescent place. From 1918 to 1926, during the first great period of labor militance of the Chinese industrial working class, Shanghai had 638 recorded strikes. Tianjin had 14.[1] At the end of the Japanese occupation, and during the period of severe inflation in 1947–48, it sometimes seemed that all Shanghai was on strike. Tianjin's labor struggles during this period were scattered and quickly suppressed. Such relative inactivity is usually explained by the conventional wisdom, communicated to the researcher by people of every background in Tianjin, that "Northerners are just more conservative."

Yet this statement is not a sufficient description of working-class consciousness. Tianjin workers, as the previous chapters have shown, furthered their own interests through shifting alliances based on native place, kinship, patronage, and class. Many of these alliances did not involve overt conflict across class lines, but they all reveal a degree of conscious strategy on the part of powerless newcomers to the urban workplace.

At several points in the history of the Tianjin working class, strategic planning expanded to include organized labor activity. Both the formation of unions and the staging of strikes are part of the history of working-class

Tianjin, and a careful examination of working-class militance makes Tianjin seem a far from quiescent place. The militance was, however, limited in space and time. Of the workers whose lives have been explored in this study, only those in the largest manufacturing units engaged in organized, class-based protest. Cotton and flour mills, match and carpet factories had strikes; Santiaoshi metalworking shops and individual transport guilds usually did not. The need for a critical mass of workers before certain types of organized activity were practical, and the small size of most of Tianjin's manufacturing units, contributed to the relative weakness of labor activity. In addition, the lack of an artisanal tradition, the strength of vertical alliances, and the institutionalized violence of the workplace combined to keep workers in small shops from giving collective, class-based expression to their dissatisfaction.

Even in large workplaces, organized labor protest was mostly confined to two brief periods, in 1925–26 and 1946–48. In the mid-1920's, thousands of workers participated in political marches and rallies. Cotton mill workers struck the Yu Da Mill in August 1925 and damaged the physical plant so badly that it shut down for several months. Smaller-scale protests occurred in the 1930's. With factories closing throughout the city because of the Depression, match workers barricaded themselves in their dormitories and went on a defensive hunger strike to avoid layoff and eviction, while discharged cotton mill workers at Heng Yuan refused to leave factory housing until arrested. During the Japanese occupation, strike activity was replaced by "soaking mushrooms" and stealing. When the Nationalists returned in 1945, bringing inflation with them, strikes engaged larger numbers of workers than at any earlier period.

Since organized labor activity was confined to large workplaces and limited to short intervals, it clearly cannot be taken as the exclusive measure of working-class consciousness. Nevertheless, the history of the Tianjin working class is incomplete without an account of why labor protest took the forms it did—and played so limited a role. Large factories offered the most likely ground for the development of an organized labor movement. At the same time, it was in the mills and factories that the constraints on successful worker organizing became clearest.

In examining protest in large factories, we must trace three sets of relationships. Bonds between workers, of the kind explored throughout this study, sometimes helped shape formal labor protest, although they could also work against it. The relationship of workers to dominant groups, including foremen in the factories, reform-minded GMD bureaucrats, and armed government troops, created an environment that encouraged some types of worker action, made others unthinkable, and helped determine the timing of working-class protest. Finally, the relationship of workers to outside political organizers became a crucial element in structuring labor protest in certain periods. None of these relationships was static over the three decades before 1949. Structural changes in the workforce, repression of outside organizers and inconsistency in their strategies, and instability in the dominant classes helped give working-class activity in Tianjin a particularly episodic and scattershot quality. Yet in each period, workers reacted to the possibilities before them and helped enlarge those possibilities through their own actions. Protest was constant, but its form varied as the larger political and economic environment provided some opportunities and closed off others.

THE 1920'S: COMMUNISTS AND COTTON MILLS

The early 1920's, a time of rapid industrial development for Tianjin, was also the period in which the CCP was founded and rapidly expanded its influence among urban factory workers. In Tianjin, CCP organizers helped initiate a union drive in the cotton textile industry. Local labor organizing was spurred by national political ferment when the May 30th Movement of 1925 swept China's urban centers. Ultimately, though, it was the regional logic of warlord politics that prevailed, destroying the possibility of an active labor movement.

In the early 1920's, students involved in the nascent Communist movement targeted the six Tianjin cotton mills for union organizing. The method they chose was education; they founded workers' schools in the vicinity of the mills and recruited workers to learn how to read. The first school was opened in 1921 by two young men, Yu Shude and An Ticheng, who had recently returned from study in Japan. It operated for about a year before being closed down by the authorities. By the time it closed, Yu and An had joined the Communist Party, and the workers' school had come under the direct leadership of the Beijing CCP.[2]

By early 1924, the CCP had entered into a formal coalition with the Guomindang, and Communist organizing work in many Chinese cities gained momentum. In Tianjin, activists founded a Local Executive Committee of the Socialist Youth League and a Local Executive Committee of the CCP. The former concentrated on student work, while the party's Executive Committee assigned cadres, usually from an intellectual background, to organize railroad workers, printers, dockworkers, and mill operatives. Again, initial contact was made with mill workers by founding two common schools (*pingmin xuexiao*). One, in the neighborhood of Bao Cheng and Yu Da on the east side of the Hai River, was run by Li Peiliang.

Lu Shaoting opened another near Yu Yuan and Bei Yang on the river's west bank. Both men were Hebei natives (Li was from Tianjin) who had joined the CCP after a period of activity in the student movement.[3]

Li and Lu used a variety of methods to attract mill workers to their classes. They stood on street corners at quitting time and talked about the value of literacy. They interviewed workers in their homes. They posted ads across from the factory gates, offering free tuition, paper, and pens. Li Peiliang's school was located in two newly constructed small rooms in back of the mills. By the time it opened for formal classes in the spring of 1925, Li already knew a group of workers and had begun to talk to them about union organizing.[4]

Three Bao Cheng workers who visited Li often before the school opened were Shen Yushan, Dong Zhaoyi, and Ji Zhaosheng. Although it is not known what drew them to the Common School, together they embodied a number of characteristics of Bao Cheng's diverse labor force. The mill was run by people from Shanghai, and the high-ranking staff and skilled workers were all southerners who earned relatively high wages. Northerners, from Henan, Shandong, and Hebei villages, all earned lower pay but had little else in common. Members of each group socialized and swore brotherhood with people from their own native area. Shen was a southerner who made a relatively high salary, 24 yuan a month, repairing machines in the reeling room. He had a certain amount of prestige among the southern workers. Dong and Ji also worked in the reeling room, where 60 percent of the workforce was concentrated. After extensive conversations with Li about conditions in the factory, the three agreed to recruit pupils for the Common School, Shen concentrating on southerners and the other two on ordinary reeling room workers. They attracted several dozen pupils to the school's opening session. Ji also arranged for someone from his home county in Shandong to cook and clean for Li.[5]

Each pupil who attended one of the Common Schools was given a 1,000-character primer. Aside from teaching literacy skills, Li and Lu used class time to advocate forming a union, secretly if necessary. Li argued with workers who insisted that conditions in the factory were their "fate," and told them that a union would give them more power at work: "It's easy to break one chopstick, but not a bunch together." After class, Li continued to meet privately with Shen, Dong, and Ji, and within a few months all of them had joined the CCP.[6]

Over a period of several months, the Common School pupils mobilized several hundred activists in the cotton mills. All of them were male; without a group of women labor organizers, it was difficult to contact the small number of women who were millhands. By April 1925, a union was organized in Bao Cheng, with about 1,800 members, two-thirds of the total workforce. Membership cut across the usual factional lines in the mill; Shen Yushan, for instance, convinced southerners to join by telling them that anyone who sided with the owners was a scab. Because of his standing in the factory, other workers did not dare oppose him. Each workshop had a union committee of several members; workers paid dues of one mao a month. A successful three-day strike in May, over a cut in wages, increased the prestige of the union. Other mills quickly organized as well. In May, representatives from all the mills except Yu Da met at Li's Common School to found the Tianjin Textile Union.[7]

In the late spring and summer of 1925, Chinese cities were caught up in protests engendered by the May 30th Incident in Shanghai. Anti-imperialist demonstrations temporarily displaced economic issues in the Tianjin labor movement, but unionization continued apace. Carpet workers, printers, sailors, and railroad workers formed unions during this period, guided by young CCP organizers. A sailors' strike in July against a British steamship company shut down a good portion of Tianjin's trade. Thousands of millhands, in highly organized groups, joined three marches in June and one in August to protest the events of May 30th. At these demonstrations, several tens of thousands of people marched across the city, skirting the British and Japanese concessions, where nervous armed guards blocked their way. Workers shouted slogans denouncing imperialism and the unequal treaties, and carried placards advocating a boycott of Japanese goods. They heard speeches by several party activists, but also listened to a representative of the Tianjin Chamber of Commerce. Their parade marshal was a teacher from the School of Law and Government. The marches involved workers in the wave of political activity sweeping Chinese cities, but did not pit them directly against the millowners or raise economic issues of concern to workers in particular.[8]

Politics and economics soon intersected, however, in a July strike at the Bao Cheng Mill. While union officials were meeting to plan a demonstration of support for striking workers in other cities, the leader of a small group from the day shift sent a report that the factory had suddenly fired a woman worker for leaving her machine to eat. She asked the union for help. The workers hastily elected representatives to go to the management offices and demand her job back, but guards barred their way and threatened them with a lockout.

That night the millhands decided to strike. They gathered at the factory gate between the night and morning shifts, marched to nearby saltyards for a morning meeting, then went back to the plant in the afternoon to discover they were locked out. A number of workers got into a scuffle with the factory guards, rushed into the factory yard, and destroyed the management office. Then they returned to the saltyards. After five days on strike, with the help of CCP activists mediating as "student representatives," the workers achieved their goals. The woman was given her job back, the factory rescinded a wage cut, and management officials agreed not to beat or insult workers, as well as to allow them to stop their machines and take a lunch break.[9]

Smashing Yu Da

By summertime only one cotton mill, Yu Da, remained unorganized. Tight control by the Japanese management and the hindrance of Zhao Kuigao, the chief foreman and a member of the Green Gang, impeded efforts to organize secretly there. When Li Peiliang called union representatives from the other mills together to discuss this deadlock, however, they devised a solution that made use of family networks in Yu Da. If Xiang Ruizhi were approached properly, the millhands told Li, he would be invaluable in organizing Yu Da workers. He and his three brothers were all employed in the mill, and his father was a cook in one of the kitchens where workers purchased hot meals. Known as the Five Tigers of the Xiang Family, they counted many fellow natives from nearby Baodi county among their workmates.[10]

In July 1925 another Yu Da worker brought Xiang to the Common School. Li Peiliang asked him about conditions in the mill, then said, "I've heard that Yu Da workers can't organize because they are afraid of Zhao Kuigao." Xiang flushed and replied that he could organize the mill in spite of "that goddamned Zhao Kuigao." Within a few weeks he had secured the support of his father and most of his brothers, and used his father's kitchen as a place to talk openly about the union and sign workers up. A successful organizing drive in Yu Da completed the unionization of Tianjin's six cotton mills. In early August, Tianjin's cotton mill workers joined representatives of more than 20 unions in forming a city-wide General Labor Union (GLU), with a CCP organizer named An Xingsheng in charge.[11]

On August 11, 1925, the newly organized Yu Da union presented five demands to the mill management: an office for the union, eight hours of work and four of study each day, an hour of rest for meals, and an increase in wages. In addition, they asked that the management send a telegram to British and Japanese factories in Shanghai, which had locked out their workers since May 30th, to demand that they reopen.

Accounts differ as to what happened next. A Japanese version holds that the Japanese chairman of the company accepted all the demands, but granted a slightly lower wage increase than the workers wanted. Chinese workers recall that the management balked at sending a telegram to Shanghai. In any case, when workers finished the day shift and started out the gate to meet in the saltyards, they discovered that more than 100 policemen were blocking the road. The factory management had asked local warlord Li Jinglin for assistance, and he had sent these forces in response. Union officials then decided to call a strike, and sent messengers to neighboring Bao Cheng and to Yu Yuan and Bei Yang across the river for help.[12]

As they started to pass the warlord troops, some workers taunted them for supporting a Japanese millowner against their countrymen. Insults were exchanged, the troops opened fire, Xiang Ruizhi's older brother and two other picketers were wounded, and a large group of enraged workers chased some of the troops and the factory security force into the mill courtyard. The troops barred the gate to prevent more workers from entering.[13]

When workers from the Bao Cheng Mill arrived, they could hear the sounds of the mêlée from the factory courtyard. Pressing forward, they pushed down a section of the south wall of the factory and rushed in, joining the workers in hand-to-hand fighting with the troops. Some workers grabbed pickaxes from inside the plant, while others cut the phone lines. They destroyed the factory office, ripping up cloth, clothes, and account books; the engine room and the water pump room were also badly damaged. The *North-China Herald* report later described the scene as follows:

The cotton milling machinery crumpled up before them like wooden houses in a tornado and in a few minutes was mostly a tangled mass of broken machinery, spindles, and debris. . . . More than 75 per cent of the window panes in the entire establishment, including wire reinforced glass, were smashed with bricks, which lay about the interiors adding to the mess. What was once a typewriter was partly flattened and crushed steel keys and types, evidently the result of a fairly effective crow-bar.

By the time workers from the mills across the river arrived, the fighting had stopped, most of the troops had fled, and the workers had acquired ten rifles, three pistols, and two hostages, a military policeman and a Japanese doctor.[14]

Government reaction was swift. That night an official named Chen visited Xiang Ruizhi, offering his services as mediator in return for the release of the hostages, and warning that this incident could have international repercussions if it were not resolved. Xiang let the prisoners go. Workers from the various mills returned to their homes, promising to come back the next day for a meeting. But when millhands from the west side of the river tried to cross over at dawn the following day, they discovered that the military police had pulled all the ferry boats out to the middle of the river and anchored them there. While workers were swimming out to retrieve the boats and ferrying themselves across, armed troops ambushed east bank workers who had already massed in the saltyards, forcing them to retreat into the Yu Da Mill. There most of the strike leaders were arrested. West bank workers arrived just in time to be chased into a local temple by firing troops.[15] The *North-China Herald*, while blaming the millhands for attacking the troops with stones and mud, nevertheless decried the horror of the ensuing "indescribable scene of panic": "Unable to get away from the rifles of the police, the leading ranks of the rioters turned to fight those behind. While the unlucky ones dropped dead or wounded, a number jumped into the Haiho River to avoid the bullets and many are believed to have been drowned."[16]

Damage to the Yu Da Mill was later estimated at more than 500,000 taels. At least ten workers were killed in this incident, several dozen wounded, and more than 400 arrested. "It appears that many wounded were carried into the country, fearing arrest," reported the *North-China Herald*. Xiang Ruizhi fled directly from the saltyards to his native Baodi county, but on his return several months later he was arrested and tortured by having hot pepper-water poured in his ears. Ji Zhaosheng, one of the early Common School activists and a CCP member, was easily identified by the head of Yu Da security because he was pockmarked and spoke with a thick Shandong accent; he was arrested. Although most workers were released almost immediately, Xiang, Ji, and eight other activists were held until the end of 1925. Immediately after the incident at Yu Da, Li Jinglin closed down all unions in the Chinese part of the city, put those in the concession areas under police surveillance, closed down the Guangdong Guild, which had been an organizing center for the sailors' strike, and held a number of student leaders for questioning about their CCP connections. The Common Schools, site of the CCP's most successful recruiting and organizing efforts, were closed as well. The Japanese Minister registered a formal protest with the Ministry of Foreign Affairs about the damage to Yu Da property.[17]

Political Repression and Worker Protest

The suppression of the Yu Da strike illustrated the extreme vulnerability of Tianjin workers to the larger political environment of the city. Although Japanese ownership of Yu Da was a factor in shaping this particular incident and government response to it, for the next 25 years the pattern was not substantially different in Chinese-owned factories. Armed municipal police or government troops were routinely called upon to prevent or forcibly suppress worker protest. During the years of the Japanese occupation, when many factories were garrisoned, the presence of troops made any type of formal organizing impossible. Only in periods when the elite was initially unprepared to confront worker militance, as in 1925, or too weak to do so effectively, as during the late 1940's, did workers find an opportunity to stage large-scale strikes.

In August 1925, with most union leaders in jail and all umbrella organizations closed down, open organizing of Tianjin workers came to a halt. The Yu Da Mill closed its doors for several months, throwing 1,500 millhands out of work. CCP officials from Beijing visited east bank workers to give relief funds to families of those injured in the strike. Quiet recruitment of workers into the CCP continued in several mills. At the same time, mill management tried to buy off people who had been active in the recent conflicts by promoting them to foreman and raising their wages.[18] This lull in worker organizing was purely a product of government pressure. When Tianjin was occupied by the Guominjun Third Army under Sun Yue from December 1925 to March 1926, the political constraints disappeared. The Guominjun, led by Feng Yuxiang, took a decidedly more liberal attitude toward worker organizing than the regimes that preceded and followed it. All the activists arrested after the Yu Da strike were released immediately. Though the CCP itself remained secret, it worked freely through organizations like the General Labor Union.[19]

The GLU established its headquarters in the Dadong Hotel, in the Chinese city. The CCP moved out of the relative safety of the concessions into the same building. Unions for millhands, carpet weavers, painters, and printers were quickly restored, and organizing was begun among rickshaw pullers, Santiaoshi ironworkers, and woodworkers, bringing more than 30,000 workers under the leadership of the GLU. The union published two periodicals, *Workers' Tabloid* and *Workers' Life*.[20] Announcing an ambitious new organizing agenda, *Workers' Life* declared: "Whether you work in a modern-style enterprise, as a worker or apprentice in a handicraft workshop, as a rickshaw puller or as a shop apprentice—if you sell your labor power to live, you may organize under our banner!"[21] For a brief period, it seemed that the fragmentation of the Tianjin working class might be overcome by mobilizing workers into one big union.

In this period of relatively unhindered labor activity, union organizers noted two recurrent problems. One was the tendency of newly organized workers, particularly young men, to express their discontent by damaging factory equipment. The other was the danger that worker activists would be found out by foremen and fired before they could complete the organizing process. *Workers' Life* warned that individuals who failed to respect union discipline and flouted factory rules would be regarded as saboteurs, while those who reported union secrets to the management would be treated as running dogs. Special meetings were held for young cotton and carpet workers to explain the necessity of disciplined action rather than mob violence.[22]

This period of open activity came to an abrupt end in March 1926, when Tianjin was reoccupied by Chu Yupu of the Fengtian warlord clique. Once again, political constraints curtailed worker organizing. Unions went underground; the CCP moved its headquarters back to the concessions. From November 1926 to January 1928, the local party organization was destroyed eight times, and a number of Communist and revolutionary Guomindang leaders were executed.[23]

Nevertheless, sporadic strike activity continued in the cotton mills, much of it under clandestine CCP leadership. As in the 1925 campaigns, the most successful organizing made use of preexisting networks in the mills. The Yu Yuan Mill, for instance, had three strikes in 1926. One of the leading activists was Zuo Zhenyu, who joined the union at the urging of a member of the factory party committee. With Zuo came his seven sworn brothers, who had grown up with him.[24]

Two of the Yu Yuan strikes were confined to a single workshop. The third, which required a great deal of advance planning, concerned demands for higher wages, paid holidays, a meal break, a night school, and an end to arbitrary firings. Taking a lesson from the failure of the Yu Da strike, workers stayed at their machines and blockaded the factory doors with raw cotton, which would ignite if troops outside opened fire. When the head of the personnel department stood outside the weaving room cursing the workers, they hauled him in through the window and kept him hostage. Although the workers' demands for a raise and holiday pay were granted after two days, warlord troops arrested pickets outside the factory and killed several of them.[25] Even worker activity that was well-supported and highly organized could enjoy only temporary success in an environment of sustained political repression.

As late as 1927, the Communist Party in Tianjin had 24 branches and 459 members, of whom "a large proportion" were workers. Ultimately, however, CCP activists in the cotton mills found themselves cut off from an increasingly beleaguered party leadership. Many politically active mill workers were fired for union activity or forced to flee the police after the suppression of a strike. Si Chengxiang, a millhand at Yu Yuan and Bei Yang mills and a CCP member, was arrested with four other Bei Yang union leaders and two outside CCP organizers in January 1927. Accused of possession of suspicious political leaflets, they all pretended to know little about one another. After one of their number was released for lack of evidence, another declared that the released man (already long gone) was an oil vendor who had left the leaflets in his house. He further pretended to be illiterate and unable to tell the difference between a political leaflet (*chuandan*) and a bill for oil (*zhangdan*). Although the exasperated authorities eventually released this group, the episode brought their mill organizing to an end. Si changed his name and got a new job in the Yu Yuan Mill, but other activist millhands were reduced to hawking goods on the street in order to survive.[26]

The Tianjin millhands of the mid-1920's, a factory workforce made up mostly of young men from the countryside, proved very amenable to CCP-guided organization. Attempts to mobilize these workers were particularly successful when the organizers made use of family and native-place networks to circumvent the vertical bonds and factional divisions in the mills. Many millhands became active in unions, while a small but important core of activists was recruited into the CCP. Workers devised their own demands to present to mill management, mostly concerned with wages and working conditions. But their protests sometimes reflected larger political issues in Tianjin and other cities; they joined in city-wide anti-imperialist demonstrations and carried their anti-Japanese sentiments into at least one important strike. Whereas early worker activity had frequently damaged factory property, workers became increasingly disciplined and versatile at using the threat of violence without resorting to outright destruction. Most strikes, in this period as later, took place inside the factory itself.

The cotton mills, at this time still in a period of expansion, could afford to grant some worker demands without undue strain. The initiative in pressing for better conditions lay with the workers, in contrast to the situation of the 1930's, when workers responded defensively to factory layoffs and closings. Constraints on organizing activity in Tianjin factories during the 1920's were not economic, but political. Warlord troops used armed force to suppress strikes in both foreign- and Chinese-owned mills. Ultimately, armed suppression put stringent limits on worker organizing, while destroying the CCP organization that had helped inspire it. The CCP was forced to transfer many of its experienced cadres out of Tianjin to safety, while local-level activists were fired, arrested, or compelled to flee. The party could not develop the kind of sustained contact with mill workers necessary to build a strong union organization. Worker discontent made the labor movement of the 1920's possible, but that movement was shaped—for better and for worse—by the CCP, and was finally destroyed by the warlords who garrisoned Tianjin.

THE NANJING DECADE:
REFORMERS, LAYOFFS, AND LOCKOUTS

In 1928, the Guomindang completed the nominal unification of China, and Shanxi warlord Yan Xishan acquired control of Tianjin. During the decade that followed, CCP activity among factory workers was insignificant. The main impetus for union organizing came instead from the Guomindang government, which shaped an official union movement in an attempt to control the workforce. Workers, on the defensive in an increasingly troubled economy, nevertheless made use of the government labor apparatus to defend their jobs. Militant activity, much of it aimed at preventing layoffs, was once again confined to the largest mills and factories.

One of the first acts of the Guomindang municipal government was to organize new unions. By 1928 the city had 76 unions with 21,580 members, and by the following year the number of unionized workers was 22,431. This number included industrial workers, communications workers, and a third category the government called "vocational" (*zhiye*) workers: printers, tanners, bleachers, freight haulers, and service workers. Slightly more than half the total were cotton mill workers. A new General Labor Union was founded in August 1928.[27]

Although the organizational structure and sometimes the rhetoric of these new unions resembled those of the mid-1920's, the intent of the government officials who controlled them was significantly different. Foremost among their concerns was the eradication of CCP influence. A government report on unions noted that at its inception in 1925, the workers' movement had been controlled by Communist elements. After Jiang Jieshi's 1927 coup, the "loyal comrades" (Guomindang members) became more active, especially in organizing railroad workers. In 1929 the new GLU leadership warned that "even now, in the shadows of this city, lurk the seeds of a Red insurrection. . . . They have the charm to bewitch the minds of youth, and the tactics to trick the peasants and workers. A disease in one's vital organs is very difficult to cure."[28]

The surest way to prevent the spread of this disease, the authorities felt, was not merely to organize workers, but to provide them with political training. This government approach to the problem of labor control sometimes conflicted with the desires of factory owners, who would have preferred no unions at all. In enterprises of all sizes, workers frequently organized in the face of management opposition, but they could count on support from the municipal government as long as they stuck to a certain agenda, summarized in the slogans put forward at the second city-wide meeting of the GLU:

Workers of the whole city, unite!
Down with imperialism!
Repudiate the unequal treaties!
Promote cooperation between labor and capital!
Eliminate class struggle!
Down with the compradore class!
Stamp out the CCP!
Guarantee workers' livelihood!
Raise the status of workers!
Eliminate the contract labor system!
Long live the liberation of workers!
Support the Guomindang![29]

Those unions deemed most successful by government investigators were located in the larger factories, had a hard-working staff, and usually received a direct factory subsidy to cover union expenses (although dues were often collected as well). The Yu Yuan union, touted as a model in a 1929 government report, had an elected executive committee of nine workers, five branch unions, and sections in charge of organizing, propaganda, training, and general affairs. The factory gave the union 200 yuan a month and contributed additional funds for special expenses. Total membership in 1931 numbered 4,725 men and 886 women; 39 of the men (but none of the women) were members of the Guomindang.[30]

Organizing in handicraft industries and among seasonal workers was more difficult. Most intractable of all was a freight haulers' branch union, whose members were described in a government-sponsored report as "ignorant and unorganized people who don't know what a union should be." In such cases the union structure became a mere formality imposed from above.[31] Sometimes it was not possible for government organizers to establish a union at all. A 1932 government report estimated that of 200,000 workers, coolies, and handicraft workers in Tianjin, only about 16 percent were organized. Of these, three-quarters were in industrial unions.[32]

Promoting the workers' livelihood while at the same time eliminating class struggle was a difficult mandate. But the municipal government, through its Bureau of Social Affairs (BSA), founded in August 1928, offered itself as a mediator in disputes between capital and labor. The Bureau, staffed by moderates with an interest in social work, was also in charge of social survey work and some welfare enterprises. In any labor dispute, a committee was to be established with members from the BSA, the Public Security Bureau, and the contending parties. Either of the parties involved could request mediation, or the committee itself could initiate the process. It was then required to conduct an investigation and reach a decision within two days. If either of the parties was dissatisfied, they were invited to appeal to a second committee, which had representatives from the city government, the Guomindang party branch, the local court, and capitalists and workers not affected by the dispute. Workers were not permitted to strike during the mediation period, but neither could the management fire them or lock them out. Industries supplying the military, as well as workers in public utilities and transport, were not permitted to strike at all.[33]

As an elaborate new labor bureaucracy took shape in Tianjin, its organizers were careful to ensure that it would not be controlled by activists with Communist sympathies. Each prospective union member was required to fill out a form giving his or her personal history in the workers' movement. In addition, the municipal Guomindang Bureau (*dangbu*) helped fund an exhaustive investigation to determine if there were "counterrevolutionary" activities among the GLU members.[34]

Even if these measures were not completely effective, other forces worked to undermine what was left of CCP influence in Tianjin factories. Some CCP members among the millhands and printers left the party and became active in the GMD and the new unions.[35] Surveillance and arrests of the CCP leadership, fierce but sporadic under the warlords, became more systematic under the GMD. By opening mail, staking out the CCP mailbox, and following the courier who came to pick up letters, the head of the Special Agent Division of the Public Security Bureau in 1929 succeeded in arresting more than 30 CCP members, several of them key worker activists.[36] It became extremely difficult for the CCP to maintain a presence in the factories. In 1932, reporting on a series of Tianjin strikes, a party publication located in one of the soviet areas commented that the CCP had not been in any way involved in these activities, and that after a month-long flour mill strike the Tianjin party branch still did not even know the addresses of the mills involved.[37]

The combination of a new union structure, a mediation procedure, and the meticulous rooting out of CCP activists effectively kept worker protest within controllable bounds. According to government statistics, in the last four months of 1928 the city had seven disputes between owners and workers, but only one resulted in a strike. The following year saw 54 disputes, including three strikes and 29 work stoppages; by 1930 the number of disputes was down to 31, with three strikes and four stoppages. Almost 90 percent of these disputes, whether they resulted in strikes, stoppages, slowdowns, or merely formal complaints, were concerned with "conditions of employment"; none had any obvious connection with outside political organizations or movements. Of these 92 disputes, 67 percent were mediated by the BSA, and the remainder were handled by the BSA in cooperation with the local court and the mediation committee. Almost a third resulted in the complete satisfaction of worker demands, while another third won them partial gains. Only 12 percent resulted in complete defeat for workers.[38]

These bland statistics conceal a situation in which workers were increasingly on the defensive. BSA proclamations concerning labor in 1929 pointed to large-scale firings as the most serious cause of disputes. Many smaller enterprises routinely discharged their employees at the Mid-Autumn Festival and at New Year's. In March and April 1929 an additional round of firings in factories and shops targeted workers who had joined unions, to the dismay of BSA officials. But most cases involved factories forced to shut down by economic difficulties. The BSA investigated 33 such cases in 1929, almost three-fourths of them in the figured weaving industry, where a glut on the market and insufficient capital led to many closings. In each of these cases, BSA officials either ordered the company to take the workers back, or accepted the inevitable and tried to get severance pay and traveling expenses for the discharged workers. The officials were less sympathetic if workers struck outright; then the usual procedure was to call the police to suppress the strike and at the same time sponsor negotiations.[39]

As the effects of the world Depression deepened in the 1930's, the threat of layoffs and closings spread to the cotton mills. In the summer of 1933, workers in every Chinese-owned mill in Tianjin went out on protracted strikes. At the Heng Yuan Mill, workers not surprisingly objected to a BSA proposal that their wages be reduced to 80 percent of their usual earnings. They stopped work, but the municipal government backed the BSA in its proposal, presumably feeling that a pay cut was preferable to layoffs. The following month the factory declared that because of financial losses it was suspending operations for six months, but agreed to reopen if it could pay workers three-quarters of their usual wage. This time, convinced that their jobs were in danger, the workers agreed.[40]

Workers resisted cutbacks in other mills as well. At Bao Cheng the management decided to abandon an experiment with three eight-hour shifts and return to the system of two 12-hour shifts. When the workers objected, the management locked them out for more than a month, then laid off 600 workmen and permitted the remainder to come back to work on 12-hour shifts. Extensive mediation by the local GMD and government did not win the laid-off workers their jobs back, but did secure severance pay, travel expenses, and the right of first rehire for the discharged millhands.[41]

The best-organized strike of the summer of 1933 took place at the Yu Yuan Mill. Like other millowners, the Yu Yuan management announced their intention to cut back production, in this case by eliminating night work and having the two shifts work alternate weeks. A small group of workers, without waiting for approval from the union, organized a work stoppage. They arranged for the cooks to smuggle in 200 small knives with the noon meal. The cooks, some of whom were sworn brothers of the mill-hands, concealed the knives in barrels of rice gruel. As soon as the workers were armed, they shut the managers and staff in an inner room, using them, as one worker explained, "as a kind of 'deposit' (*yajin*)." When they got hungry in the evening, they took flour from the sizing department (it was normally used to make sizing starch), occupied the staff kitchen, and made themselves wheatcakes. But in the middle of the night several hundred police arrived, forced the workers out of the factory, and arrested 73 strike leaders. The management subsequently attempted to close the factory and fire the entire workforce, but in a government-arbitrated settlement agreed instead to lay off more than 1,000 workers and resume operations.[42]

Although little is known about the relationships between workers involved in these strikes, it is clear that when confronted with the threat of losing their jobs, they were capable of taking coordinated action. As the cotton mill crisis worsened in 1935, though, workers were forced into an increasingly reactive posture. Instead of striking to defend existing jobs, they found it necessary to appeal to the BSA for restoration of jobs that had been taken from them by abrupt factory closings. Eight hundred Bao Cheng workers marched first to the BSA, then to the municipal government offices, to protest the closing of their mill. The head of the BSA arranged for them each to be fed a half-catty wheatcake and a chunk of pickled vegetables, but could do little about their situation. The municipal government ordered the mill management to pay them back wages. Bao Cheng eventually merged with the Japanese-run Yu Da Mill, and hired workers from other parts of China.[43]

In January 1935, the Yu Yuan management announced that the mill was closing, and workers followed the same route as the millhands from Bao Cheng. Demanding a definite time limit to the work stoppage and a guarantee that the factory would reopen, they sent their union officials to the BSA and to the GMD party headquarters. The GMD Party Bureau (*zhengdang ju*) promised to sponsor negotiations between workers and owners, but the factory owners delayed a settlement as long as possible, sending key personnel to Beijing on a business trip. The BSA ordered the recalcitrant managers back to Tianjin. Workers eventually were granted rights of rehire, severance pay, and travel expenses, but those who complained about the size of their final paychecks were warned by the GMD

Party Bureau not to start any more incidents. It was 20 months before the mill reopened under new Japanese owners, who agreed under pressure to rehire some former workers for a trial period of six months.[44] With most mills in Tianjin having been sold to Japanese owners, and even Chinese-owned mills like Heng Yuan undergoing major changes in hiring patterns (see Chapter 6), government guarantees of rehiring rights were virtually impossible to enforce. Although at least some leaders of government-sponsored unions attempted to act energetically to defend cotton mill jobs, the entire government apparatus of cooperative unionism was overwhelmed in the economic crisis of the 1930's, and workers were left with very little room to maneuver.

Worker protest in this period was partly shaped by the constraints of a serious economic crisis, but it was informed by older rhythms as well. The end of the lunar year was a time when conflicts in many factories and shops took place over the size of New Year's bonuses. When a factory's economic health was not in immediate jeopardy, BSA officials sometimes audited factory records and ordered the management to pay a higher bonus. But they dealt harshly with workers who struck for bonuses rather than appealing for them, sending police to arrest strike leaders before undertaking to mediate disputes.[45]

In one such New Year's strike, workers showed considerable ingenuity in developing a form of protest that would win them maximum government attention while avoiding suppression. The conflict began in January 1935 at the Bei Yang Match Factory, when the owners announced that they would stop work ten days before the Chinese New Year to clear accounts. Workers suspected that the early holiday closing portended economic trouble and that the plant might not reopen. On January 19, several hundred men and women outworkers—that is, workers employed in packing matches who did not live on the factory grounds—refused to leave the factory until they were paid. As was its practice, the BSA sent police to put down the strike, threatening to send the workers (including about 40 "women workers who had blindly joined in") home. This particular protest was settled when every worker was given one yuan holiday pay.[46]

True to the fears of the workers, however, the manager resigned at the beginning of February and the company was taken to court by its creditors before it could reopen. After government intercession, the factory's Board of Directors agreed to pay both resident workers and outworkers a certain amount for living expenses while the factory remained closed. But the factory was slow about issuing payment for food, and on March 4 the workers grew impatient. Leaving the women workers to guard the factory, several hundred men marched to the GMD Party Bureau to demand aid money and a definite date for the reopening of the factory. The management promised to pay up and make a decision about reopening, but neither money nor a decision was forthcoming.[47]

Many workers were still living in a factory-owned dormitory at this time. With negotiations dragging on, 500 workers of both sexes went on a hunger strike. Refusing an offer of food money from the BSA, they demanded their back wages. This time the Mayor himself called in the chairman of the factory's Board of Directors and demanded that he issue the workers money for food. But the workers continued their hunger strike for a second day, under the leadership of the union, because the company had not yet paid back wages and living expenses or issued a reopening date. They spent the second day of the hunger strike lying on their dormitory beds, and were only persuaded to eat when the factory gave them a temporary payment of one yuan each.[48]

In spite of their resourcefulness in garnering attention from the city government and the press, however, Bei Yang match workers were finally laid off. A BSA representative told them that the company was in serious financial trouble, and asked them to please "put up with some temporary pain" and hope that the factory could reopen in the future. As with other factories that shut down, workers received severance pay, and in addition the factory paid them back living expenses. They agreed in turn to vacate the factory peacefully. Although the factory reopened 15 months later, it is not known whether the hunger strikers ever got their jobs back.[49]

Like the millhands, match workers had used various forms of protest, the union structure, and government mediation to the fullest extent possible; like the millhands, they found themselves unemployed nonetheless. The economic crisis of the 1930's clearly hampered the effectiveness of worker organization, even with a government and union structure that was willing to represent the interests of workers as long as those interests stayed within politically acceptable bounds. Many workers laid off in the mid-1930's used their travel allowances to return to their home villages; high turnover in the workforce, so characteristic of 1920's Tianjin, contributed to lack of continuity in the workers' movement of the 1930's as well. When some of these workers returned to Tianjin several years later, after the Japanese invasion, they had to make their way in an occupied city where the balance of political and economic power had changed once again, and with it the possibilities for organized worker action.

THE 1940'S: OCCUPATION AND GUOMINDANG REPRISE

During the Nanjing Decade (1928–37), the government had done its best to transform unions into instruments for control of the workforce and maintenance of labor-capital cooperation. To the Japanese who occupied

North China in 1937, however, even these benign unions were dangerous organizations "controlled by radical elements, bent on creating disturbances." The Japanese military authorities banned all labor organizations in North China in March 1938.[50] As working and living conditions deteriorated rapidly over the next eight years, strikes ceased to be a feature of Chinese working-class life, replaced by indirect forms of protest such as "soaking mushrooms," stealing, and occasional acts of sabotage.

The most obvious reason for the decline in open protest was the increasingly effective suppression. "The Japanese regarded strikes not as economic but as political, with Communists or the Eighth Route Army involved," comments former millhand Chen Zhi. Zhang Chunfeng participated in a strike with other cannery workers in 1943 for more food and an end to beatings, but after the strike ended the Japanese "conducted interrogations, figured out who some of the organizers were, and sent them off to the special agent organizations."[51] Strikes were not merely illegal, to the Japanese they were treasonous, and penalties were meted out accordingly.

Another cause of quiescence in the large plants was high turnover. Especially in the first few years of the occupation, the mills competed for labor, and millhands moved around a great deal (see Chapter 6). They also returned to their native villages when the harvest was good, or when they felt that the countryside might be safer than the city. Finally, they left when they feared they might be caught for stealing and sent to the military police, or to Japan or Manchuria as corvée labor.[52] This high degree of mobility, perhaps best viewed as a flight from intolerable conditions rather than a search for better ones, decreased the likelihood of long-term clandestine organizing.

A final factor in the absence of organized protest was sheer physical debilitation, brought on by long, tense hours of work and a worsening food supply. Workers had little energy for any activity beyond that necessary to sustain life. Han Ruixiang, who worked at a Japanese-owned cotton mill, recalls that

during the occupation one of the Japanese organized a big brass band. In order to get people to join, they would give two steamed buns to everyone who came. Some people came for the steamed buns. It wasn't easy to get two steamed buns to eat. But as soon as you blew on the instruments it took a lot of effort, more than the steamed buns could provide. So after that no one came.[53]

Even under these circumstances, factory workers did not abandon efforts to make their lives more bearable. But they usually chose forms of protest that could secure the maximum return while avoiding confrontation with the military authorities. Aside from the slowdowns and stealing described in Chapter 6, workers occasionally took part in acts of arson, burning cotton warehouses or sabotaging machinery. Underground GMD workers participated in some of this work.[54] But most worker activity was directed at the short-term goal of survival until the Japanese were defeated.

Official Unionism and the Scope of Protest, 1945–49

When the Guomindang government reoccupied Tianjin in 1945, it brought with it the full panoply of labor institutions that had characterized the Nanjing decade: an officially sponsored union movement, a Bureau of Social Affairs to mediate disputes, and a municipal government ready to use both persuasion and force to ensure peace in the workplace. The government took over direct operation of seven cotton mills from the Japanese, and unions in those mills were among the first established after the victory. Most other large factories and many small ones were unionized as well; the number of organized workers totaled 44,148 in September 1946. A city-wide Textile Union was founded in April 1947, a General Labor Union in August.[55]

With the institutional structure came a set of procedures and an ideology that resembled those of a decade earlier. Foremen and skilled workers, rather than rank and file members, were instrumental in organizing and controlling branch unions.[56] Labor disputes were to be mediated by a committee made up of two labor officials, three owners, and three government representatives. Public transport workers, and any other workers whose disputes were being mediated, were forbidden to strike. Unions were not permitted to call strikes or slowdowns during "extraordinary periods," with the nature of those periods left unspecified.[57] The slogan of the union at the Yi Zhong Tobacco Company (formerly the British and American Tobacco Company) summed up the desirable parameters of union activity: "Don't insist, don't be excessive, don't transgress the law, and don't let the workers go unrestrained" (*bu qiangqiu, bu guofen, bu yufa, bu renzong gongren*).[58]

Such restraint was supposed to result in a shared sense of national purpose, extending across class lines, which would promote higher productivity and increased benefits. *Workers' Weekly*, the magazine of the official labor movement, printed a factory owner's reflections in which he quoted Sun Yatsen as saying that there were really no capitalists in China, only the "big poor" and the "small poor." In a situation like this, the owner went on, labor struggles were inappropriate; instead, workers and owners must cooperate to produce more food and clothing for everyone. In this world of cooperation, owners helped finance union-sponsored welfare facilities, which were more elaborate than those of the 1930's. Unions in the larger factories staged New Year's performances, founded ball teams, co-ops, martial-arts clubs, and opera troupes, and even offered cheap haircuts.

The owners, asserted one worker in *Worker's Weekly*, should realize that it was in their interests to fund all this. Attending to the cultural life and housing needs of the workers would help increase production and avoid strikes.[59]

The structure and ideology of institutionalized unionism had definite limitations, however, which were clearly perceived even by official labor leaders. The gap between the outlook of municipal government officials and workers became clear at the end of 1946. In a major speech to worker representatives, Tianjin's new mayor outlined nine objectives of labor activity: to promote labor-capital cooperation, increase production, raise the technical and educational level of workers, preserve labor discipline, protect the factories, abide by government decrees, assist in the implementation of government decrees, serve society at large, and (for GMD members in the movement) observe party regulations. He did not mention that a union might also concern itself with pay and working conditions. An informal exchange followed, in which a worker representative from the Jibei Power Company, although so embarrassed at speaking out in public that "his face and ears were red," managed to stammer out that at his plant the company had delayed raising workers' wages, in spite of an agreement to do so. He was echoed by another worker who pointed out that laborers worked to earn a livelihood; his hope was that government policy would help to make that possible. Other workers chimed in, respectfully registering their dissatisfaction with wages that remained unadjusted for the severe inflation then raging. The mayor and the director of the BSA listened politely, asked some follow-up questions, and encouraged the workers to use "an experienced and prudent spirit to gain the trust of both labor and capital and think of a way to solve the problem."[60]

The muted frustration of these labor leaders at the lack of official attention to economic issues was echoed in much less tractable form in the factories and streets of Tianjin. Labor disputes erupted continuously: 70 in the last two months of 1945, 200 in 1946, 118 in 1947, and 79 in the first four months of 1948. The main cause of worker dissatisfaction changed over time. In 1945, almost two-thirds of the disputes began because workers demanded discharge allowances when factories shut down at the end of the war. In 1946, the peak year of unrest, the leading problem was wages (38 percent), followed by layoffs (22 percent). As more factories were affected by electricity and raw material shortages, in 1947, layoff disputes grew to more than half the total, while wage conflicts declined to 29 percent. This tendency sharpened in the first four months of 1948 (61 percent layoffs and 22 percent wages). Other causes of conflict included demands for severance pay and resumption of work.[61]

One of the main sources of discontent was inflation. The cost-of-living index for workers in July 1946 was more than 4,000 times higher than that of the base period in 1937, and it continued to rise steadily.[62] By July 1947, the average monthly wage of an ordinary skilled worker in a government cotton mill was equivalent to 236.4 catties of cornmeal. In a privately owned mill, the wage was worth 210 catties; in a small enterprise, it could buy only 157 catties. The pay earned by workers in the tiniest shops was worth only about 40 catties. These figures ranged from one-eighth to one-third of 1936 wage levels.[63] Prices fluctuated weekly, even daily, so that wages agreed upon one month were almost worthless the next. Although the government quickly established a Wage Arbitration Committee, mandated to settle wage disputes on the basis of the workers' cost of living index, arbitration and enforcement could not keep pace with inflation.[64] It became standard practice for factories to circumvent the effects of inflation by paying workers partly in flour, cloth, coal, and other goods, but then the focus of dispute shifted to the current market value of such goods.[65] Under these circumstances, the early enthusiasm that many workers felt for the Guomindang—the feeling that this was a legitimate Chinese government which deserved support—quickly dissipated.[66]

Superficially, the contours of both the labor movement and worker unrest from 1945 to 1949 resembled those of the Nanjing decade. Like their 1930's predecessors, workers expressed some of their dissatisfaction through a union structure that was closely tied to management. Workers of both generations were hemmed in by notions of legality that provided procedures for mediation but also limited their right to strike. Most important, both cohorts of workers were constrained by a troubled and unstable economic climate, so that most of their activity was devoted to preventing a further deterioration in their standard of living, rather than demanding improvement.

However, the internal dynamics of worker protest had changed greatly by the late 1940's. Although verifiable statistics are difficult to come by, many observers indicate that the labor force after the war was older and more stable than that of any previous period. Many of the child workers hired under the Japanese had now reached young adulthood and had years of factory experience behind them. Workers who had moved from mill to mill and from city to countryside now settled in Tianjin, sometimes in factory housing, and brought their families in from the villages.

Initially this migration grew out of the optimism and improved economic conditions that followed victory over Japan. Later, as inflation made life more difficult, workers may have elected to remain in the city because most of their home villages were in the war zone, or in the hands of the

Communists. Whatever their reasons, they now had a home in Tianjin and therefore more of a stake in the outcome of struggles over wages. They were also older, more sophisticated in the ways of the workplace, and perhaps less easily intimidated than the child and adolescent workers of earlier periods.[67]

Workers may also have been encouraged to protest more vociferously than in previous years because of the relative weakness of the Guomindang government. Compared to that of the Japanese occupation period, effective government control over the workplace was much weaker. Mired in a civil war, surrounded by Communist-controlled areas in the North China countryside, GMD officials might well have felt the need to grant some worker demands so that workers would not transfer their allegiance to the Communists.

A third factor in the nature of worker protest was the renewed presence of CCP organizers in most Tianjin factories. This network of organizers had begun to develop in schools and workplaces in the final years of the Japanese occupation. Their leadership was located not in Tianjin, but in the Central Hebei base area or one of the other base areas in North China. As in the 1920's, most initial urban recruits to the party came from student backgrounds, but near the end of the war many of these students, responding to a CCP directive to "go among the workers," found factory jobs.[68]

CCP Organizing in Tianjin Mills

One such worker was a woman named Su Geng, who went to work in the Shuang Xi Cotton Mill (later known as Cotton Mill #5 under the Guomindang) and remained there until the summer of 1946, when she had to flee to the Liberated Areas. Su's father was a staff member in a factory. When she finished junior high school she couldn't afford to continue her schooling. Unlike many young student activists who came from upper-class backgrounds and would have been easy to spot as suspicious characters, Su was a natural choice for factory work.

In Shuang Xi, Su Geng initially did not engage in any organizing activity. She slowly made friends among her fellow workers. Like other CCP members, she kept in touch with the party through single-line vertical contacts. Party members working in the same mill frequently did not know of one another's existence. This form of organization was intended to minimize damage to the CCP network if one person was arrested. But it was also a product of the fact that during the occupation, the Urban Work Department of every base area sent people into Tianjin. Sometimes people from different base areas would discover each other in the process of doing factory work. When this happened, the organization that had developed more extensive contacts in the particular workplace would remain and the other one would withdraw. Party organizers in the Liberated Areas also sought out workers who returned to their home villages from Tianjin for New Year's, running classes for them and assigning them tasks once they returned to the city.[69]

The leadership of the base areas and direction of CCP work in Tianjin were not united until after the Japanese surrender, when the Tianjin Work Committee (*Tianjin gongzuo weiyuanhui*) was formed under the leadership of the Central Hebei Base Area. By this time more than 1,000 underground CCP members were at work in the city. The Tianjin Work Committee had subcommittees that worked among students, sympathetic members of the elite, workers, and urban residents whom it was difficult to reach through their place of work, like handicraftsmen and unemployed workers. Workers in large factories and on the railroads were contacted by the Workers' Committee. Santiaoshi workers, when they were contacted at all, were reached through the Urban Residents' Committee. Most workers in small shops, however, remained beyond the reach of the CCP network.[70]

Su Geng, and other party cadres scattered throughout Tianjin factories, slowly began to talk to other workers and recruit them into the CCP. Su "developed" three or four members, one of whom became her husband. Sun Shaohua, a woman millhand who had begun work in 1936 at the age of eight, met Su in 1945. This was not Sun's first contact with CCP members, however. A year earlier, two women had come to work in the factory. One of them, who was very tall and "looked like a man," explained to the workers that she was fleeing an unhappy marriage. The two women lived together in the factory dormitory and worked in the weaving mill. During lunch hour they would come to the spinning workshop, teach the girls and women there to read, and tell them stories. The tall woman also entertained them with renditions of Beijing opera. Sun, sixteen years old at the time, thought the two were unusual because not that many educated people had contact with workers. Although she had no idea they were CCP members, she was not surprised when they suddenly left the factory after less than a year. She later learned they had fled to the Liberated Areas. It was soon afterward that Su Geng came to the mill and continued the work of storytelling, mixed with news about the Eighth Route Army and the impending Chinese victory over Japan. Sun Shaohua herself joined the CCP in 1946, just before a major summer strike that exposed many CCP workers and forced them to seek work in other mills.[71]

This protracted building of CCP networks in the mills helped shape the struggles of the late 1940's. Party members, whether sent in from outside or "developed" within the workplace, helped initiate and direct demands for higher wages, and also assisted in attempts to wrest power from the official union leadership. They did not necessarily take the lead in every struggle; they responded to existing causes of worker discontent rather than attempting to impose a political agenda from without.

Strike Activity

In some of the mills, CCP members joined with non-party workers to form "progressive unions," loosely organized groups that led worker struggles and competed with the ineffective government-sponsored unions. At Ren Li, a wool mill, the official union came under attack in 1946 because workers felt it was not adequately representing their interests. The mill, run by a Chinese entrepreneur who had studied in Germany, automatically deducted 50 cents from each worker's monthly paycheck and deposited it in an enforced savings account, to be redeemed in the future. With mounting inflation, workers feared that their savings, already accumulated over a period of ten years, "were no longer enough to buy a bag of toothpowder, let alone a bag of flour." When the official union was established, many of them demanded that the union negotiate with the owner to issue them ten bags of flour each in lieu of the rapidly depreciating cash. The owner refused; the union declined to press the issue further.[72]

At this point, some of the workers (later identified as CCP members) suggested that the workers take action on their own, independent of the union. In April 1946 the workers barricaded themselves in the factory, refusing to let the managers leave their offices and denying them food. When union officials tried to persuade them to relent, the strikers replied that if the union had represented them properly, they would not be in this situation. Exasperated, the union officials accused them of "using peasant methods inappropriate to city life and treating the capitalist like a landlord." After a 12-hour strike, the owner consented to issue a considerable sum of cash to each worker.

The strike settlement did not heal the rift that had emerged between the union leadership and the rank and file. Union officials accused the CCP of provoking the strike; workers took a complaint about the union leadership to the Bureau of Social Affairs. Eventually the head of the union lost the support of the GLU and the BSA and was removed from his post.[73]

One of the workers active in these events was Yang Chunlin, who had worked in the mill for 12 or 13 years. Identifying him as a talented activist, representatives of both the GMD and the CCP came to him secretly and asked him to join. Although he disliked the GMD, he was afraid a blunt refusal would get him into trouble, so he told the recruiters that he was the kind of person who only understood how to eat and work, and did not aspire to membership in any organization. To the CCP recruiter, who had also been a leader in the strike, he said that he would consider joining. After a night of reflection, he decided that if he joined the CCP at least he could always flee to the Liberated Areas if his union work got him into trouble, whereas if he joined no party he would have no means of escape. He joined the CCP and stayed at Ren Li until October 1948, when he fled to the Liberated Areas to avoid arrest.[74]

The pattern of protest and CCP participation was similar in the cotton mills. Party members joined many of the clubs established by the unions, and used them as means to befriend other workers. In contrast to the situation in the 1920's, they were present inside the factories over a period of several years, and they learned to identify local issues and activists in each place. Also unlike the CCP of the 1920's, this organization had many female cadres. As a result they were able to organize women millhands, whose numbers had increased greatly during the intervening years, and encourage them to take an active role in factory struggles. One woman millhand-turned-cadre feels that women were easier to organize than the men, because male millhands were already entangled in gang membership and the GMD. Women, less politically experienced and more "pure," were easier to work with. In at least one mill the CCP organizers decided to concentrate their efforts on the spinning factory, where the workforce was half women.[75]

Although most struggles in Tianjin mills during this period grew out of dissatisfaction with wages and layoffs, they also reflected preindustrial practices and rhythms. Workers in Cotton Mill #2 struck in June 1946, when a worker was killed in an industrial accident, and refused to resume work until the management promised to provide a large funeral, a good-quality coffin, and payments to his family.[76] Waves of strikes continued to accompany traditional festivals like the Mid-Autumn Festival and New Year's, as workers demanded larger holiday bonuses and protested if the amount was less than those granted in other factories.[77]

Many protests also reflected traditional native place divisions in the workforce, exacerbated by economic competition. In January 1947, for instance, workers at Cotton Mill #4 (formerly the Shanghai Cotton Mill) staged a slowdown to oppose the hiring of a new group of workers from Shanxi. The management argued that the hirings were necessary because of a shortage of workers and skilled personnel. Local workers were angry because many people had lost their jobs at the mill, and instead of rehiring them the management was recruiting in another province. They put forward a demand to the union that the new workers not be permitted to begin work, but while negotiations over the issue dragged on, 200 impatient workers organized a slowdown. The next day, the same group of activists, wielding wooden clubs, first tried to persuade other workers to join them and then got into an altercation with the factory security force. Three security guards, one staff member, and two workers were wounded in the fray. With help from the military police and the municipal GMD headquarters, the workers were subdued and 18 of them were fired. It is not known whether underground CCP members active in this factory participated in this particular protest. But it is clear that even 1940's conflicts in the modern sector could be colored by traditional regionalism.[78]

Sporadic group violence, so characteristic of workplace relations and nonworking life, continued to spill into working-class protest as well. In March 1947, workers from a number of industries attacked the office of the municipal Party Bureau, though the cause of their frustration is unclear. In November 1947, 80 workers at a chemical factory, including women as well as men, beat the director of the BSA Labor Department out of dissatisfaction with his mediation of a lockout at their plant. As a result, the BSA closed down the factory union and refused to mediate any more disputes on the workers' behalf.[79] The penchant for violent expression of discontent exhibited by workers in some of these struggles probably caused as much consternation among underground organizers as it did among government authorities, since it invariably provoked government repression.

If these traditional patterns were important in shaping militant action, they were of far less concern to GMD authorities than the threat of an organized Communist movement with a base of support in the working class. As the Guomindang began to lose ground in the civil war outside Tianjin, repression within the city tightened, as did government surveillance of large workplaces. In June 1947, martial law was declared in Tianjin, and a curfew was imposed. Although the restrictions were partly lifted later, the government reimposed martial law intermittently through the end of 1948.[80] In February 1948, 83 CCP members were arrested and charged with planning a general strike. Among those detained were workers on the railroad and the docks, factory laborers, freight haulers, and coolies. One organizer, Ma Yanchi, confessed that he had been sent to Tianjin by the Central Hebei Military District Political Department to take charge of propaganda, to develop organizations in the factories, and to recruit CCP members.[81]

Throughout 1948, jittery government authorities tightened their supervision of the large factories. Government patrols were stationed in the factories; soldiers searched workers on the shop floor and on the way to work; workers were required to carry identity papers. Foremen in the factory were instructed to report worker activists to the authorities, particularly if there was any suspicion that they were connected to the Eighth Route Army.[82] Strike activity abated as heightened surveillance, the arrest of organizers, and increasing CCP preoccupation with the civil war all took their toll.

Even at its height, organized militance in Tianjin factories involved many workers who were casual participants rather than committed activists. Li Guilan, who joined in the 1947 strike at Cotton Mill #4, describes her experience this way: "I saw what they did, and I did it too. The workers ran out, and I ran out too. I was small; I didn't understand things." For every worker activist, there were hundreds more who, like male millhand Gao Fengqi,

joined in strikes, but only to join in the excitement. We didn't know what it was all about. . . . In 1948, a strike started in the weaving mill. . . . We were just working when people came over and hid in a corner. We didn't know what was happening. We didn't dare move. Later we found out it was a strike. It was over wages. It was successful. We didn't know who had organized it. Maybe someone who worked in the weaving mill knows. I was in the spinning mill.

Preoccupied with daily survival strategies, workers were often oblivious to larger political events. Many workers, while they might have heard of or even joined protests in their own factories, were unaware of the role of CCP organizers in instigating them. "We didn't understand anything about national affairs," recalls Gao. "And we didn't dare speak. We only knew how to work."[83] Communist organizers were better integrated into the workforce than at any previous time, and an older, more stable workforce was more skilled at devising strategies. Protest was more sustained than ever before. But even though militant activity was an important feature of Tianjin working-class life in the 1940's, the level of commitment and consciousness which shaped that activity varied from worker to worker. Ultimately, working-class protest played virtually no role in the political fate of the city. In January 1949, after a two-month siege, the People's Liberation Army entered Tianjin.[84]

Organized working-class protest, of the sort easily visible to historians, was limited in scope and duration in pre-Liberation Tianjin. The experience of most of the working class most of the time should be sought elsewhere, in the structures and relationships of the workplace, as well as the rhythms and passages of nonworking time. These offer many clues to the relative lack of overt militance. The fragmentation of the working class into a number of different sectors with widely varying experiences made the development of any unified working-class activity unlikely. Among artisans, as Chapters 3 and 4 have noted, the small workplace size and the weakness of guild institutions and practices, as well as the economic fragility of the entire handicraft sector, made cross-class alliances more common than class-based protest. Casual laborers and outworkers were a significant percentage of the working class, but they remained marginal in the sense that their working lives were discontinuous and not limited to a single occupation. In fact, discontinuity characterized the careers of workers in every sector, since most were first-generation rural immigrants who returned to their native villages when life in Tianjin became too difficult.

If some features of working-class structure militated against organized protest, however, others were more ambiguous. Rural ties could give workers less of a stake in urban workplace struggles and could bind workers to owners, but in large workplaces they could also be used to organize networks of discontented workers. As our study of protest in the 1920's cotton mills has shown, newness to an urban working-class environment did not in itself make workers innately conservative or dampen protest.

Vertical patronage, another characteristic of Tianjin workplaces, worked the same way. Loyalty to a foreman, or fear of him, could prevent a worker from joining with others in protest. But if a powerful worker with prestige and connections in a factory, like Shen Yushan in the Bao Cheng Mill of the 1920's, decided to throw his prestige behind union organizing, he brought with him everyone he had promised to patronize and protect. As for violence, a ubiquitous feature of the workplace that kept many workers quiet, it could become a tool of workers in struggle as well as a means for their suppression. Under the right circumstances, rural ties, vertical patronage, and violence all contributed to the shape of organized working-class protest.

Ultimately, the history of working-class protest in Tianjin cannot be entirely explained by reference to this or that structural factor. It must also be understood as the product of the particular economic and political history of Tianjin. Organized worker action, like the working class itself, was responsive to, even dependent on, the larger environment. Outright repression and more subtle cooptation on the part of Tianjin's many governments helped to determine the parameters of protest. Outside organizers, notably the CCP, gave shape and direction to worker discontent. Neither repression nor mobilization was constant over time, and their interaction for each period of working-class history must be analyzed separately.

Yet working-class militance was not exclusively a product of these political relationships either. Outsiders influenced but did not create worker protest; they should be seen as limiting or enabling rather than determining. Workers certainly had enough grievances to fuel extensive activity.

When governmental power could be circumvented or held at bay, and when CCP organizing was intelligent, consistent, and yet flexible, then those grievances no longer seemed the inevitable products of fate. They became unnecessary, intolerable, and sometimes even correctable.

Protest became possible for different sectors of the working class at different times. Among the most militant workers in large enterprises, gender helped structure and limit participation. Women were excluded from many of the networks that were used to mobilize men; on the other hand, they were not so completely enmeshed in the structure of patronage that kept so many men inactive. It took a conscious organizing effort on the part of CCP cadres to bring women into formal workplace struggles; when women became involved, however, their actions clearly showed that the early lack of militance was a product of social, not "natural," constraints.

The contours of organized working-class action in Tianjin can be retraced. Large workplaces, an experienced workforce, respected leadership, and a proper external political context did produce militant activity. But the nature of the working-class consciousness which animated that activity remains vague and not very accessible. Government officials eager to suppress worker militance before 1949, and government officials eager to glorify it after 1949, were quick to attribute to workers a high degree of class consciousness and a natural sympathy to Marxism-Leninism. So much of the surviving historical material on worker activism has been shaped by these assumptions that a retrospective reconstruction of consciousness is all but impossible. Even interviewees, very much influenced by 30 years of class education campaigns, have a difficult time recalling how the world looked to them in prerevolutionary times.

Yet it seems clear that what mobilized workers in periods of action was not an abstract commitment to a revolutionary ideology, but the concrete possibility of doing something about the immediate conditions of their working lives. Marxism-Leninism came to the workers in the form of a teacher who taught them to read, or a fellow worker who told them stories about the Eighth Route Army. Workers had (and, one could argue, still have) little understanding of Marxism-Leninism as a tool for analyzing the world or a program for revolutionary action.

Did Tianjin workers, as E. P. Thompson has put it, "as a result of common experiences (inherited or shared), feel and articulate the identity of their interests as between themselves, and as against other men whose interests are different from (and usually opposed to) theirs"?[85] Sometimes. Tianjin workers saw themselves as rooted in a variety of relationships. Some represented continuity with their rural past, some the search for survival in the workplace. Those networks could be put to a variety of uses;

securing cross-class protection was one, and forging alliances for change was another. "Common experiences" and "identity of interests" did not always seem to organize themselves along class lines. When they did, then workers articulated their own interests against those not only of the factory owners, but of the government. But this perception of interests as structured by class was situational, and therefore transient in the constantly changing political environment of Tianjin.

When the CCP took power in 1949, it was able to deliver what the Guomindang had promised but could not provide: stable jobs, a wide range of welfare facilities, safety from daily violence in the workplace, and cooperation between workers and those who controlled production. Ironically, under these circumstances of relative stability, workers ceased to perceive their demands as mediated by class. Class consciousness became formulaic, a way of understanding the sufferings of the past and creating the possibilities of the future, but not a means of interpreting the experience of the present. Although arguably classes and class struggle did not cease to exist under socialism, the terms themselves were appropriated by the state for larger political purposes; they were not used by workers themselves to describe their own post-1949 experience.[86] At last, workers had the patronage, protection, and stability that had been so elusive in prerevolutionary Tianjin. Class consciousness, and the organized worker militance it had helped to shape, were safely confined to the history of the bitter past.

REFERENCE MATTER

Letter of Guarantee for Wang Mobin

Entered factory: First day of second month, 1935.

The signer of this letter, Han Yingru, guarantees that Wang Mobin, age seventeen, of Hebei province, Tianjin county, Haixia village, wishes to enter this honorable factory to study industrial craftsmanship (*gongye shouyi*), and is willing to respect the rules of the factory. If he violates any of the rules below, from the day of the signing of this letter of guarantee, the guarantor will assume complete responsibility and will not go back on his word. Regretting that an oral promise is not enough, he signs this guarantee letter as proof.

> GUANGDA FACTORY: (seal)
> GUARANTOR: (seal)
> ADDRESS:
> INTRODUCER: (seal)
> ADDRESS:

The factory rules are as follows:

1. The term of apprenticeship in this factory is three years. Before the apprenticeship is completed, it is not permitted to arbitrarily discontinue one's study. If

---

NOTE: This contract is an unnumbered item in the Santiaoshi Archives. Guangda gongchang, which was on Santiaoshi Avenue, made lamps, and was neither an ironworks nor a machine factory. But the terms of contracts signed in those shops were substantially the same. A copy of a 1948 contract for Guo Tian Xiang Machine Works is reproduced in *Tianjin* [22], Sec. 9, 5. The Guangda contract has been reprinted here instead because it survives in the original and was not edited for the purposes of later political campaigns.

for some reason the apprentice discontinues his study midway, he must, by the rules of the factory, pay back 15 cents per day to make up for the expense of his food.

2. In the past, apprentices in this factory have received no wages. Now, in order to promote the enterprise and encourage the apprentices, from the day that the apprentice enters the factory, for the first year each month he will receive one yuan pocket money (*lingfei*). The second year each month he will receive 1.50. The third year he will receive two yuan each month. Aside from this special gift, if apprentices perform their work carefully, when it is examined and recorded they will receive an additional monthly reward, no matter when they arrived.

3. The apprentices of this factory, aside from taking the holidays provided for in the rules, are not permitted to stay away from work without leave or good reasons, nor to ask for leave to return to their native place. If there is a wedding, a funeral, or some other matter, they must first come to the factory with the introducer and the guarantor to report it, and then they can go, but not for a period exceeding one month.

4. If during the period of study the apprentice becomes sick or has an accident, without exception the problem will be handled by the guarantor. This factory will assume no responsibility.

5. If the apprentice of this factory steals the property of the factory or violates police regulations or absconds, the guarantor will take responsibility for indemnifying the factory for the full amount. If he has violated police regulations he must be sent to the government offices. [Note: It is not clear whether this stipulation refers to the apprentice or to the guarantor.]

6. If the factory management discovers that an apprentice of this factory, during the period of study, does not study diligently or has no intention of studying, then it may immediately discharge the apprentice. The apprentice must immediately clear his food bill and leave the factory. No excuses or deceitful arguments will be accepted. Furthermore, he will not be able to ask for the special gift or pocket money.

7. If an apprentice of this factory repeatedly takes days off, they will be noted and will have to be made up. Those who have completed three years will be permitted to become craftsmen.

Signed: (Guarantor)

First day of the second month, twenty-fourth year of the Republic (1935).

Notes

Complete authors' names, titles, and publication data for the works cited in short form are given in the Bibliography, pp. 285–301. The following abbreviations are used in the Notes and in the Bibliography:

BGCQ   *Beiguo chunqiu* (Northern Annals)
BYGR   *Banyun gongren gonghui cankao ziliao* (Reference material on the work of the Transport Workers' Union)
CCP   Chinese Communist Party
CEB   *Chinese Economic Bulletin*
CEJ   *Chinese Economic Journal*
CYB   *China Year Book*
ILO   International Labor Organization
JJZK   *Jingji zhoukan* (Economic Weekly)
NWSS   *Nankai Weekly Statistical Service*
PRC   People's Republic of China
SHYK   *Shehui yuekan* (Social Monthly)
TJWS   *Tianjin wenshi ziliao xuanji* (Selected materials on the culture and history of Tianjin)
WSZL   *Wenshi ziliao xuanji* (Selected materials on culture and history)
YWCA   Young Women's Christian Association
YSB   *Yishi bao*
ZMTS   *Zhongguo mianfang tongji shiliao* (Historical statistical material on Chinese cotton spinning)

INTRODUCTION

1. Thompson, *English Working Class*, 11.

2. *Ibid.*, 9–11. For a further discussion of Thompson's conceptualization of class, see his "Eighteenth Century English Society." See Note 9 below for extensions of Thompson's discussion to the female half of the working class.

3. "The working class made itself as much as it was made." *English Working Class*, 194.

4. In summarizing the entire development of working-class historiography in the past twenty years as an extension of Thompson's work, I am of course oversimplifying and risking distortion. Some of the most important contributors to the field, like E. J. Hobsbawm, are contemporaries rather than disciples of Thompson. Others, like Herbert Gutman, have been influenced deeply by Thompson but have produced work that is far more than derivative. Still others, like Peter Stearns, differ markedly from Thompson in scholarly approach and political orientation. Yet Thompson's work has been so influential that it seems to me the most useful starting point for a discussion of the field.

5. Representative works include Hanagan, *The Logic of Solidarity*; McDougall, "Consciousness and Community"; Scott, *The Glassworkers of Carmaux*; Sewell, "Social Change and the Rise of Working-Class Politics"; Bell, "Worker Culture and Worker Politics"; Louise Tilly, "*I fatti di maggio*"; Robert Johnson, *Peasant and Proletarian*; Koenker, *Moscow Workers*; Zelnik, *Labor and Society*; Montgomery, "To Study the People"; Gutman, *Work, Culture, and Society*; Rodgers, "Tradition, Modernity and the American Industrial Worker."

6. See, for example, the work of Gutman, Robert Johnson, and Koenker.

7. Representative works are those of Scott, Hanagan, Sewell; also Aminzade, "French Strike Development."

8. The work of Sewell, Robert Johnson, and Dublin, *Women at Work*, is exemplary in this respect.

9. Tilly and Scott, *Women, Work, and Family*; Dublin; Humphries, "Class Struggle"; Pleck, "Two Worlds in One"; Tilly, "Paths of Proletarianization" and "Women's Collective Action and Feminism in France, 1870–1914"; in Tilly and Tilly, eds., *Class Conflict*, 207–32.

10. See, for example, Bythell, *The Sweated Trades*.

11. Thompson, "Time, Work-Discipline, and Industrial Capitalism," 85 and *passim*; Hobsbawm, "Custom, Wages and Work-Load," in *Labouring Men*, 405–36; Gutman.

12. See, among others, Aminzade; Bonnell, *Roots of Rebellion*; Cronin, "Labor Insurgency and Class Formation" and "Theories of Strikes"; Hanagan and Stephenson, "The Skilled Worker"; Robert Johnson; Koenker; McDougall; Montgomery, "Strikes in Nineteenth-Century America"; Reddy, "Skeins, Scales, Discounts, Steam"; Sewell; Shorter and Tilly, *Strikes in France*; Zelnik.

13. Richard Johnson, "Thompson, Genovese, and Socialist-Humanist History," esp. 90–91, 97; also see letters and replies in *History Workshop*, Nos. 7–9 (1979–80).

14. For various perspectives on this criticism, see Fox-Genovese and Genovese, "Political Crisis of Social History"; Judt, "A Clown in Regal Purple"; Eley Nield, "Why Does Social History Ignore Politics?"; Hochstadt, "Social History and Politics."

15. Chesneaux, *The Chinese Labor Movement*; Shaffer, *Mao and the Workers*; Ming Chan, "Labor and Empire"; Thomas, *"Proletarian Hegemony"*. The work of the China Labor Movement History Research Group is published in their journal, *Chugoku rōdō undōshi kenkyū* (Research on China labor movement history), Nos. 1–12 (1977–83). Chesneaux, Shaffer, and Chan are ably summarized and discussed in Shaffer, "The Chinese Working Class." The classic studies of the Chinese labor movement are Nym Wales, *The Chinese Labor Movement*, and Deng Zhongxia, *Zhongguo zhigong yundong jianshi*.

16. A recent work that traces CCP policy toward labor through periods of both militance and quiescence is Thomas, *Labor and the Chinese Revolution*.

This Introduction does not discuss the work on labor history done in the PRC since 1949, although the case studies in this book do draw on and discuss some of those sources. Large numbers of interviews and documents were collected in the course of class education movements in the PRC. Most focus on the difficult daily lives of the workers, their formal labor activities, and the role of the CCP in organizing them. Although they provide material unobtainable elsewhere, they often reduce the dynamics of working-class struggle to the simple polarities of monolithic oppression and united resistance. The recent resurgence of the historical profession in China raises the possibility that working-class history may soon be investigated in a broader and deeper fashion by Chinese scholars.

17. Alistair Reid points out that lack of organization and action may be products of the way capitalism itself develops. Whereas Marx stressed the increasing homogeneity of the working class under capitalism, he put less emphasis on its tendencies toward fragmentation: an increasingly complex division of labor, "compounded by sexual and cultural divisions." The uneven development of capitalism makes machine operatives always a minority; workers compete with one another for employment; all of this suggests to Reid that "defeat is the normal . . . condition of the working class under capitalism," and that "without consciously formulated politics and alliances, it can only sustain short-term sectional revolts." Reid, "Politics and Economics," 359–61.

18. Strand, private communication, July 22, 1984; Selden, "The Proletariat," 111.

19. Eley and Nield, 270.

20. This point is well illustrated by the ongoing discussion of the militance of the Russian working class. Whereas the Bolsheviks explained the workers' revolutionary fervor as a sign of the maturing of the proletariat, scholars like Von Laue and Haimson have argued (as did the Mensheviks) that militance grew out of discontent brought in from the villages and exacerbated by the strains of factory life. Robert Johnson and Zelnik have each complicated the argument by suggesting that Russian workers did not travel a one-way road leading from village to factory, but maintained dual attachments and a mixed, often volatile, sense of injustice. Bonnell stresses the frustration of workers with trade union organizations; Koenker points to the incremental nature of the process by which workers were radicalized. Collectively, the meticulous research and varied conclusions of these scholars remind us that no single factor, either structural or ideological, can account for worker militance. See the works of these scholars listed in the Bibliography.

21. Strand has asked such questions about the genesis of protest among the rickshaw pullers of Beiping. Strand and Weiner, "Social Movements and Political Discourse."

22. A book on the women cotton mill workers of Shanghai that deals with these issues is Honig, *Sisters and Strangers*. The book had not yet been published at the time of this writing; all citations of this work are taken from the dissertation on which it was based.

23. For an eloquent warning against the notion of a depoliticized working-class culture, see Eley and Nield.

CHAPTER ONE

1. Michie, *Life in a China Outport* (McLeish, 1917), cited in O. D. Rasmussen, *Tientsin*, 37. The city was known as Tientsin by nineteenth- and twentieth-century Western residents; in the romanization system now in use in the PRC, the name is spelled Tianjin. The latter spelling is used throughout this study except when quoting pre-1949 Western sources.

2. In the Neolithic period, 5,000 years ago, the coastline near Tianjin was 50 kilometers farther west than it is today. Since 1957 archeologists have found four successive embankments of shells left behind as the coastline advanced. Tianjin [17]; interview with Li Shiyu, who discovered one of the original shell embankments, Oct. 21, 1980.

3. The total annual rainfall is 560 mm per year. Bao Juemin, "Tianjin zhi qihou." From the beginning of the Ming dynasty until 1949, there were 72 recorded floods in Tianjin. Qiao Hong, "Ming Qing yilai."

4. Rasmussen, 292.

5. My thanks to Wang Yufeng and Lu Xinmin respectively for writing these two rhymes down for me.

6. Cranmer-Byng, ed., *An Embassy to China*, 82.

7. Nieuhoff, "The Embassy of Peter de Goyer," 257.

8. Unless otherwise indicated, material for the following discussion on the early history of Tianjin is drawn from Tianjin [17], 1–25, and Tian Hongshi, "Tianjin gaishu."

9. Eberhard, *A History of China*, 266–67.

10. I am indebted to Carl Crook for first calling this rhyme to my attention.

11. See Linda Grove, "Managerial Practices among Traditional Merchants and Modern Capitalists in North China" (forthcoming), which will include a discussion of the Changlu salt merchants in Tianjin.

12. The system originated in Tianjin when a merchant buying dye from Sichuan had to pay for it with silver. Transporting silver from Tianjin to the interior was cumbersome and dangerous; the remittance system made it possible to transport paper drafts instead. These Shanxi banks remained very popular in Tianjin until the end of the nineteenth century. Shanxi merchants in Tianjin also dealt in satins, skins and furs, tea, and dry goods, and ran pawnshops. For further information about Shanxi banks in Tianjin, see Yang Lien-sheng, *Money and Credit in China*, 82–85. On other native banks in China, see *Tianjin wenshi ziliao xuanji* (hereafter *TJWS*), No. 20 (Aug. 1982), 90–168.

13. The two composite portraits of Tianjin that follow are based upon the following sources: Henry Ellis, *Journal of the . . . Late Embassy to China*; Sir George Staunton, *An Authentic Account*, I, 279; a tour of Tianjin given Linda Grove and me by Bao Juemin, Jan. 24, 1980; Wang Xiushun and Zhang Gaofeng, "Tianjin zaoqi," *TJWS*, No. 16 (Aug. 1981), 61–73; interview with Xu Jingxing, May 19,

1981; and my own two years' residence in Tianjin. Other published sources are cited where appropriate.

14. Staunton, 256.

15. Cranmer-Byng, 83; Staunton, 278–79.

16. Ellis, 69.   17. *Ibid.*, 69–70.

18. Staunton, 276.   19. *Ibid.*, 268–69.

20. *Ibid.*, 276. Spellings in this and subsequent quotations are reproduced from the original texts.

21. Ellis, 155.

22. *Ibid.*, 154.

23. *Ibid.*, 155.

24. Tianhou is supposed to have been born in the first year of the Song dynasty in the county of Putian near the Fujian coast. By 987 she was being worshiped as a local spirit who had jurisdiction over drought and rain, boats, pestilence, and male offspring. The location of her native place near the sea accounted for her early association with sailors. After the Southern Song, her influence spread. In the Yuan, with the policy of sea transport for grain from the south, she became the highest protective spirit for seagoers and her other duties faded. Later her powers re-expanded to include the protection of children and smallpox vaccinations. With the advent of steamships and increased safety in shipping, she became exclusively a provider of sons. Yu Henian, "Tianjin Tianhou gong kao."

25. Wang Yuanzeng, cited in *Tianjin ribao*, March 9, 1980.

26. Population figures from 1860 to 1937, not including the foreign concessions, may be found in the *Chinese Economic Journal and Bulletin*, 20, No. 3 (March 1937). Figures from 1938 to 1947 are cited in Tianjin [20], 2. The population of the foreign concessions from 1927 to 1939 is given in *CYB*: 1928, 915–16; 1931, 73–74; 1935, 347; 1939, 158–59; Tenshin Nihon shōgyō kaigishō, *Tenshin shōgyō annai furoku*, 7. In 1927 Tianjin ranked after Wuhan, Shanghai, Hangzhou, and Guangzhou; Tenshin Nihon shōgyō kaigishō, *Tenshin gaikan*, 6. In 1935 it ranked after Shanghai and Beiping; Zai Tenshin Nippon taikoku soryojikan, 16, hereafter Zai Tenshin. In 1947 it ranked after Shanghai only, and was followed by Beiping, Guangzhou, Shenyang, Nanjing, and Chongqing; Tianjin [20], 2.

27. The Chinese coast north of the Qiantang River was mostly sand, except for the Shandong peninsula, and there were not many good port sites. The Nanyun, Beiyun, Daqing, and Ziya rivers were all used for internal river shipping in the first half of the twentieth century; the Yongding was only deep enough for small boats; Bao Juemin, "Tianjin gangkou" and "Tianjin zhi qihou"; Rasmussen, 103. Pre-1949 attempts to bring the Hai River under control are described in Feng Guoliang and Guo Tingxin, "Jiefangqian Haihe."

28. Liu Guhou, "Tianjin gongshangye de niaokan," 3; Wang Huaiyuan, "Jiu Zhongguo shiqi Tianjin," Part 1, 85; Bao, "Tianjin gangkou."

29. Rev. John Innocent, *The Chinese Times*, 1890, cited in Rasmussen, 37–38; Michie, *The Chinese Times*, Nov. 3, 1888, cited in *ibid.*, 44. For the dates on which the concessions were ceded, expanded, and returned to China, see Hershatter, "The Making of the Working Class," 458.

30. Drake, *Map and Short Description*, 3; *Peking and the Overland Route*, 121. On the growth of the British concession, see *TJWS*, No. 9 (June 1980), 1–53. For a memoir of life in the British concession during this period, see Hersey, "Homecoming."

31. The first foreign newspaper in Tianjin was *The Chinese Times*, which ran from 1886 to 1891. Further information about the Tianjin press can be found in Rasmussen, 109–11, 259–63; Albert Feuerwerker, *The Foreign Establishment in China*, 109; Arnold, *Commercial Handbook of China*, I, 312ff.; Wang Yunsheng and Cao Gubing, "Ying Lianzhi," and three recent articles in *TJWS*, No. 18 (Jan. 1982), 39–110.

32. Interview with Israel Epstein, Dec. 7, 1980.

33. *TJWS*, No. 3 (June 1979), 106–14; interview with Israel Epstein, Feb. 7, 1980. On non-Jewish Russians in Tianjin, see Du Lijun, "Bai E zai Tianjin."

34. The Tianjin Massacre is treated in detail in several English-language works. For a recapitulation of contemporary accounts, see Rasmussen, 45–53. Scholarly accounts include Paul Cohen, *China and Christianity*, 229–61, and John K. Fairbank, "Patterns Behind the Tientsin Massacre." For more general background on missionary activities in Tianjin, see Rasmussen, 247–58. A recent account appears in three articles in the *TJWS*, No. 2 (Feb. 1979), 142–87.

35. Gao Bohai, "Tianjin maiban Gao Xingqiao fajiashi." On the development of the Japanese concession area, see Sun Limin and Xin Gongxian, "Tianjin Rizujie gaikuang"; on the development of the Quanyechang commercial quarter, see Zhang Gaofeng, "Quanyechang yidai de bianqian."

36. *Peking and the Overland Route*, 119. Accounts of the Boxer Rebellion in Tianjin include Rasmussen, 113–230, who reproduces an eyewitness account of the siege by William McLeish; three short memoirs in *TJWS*, No. 8 (April 1980), 8–19; and an extensive account based on interviews with former Boxers, written at Nankai University in 1956: Nankai daxue [3].

37. Bao Juemin, "Tianjin gangkou."

38. *Jicha diaocha tongji congkan*, 1, No. 5 (Nov. 1936), 7. Tianjin was the provincial capital from 1913 to 1935, first of Zhili and after 1928 of Hebei. During the warlord conflicts of the early 1920's, many northeast corner merchants moved to the protected business environment of the concession areas, and the northeast corner declined once again. Wang Xiushun and Zhang Gaofeng, 71–72.

39. "Zhongshan Lu man bu" (A Stroll Along Zhongshan Road), *Tianjin ribao*, Sept. 25, 1980; Nankai daxue [2].

40. For a history of Nankai University, see *Nankai daxue* [4]. For a series of short reminiscences, devoted mostly to the career of Nankai president Zhang Boling, see *TJWS*, No. 8 (April 1980), 72–211.

CHAPTER TWO

1. Rasmussen, 283.

2. Wang Huaiyuan, I, 70. For a more detailed discussion of foreign trade in Tianjin, see Hershatter, "The Making of the Working Class," 32–38, 460–61.

3. On the total value of trade from 1867 to 1948, see Hsiao Ling-lin, *China's Foreign Trade Statistics*, 177–78.

4. Wang Huaiyuan, I, 78–80; II, 3, 33. On the munitions trade, see Mi Luzhai, "Yan Xishan," 66–68.

5. Wang Huaiyuan, I, 74–75; II, 40–42, 44. In 1936, about one-fifth of North China's total agricultural and pastoral production was traded through Tianjin. Half was exported, a quarter transshipped, and a quarter consumed in Tianjin. Zai Tenshin, 19–22, gives a detailed breakdown of 1936 imports and exports.

6. For an analysis of Tianjin trade during the Depression, see Wu Ziguang, "Jingji konghuangzhong Tianjin," 1–11. Imports in 1936 showed a 12.6 million yuan drop from 1935 levels, much of it caused by a diversion of goods into smuggling. Wang Huaiyuan, II, 33.

7. Hershatter, "The Making of the Working Class," 37; Zai Tenshin, 16.

8. Zai Tenshin, 16, 31–42; Wang Huaiyuan, III, 98–106.

9. On the Customs Service, see Li Bingzhi, "Diguozhuyi kongzhixia Tianjin," 54–68.

10. Tian, 10; *JJZK*, No. 51 (Feb. 21, 1934); Wang Huaiyuan, I, 85; II, 32, 43; III, 109; Liu Guhou, "Tianjin gongshangye zhi niaokan," 3–5; *CYB 1921–22*, 768; Chesneaux, *Chinese Labor Movement*, 35.

11. The history and activities of several of Tianjin's foreign firms, and the careers of their compradores, are given in *TJWS*, No. 9 (June 1980), 79–145.

12. Ruan Weijing, "Meishang Da Lai Yanghang"; Wang Huaiyuan, II, 32. For a history of another foreign firm see Huang Xianting, "Sanshi nianlai yingshang."

13. Major Tianjin banks included the Hong Kong and Shanghai Banking Corporation (British, founded 1880), the Chartered Bank of India, Australia, and China (British, 1882), the Deutsch-Asiatische (German, 1897), Yokohama Specie Bank (Japanese, 1898), Russo-Asiatic (Russian, 1897), and City Bank (U.S., 1913); Tian, 6; *JJZK*, No. 49 (Jan. 31, 1934); Wang Huaiyuan, II, 32; *TJWS*, No. 9, 69–78; Wu Shicheng, "Tianjin zhi zhibi," 27–33; Chang Nan, "Yingguo Huifeng Yinhang de jingji lüeduo."

14. Tian, 7; Tianjin [8], 199–209, 231–51; Nankai daxue [2]; Zheng Yufu, *Tianjin youlan zhi*, 201–4; Xu Jingxing, "Tianjin jindai gongye," 137–39; Li Shaomi and Ni Jinjun, "Tianjin zilaishui shiye jianshi."

15. Rasmussen, 83, 286; *CYB 1914*, 106; *CYB 1924*, 225; Xu Jingxing, "Tianjin jindai gongye," 134–36.

16. Of the egg factories, the British-owned International Export Company, or *Heji Yanghang*, is perhaps the most famous. See Liao Yizhong, Lu Wanhe, and Yang Sishen, eds., "Tianjin Heji Yanghang shiliao." On the egg export trade, see *CEJ*, 11, No. 3 (Sept. 1932), 172, and *Chinese Economic Journal and Bulletin*, 14, No. 3 (Sept. 1936), 213. On nut sorting, see *Chinese Economic Journal and Bulletin*, 4, No. 5 (May 1929), 433, and *CEB*, 16, No. 18 (May 3, 1930), 223–26. On the British and American Tobacco Company, see Cochran, *Big Business in China*; and Xiao Zhuwen, "Tianjin Yingmei Yangongsi." The Kailuan mines had their offices in Tianjin but their mining operations in Tangshan. Since they did not directly affect the development of the Tianjin working class, they are not discussed here as a Tianjin industrial investment.

17. *JJZK*, No. 51 (Feb. 21, 1934). A statistical analysis of foreign investment in Tianjin on the eve of the war is given in Wang Huaiyuan, II, 29. For a list of major foreign enterprises and their levels of capitalization, see Zai Tenshin, 13–16.

18. The classic discussion of joint official-merchant enterprises is Feuerwerker, *China's Early Industrialization*.

19. On Li Hongzhang's activities in Tianjin, see Spector, *Li Hongzhang and the Huai Army*, 139, 160–63; Tian, 7; Hummel, *Eminent Chinese*, 466; Xu Jingxing, "Tianjin jindai gongye," 125–34; Tianjin [8], 179–88.

20. Xu Jingxing, "Tianjin jindai gongye," 125–34; interview with Xu Jingxing, May 10, 1981. By "modern," Xu means "factories that use power and machines to engage in production and hire a large number of workers." He adds, how-

ever, that the arsenal was not a capitalist enterprise since it did not engage in commodity production, exchange, or profit-making.

21. Interview with Bian Huixin, conducted by Linda Grove and myself, March 17, 1980.

22. MacKinnon, *Power and Politics*, 37–61 and 163–79. MacKinnon argues that "the political power structure of late Imperial China fell, in the North especially, with Yuan Shikai in 1916 and not with the dynasty in 1911–12" (234). My own examination of events in Tianjin confirms that little changed locally in 1911, particularly with respect to industry and commerce. Because Yuan's career and that of his chief industrial assistant, Zhou Xuexi, span both sides of the 1911 divide, I have treated them here as a transitional group between Qing officials and Beiyang warlords. Also see Ch'en, *Yuan Shih-k'ai*, 55–76.

23. For information about Zhou's career, see Zhu Chunfu, "Zhou Xuexi"; Tian, 7–11; MacKinnon, 163–79; Xu Jingxing, "Tianjin jindai gongye," 142–45; Li Zhidao, "Zhongguo shiye yinhang"; Tianjin [8], 162–78; Rasmussen, 269–71.

24. MacKinnon, 163–65, 173.

25. For a summary of the period and the secondary literature in English, see Sheridan, *China in Disintegration*, 20, 57–106, 298–300.

26. This discussion of warlord economic activities is based upon the following sources: Zhu Chunfu, "Beiyang junfa dui Tianjin"; Zhao Shixian, "Junfa Wang Zhanyuan"; Dong Quanfu and Liu Shenzhi, "Cao Kun jiazu"; Chen Shiru, "Cao Kun jiazu dui renmin"; Wang Zishou, "Tianjin diandangye"; Ji Hua, "Ni Sichong"; He Chengruo, "Ni Sichong zai Anhui." Gold dollar equivalents are given in Lee, 44; and National Government, 152–56.

27. Liu Guhou, "Tianjin gongshangye zhi niaokan," 6.

28. See, for example, two articles on the activities of Yan Xishan in Tianjin from 1928 to 1937: Yan Zifeng, "Yan Xishan"; and Mi Luzhai, "Yan Xishan."

29. For further information on the salt merchants and the "eight great families," see *TJWS*, No. 20 (Aug. 1982), 39–89, and the forthcoming work by Grove. Two case studies of wealthy twentieth-century merchants and their investments are Sun Jingzhi, "Yuanlong zhoubudian"; and Cai Muhan, "'Shenfang Cai' fajiashi."

30. For a discussion in English of the role of compradores, see Hao Yen-p'ing, *The Compradore in Nineteenth Century China*.

31. Yan Yiwen, "Sishi nian maiban"; Bi Mingqi, "Tianjin de yanghang"; Gao Bohai, "Tianjin maiban"; Liang Peiyu, "Tianjin Yihe Yanghang"; Zheng Zhizhang, "Tianjin Taigu Yanghang"; and Wei Bogang, "Tianjin Hengbin zhengjin."

32. Interview with Bian Huixin; Tianjin [3], 10.

33. Xu Jingxing, "Tianjin jindai gongye," 140–42; Wu Huan, "Guanyu wo fu Wu Diaoqing"; Rasmussen, 268–69.

34. *CEB*, 10, No. 315 (March 5, 1927), 28; Yan Yiwen, 264.

35. Interview with Xu Jingxing, May 10, 1981.

36. The conditions summarized in this section are discussed in greater detail in Hershatter, "The Making of the Working Class," 161–83.

37. See Note 26 above for references to the economic activities of warlords in Tianjin. For additional material on the involvement of warlords in the cotton mills, see Wang Jinghang and Zhang Zesheng, "Yu Yuan shachang," 173–74; Xia Shaoquan, "Guanyu Zhou Xuexi"; Nankai daxue [2]; Zhu Mengsu, "Tianjin Bei Yang shachang yange," 196; Lu Luyuan, "Bei Yang shachang," 129–30.

38. Nankai daxue [2]; Huashang shachang lianhehui, *Zhongguo mianchan tongji*,

1–5; *Jingji yanjiu zhoukan*, Nos. 30, 31 (Sept. 21, 28, 1930); Fang Xianting, "Zhongguo mian fangzhiye"; Dong Quanfu and Liu Shenzhi, 96; H. D. Fong [2], 2.

39. From 1919 to 1932, foreign exporters bought more than two-thirds of the cotton traded in Tianjin for shipment overseas and to other Chinese ports. Fang Xianting, "Tianjin mianhua yunxiao gaikuang."

40. Dong Quanfu, 96–97; *CEB*, No. 196 (Nov. 22, 1924), 10; Minami manshū tetsudō kabushiki kaisha, *Hokushina kōjō jittai*, 28; Liu Guhou, "Tianjin gong-shangye de weiji," 44; Fong [2], 1.

41. The discussion that follows is based upon Leonard T. K. Wu, "The Crisis in the Chinese Cotton Industry," as well as upon the specific citations given.

42. For data on the price decline, see Tianjin [9], 564; and He Lian, "Bai yin zhengshui."

43. A 1932 study of 122 textile mills in China yielded the following figures on capitalization of cotton mills:

Ownership	Number of factories	Avg. capital per factory (yuan)
Chinese	78	1,836,911
British	3	4,720,767
Japanese	41	9,061,869
TOTAL	122	AVG. 4,335,885

Fang Xianting and Chen Zhenhan, "Zhongguo gongye xianyou kunnan de fenxi." On Japanese and Shanghai yarn, see Wang Zijian, *Minguo 23 nian de Zhongguo*, 44–45. In 1929, two years before the invasion of the Northeast, 13.51 percent of Chinese textiles were going to Northeast markets. For individual Tianjin mills like Bao Cheng, the percentage was much higher. Fang Xianting, "Zhongguo mian fangzhiye"; Tianjin [9], 563.

44. Leonard Wu; Fang Xianting, "Zhongguo mian fangzhiye," 188; Wan Xin-quan, "Tianjin shi shuijian gaikuang," 1.

45. Leonard Wu. For a comparison of the average output per spindle per day of Japanese- and Chinese-owned mills in Shanghai and Tianjin, see H. D. Fong [1], 95. For a comparison of weaver productivity in Japanese- and Chinese-owned mills, see Fang Xianting, "Zhongguo mian fangzhiye."

46. For an analysis of the shortage of circulating capital, see Ding Gu, "Zhong-guo gongye de liudong"; and Fang Xianting, "Zhongguo mian fangzhiye." For a detailed account of the problems of the Yu Yuan mill, see H. D. Fong [2], 2; Tian-jin [9], 562–63; Wang Jinghang, 175–79; Mian Er, *Changshi 1918–1949*, 9–10, 55–57.

47. Fong [1], I, 319, cited in Fong [4]. The mention of the contract labor system refers to practices in Shanghai, not Tianjin. For a further discussion of manage-ment problems see Du Wensi, *Ping Jin gongye diaocha*, 23–24. For an account of this type of management system in the Heng Yuan Mill, see Dong Quanfu and Liu Shenzhi, 97–99.

48. For details on this crisis, see Hershatter, "The Making of the Working Class," 174–75.

49. "Japan Developing North China Cotton Industry," *Far Eastern Survey*, 5, No. 17 (Aug. 12, 1936), 185; "Tientsin Slowly Emerging as a New Textile Center," *Far Eastern Survey*, 6, No. 1 (Jan. 6, 1937), 11. For details of the Yu Yuan pur-

chase, see Tianjin [9], 561–63, and Wang Jinghang and Zhang Zesheng, 178–79. On new mills, see Minami manshū, 31–32; "Japan Developing North China Cotton Industry" (cited above); "Tientsin Slowly Emerging" (cited above); Rockwood Q. P. Chin, "Cotton Mills, Japan's Economic Spearhead," *Far Eastern Survey*, 6, No. 23 (Nov. 17, 1937), 263.

50. This percentage is derived from figures given in Minami manshū, 26, 30–33, and 36, and differs from figures given in Shanghai shi mian fangzhi, *Zhongguo mianfang tongji shiliao*, hereafter *ZMTS*.

51. Zhang Xuyu, "Wo shi yige fangzhiye de gongren," 12; Minami manshū, 37, 49, 86; Lu Luyuan, 132.

52. Ji Guangzhi, "Jiu Zhongguo shiqi de Tianjin," 21.

53. Zhu Mengsu, 200; Tianjin [12], 99. For a mill-by-mill account of late wartime troubles, see Tianjin [4], 195–201; Dong Quanfu and Liu Shenzhi, 111. The estimates of spindle capacity are from Li Luozhi and Nie Tanggu, *Tianjin de jingji diwei*, 252. This work, sponsored by the Nationalist government at the end of the war, indicates that the 1942 figure is for Japanese-owned mills only, but gives no source for either figure. Despite the problems in making exact statements, it seems safe to say that there was a dramatic increase in spindle capacity until the outbreak of the Pacific War, and then a decrease because of the meltdowns, but that the occupation nevertheless brought a net increase in spindle capacity to Tianjin. The estimates of spindles and looms in operation at war's end include only the Japanese-owned mills, so the actual figures must have been higher. "Report of the China Textile Industries, Inc., for 1946," cited in China Correspondent Monthly Reports (April 1947), C13/2/75, ILO Archives, Geneva, 3.

54. *Ibid.*, 2, 3, 9. The Yu Da and Bao Cheng mills became part of a single enterprise.

55. Barnett, *China on the Eve of Communist Takeover*, 57, 56; Gao Erfu et al., "Jiefang qianxi yanyan yixi."

56. "Report of the China Textile Industries," 4, 15; Tianjin [4], 196.

57. Barnett, 56. Power was supplied by the Jibei Dianli Gongsi, a government-operated utility. Mian Si (Cotton Mill #4), "1946 nian ben chang," and "1947 nian ben chang," Bao Jingdi, in *Fangzhi jianshe* (Oct. 15, 1948), cited in *BGCQ*, 2, No. 1 (Jan. 1960), 102.

58. *BGCQ*, 2, No. 1, 103.

59. *Ibid.*, 105. According to Barnett (53–54) the Tianjin business community believed that this discrimination against Tianjin was intentional. Since import quotas for each region were set nationally, they asserted, the government was using the system to favor the "business interests of government officials in Shanghai," and to keep the risks to government investment to a minimum in the politically precarious North.

60. A cogent discussion of various definitions of imperialism as applied to China can be found in Cochran, 5–6, 202–7.

61. He Chengruo, "Ni Sichong," 189; Liu Guhou, "Tianjin gongshangye de weiji," 44; Fang Xianting and Chen Zhenhan, "Zhongguo gongye xianyou"; Wu Ao [2], 1–4.

62. For an example of this argument see Lu Dangping, "Fazhan Tianjin gongshangye," 1–4. In 1929 Lu observed that outside the concessions, Tianjin had 2,148 factories, with capital totaling 31,406,944 yuan, or about 10,000 yuan

apiece. The city had 20,000 stores, with a total capital of 22,230,468 yuan, or about 1,000 yuan apiece.

CHAPTER THREE

1. For a preliminary discussion of all these sectors of the labor force, see Lieberthal, *Revolution and Tradition*, 11–25.

2. In carpet weaving, however, 22 of 303 workshops employed more than 100 workers. *NWSS*, 2, 29 (Oct. 28, 1929), 4. For statistics on the number of workers per enterprise, see H. D. Fong [7], [3], and [6]; Du Wensi, *Pingjin gongye diaocha*, 61–79; *CEJ passim*; *CEB passim*.

3. Almost 7,000 additional carpet weavers went uncounted in the survey on which these figures are based (see source note to Table 2). When other industries like brick-, button-, and glass-making, electroplating, mat weaving, soapmaking, and tanning are included, the total number of artisans may be as high as 30,000. *NWSS*, 3, No. 42 (Oct. 20, 1930), 201, 204; *CEJ passim*; *CEB passim*.

4. Fong [3], *passim*; *CEB*, 1924–35 *passim*; *CEJ*, 1927–32 *passim*; *CYB*, 1912–39 *passim*.

5. Later it was disrupted by warlord conflicts, the worldwide Depression, and the Pacific war. Fong [7], 13; Rui Chongzhi, "Tianjin ditan gongyede xingqi."

6. Fong [6], 24.

7. Just before the Japanese invasion, for instance, tanneries and weaving workshops suffered from the loss of the Manchurian market, Japanese smuggling, and heavy Guomindang taxation. At the same time the ironworking industry, apparently unaffected by all these factors, entered one of its most prosperous periods (see Chapter 4). See *Guoji laogong tongxun*, 16 (Jan. 1936), 46, 57, 73; 18 (March 1936), 84; and 22 (July 1936), 60.

8. Fong [3], 25.

9. Lieberthal found that in 1943 and 1949, more than half the workforce was employed in small or medium-sized enterprises. Lieberthal, *Revolution and Tradition*, 12; and "Reconstruction and Revolution," 27–29.

10. In 1928 the six mills had 226,808 spindles and 1,310 power looms. Nationally, Tianjin accounted for about 6 percent of China's total spindle capacity and 6–7 percent of the national mill workforce from 1924 to 1930. It ranked third or fourth among national textile centers, after Shanghai, Wuhan, and in some years Qingdao. Tianjin cotton mills in 1928 consumed 6.73 percent of the raw cotton used by all Chinese mills, producing 6.03 percent of the yarn and 5.94 percent of the cloth. During the same period, Shanghai accounted for more than half the nation's spindles and millhands. On the national standing of Tianjin and Shanghai, see H. D. Fong [1], 16f, 114. On capitalization and size of the workforce, see H. D. Fong [5], 10. Spindlage and percentages of national raw material are given in *NWSS*, 2, No. 28 (Oct. 21, 1929), 1. The number of looms and Tianjin's percentage of the national workforce are given in *ZMTS*, 5, 11, 15. The percentage of industrial investment is for the year 1929, and is derived from Wu Ao [4]. Statistics on motor power are from a Bureau of Social Affairs 1933 survey, cited in *BGCQ*, 2, No. 1, 93. The sexual composition of the workforce is derived from Wu Ao [4], Tianjin [19].

11. Between 1915 and 1925, ten flour mills were built in Tianjin, although a

resurgence in foreign flour imports after World War I forced six of them to close by 1932. Dong Changyan, *Tianjin mianfen gongye zhuangkuang*, 9–10, 14, 16, 20; Wu Ao [4]; Tianjin [19].

12. The match industry in 1928 had five plants and a total capital of 1.5 million yuan, more than half of it divided between two of the factories, Tan Hua and Bei Yang. Wu Ao [2], 6, 29, 45; Wu Ao [4]; Tianjin [19].

13. One cotton mill, the Yu Da, and one match factory had substantial amounts of Japanese capital. On cotton see Chapters 2 and 6; on matches, see Wu Ao [2], 58–59. The British and American Tobacco Company (BAT) opened a Tianjin branch in 1921 on the banks of the Hai River. By 1930 it employed about 4,000 workers. The Japanese-owned Tōa Company, opened in 1918, also had several thousand workers. Xiao Zhuwen, "Tianjin Yingmei Yan Gongsi," 168–69; *CYB*, *1931*, 523–24. On BAT operations in China, see Sherman Cochran, *Big Business in China*. All available investment figures are for BAT as a whole, not just the Tianjin plant. On the Tōa Company, see Zheng Qinan, "Jingji bu jieshou," 14.

14. On cotton mills, see Chapter 2. On flour, see Gao Erfu, 160–63, and Du Wensi, 3. On matches, see Wu Ao [2], 59. On tobacco, see Xiao Zhuwen, 169; Zheng Qinan, 14; and Gao Erfu, 163–66.

15. Wu Ao [4]; Tianjin [19]. But the number of women in all sectors of the workforce was consistently underestimated in social surveys. In 1929, for instance, the Bureau of Social Affairs found only 2,606 women in the industrial workforce, most of them in the textile mills. Yet the 1927–28 study of women industrial workers by T'ao Ling and Lydia Johnson, which covered cotton mills, military uniform factories, wool spinning factories, match factories, walnut warehouses, tobacco factories, and a variety of other establishments, found 10,450 women and girls employed. The authors believed that this was only a fraction of those actually working. *NWSS*, 3, No. 17 (April 28, 1930), 85–86; Lydia Johnson, letter to Sarah Lyon, Dec. 1, 1927, World YWCA Archives, Geneva, China 1926–29: Correspondence, Minutes, Reports III, mimeo.; T'ao Ling and Lydia Johnson, "A Study of Women and Girls," 519–28. For further discussion of the role of women in the Tianjin workforce, see H. D. Fong [5], 21; and [7], 23–24; *YSB*, March 26, 1937, 5; Zhang Xuyu, "Wo shi yige fangzhiye de gongren," 12; *YSB*, Aug. 26, 1947, 4, Sept. 1, 1947, 4.

16. H. D. Fong found in 1929–30 that 94 percent of the hosiery knitters, 92 percent of the carpet workers, and 77 percent of the handloom weavers were from the Hebei countryside. Most of the remainder came from Shandong. Apprentices showed approximately the same pattern. Ninety-six percent of the hosiery knitters who were not Tianjin natives had resided in the city for ten years or less; the figure for handloom weavers was 86 percent. H. D. Fong [3], 64; [7], 55; [6], 50, 63.

17. Fong [7], 55; [3], 64; on ironworkers, see Chapter 4.

18. Fong [7], 46; [6], 53; [3], 59.

19. "Wages in Tientsin Industries," *Chinese Economic Monthly*, 3, No. 10 (Oct. 1926), 418; H. D. Fong [1], 115; Minami manshū, 57–59, 108; Wu Ao [1], 208. No similar data exist for the flour and match industries, although a 1931 survey of one flour mill found that half the workers were from Tianjin county and nearby Jinghai county, with the rest from scattered Hebei and Shandong counties. Wu Ao [3], 62.

20. Wu Ao [4], section on *hukou* (population).

21. Wu Ao [1], 195; Tianjin [23], 35.

22. Interview with Ji Kailin, Nankai Daxue jingji yanjiusuo, Dec. 29, 1980.

23. Wu Ao [1], 208; interview with Gao Fengqi, Jan. 17, 1981; Ji Kailin.

24. Fong [7], 54, 42; [6], 23; [3], 67; *CEB*, 9, No. 305 (Dec. 25, 1926), 371–72; 11, No. 344 (Sept. 24, 1927), 168–69; 10, No. 314 (Dec. 26, 1927), 105–6; 10, No. 308 (Jan. 15, 1927), 36; Nankai Daxue [2]; Du Wensi, 61–79.

25. Fong [7], 57–59; [6], 63–67; [3], 63–67. On apprenticeship conditions in the ironworking and machine-making industries, see Chapter 4 below.

26. On the unemployment of former apprentices, see Fong [7], 67, and Chapter 4 below.

27. Wu Ao [4]; Fong [6], 51; [7], 44; [3], 58.

28. *Baogong huikan*, 160 (Dec. 1926), cited in Wang Qingbin, *Diyici laodong nianjian*, 570–71; Zhou Xuehui, "Tianjin Hua Xin Fangzhi Gongsi shimo" (The Story of the Hua Xin Spinning Company in Tianjin), cited in Zhu Chunfu, "Beiyang junfa dui Tianjin," 26; Wang Jinghang and Zhang Zesheng, 174; Mian Er, *Changshi 1918–1949*, 17–18. The terms "apprentice" (*xuetu* or *tugong*) and "child worker" (*tonggong*) are used interchangeably in the sources for the period before the occupation. Another term, "trainee" (*yangchenggong*), came into use under the Japanese and persisted until Liberation. It, too, is used loosely to refer to all young workers. This relaxed use of terms makes it difficult to determine how many child workers were unpaid but taught a skill, and how many were paid a pittance to perform odd jobs.

29. *Baogong huikan*, 571.

30. Nagano Hogara, *Shina rōdōsha yo rōdō undō* (Chinese laborers and the labor movement) (1925), cited in Wang Qingbin, 228. In the original, the columns for workers under and over 15 were mistakenly reversed, giving the impression that child workers were consistently paid higher wages than adults.

31. Wu Ao [1], 12, 39–44; Deng Qinglan, ed., *Tianjin shi dierci*, 67. Both surveys were sponsored by the municipal Bureau of Social Affairs; the 1933 survey did not include weavers. Although the 1929 figures showed a decline from 1926 levels, they were high compared to the percentage of child labor in mills in Shanghai (5.7 percent), Wuhan (4.6 percent), and Qingdao (7.3 percent). Given the low percentage of women workers in the Tianjin mills at this time, it may be that young male workers partially fulfilled their role. Fong [1], 149.

32. Ji Kailin; interview with Zhang Chunfeng, Jan. 21, 1981; interview with Cheng Changli, Jan. 17, 1981; Gao Fengqi; interview with Han Ruixiang, April 1, 1981.

33. Interview with Zhang Wenqing, Cotton Mill #2, Jan. 21, 1981.

34. Han Ruixiang, April 1, 1981.

35. Ji Kailin.

36. Han Ruixiang, April 1, 1981; Mian Si, "1946 nian." On a similar situation in Shanghai, see Honig, "Women Cotton Mill Workers," Chapter 2.

37. Fong [1], 116.

38. On the experience of women cotton mill workers in Shanghai, see Honig, "Women Cotton Mill Workers." The other southern mill centers were not far behind: 68 percent of Wuxi millhands were women, and the percentages for Nantong and Wuhan were 56.5 and 42.4. Fong [1], 149.

39. In 1930, women made up only 6.4 percent of the Qingdao cotton mill workforce. Fong [1], 149; Minami manshū, 57–59, 92, 102, 111, 118, 128, 131, 135,

145, 150, 153; Tianjin [4], 123, 195–200. In the latter two surveys, children were not listed separately from adult men and women.

40. Yet in North China, Japanese ownership did not at first lead to increased female employment. In Qingdao, where there was substantial Japanese investment in the textile mills in the 1920's, the millhands were almost all men. And in the Yu Da Mill in Tianjin, in spite of Japanese investment and management as early as 1926, by 1929 women accounted for only slightly more than 7 percent of the workforce. Fong [1], 149; Wu Ao [1], 12, 39–41.

41. Honig, Chapters 2 and 5.

42. Women with bound feet numbered 146,191 of a total female population of 543,366. Wu Ao [4], section on *hukou*. Also see Elizabeth C. Wright, "Annual Report, Tientsin, 1921," World YWCA Archives, Geneva, China 1920–1922: Reports, mimeo., 3/68, 2; Israel Epstein; Honig, Chapter 1.

43. A survey of 87 male cotton workers and their families conducted in Tianjin in 1929–30 found that husbands provided 74.7 percent of the family income, whereas wives and children of both sexes contributed only 16.5 percent. (The remainder came from other household members and from nonwage sources.) Although it is not specified what work these wives and children did, the small percentage of total family income they earned leads one to surmise that they took in handicraft work on a piecework basis or joined the city's casual labor force, rather than working at full-time factory jobs. Fong [1], 136. For a comparison with income contributed by working women in Shanghai, see Honig, Chapter 5.

44. Honig, Chapter 1.

45. Fong [3], 58; [7], 45; [6], 51.

46. On 1938 sex ratios, see Tianjin [26], II, 5–6. The district numbering system for the 1930's and the Japanese occupation, and the industry distribution within each district, are derived from Deng Qinglan, 5, and Tianjin [25], 10.

47. *CEB passim, CEJ passim*, Du Wensi, 61–79; Fong [6], 19; [7], 48; [3], 27; Li Pu Lung, *The Brick Industry*, 6.

48. Wu Ao [3], 12, 42, 50, 62; [2], 30, 45; [1], 39–41, 49.

49. Zhang Wenqing; Han Ruixiang, April 1, 1981; interview with Li Guilan, Cotton Mill #4, June 16, 1980; interview with Zhang Jiagui, Cotton Mill #2, Jan. 17, 1981; Zhang Chunfeng; Honig, Chapter 5.

50. Han Ruixiang, April 1, 1981; Zhang Chunfeng; Gao Fengqi; Ji Kailin.

51. Derived from statistics in Fong [5], 17–19.

52. Fong [6], 60, 53–55; [7], 46–47; [3], 60.

53. Wu Ao [1], 70. In 1929 Fong examined records of four Tianjin mills and discovered that the number of millhands who left in a given year ranged from a low of 6.6 percent to a high of more than 75 percent. The separation rate was high, unstable, and occasionally must have reflected major upheavals at a particular mill. Fong [1], 121. For another argument that the turnover rate was high during this period, see Mian Er, *Changshi*, 12.

54. Fong [1], 122.

55. *Ibid.*, 123–24.

56. Han Ruixiang, April 1, 1981.

57. Interview with Chen Zhi, June 16, 1980.

58. Han Ruixiang, April 1, 1981.   59. *Ibid.*; Zhang Chunfeng.

60. Han Ruixiang, April 1, 1981.   61. T'ao and Johnson, 522.

62. Colonel C. L'Estrange Malone, *New China, Part II*, 13–14.

63. Lydia Johnson, letter to Mary Dingman, May 20, 1931, Box 11/115, World YWCA Archives, Geneva.

64. Such interviews reflect more than 30 years of political education about the misery of workers in "the old China." Interviewees frequently point out that their social status was low: "The term 'stinking' was added to the term 'worker.' In society the idea was current that good people didn't become workers, good iron didn't make nails" (Ji Kailin). It is not clear, however, that consciousness of their low social status was of daily concern to them at the time. The only means of ascertaining the attitudes of workers toward their jobs before Liberation is to invite comparisons with other jobs they might have been able to find.

65. Han Ruixiang, April 1, 1981. Han was literate and held a low-level staff position in a cotton mill, and so the jobs he could hope to find differed from those available to most millhands.

66. Interview with Xu Jingxing, May 10, 1981; Han Ruixiang, April 1, 1981.

67. Chen Zhi.

68. Interview with Chen Yihe, April 18, 1980.

69. Chen Zhi.

70. Gao Fengqi.

71. On women in the Tianjin manufacturing sector, see T'ao and Johnson, 521–25. On the tobacco factories, see Xiao Zhuwen, 181–84. On women in the egg industry, see Liu Chin-t'ao, *Egg Industry in Tientsin*, 8; and Liao Yizhong et al., "Tianjin Heji Yanghang," 60–69. For a comprehensive study of the match industry which includes a discussion of women's role, see Wu Ao [2]. Information on women printers comes from Chen Yihe.

72. Ji Kailin.

73. Zhang Jiagui.

74. Han Ruixiang, April 1, 1981.

75. Interview with Sun Qingkui, Cotton Mill #2, Jan. 17, 1981.

76. Zhang Chunfeng.

77. Zhang Jiagui.

78. Ji Kailin.

79. The lack of consistent migration statistics makes it impossible to determine exactly what percentage of peasants migrated alone, or lived alone once in Tianjin. Interview data indicate, however, that even those peasants who arrived alone both depended upon local relatives for work introductions and maintained an economic relationship with urban relatives, or their rural kinfolk, or both. The discussion that follows, however, focuses on those peasants who migrated or lived in family groups, since their experience is more accessible and since the qualitative data indicate that they made up the majority of immigrants.

80. *JJZK*, No. 213 (April 14, 1937). The surveys included were conducted between 1922 and 1928.

81. The statistics on total city population and household size are given in the following sources: Wu Ao [4]; "Zui jin Zhongguo renkou de xin guji" (A new estimate of the recent Chinese population), *Shehui kexue zazhi*, 6, No. 1 (March 1935), 246–47; "Zui jin Zhongguo zhi renkou tongji" (Recent Chinese population statistics), *Tongji yuebao*, 1, No. 1 (1929), 46; *YSB*, June 10, Sept. 26, 1935, March 22, June 20, July 19, Aug. 18, Nov. 17, Dec. 17, 1936, Jan. 15, Feb. 17, March 14,

April 14, June 13, 1937, all citations on p. 5; Cheng Haifong, China Correspondent Monthly Reports (Aug. 1947), 23, ILO Archives, C13/2/79, 23. Some of these estimates include suburban districts.

82. Feng Huanian Xiansheng jiniance, 492; Wu Ao [1], 49–50; *YSB*, July 7, 1935, 5. These surveys did not have a uniform definition of household. Feng Huanian's survey, for instance, included only people who lived and ate at home every day (p. 490), whereas the *YSB* survey defined a household as an "economic unit," whether or not the members were related or all living together.

83. See sources in note 81, with the exception of Wu Ao and *YSB*, Jan. 15 and June 13, 1937, which do not provide sex ratios.

84. Tianjin [10], 4; *YSB*, Jan. 14, 1948, 4, and Oct. 15, 1948, 5.

85. Tianjin [11], 14; *YSB*, Jan. 14, 1948, 4, and Oct. 15, 1948, 5.

86. Feng Huanian, 493, 495.

87. Interview with Chen Guilan, Nov. 2, 1980. A rich account of childhood in the family of a Tianjin street vendor and the lives of casual laborers is given in Xin Fengxia, *Reminiscences, Xin Fengxia huiyi lu*, and *Yishu shengya*.

88. Chen Yihe.

89. Zhang Wenqing; Wu Ao [1], 348; Fong [1], 135–36. Feng Huanian's survey of 132 handicraft worker households in 1927–28 substantiates this point. While almost 87 percent of the household's income came from the major earner, who was invariably a man, the amount contributed by children and wives made it possible for the family to meet its expenses. Of 260 family members who were employed, 182 were men, 78 were women. The men worked, among other things, as carpenters, weavers, barbers, tanners, metalworkers, cobblers, painters, and coolies. The women spun yarn, knitted, glued matchboxes, and rolled cigarettes. Of the five families in the group with the highest income, four had working wives. Feng Huanian, 493, 495–96, 502.

90. Chen Guilan; interview with Gao Renying, former secretary of the Tianjin YWCA, April 21, 1980; Feng Huanian, 497.

91. Feng Huanian, 489, 501, 503–4.

92. Chen Guilan; Feng Huanian, 521. Feng's survey found that 7 percent of the families lived in brick houses, 15 percent in limewash houses, and 78 percent in mudwash houses.

93. *Beiping ribao*, April 18, 1935, reprinted in *Laodong jibao* (Labor quarterly), No. 5 (May 1935), 138.

94. *YSB*, Jan. 20, 1935, 9.   95. Feng Huanian, 521–22.

96. Feng, 522.   97. Feng, 522–23; Chen Guilan.

98. *Jingji yanjiu zhoukan*, No. 18 (June 29, 1930). Working-class food, like clothing and fuel, changed very little right up until Liberation. For a very similar list dating from 1946, see *Huabei laodong*, 1, No. 2 (Feb. 25, 1946), 7.

99. Feng Huanian, 510–11, 515; Tianjin [6].

100. Chen Guilan.

101. Tianjin [21]; Chen Guilan; Feng Huanian, 510–11; Wang Da, "Tianjin zhi gongye," 117; Wu Ao [1], 344; interview with Li Shiyu, March 24, 1981.

102. Feng Huanian, 490, 500, 527; Chen Guilan.

103. Feng Huanian, 522–23; *Beiping ribao*, April 18, 1935, cited in *Laodong jibao*, No. 5 (May 1935), 137.

104. Chen Guilan.

105. Feng Huanian, 517–19; *Jingji yanjiu zhoukan*, No. 18 (June 29, 1930); Wu Ao [1], 343–44.

106. Chen Guilan.

107. Zheng Yufu, 5.

108. "Gongce wenti" (The problem of public toilets), *Tianjin shi zhoukan*, 6, No. 7 (March 20, 1948), 12–13.

109. Zheng Yufu, 219–21; Wu Ao [1], 346–47; Feng, 527.

110. Chen Guilan.

111. *YSB*, June 30, 1936, 9; *Tianjin shi zhoukan*, 4, No. 1 (Aug. 23, 1947), 15; T'ao and Johnson, 525.

112. Tianjin [11], 6–7, 10.

113. *Ibid.*, 12, 16.

114. *SHYK*, 1, No. 1 (July 1929), 54; *YSB*, April 2, 1948, 5.

115. Tianjin [21].

116. Fong [5], 15–16; Tianjin [21]; Cheng Haifong, "Visit to Peiping, Tientsin and Tsinan, 21 May–14 June 1935," ILO Archives, mimeo., C1802/3, 11; *Guoji laogong tongxun*, 4, No. 4 (April 1937), 102–3; *Central China Daily News*, May 28, 1941, cited in Cheng Haifong, China Correspondent Monthly Reports, May 1941, ILO Archives, mimeo., C1803/122, 28; *Huabei laodong*, 1, No. 1 (Jan. 1946), 23, and No. 2 (Feb. 1946), 15; Cheng Haifong, China Correspondent Monthly Reports, Sept. 1946, ILO Archives, mimeo., C1803/176, 5.

117. Elizabeth Wright, "Quarterly Report, August–October 1920," World YWCA Archives, China 1918–1921: Minutes, Reports, mimeo., 3/67.

118. Letter from Grace Coppock, Dec. 3, 1920, World YWCA Archives, China 1918–1920: Correspondence, mimeo., 3/65.

119. Israel Epstein.

120. Cheng Haifong, China Correspondent Monthly Reports, Aug. 1939, ILO Archives, mimeo., C1803/101, 4; Sept. 1939, C1803/102, 3; March 1940, C1803/108, 4; May 1940, C1803/110, 3.

121. *Tianjin shi zhoukan*, 7, No. 6 (June 5, 1948), 10–11; *YSB*, June 21, 1947, 4; Jan. 19, 1948, 3; Jan. 22, 1948, 3; June 17, 1948, 5; A. Doak Barnett, *China on the Eve*, 58.

122. Tianjin [24]; Nankai Daxue [2]; Tianjin [8], 8–17.

123. *SHYK*, 1, No. 1 (July 1929), 31–32; *YSB*, May 16, Aug. 11, 1936, 5.

124. Wu Ao [4]; Nankai Daxue [2]; *Tianjin shi zhoukan*, 5, No. 1 (Nov. 15, 1947), 4–5; 1, No. 7 (Jan. 25, 1947), 12–13.

125. *YSB*, Jan. 20, 1935, 9; Jan. 1, 1936, 5; *Tianjin shi zhoukan*, 4, No. 9 (Oct. 18, 1947), 10; 5, No. 1 (Nov. 15, 1947), 4; 7, No. 6 (June 5, 1948), 10.

126. *YSB*, Jan. 1, 1936, 5; *Tianjin shi zhoukan*, 1, No. 7 (Jan. 25, 1947), 12–13; 5, No. 1 (Nov. 15, 1947), 4.

127. *Tianjin shi zhoukan*, 4, No. 9 (Oct. 18, 1947), 10.

128. *Ibid.*, 1, No. 7 (Jan. 25, 1947), 13; *YSB*, Jan. 1, 1936, 5; Jan. 20, 1935, 9; *Tianjin shi zhoukan*, 5, No. 1 (Nov. 15, 1947), 4.

129. *YSB*, July 7, 1935, 9.

130. *Tianjin shi zhoukan*, 5, No. 1, 4; 1, No. 7, 12.

131. *YSB*, July 7, 1935, 9; *Tianjin shi zhoukan*, 1, No. 7, 13.

132. *Tianjin shi zhoukan*, 1, No. 7, 13; 5, No. 1, 4; 4, No. 9, 11.

133. Tianjin [21].

CHAPTER FOUR

1. An earlier version of this chapter was published in *Modern China*, 9, No. 4 (Oct. 1983), 387–419.

2. Santiaoshi was sometimes mentioned in municipal surveys in the 1920's and 1930's, but as a marginal sector of local industry it never commanded much attention. This situation changed after Liberation. As early as the "three-anti/five-anti" campaign in 1951, certain Santiaoshi shopowners had been singled out as members of GMD-affiliated groups or secret societies or both. In 1957 an exhibition mounted as part of the anti-rightist campaign criticized the feudal conditions under which Santiaoshi apprentices labored. A lengthy report on Santiaoshi was compiled in 1958 by a team of students from the Nankai University History Department.

By the early 1960's the district had its own museum, devoted to exposing the evils of the pre-Liberation metalworking trade. Fictionalized accounts and journalistic articles emphasizing the suffering of the apprentices were written about Santiaoshi. Local activity peaked during the Cultural Revolution. The district museum, endorsed by such diverse figures as Zhou Enlai and Chen Boda, became a pilgrimage site for groups of Red Guards from throughout the country. The museum staff was expanded so that it could reinterview any worker who had ever labored in Santiaoshi. A substantial archival collection was assembled; it included interview notes, financial records from several factories, and artifacts. One former workshop was reconstructed on the original site and opened to visitors. Several workers became famous on the local lecture circuit as "typical Santiaoshi apprentices," who exposed the evils of pre-Liberation capitalists and condemned the "black line" of collaboration with the capitalist class espoused by Liu Shaoqi. (One of the major documents attacked during the Cultural Revolution was a series of talks given by Liu Shaoqi in Tianjin in April and May 1949. In these talks he outlined a party policy under which capitalists were to be given an active role in the building of post-Liberation industry. During the Cultural Revolution these talks were condemned as a distortion of party policy that advocated class collaborationism. Since the talks had taken place in Tianjin, much local effort was expended to prove that Tianjin capitalists were unworthy of party support in any form.) Well after the Red Guards had gone home, as late as 1979, the area continued to be the subject of scholarly-cum-political inquiries about capitalist exploitation.

3. On the organization of small-scale industry in China, see Yoshinobu Shiba, "Ningpo and Its Hinterland"; W. E. Willmott, *Economic Organization in Chinese Society*; Richard Tawney, *Land and Labour in China*, 114.

4. Steven R. Smith, "The London Apprentices"; William H. Sewell, Jr., *Work and Revolution in France*, Chapter 2; and Ezra Mendelsohn, *Class Struggle in the Pale*.

5. On these functions of guilds in 1920's Beijing, see John Stewart Burgess, *The Guilds of Peking*. On the religious, commercial, corporate, and community-service functions of guilds in nineteenth-century Hankow, see William T. Rowe, *Hankow*, 289–321. (The Hankow guilds were, however, local origin and trade guilds rather than craft guilds.) On guilds as regulators and protectors in fifteenth- and sixteenth-century Europe, see Robert S. Duplessis and Martha C. Howell, "Reconsidering the Early Modern Urban Economy." The literature on artisan militance in Europe is vast. Works employing widely varying approaches that I have

found particularly helpful include E. P. Thompson, *Making of the English Working Class*; William H. Sewell, Jr., "Social Change and the Rise of Working-Class Politics"; Michael Hanagan and Charles Stephenson, "The Skilled Worker and Working-Class Protest"; and Ronald Aminzade, "French Strike Development and Class Struggle."

6. The vast amounts of printed material generated in Santiaoshi's 25 years of political prominence range from crudely political denunciations of Liu Shaoqi, through sensationalistic accounts of workers eating dead pickled rats that had fallen into a vat of salted vegetables, to attempts to calculate the rate of exploitation of surplus value in an ironcasting shop. Although the quality of historical investigation is at best uneven, these materials, used critically, make it possible to begin to explore the experience of handicraft workers in Tianjin.

The material in the Nankai University report (Tianjin [22]) includes oral history interviews with old Santiaoshi workers and factory owners, as well as material culled from the company books of Jin Ju Cheng Ironworks. Repetitive and rambling, it is nevertheless the best compendium of material about the district. Several articles about Santiaoshi in Chinese are based entirely or in part on this report. They include Lin Kaiming, "Guanyu Tianjin Santiaoshi"; Xu Jingxing, "Tianjin jindai gongye"; Nankai Daxue [5]; and Gu Jinwu, "Shilun jiefang qian Tianjin Santiaoshi." Since these articles present no new data, they are not cited in this chapter unless the analysis presented by the authors is under discussion. Fictional accounts of Santiaoshi include Wang Xirong et al., "Jiefang qian Santiaoshi tugong," and Ren Pu, *Santiaoshi*.

7. Ji Guangzhi, "Jiu Zhongguo shiqi de Tianjin," 27.

8. Tianjin [22], Sec. 1, 3.

9. *Ibid.*, Sec. 1, 3–5.

10. *Ibid.*, Sec. 1, 6–7.

11. After the suppression of the Boxer Rebellion, a foreign-run provisional municipal government controlled Tianjin for two years. It tore down the old city walls and sponsored a great deal of construction. In addition, many of the concession areas expanded, creating a sizable demand for pipes, stoves, and other metal tools and construction materials.

12. For a detailed description of ironcasting technique throughout China in the 1920's, which seems substantially the same as that practiced in Santiaoshi, see Rudolf P. Hommel, *China at Work*, 13–32. Some of these techniques apparently date from the first few centuries A.D.

13. Tianjin [22], Sec. 1, 26–27.

14. Unless otherwise noted, this discussion of Jin Ju Cheng is based on the following sources: Tianjin [22], Sec. 5, 1–12; my notes on interviews with former Santiaoshi capitalists conducted by the staff of the *Tianjin wenshi ziliao xuanji* on March 26 and April 17, 1980; personal interview with Ma Yunlong, April 19, 1980; and a near-complete set of Jin Ju Cheng account books (1897–1956) in the archives of the Santiaoshi History Museum (hereafter Santiaoshi Archives).

15. Tianjin [22], Sec. 2, 2; Ma Yunlong.

16. In 1900 the shop bought 76,507 catties of iron, but by 1906 purchases had nearly doubled, reaching 135,745 catties. The volume of business transacted went from about 7,000 strings of cash per year in 1900–1904 to more than 12,000 in 1905–6. Profits recorded in the company books swelled from 1,043 strings in 1901 to 1,818 strings in 1906, and then to more than 39,000 strings by 1910.

17. Tianjin [22], Sec. 1, 8; Sec. 2, 5–10.

18. *Ibid.*, Sec. 1, 13–14; Sec. 2, 7–10.

19. *Ibid.*, Sec. 2, 10; Ma Yunlong.

20. Tianjin [22], Sec. 2, 18–19, Sec. 3, 1; Ma Yunlong.

21. Tianjin [22], Sec. 3, 1–6, gives details of many of these divisions and subdivisions.

22. Ma Yunlong.

23. Tianjin [22], Sec. 3, 3–4; Ma Yunlong; Zeng Tiechen, "Tianjin zhi jiqiye."

24. Tianjin [22], Sec. 2, 22–23; Chen Yihe.

25. Tianjin [22], Sec. 2, 25.

26. Wang Da, "Tianjin zhi gongye," 185.

27. On these bigger shops, see Deng Qinglan, 262–64; *Shehui tongji yuekan* (1940), 2, 24–26; Minami manshū, 589–637.

28. Zeng Tiechen, 4–8; Wu Ao [4]. These statistics did not include the concessions, which according to the same survey had only 24 ironworks and six machine-building plants.

29. Whether because their criteria were stricter (they may have excluded purely household-based metalworking shops) or because their investigators were not as thorough, they included only 99 ironworking shops and 43 machine-building factories. More than one-third of each were in District Three, the Santiaoshi area. The results of the survey can be found in Deng Qinglan, *passim.*

30. Ma Yunlong. For a more detailed discussion of the transport guilds and their bosses, see Chapter 5.

31. Ma Yunlong.

32. *Ibid.*

33. Tianjin [22], Sec. 3, 6–9, n.p. During the occupation the Japanese constructed 75 of their own machine factories, most of them also small-scale. They reportedly employed close to 10,000 Chinese workers. Most of these factories were outside Santiaoshi. Zhen Ji, "Shengli qian Tianjin."

34. Interview with Chen Wenbing, July 10, 1980.

35. Guo Dongbo, of Guo Tian Xiang Machine Works, became head of the guild, but it later split into two organizations, one for machine building and one for ironcasting. Shi Yukai headed the latter, and apparently contrived to keep the best jobs for his own ironcasting shop. Tianjin [22]; Ma Yunlong.

36. Tianjin [22]; Ma Yunlong.					37. Ma Yunlong.

38. Chen Yihe.					39. Ma Yunlong.

40. The rather high estimate of 83 shops probably includes some household-based ones. Tianjin [22]; interviews with former Santiaoshi capitalists conducted by the staff of the *TJWS*, March 26 and April 17, 1980; Ma Yunlong.

41. *YSB*, July 30, 1948, 5.					42. Ma Yunlong.

43. *YSB*, July 30, 1948, 5.					44. *YSB*, July 13, 1948, 5.

45. *YSB*, Aug. 3, 1948, 5.					46. Tianjin [22], Sec. 1, 6.

47. Tianjin [22], Sec. 9, 1–2; *Guo Tian Xiang diyiben xuetu mingmu* (The first apprentice list volume), Santiaoshi Archives.

48. In 1956 many tiny shops in Santiaoshi were consolidated into a few larger factories as part of the joint state-private ownership campaign.

49. Tianjin [22], Sec. 9, 1; "Santiaoshi lao gongren tongji biao" (Statistics on old Santiaoshi workers), Santiaoshi Archives, A2 (73). A2 refers to a file, and numbers within parentheses to specific items within the file. The statistics were apparently collected in the early 1970's.

50. Tianjin [22]; Santiaoshi Archives, A2 (33,36,41,66).
51. Tianjin [22], Sec. 9, 2; Santiaoshi Archives, A2 (2,8,10,14, and 22).
52. Interview with Liu Bingwen, July 10, 1980.
53. Tianjin [22], Sec. 9, 2. 54. Liu Bingwen.
55. Ma Yunlong. 56. Chen Yihe.
57. *Guo Tian Xiang diyiben xuetu mingmu.* These ages are probably calculated according to the traditional Chinese method, where a child is considered a year old at birth and gains another year at Chinese New Year. Therefore by Western reckoning the average age is probably a year or more younger than that indicated here.
58. Chen Yihe. 59. *Ibid.*
60. Burgess, 155–68. 61. Tianjin [22], Sec. 9, 7.
62. Wang Weizhen, in Tianjin [22], Sec. 9, 5.
63. Tianjin [22], Sec. 9, 8.
64. *Guoji laogong tongxun*, No. 12 (Sept. 1935), 53–55.
65. *YSB*, June 30, 1936, 5.
66. *Guoji laogong tongxun*, No. 24 (Sept. 1936), 54–55.
67. *YSB*, Feb. 26, 1937, 5. 68. Chen Yihe.
69. *Ibid.* 70. *Ibid.*
71. Several of these accounts are summarized in Tianjin [22], Sec. 9.
72. Chen Wenbing; Santiaoshi Archives, A2 (13).
73. Tianjin [22], Sec. 9.
74. *YSB*, Nov. 6, Nov. 24, and Dec. 25, 1936, 5.
75. *Laogong yuekan* 4, No. 7 (July 1935), 4–5, 11, 17.
76. *YSB*, Sept. 12, 1935, 5; March 30, 1937, 5; June 19, 1937, 5.
77. Chen Wenbing. 78. Wang Qingbin, 580.
79. Liu Bingwen. 80. Chen Yihe.
81. Chen Wenbing.
82. Tianjin [22], Sec. 9, 4, gives the ratio of apprentices to workers in several factories as follows:

Factory	Year	Apprentices	Workers	Ratio
Quan Sheng De Machine Works	1920	40	1(owner)	40:1
Guo Tian Xiang Machine Works	1940	160	40	4:1
Rui He Cheng Machine Works	post-1945	20	1	20:1

On apprentices in Beijing, see C. C. Chu and Thomas C. Blaisdell, Jr., *Peking Rugs and Peking Boys*, special supplement to *Chinese Social and Political Science Review* (April 1924), cited in Burgess, 166–67, and S. D. Gamble and J. S. Burgess, *Peking: A Social Survey* (New York, 1921), cited in Burgess, 167.
83. Liu Bingwen; Tianjin [22], Sec. 9, 4; Lynda Shaffer, "The Chinese Working Class," 462–63; Burgess, 167.
84. Chen Wenbing.
85. Lu Dangping, *Tianjin gongshangye*, Chapter 8, 1–4.
86. A 1929 survey of Santiaoshi shops indicates that 13- and 14-hour days were common. *SHYK*, 1, Nos. 3–4 (1929), 4–7, 26–29. A 1935 survey of Tianjin machining and ironcasting shops found that their working hours were as follows: of 142 shops, 18 worked 11-hour days and 40 worked 12-hour days. Eleven of the

ironcasting shops worked 14-hour days. Deng Qinglan, 101. Beijing carpet-weavers worked similar hours. Chu and Blaisdell, 24, cited in Burgess, 161–62.

87. Liu Bingwen.

88. The available wage data for Santiaoshi factories are so scattered and inconsistent that they do not lend themselves to systematic analysis. A 1929 survey calculated the average wage for a machinist as 11 yuan a month, with a range from one to 45 yuan according to skill. A 1935 survey of 142 machining and ironcasting factories in Tianjin put the average wage for machinists at nine yuan a month and for ironcasters at 8.50. Other surveys provide estimates whose averages vary as much as ten yuan per month in either direction. The number and location of factories varied from survey to survey, and averaging methods were frequently unexplained. In addition, we know from interview accounts that within factories, wages varied greatly according to an individual craftsman's skill. Finally, New Year's bonuses and other holiday gifts, standard in almost all Tianjin factories and trades, were a substantial part of a worker's yearly income but are unspecified in most of the surveys. It therefore seems useful to rely on workers' accounts of their own economic status rather than to depend on the treacherous security of wage data. In this connection the marital arrangements of Santiaoshi craftsmen provide an important clue. Zeng Tiechen, 24; Deng Qinglan, 88; Lu Dangping; Wang Qingbin, 242, 582; Ma Yunlong.

89. Chen Wenbing.

90. Ma Yunlong.

91. *Ibid*.

92. Chen Wenbing. On the Yi Guan Dao in the cotton mills, see Chapter 6.

93. Chen Yihe.

94. Tianjin [22], Sec. 10, 4; Santiaoshi Archives, A2 (10); Chen Wenbing.

95. Chen Wenbing; Tianjin [22], Sec. 10, 4; Chen Yihe.

96. Chen Wenbing.   97. Ma Yunlong.

98. Tianjin [22], Sec. 10, 3–4.   99. Chen Yihe.

100. Tianjin [22], Sec. 10, 6–11.   101. Burgess, 31, 205.

102. *Ibid*., 175–85, 211. In his study of Marseille workers, Sewell located the source of artisan militance in a "crisis of expansion," as migrants moved into and transformed trades where a tightly knit traditional culture had dominated. In Santiaoshi this type of traditional urban working culture did not exist. Everyone in the trade was an immigrant, and they brought with them rural ties that militated against protest. Sewell, "Social Change."

CHAPTER FIVE

1. Rickshaw pullers, who were not organized into guilds, nevertheless formed a significant part of the working class in Tianjin. Their numbers were estimated at 45,000 in 1935 and 73,000 in 1946. Most pullers could not afford their own rickshaw, but rented one from a garage for a set daily fee. The garage paid the nine transport taxes—one for each district and concession—so that the puller could move freely throughout the city. In return the garage charged rental fees that were sometimes more than a worker could make in a day's pulling. For statistics on the number of pullers and their rental arrangements, see *Dierci Zhongguo laodong nianjian* I, 189–90; Wan Xinquan, "Tianjin shuijian gaikuang"; *Beiping ribao*, April 18, 1935, reprinted in *Laodong jibao*, 5 (May 1935), 137; Cheng Haifong, "Visit to

Peiping, Tientsin and Tsinan," 14; Kōain Kahoku renraku, *Kahoku rōdō mondai gaisetsu*, 92; *Huabei laodong*, 1, No. 1 (Jan. 1946), 14.

2. The transport workers remain, for the historian, the most elusive of all those who labored in Tianjin. "It is difficult to write about the transport guilds," lamented a journalist in 1947, "not only because their history is long and their present circumstances are complicated, but because documents mention nothing about them, and one cannot find any reference material." Tianjin [15], Part 1, 7. The author of this article compensated for the lack of written material by interviewing members of the transport guilds, but that avenue of research is no longer open. The industry has been completely reorganized since 1949, and many of the workers have moved on to other trades.

Like other sectors of the working class, transport workers have had their history codified in post-Liberation stories and plays, in which the bosses of the transport guilds mercilessly persecute the coolies in their employ. See, for example, Tianjin [16], for an idealized operatic account of a 1948 strike in the Tianjin freight yards. Workers took an active role in writing and acting in early versions of this opera, which retains much of the flavor of Tianjin working-class language. For a history of the play and its leading actor, see *Tianjin ribao*, Aug. 2, 1980, 4.

3. Lieberthal, *Revolution and Tradition*, 22.

4. Interview with Xu Jingxing, May 10, 1981.

5. The term transport guild is a loose translation of the Chinese term *jiaohang*, which literally means "foot trade." The literal translation unfortunately does not convey the sense of a highly organized and regulated group. Lieberthal (*Revolution and Tradition*, 22) has translated it as "coolie association," but the jiaohang were neither run by the coolies nor based upon principles of free or equal association. Although the jiaohang differed in some respects from the classically organized Chinese guilds (for example, they had no apprenticeship system), they did fit John Stewart Burgess's general description of a local association of "craftsmen, merchants, or professionals, organized for the purpose of furthering their mutual interests, primarily economic, and of mutually protecting the members of their representative crafts, trades or professions, and of working out regulations and procedures to be followed by the members with such ends in view." Burgess, *Guilds of Peking*, 19.

6. Unless otherwise indicated, the discussion of guild history that follows is based upon two sources: a two-part study of the transport guilds published in 1947, Tianjin [15]; and a 1965 study, Tianjin [18], esp. 1–5.

7. Tianjin [15], Part 1, 7, mentions that since the *fuzi* made very little money taking care of official luggage, the government granted them specific territories to assure them of an adequate income. The same article (7–8) mentions the role of the guilds in maintaining public order during the Taiping assault on the Tianjin suburbs; it suggests that this may also have been a factor in the government's granting of special rights to the guilds. Yet government sanction of the guilds clearly predates the Taiping Rebellion.

8. The date of the establishment of the Four Gates system is unclear, as are many details of its operation. See Tianjin [15], Part 1, 7; and Tianjin [18], 1–2.

9. Tianjin [15], Part 1, 7.

10. Like the Chinese municipal government, the concession governments also taxed the guilds in their areas. An Lifu, *Tianjin shi banyun*, 2.

11. For details of railroad station construction, see Tianjin [18], 3. A fourth

station was constructed during the Japanese occupation. On railroad guild formation, see An Lifu, 2.

12. Noah Fields Drake, n. p.

13. *BYGR*, 24.

14. When cotton mill workers were fired or left the mills during the busy summer transport season to seek quick money, they often came to the riverbank to hire out as coolies on a casual basis. They were not part of the guild membership. Performing coolie labor along the riverbank was also the first point of entry into the working class for people without connections coming from the countryside.

15. *BYGR*, 24–25; Zai Pekin Dai Nippon, 42–44, 48–49; An Lifu, 2; Zheng Yufu, 206–7; Tianjin [18], 3.

16. Xue Buqi, *Tianjin huozhanye*, 101.

17. For descriptions of the railroad guilds, see Tianjin [18], 3; Kōain Kahoku, 102–3, *BYGR*, 27–31.

18. Tianjin [18], 3.

19. The same was not always true of the dockside guilds, which practiced the "Big Grab" (*da zhua*), a term that meant stealing part of what they moved. In the late 1940's, when the transport bosses took advantage of their connections with the military police to "grab" as much as several hundred million yuan worth of goods at a time, some steamships reportedly did not dare to unload at Tianjin, going instead to Dagu or Qinwangdao. Tianjin [15], Part 2, 6–7. For a discussion of the guilds and the warehousing industry, see Xue Buqi, 101–2.

20. *BYGR*, 5. Most factories used these guilds. Some large factories that needed coolies to move goods inside the factory, such as the Yu Yuan Mill, hired coolie labor by throwing a bundle of numbered sticks into a crowd of coolies at the gate each morning and hiring the ones who successfully scrambled for them. For a description of this procedure, see Fong [1], 120.

21. Ruan Weijing, "Mei shang Da Lai Yanghang," 10, 14.

22. The number of guilds and bosses is given in Tianjin [18], 3; the total number of workers is from Tianjin [15], Part 2, 6. A June 1947 survey conducted by the Bureau of Social Affairs listed 64,955 transport workers, 30,601 rickshaw pullers and sanlunche pedalers, and 1,105 dockworkers. These totals vary greatly from survey to survey. Tianjin [20], 8. For a list of the major guilds in 1946, see Tianjin [18], 8–14; for major guilds in 1947, see Tianjin [15], Part 2, 6; for a more detailed survey of the guilds in District #2 at Liberation, see *BYGR*, 7–9.

23. Tianjin [15], Part 1, 8. On the longevity of certain guilds, see Tianjin [18], 7–8. On rights of sale, see An Lifu, 3.

24. Tianjin [15], Part 1, 8; An Lifu, 3; *BYGR*, 6, 19–20. Workers, or those without slips, also participated in rumbles over turf.

25. Tianjin [18], 7; An Lifu, 3; *BYGR*, 6, 19. For a study of the structure of two guilds, see *BYGR*, 19–22.

26. Tianjin [18], 17–18; An Lifu, 4.

27. *YSB*, Aug. 4, 1948, 5.

28. There are two extant surveys of transport workers in Tianjin. The first, conducted by the Japanese Embassy in Beijing in 1941, covers several samples (of varying size) of workers employed by the Kahoku Unyu Kaisha (North China Transportation Company). These workers were actually supplied to the company by the transport guilds on a subcontracting basis. The second survey was conducted in September 1949 by the Transport Workers Union. It included a random sample of

2,175 workers drawn from among the freight haulers, rickshaw pullers, dock workers, railroad workers, and sanlunche drivers. The representativeness of these samples cannot be evaluated, but because they are the only data on a very elusive sector of the working class, they have been included here. The social characteristics of this group in the late nineteenth and early twentieth centuries may well have differed from those summarized below. The 1941 data can be found in Zai Pekin, the 1949 data in *BYGR*.

29. Of 1,083 transport workers at the Tianjin railroad station in 1941, 62 percent came from Tianjin proper. Most of the remainder came from nearby counties. Zai Pekin, 233. In the 1949 samples, only 20 percent of the freight haulers, 34 percent of the dock workers, and 15 percent of the railroad workers listed their previous occupation as "peasant." Lieberthal has interpreted this to mean that most of the workers were of urban origin. He fails to note, however, that a large group in the same sample were former industrial workers (32 percent, 39 percent, and 7 percent, respectively), and that many of these people had probably been born and raised in the countryside, come to the factories of Tianjin, then been discharged and forced to seek work as coolies. Lieberthal, *Revolution*, 33; *BYGR*, 44.

30. In the 1941 survey, the ages of 1,543 workers were surveyed. Fifty-six percent of them were between the ages of 25 and 44. In the 1949 survey, 59 percent of the freight haulers, 63 percent of the dock workers, and 62 percent of the railroad workers were between the ages of 26 and 45. Zai Pekin, 243; *BYGR*, 42.

31. The 1941 survey set the literacy rate at 13 percent for a sample of 3,086 workers. In the 1949 sample, the illiteracy rate was 64 percent for freight haulers, 54 percent for railroad workers, and 86 percent among the dock workers. Zai Pekin, 246; *BYGR*, 45.

32. Ninety-three percent of 1,586 workers surveyed in 1941 were married; 82 percent of these resided with their families. In the 1949 sample, the percentages of married freight haulers, railroad workers, and dock workers were 73 percent, 63 percent, and 79 percent, respectively. Zai Pekin, 242; BYGR, 44–45. These surveys also provide data on household size, but no clear pattern emerges from them.

33. Zai Pekin, 49.

34. *Ibid.*, 234–35.

35. For previous occupations of a sample of transport workers, see *BYGR*, 44. The same survey notes that most transport workers were drawn from the ranks of factory and handicraft workers who had become unemployed. Among transport workers, freight haulers and railroad guild workers were making the most money at Liberation. Dockworkers were having temporary difficulties because of the disruption of sea traffic, but were normally better off than sanlunche drivers and rickshaw pullers. *BYGR*, 41. The same 1949 survey of transport workers clearly indicated that rickshaw pullers and sanlunche drivers were the worst-off transport workers. Although some people pulled rickshaws only until they could find better work, the rickshaw pullers surveyed in this study were older than the other groups (almost half were over forty-six), and many had been pulling rickshaws for more than 20 years. The sanlunche drivers were more likely to be transient. Forty-four percent of the rickshaw workers were unmarried, and the author of the survey attributes this to their low earnings. For complete statistics, see *BYGR*, 41–45.

36. For a discussion of the percentages appropriated by various guild bosses, see Tianjin [18], 15; *BYGR*, 13–15, 28.

37. In 1935 an ILO inspector commented: "Rickshaw coolies, dockers, and contract workers in mines are more miserable than the factory workers. Their wages are low and treatment . . . poor. The miners and dockers are all under the exploitation of the contractors, while the rickshaw coolies have to pay a heavy rent for the rickshaws out of their pitiful earnings." Cheng Haifong, "Visit to Peiping, Tientsin and Tsinan," 41.

38. *YSB*, July 8, 1936, 5.

39. Israel Epstein.

40. "Report of the YWCA in China for 1921," World YWCA Archives, China 1920–22, Reports, 68, mimeo.

41. *YSB*, July 14, 1948, 5; a similar case is reported in *YSB*, Oct. 23, 1936.

42. Colonel C. L'Estrange Malone, *New China*, Part II, 9.

43. *Beiping ribao*, April 18, 1935, reprinted in *Laodong jibao*, No. 5 (May 1935), 136–38. For other accounts of conflicts between rickshaw pullers and the police, see *YSB*, Jan. 29, 1935, 9, and *Tianjin shi zhoukan*, 3, No. 9 (July 26, 1947), 13.

44. For reasons similar to those given in Chapters 3, 4, and 6, no attempt has been made here to correlate the available unsystematic wage data with cost-of-living figures, or to compare them rigorously to the equally unsystematic data available for other occupations.

45. Tianjin [15], Part 2, 7.

46. *BYGR*, 27; An Lifu, 5; Zai Pekin, 49; *YSB*, Aug. 4, 1948, 5.

47. Most of the major firms in the city, including the cotton mills, had all their moving handled by a specific guild. Tianjin [18], 14.

48. Zhang Shou, *Jin men za ji*, II, 39–40. The term hunhunr is a localism and is difficult to translate. *Hun* may mean variously "dark, opaque, blackened, blurred," or "to drift along or through."

49. This discussion of hunhunr customs and activities, unless otherwise noted, is based on Li Ranshi, "Jiu Tianjin de hunhunr," 187–209. This "study" is quite possibly based upon inherited fragments of truth, fiction, and retrospectively mythologized behavior. Posture and the creation of reputation are, of course, legitimate historical subjects. The hunhunr as myth certainly affected the twentieth-century behavior of the transport guilds *as if* the tales of their nineteenth-century exploits were literally true.

50. Various versions of the struggle are recounted in Li Ranshi, 196; An Lifu, 4; Tianjin [18], 20; Zai Pekin, 276.

51. A story dating from the turn of the century recounts that one hunhunr-cum-transport-boss, when he was being beaten in the *yamen*, let out an "aiya!" Everyone present, the story goes, felt that he had not lived up to the requirements of stoic behavior. The officials stopped beating him in disgust, the assembled multitudes jeered him, and he had to turn over the right to operate the transport guild to someone else. Tianjin [15], Part 2, 7–8.

52. "Pekin Tenshin shisō dantai chōsa," 427–28. For a slightly different version of the Tianjin Massacre executions, which asserts that 18 hunhunr volunteered to be executed in return for payments to their families, see Li Ranshi, 191. In this account, a widow of one executed hunhunr was cheated on her payment and subsequently became a hunhunr herself. Many legends grew up about her pluck and prowess. In one, the owner of a factory told her she could have as many reeds as she could carry, and she walked off with a pile of more than 100 catties. She was

one of a handful of women hunhunr, this particular brand of behavior being generally reserved to men.

53. Zai Pekin, 276.

54. The earliest branch was in Anqing, and it was first called the Anqing Dao
You Hui, then the Anqing Bang, then the Qing Bang. Interviews with Li Shiyu,
April 16, 1980, and March 24, 1981. For the putative origins of the Qing Bang, see
Jean Chesneaux, *Secret Societies in China*, 45–47. Chesneaux, 50–51, explains that
"By a graphic slip . . . the simple character *ching* which figured in the founder's
name was replaced by another pronounced in the same way but meaning 'green.' In
the twentieth century this impressed itself even more easily than it would otherwise have done by virtue of the fact that by a similar slip the Triad or Hung-bang
[*sic*] was more and more often called the 'Red Band.'" (The "founder's name" to
which Chesneaux refers was actually the place name "Anqing.") Li Shiyu adds that
the characters *qing* (green) and *hong* (red) were often used together in such gang
phrases as "Is your wound *qing* (black and blue) or *hong* (bleeding)?"

55. Ma Chaojun, *Zhongguo laodong yundong shi* (History of the Chinese workers'
movement) (Chongqing, 1942), 74–77, cited in Chesneaux, 47–50.

56. Chesneaux, 48–49; "Pekin Tenshin," 429, 437.

57. A 1941 investigation of the Qing Bang in Tianjin estimated that it had
500,000 members, or roughly a quarter of the city's population. Their occupations
were given as follows: Laborers (including transport workers), 50 percent; no occupation (supported by proceeds from gang activities), 5 percent; people who ran
amusement halls or brothels, 20 percent; army, government, police, and railroad
workers, 5 percent; post office, commerce, self-employed, 12 percent; Chinese employees of concession governments, 3 percent; other, 5 percent. "Pekin Tenshin,"
439–40.

58. *Ibid.*, 430.

59. Israel Epstein.

60. For an example of the latter, see Chapter 6. A 20-year struggle between gang
bosses Yuan Wenhui and Li Guanghai is recounted in Liu Jingshan, "Hanjian eba
Yuan Wenhui de yisheng" (The life of traitor and local tyrant Yuan Wenhui),
TJWS, No. 18 (Jan. 1982), 208–11.

61. For more information on the political activities of the Qing Bang, see Pekin
Tenshin, 429–31, 434–39, 444–47. On the collaborative activities of Yuan Wenhui,
see Liu Jingshan, 205–8. On Qing Bang collaborative activities in Hankou, see
William T. Rowe, "The Qingbang and Collaboration," 491–99.

62. For information about the gangs and their connections with transport guild
bosses, see Tianjin [18], 4, 21; *BYGR*, 16, 29; *Jinbu ribao*, March 29, 1951, 1, and
Liu Jingshan, 202–3. Yuan Wenhui, born in the south city in 1901, was raised by
an uncle who was the boss of the Lu Zhuangzi guild. This guild monopolized
transport in the northern part of the Japanese concession and the south city. Yuan
worked as an office attendant at the guild by day, and as an attendant in his uncle's
gambling den by night. Ba and Zhai were executed on March 31, 1951, during a
campaign to suppress counterrevolutionaries. Ma and Yuan were also executed
after Liberation. *Jinbu ribao*, March 31, 1951, 1; Tianjin [18], 29.

63. Lieberthal, *Revolution*, 23.

64. This is not to imply that the Qing Bang had no structure or rituals of its
own, only that it had no independent organizational agenda. Information on the

rituals and genealogy of the Qing Bang, as well as a highly stylized account of its history, can be found in *Banghui shouce si zhong*; Yi Sumin, ed., *Qing bang kao shi*; *Qing pu jiyao*; and *Qing hong bang kao yi*. These reprints of secret society manuals are prescriptive rather than descriptive, and contain little information on the interaction of the gangs with other social institutions.

65. Li Shiyu, April 16, 1980, and March 24, 1981; Lieberthal, *Revolution*, 23.

66. Li Shiyu, April 16, 1980, and March 24, 1981.

67. Israel Epstein.

68. On heroism in the guilds, see *YSB*, Aug. 4, 1948, 5. On mutual loyalty, see "Pekin Tenshin," 440.

69. Zai Pekin, 275.

70. Lieberthal, *Revolution*, 23–24.

71. These figures are from a 1941 study. Of the estimated 250,000 gang members who lived by manual labor, 220,000 worked in factories, while the remaining 30,000 were dockworkers, redcaps, boat owners, and laborers on steamboats. "Pekin Tenshin," 440.

72. Lieberthal, *Revolution*, 25.

73. *YSB*, Aug. 4, 1948, 5. The following portrait of violence in the guilds is drawn almost exclusively from newspaper accounts, which inevitably present an episodic and fragmented picture. They are of little help in imposing a sense of analytic coherence on guild violence, but they do help to define its scope.

74. Zhang Shou, *Jin men za ji*, III, 41.

75. Tianjin [15], Part 1, 8.

76. *YSB*, July 24 and Nov. 5, 1935, 5.

77. *YSB*, Oct. 3, 1935, 5; March 16, 1936, 5; April 13, 1936, 5; Feb. 22 and 23, 1937, 5; Jan. 26, 1948, 4; May 10, 1948, 5.

78. *YSB*, Nov. 23, 1935, 5.   79. *YSB*, March 21, 1936, 5.

80. *YSB*, April 1, 1936, 5.   81. *YSB*, March 14, 1948, 5.

82. *YSB*, July 23, 1948, 5.

83. *YSB*, Aug. 4, 1948, 5; Tianjin [18], 19.

84. *YSB*, March 24, 1936, 5.

85. *YSB*, Oct. 29, 1935, 5; July 29, 1947, 4.

86. Tianjin [15], Part 2, 7.   87. Tianjin [18], 19.

88. *Ibid.*, 21–22.   89. *YSB*, Sept. 24, 1935, 5.

90. *YSB*, Nov. 19, 1936, 5.   91. *YSB*, April 20, 1937, 5.

92. *YSB*, Dec. 30, 1935, 5; Nov. 15, 1936, 5.

93. *YSB*, Sept. 1, 1936, 5. Similar acts of violence characterized the relationship between rickshaw pullers and rental garage owners, and that between the pullers themselves, who were not above stabbing one another in conflicts over a parking place. As with the guild workers, family members were frequently involved in these altercations. See *YSB*, Feb. 2 and Aug. 6, 1936, 5; Aug. 1, 1948, 5.

94. Zhang Shou, *Jin men za ji*, III, 41–42.

95. He Zechun, *Kaocha geji gonghui*, 12–13, 39–43.

96. *YSB*, Nov. 22, 1935, 5; June 10, 1937, 5.

97. *YSB*, March 11 and April 18, 1936, 5; Tianjin [15], Part 1, 7.

98. *YSB*, April 29, 1936, 5.

99. *YSB*, April 30, May 4, May 7, May 26, 1936, 5.

100. *YSB*, Aug. 23, Oct. 29, Nov. 28, Dec. 1, 1936, 5; May 28, 1937, 5.

101. Tianjin [26], 53.

102. *Ibid.*, 44–51; Tianjin [18], 6–7.

103. Tianjin [15], Part 2, 7; "Zhengdun jiaohang" (Reorganize the jiaohang), *Tianjin shi zhoukan*, 4, No. 6 (Sept. 27, 1947), 3–4. Before and after the war the government also attempted to register and regulate the number of rickshaws, and after the war it issued directives requiring that rickshaws be replaced by sanlunche. For accounts of these efforts, see *YSB*, June 21 and Dec. 4, 1935, 5; May 27, 1937, 5; Jan. 21 and May 20, 1947, 5; March 22 and April 3, 1948, 5; *Tianjin shi zhoukan*, 2, No. 2 (March 15, 1947), 6.

104. Tianjin [15], Part 2, 7.

105. For details of that campaign, see Lieberthal, *Revolution*, 60–77.

CHAPTER SIX

1. On the transience of the millowners, see Chapter 2; on turnover among mill-hands, see Chapter 3.

2. For a description of worker adaptation in U.S. factories, see Herbert G. Gutman, *Work, Culture and Society*, 7–65.

3. H. D. Fong [1], 118–19; Wang Jinghang and Zhang Zesheng, "Yu Yuan shachang," 174; Ji Guangzhi, "Jiu Zhongguo shiqi Tianjin gongren zhuangkuang," 16; Wu Ao [1], 12, 39–41.

4. Fong [1], 119.

5. Zhang Jiagui; Fong [1], 120.

6. Tim Wright has developed this argument for the use of contract labor in Chinese coal mines before 1937, arguing that during the early stages of industrialization, even if no shortage of labor exists, the labor market is fragmented and intermediaries are necessary. Emily Honig has investigated the use of the contract labor system in Shanghai cotton mills, finding that it was controlled by Shanghai gangs to the detriment of capitalist and worker alike. Except for a brief period early in the Japanese occupation, the contract labor system was apparently never used in Tianjin, but foremen played a large role as intermediaries in procuring labor throughout the first half of the twentieth century. Sidney Pollard, *Genesis of Modern Management*; Tim Wright, "'A Method of Evading Management'"; Honig, "Women Cotton Mill Workers," Chapter 3; Chen Zhi.

7. Zhu Mengsu, "Tianjin Bei Yang shachang," 197; *YSB*, July 15, 30, and 31, Aug. 1, 3, 21, and 26, 1935, 5.

8. *YSB*, July 15, 18, 1935; May 20, June 8, 26, 1936; Aug. 12, 17, 23, 29, 1936; Sept. 23, 1936; Nov. 22, 1936, 5.

9. Interview with Han Ruixiang, Jan. 17, 1981; Zhang Wenqing.

10. Ji Kailin.

11. Li Guilan.

12. Zhang Wenqing.

13. Ji Kailin; Li Guilan; Zhang Wenqing.

14. Han Ruixiang, April 1, 1981.

15. Honig, 47–53.

16. *YSB*, July 30, Aug. 26, Oct. 24 and 28, Nov. 4, 1935, 5.

17. *YSB*, Dec. 2, 5, 6, 8, 1935, 5. 18. *YSB*, Dec. 14, 1935, 5.

19. *YSB*, Dec. 16, 23, 1935, 5. 20. *YSB*, Jan. 17, Feb. 5, 1936, 5.

21. *YSB*, Feb. 2, March 3, 19, 1936, 5.

22. *YSB*, April 4, 1936, 5. The labor contractors were not responsible for room,

board, or worker control; their function was apparently limited to that of hiring agent.

23. *YSB*, April 19, May 17, July 14, 17, 26, Aug. 10, 11, 12, 16, 19, 24, 1936, 5.

24. *YSB*, Aug. 18, Nov. 9, 1936, 5.

25. *YSB*, Jan. 17, 1937, 12.

26. Gutman, 22.

27. Visit to Tianjin Cotton Mill #4 (formerly the Shanghai Shachang), July 1, 1980. For a detailed description of the spinning process, see Hershatter and Honig, "Hard Times Cotton Mill Girls," 28–33. For details of the entire production process, see Honig, "Women Cotton Mill Workers," Chapter 1.

28. Fong [1], 149–50. For other studies of the sexual division of labor, see Liu Xinquan, "Huabei shachang gongren gongzi tongji"; and Wu Ao [1], 53–54.

29. The sexual division of labor varied on individual operations from mill to mill. For instance, at Shuang Xi both men and women (or, more accurately, boys and girls) did piecing, while at Bao Cheng this job was performed by men. Han Ruixiang, Jan. 17, 1981; Ji Kailin.

30. Gao Fengqi; Zhang Jiagui; Ji Kailin; Zhang Wenqing; Zhang Chunfeng; visit to Cotton Mill #4; Honig, "Women," 50–57.

31. Ji Kailin; Zhang Wenqing. For a list of the wages paid to workers of each grade in one mill, see *Gongye yuekan* (Industrial monthly), 3, Nos. 7–8 (Aug. 1946), 49. An underground CCP document in 1948 indicated that women in government-owned Tianjin mills were paid one-third less than men. Zhong gong Tianjin shi dang'anke (CCP Tianjin Municipal Archives Department), "Guanyu gongyun gongzuo zhong jige wenti de yanjiu diaocha ziliao" (Research and investigative material on several questions concerning work in the workers' movement), July 15, 1948, cited in Ji Guangzhi, "Jiu Zhongguo shiqi Tianjin gongren zhuangkuang," 19.

32. E. P. Thompson, "Time, Work-Discipline, and Industrial Capitalism," 93–94.

33. On the British case see Sidney Pollard, "Factory Discipline in the Industrial Revolution." The same methods were employed in the late nineteenth century in Italy and Russia. Donald H. Bell, "Worker Culture and Worker Politics"; Robert E. Johnson, *Peasant and Proletarian*, 81–82.

34. *YSB*, March 10, 1935, 14.

35. Zhang Wenqing.

36. Gao Fengqi; Chen Zhi.

37. Mian Si, "1947 nian bugao," Nov. 22, Dec. 12, 1947.

38. *YSB*, Jan. 17, 1937, 12. Most Tianjin cotton mills ran 12-hour shifts until 1945 and ten-hour shifts thereafter. Wu Ao [1], 14, 54–56, 102; Cheng Changli; Zhang Jiagui.

39. *YSB*, Jan. 17, 1937, 12. For a detailed description of a day in the life of a woman cotton mill worker, see Emily Honig, Chapter 4.

40. Wu Ao [1], 54–56; *YSB*, March 10, 1935, 14; Zhang Wenqing; Zhang Jiagui.

41. Wu Ao [1], 14, 103; Mian Si, "1947 nian bugao"; Zhang Wenqing.

42. Wu Ao [1], 83.

43. *Ibid.*, 181.

44. A detailed breakdown of temperature and humidity by mill and workshop is given in Tianjin [4].

45. Zhang Chunfeng.
46. Tianjin shehui ju, *Shehui ju gongbao* (Bulletin of the Bureau of Social Affairs), No. 7 (June 1, 1936).
47. Wu Ao [1], 184–85; Zhang Jiagui. Republican China had a factory law, but it was primarily concerned with the length of the workday and with regulating the presence of women and child workers, rather than with conditions on the shop floor. Even if it had mandated controls on dust and temperature—an unlikely prospect anywhere in the world in the 1920's and 1930's—it could not have been enforced, because political upheavals in China scuttled any attempts at implementation until 1945. In 1933, H. D. Fong argued that the law was wildly impractical, since it provided for eight-hour shifts, paid vacations, and the barring of women from night work. If it were ever actually enforced, he stated, it would seriously damage the textile industry. For a review of the law and its history to 1933, see *JJZK*, No. 38 (Nov. 15, 1933). For an example of a government directive requiring child care and nursing rooms in the mills in 1936 (also never implemented), see Tianjin shehui ju, *Shehui ju gongbao*, No. 9 (July 1, 1936), 13–15.
48. Israel Epstein.
49. Wu Ao [1], 105–6.
50. *Ibid.*, 54–56, 120–22; Israel Epstein.
51. Wu Ao [1], 120–22; Fong [1], 182.
52. *Laogong yuekan*, 4, No. 8 (1935), 10; *YSB*, March 10, 1935, 14.
53. Li Guilan; Han Ruixiang, Jan. 17, 1981; Zhang Chunfeng; Zhang Jiagui.
54. Zhang Wenqing.
55. Wu Ao [1], 83–84.
56. Wu Ao [1], 104–5, gives statistics on the major ailments treated at the Yu Yuan Mill in 1929. Conditions apparently did not change greatly after the occupation. According to statistics compiled in 1947 in the Yu Yuan's successor, Mill #2, 27.6 percent of the workers had respiratory infections, 3.5 percent had tuberculosis, and 38.2 percent suffered from eye inflammations. Mian Er, *Changshi*, 114.
57. Zhang Xuyu, 13; Zhang Chunfeng; zhongguo [4], 14–15; Tianjin shehui ju, *Shehui ju gongbao*, No. 7 (June 1, 1936); Mian Si, "1947 nian bugao," May 23, June 6, 1947.
58. Annual Report of the Bureau of Social Affairs, Aug. 1928–July 1929, cited in Fong [5], 16; Fong [1], 155–56; Zhang Xuyu, 13.
59. Fong [1], 154; Minami manshū, 92, 103; Zhang Wenqing.
60. Since cotton mills were the subject of far more investigation than the workshops of Santiaoshi or the transport guilds, there are more data available about prevailing wage rates in various periods. More, however, is not necessarily better, and the cotton mill data have all the same faults of internal inconsistency, variable survey populations, and lack of correlation with the cost of living or with Tianjin's changing currency systems. In lieu of an attempt to adjust for such discrepancies, this inquiry limits itself to a discussion of certain features of wage payment in the Tianjin mills: the time and piece systems, the importance of bonuses, the differences between wages paid to men and to women, and the role, in periods of economic distress, of wages paid in kind.
61. Fong [1], 127.
62. In 1930, for instance, any millhand who worked continuously for two weeks was awarded *yi gong*, which was probably equivalent to a day's wages. Nankai

daxue [2]; Fong [1], 123–24. In government-owned mills after 1945, workers received two days' extra pay for every two weeks of work; this was known as *sheng gong*. Mian Si, "1947 nian bugao," May 8, 1947.

63. Fong [1], 133; Nankai daxue [2]; Mian Si, "1947 nian bugao," Sept. 25, 1947.

64. Han Ruixiang, April 1, 1981; Ji Kailin; Zhang Wenqing.

65. Zhang Chunfeng.

66. Zhang Wenqing.

67. Ji Kailin; Mian Si, "1946 nian ben chang jianjie he diaocha," n.p.; Mian Si, "1947 nian bugao," May 30, Sept. 17, Nov. 28, 1947.

68. Mian Si, "1947 nian bugao," Nov. 15, Sept. 17, 1947; Ji Guangzhi, "Jiu Zhongguo shiqi Tianjin gongren zhuangkuang," 2, No. 3, 17; Mian Er, *Changshi*, 111–12.

69. Ji Kailin.

70. Zhang Wenqing.

71. Pollard, *Genesis of Modern Management*, 203.

72. *Heng Yuan Fangzhi Youxian Gongsi*.

73. Wu Ao [1], 56.

74. Mian Si, "1947 nian bugao."

75. *Heng Yuan Fangzhi Youxian Gongsi*.

76. Han Ruixiang, Jan. 17, 1981.

77. Han Ruixiang, April 1, 1981; Ji Kailin.

78. Zhang Chunfeng.

79. Li Guilan; Zhang Wenqing; Cheng Changli.

80. On similar broad powers of foremen in late-nineteenth-century Moscow factories, see Robert Johnson, *Peasant and Proletarian*, 86–87.

81. Zhang Wenqing. 82. Zhang Chunfeng.

83. Zhang Wenqing. 84. Wu Ao [1], 56, 123–24.

85. Zhang Wenqing. 86. Zhang Chunfeng.

87. Ji Kailin. 88. Zhang Chunfeng.

89. Zhang Wenqing. 90. Han Ruixiang, April 1, 1981.

91. Ji Kailin. 92. Han Ruixiang, April 1, 1981.

93. *Ibid*. 94. Wu Ao [1], 123–24.

95. Fong [1], 128. 96. Mian Er, *Changshi*, 83, 91.

97. Wu Ao [1], 56; *YSB*, March 10, 1935, 14. In nineteenth-century Moscow factories, the only place for workers to meet was the lavatory, which workers in one plant called "our club." Johnson, *Peasant and Proletarian*, 93.

98. Cheng Changli. 99. Ji Kailin.

100. Zhang Wenqing. 101. Cheng Changli.

102. Wu Ao [1], 13–14, 109–19; Fong [1], 133, 158, 181–89.

103. "Zhongfang Tianjin," 26. A similar report on Mill #4 is given in Mian Si, "1946 nian ben chang." On provision for burial expenses at this mill, see Mian Si, "1947 nian bugao," #4. A particularly puzzling feature of this "welfare literature" is its frequent mention of maternity benefits for women workers. See, for example, Wang Qingbin, 79, on purported benefits as early as 1926. Mian Si, "1947 nian bugao," summarizes the pregnancy policy of all government mills in 1947 as follows: Workers were to have four weeks off before giving birth and four weeks off afterward. Time off was also provided if a worker suffered a miscarriage. Workers were paid part or all of their salaries during these periods. Since there is no evi-

dence that these regulations were ever enforced, however, there is no reason to think that they were an important factor in the careers of women workers.

104. Pollard, *Genesis of Modern Management*, 202–3; Johnson, *Peasant and Proletarian*, 87–91.

105. Pollard, *Genesis*, 201.

106. Han Ruixiang, Jan. 17, 1981.

107. *YSB*, Jan. 17, 1937, 12; Zhang Wenqing; Zhang Jiagui; Cheng Changli; Ji Kailin. Post-Liberation accounts have described the experiences of these child workers in great detail, often taking them as emblematic of all Tianjin millhands. See, for example, "Tonggong ku" (The suffering of the child workers), in Zhongguo [3], 20–23.

108. Zhang Wenqing; Gao Fengqi; Zhang Jiagui; Cheng Changli.

109. Cheng Changli.

110. *Ibid.*

111. *Ibid.*; Han Ruixiang, Jan. 17, 1981.

112. On the increasing age of millhands during this period, see Cheng Changli.

113. Mian Si, "1947 nian bugao."

114. On the "underlife" of Moscow factory workers and its enrichment by these networks, see Johnson, *Peasant and Proletarian*, 94–97. He borrows the term "underlife" from Erving Goffman, in *Asylums*.

115. Ji Kailin.

116. *Ibid.*

117. Zhang Jiagui.

118. Ji Kailin; Gao Fengqi; Zhang Chunfeng.

119. Han Ruixiang, Jan. 17, 1981.

120. *Ibid.*

121. Mian Er, *Changshi*, 36, 119–20; Wu Ao [1], 129.

122. Li Shiyu, March 24, 1981; Chen Zhi.

123. Han Ruixiang, April 1, 1981.   124. *Ibid.*

125. Zhang Jiagui.   126. *Ibid.*

127. Han Ruixiang, April 1, 1981; Li Shiyu.

128. Han Ruixiang, Jan. 17, 1981.   129. Zhang Chunfeng.

130. *YSB*, Feb. 8, 1948, 4.   131. Han Ruixiang, April 1, 1981.

132. *YSB*, Feb. 8, 1948, 4; Mian Er, *Changshi*, 109.

133. *YSB*, Feb. 8, 1948, 4.

134. *YSB*, July 30, 1948, 5.   135. Zhang Wenqing.

136. Zhang Chunfeng.   137. Wu Ao [1], 127.

138. Zhang Wenqing; Mian Er, *Changshi*, 83; Zhongguo [4], 17. For a discussion of sworn sisterhood among cotton mill workers in Shanghai, see Honig, "Women," Chapter 4.

139. Chen Zhi; Zhang Jiagui.

140. Li Shiyu, a sociologist who joined the Yi Guan Dao as a high school student during the occupation in order to investigate its practices, hypothesizes that its appeal in North China cities during the war is explained by its offer of comfort during a time of uncertainty. Its followers increased after the 1939 flood and during the difficult economic conditions of the early 1940's. Members proselytized among their friends and relatives, exhorting them to "join me in heaven." Most of the members were people in the commercial sector, including a number of rich merchants. Li argues that most workers had neither the money nor the time to invest

in sect activities. Several exceptions were managers and foremen in ironworking and weaving factories, who may have brought workers in with them. Li estimates that during the Japanese occupation, as much as a quarter of the Tianjin population belonged to the Yi Guan Dao. Li Shiyu, *Xiandai Huabei mimi zongjiao*, 32–78, 87; interview with Li Shiyu, April 16, 1980, conducted jointly with Linda Grove. The Yi Guan Dao is also discussed in Lev Deliusin, "The I-kuan Tao Society." For an account of the Yi Guan Dao in Tianjin and its suppression after Liberation, see Lieberthal, *Revolution and Tradition*, 14–15, 106, 108–18. For a post-1949 Chinese account of sect activities, see Zan Daotu, "Yi Guan Dao." On recent activities of the sect in Taiwan, see David K. Jordan, "The Recent History of the Celestial Way."

141. Zhang Wenqing. Li, April 16, 1980, confirms that families often joined the sect as a unit.

142. Mian Er, *Changshi*, 87. "Jin gang" refers to the warrior attendants of Buddha.

143. William Reddy argues that large-scale pilfering in the wool mills at Roubaix in the 1830's was a continuation of the eighteenth-century food riot form, with workers centering their protests not yet on the issue of labor as a commodity, but on the prices paid for tangible products. "The success of such practices depended on a tacit communal accord that could not really be called a conspiracy, but which offered an informal tactic for imposing equity upon the owners if their pay rates dropped too low." Williams M. Reddy, "Skeins, Scales, Discounts." 211–13.

144. Wu Ao [1], 123–24.   145. Mian Er, *Changshi*, 90.
146. Zhang Chunfeng.   147. *Ibid.*
148. Chen Zhi; Cheng Changli; Zhang Chunfeng.
149. Zhang Chunfeng.   150. *Ibid.*
151. *Ibid.*   152. Zhang Wenqing.
153. Zhang Chunfeng.   154. Han Ruixiang, April 1, 1981.
155. Mian Si, "1947 nian bugao," #12.
156. Han Ruixiang, April 1, 1981.

CHAPTER SEVEN

1. Zheng Yufu, *Tianjin youlanzhi*, 30–32.

2. *Ibid.*, 32, 218; interview with Li Shiyu, Jan. 19, 1981.

3. Zheng Yufu, 33–35. The custom of "signaling prices in sleeves" (*xiuli tun jin*) originated in livestock markets in the countryside. The purpose was to keep prices secret, but local superstition held that if cattle at market found out what their selling price was, they might become angry and die of spite. The person who was proposing a price would grab the hand of his counterpart (concealed in the long sleeve of his gown) according to a prearranged pattern. If he grabbed one finger, it meant the number "one," and so on up to five. To signify "six" he separated the thumb and pinky of his negotiating partner's hand to resemble the character for six. For seven, he pressed the thumb and first two fingers together; "eight" was formed by pushing apart the thumb and index finger; and for ten he pressed all five fingers together and rotated them, indicating "twice five." The signal for "one," rotated several times, might mean 110 or 1,110, depending upon the context. Interviews with Li Shiyu, Jan. 19, March 24, 1981.

4. For a more detailed discussion of currency disorder and its effects on the

working class, see Feng Huanian, 489; *JJZK*, No. 203 (Feb. 4, 1937), n.p.; and Gail Hershatter, "The Making of the Working Class," 380–87.

5. Wang Zishou, 46; *Tianjin shi zhoukan*, 4, No. 2, 11; *YSB*, March 24, 1947, 4.

6. Zheng Yufu, 34; Li Shiyu, Jan. 19, 1981; *Joint Factory History*, 101.

7. "Chunjie zhong laoku." The following description, unless otherwise indicated, is based upon this article and on Zheng Yufu, 36–56; Tianjin [21]; and interview with Li Shiyu, Jan. 19, 1981.

8. Zheng Yufu, 213–14.

9. *Ibid.*, 46–47; Li Shiyu, Jan. 19, 1981.

10. Zhang Heqin, "Jinmen qutan cangsang lu," 117, 119.

11. According to Li Shiyu, the prototype of the *bengbeng xi* was a form called *laozi*, which entered Hebei from the Northeast and could be performed with a small group of actors and no costumes. It gradually developed into *ban bian xi*, which had costumes but did not use a full cast of actors. This form, which flourished in Hebei villages and reached its mature development in the 1930's, took root in Tianjin because of large-scale migration from the villages. It differed from "Beijing opera" or *jingxi*, which had developed originally in Hubei and is still performed with a Hubei accent. Beijing opera was also called *da xi* or "major play"; *bengbeng xi* was considered a minor form. Li Shiyu, Jan. 19, 1981.

12. Zheng Yufu, 49, 44, 42; Xin Fengxia, *Reminiscences*, 31, 35–38.

13. The origins of drumsinging are more difficult to trace than those of *bengbeng xi*. Many of the originators of the form were apparently descendants of Manchu bannermen who became impoverished under the Republic. Li Shiyu, Jan. 19, 1981. Catherine Stevens has found that one form, Beijing drumsinging, originated when singers began to move from the Hejian county countryside to Tianjin around 1880. In the first half of the twentieth century, performers moved from open-air theaters to teahouses. "Drumsinging," Stevens writes, "catered to an audience which, while it included members of the middle and lower classes, depended for much of its support on an educated and leisured elite, who engaged boxes at their favorite theaters on a yearly basis." Stevens, "Peking Drumsinging," 9, 74, 77, 81. A detailed discussion of the various drumsinging genres of Tianjin appears in Zhang Heqin, 121–38.

14. "Chunjie zhong."

15. Yao Xiyun, "Tianjin shidiao de yanbian," 163; a description of Beijing *laoziguan* in which female drumsingers performed is given in Stevens, 61–62.

16. Zheng Yufu, 42.

17. Stevens, 63–64, gives a detailed description of variety entertainments.

18. Zheng Yufu, 49–51. Additional information on the lives of performers in Tianjin may be found in Guo Rongqi, "Wode xueyi jingguo"; and Zhang Shouchen, "Huigu wode yiren shengya."

19. Zhang Heqin, 126–28. *Danxian* singing was originally developed by the Manchu bannermen. Li Shiyu, Jan. 19, 1981.

20. *YSB*, Aug. 17, 1948, 5. Though this is potentially a very significant development in the formation of working-class culture, its investigation would require a full-scale research project on local cultural history.

21. Stevens, 81, 63–64, 82, 85–100; Zhang Heqin, 127, 133.

22. Zhang Heqin, 140–41; Yao Xiyun, 160–66.

23. Zheng Yufu, 52; "Chunjie zhong"; Luo Yusheng, "Wutai shenghuo liushi nian," 181–82.

24. Yao Xiyun, 165.

25. Zhang Shou, *Jin men za ji*, II, 47.

26. *Ibid.*, 47–48. Hunhunr were frequently involved in the opening of broth-els. One famous establishment in the north city, the Tian Bao Ban, was opened jointly by a hunhunr-cum-petty-official named Tao and a former servant known only as Xiao Li Ma (Little Mother Li). After 1900 they moved the brothel to the south city. When Tao died Xiao Li Ma ran the place alone, counting such famous warlords as Cao Kun and Zhang Zuolin among her regular visitors. Xiao Li Ma had enough political influence in Tianjin to help the chief of police get his job back after he was sacked. In 1921, at the age of eighty, she still was called Little Mother Li. Li Ranshi, "Jiu Tianjin de hunhunr," 205–6.

27. Zhang Shou, 48.

28. Wu Ao [1], 44–48.

29. Wu Ao [4], *SHYK*, supp. (March 20, 1930), n.p.

30. Chen Guilan; Chen Yihe. For descriptions of the lives of prostitutes in Tianjin, see Xin Fengxia, *Reminiscences*, 16–17, 40–48, and her *Yishu shengya*, 39–48, 93–99.

31. Wang Da, "Tianjin zhi gongye," 118.

32. Song Yunpu, *Tianjin zhilue*, 356.

33. Chen Guilan.

34. *Tianjin shi zhoukan*, 2, No. 4 (March 29, 1947), 4; No. 6 (April 12, 1947), 10–11.

35. Tianjin [21].

36. *SHYK*, supp. (March 20, 1930), 1–3.

37. Wu Ao [4]. 93.7 percent of criminals of all classes were male. The population of Tianjin in 1929, excluding the foreign concessions, was 1,391,121. The number of workers was 47,519. If we double this number to account for transport workers, then laborers were about 6.8 percent of the total population. Figures on population are from the *Chinese Economic Journal and Bulletin*, 20, No. 3 (March 1937); the number of workers is from *NWSS*, 3, No. 17 (April 28, 1930), 81, 85–86.

38. Cheng Haifong, "Visit to Peiping," 11; *Guoji laogong tongxun*, 4, No. 4 (April 1937), 102–3; Tianjin [8], 12, 45, 263.

39. Tianjin [8], 59; *YSB*, Sept. 22, 1936, 5.

40. *YSB*, July 16, 1947, 4.   41. *YSB*, Dec. 31, 1935, 5.

42. *YSB*, March 4, 1935, 5.   43. *YSB*, Nov. 9, 1947, 4.

44. *YSB*, Nov. 5, 1948, 5.

45. *YSB*, June 19, 1936, 5; Tianjin [29].

46. *YSB*, Sept. 15, Oct. 9, 1935, 5.   47. *YSB*, Aug. 10, 1936, 5.

48. *YSB*, July 7, 13, 15, 1947, 4.   49. *YSB*, Feb. 17, 1948, 4.

50. Unless otherwise noted, the account of holiday customs that follows is based upon the following sources: Zheng Yufu, 68–75; Tianjin [21]; interview with Li Shiyu, March 24, 1981; Chen Pei, ed., *Hebei sheng Wuqing xian shiqing*, 26–28; Xin Fengxia, *Reminiscences*; interview with Chen Guilan, Nov. 2, 1980; interview with Ji Kailin, Dec. 29, 1980; and my own two years' residence in Tianjin from 1979 to 1981, in cases where I have verified that customs I observed were practiced before Liberation. The Wuqing material was used to analyze the similarity of urban and rural customs. A delightful and much more thorough account of holiday customs in Beijing is given in H. Y. Lowe, *Adventures of Wu*, I, 141–48, 221–32; II: 22–41, 63–74, 140–61.

51. For a description of such a scene, see Xin Fengxia, *Yishu shengya*, 1–3.
52. Chen Guilan.
53. Ji Kailin.
54. Li Shiyu tells the following story: Just before the Japanese occupation, Japanese ships frequently docked at Tianjin. Most of the ship names contained the character *maru*, which in Chinese is pronounced *wan*. During the Ghost Festival in 1936, a group of workers launched a watermelon boat that had carved into its side a political pun, *Riben wan*, which was a homonym for "Japanese ship," but was written with the characters for "Japan is finished." Li Shiyu, March 24, 1981.
55. Chen Guilan.
56. *Ibid*.
57. For elaborate descriptions of these rituals in Tianjin and in Wuqing county, see Tianjin [21], and Chen Pei, 24–25. Beijing bethrothal and wedding customs are depicted in Lowe, *Adventures of Wu*, II, 190–228.
58. Chen Guilan; Tianjin [13], 10.
59. Cheng Changli.
60. Zhang Jiagui; Ji Kailin. On this custom in Taiwan, see Arthur P. Wolf, "The Women of Hai-shan: A Demographic Portrait," in Margery Wolf and Roxane Witke, eds., *Women in Chinese Society*, 89–110.
61. The description that follows, unless otherwise noted, is drawn from Tianjin [2], 1–6; and Tianjin [21]. Neither of these sources is specific about which class of people practiced which birth customs, but interview data suggest that, as with marriages and funerals, workers were as observant as they could afford to be. Beijing birth customs are described in Lowe, I, 1–67.
62. Chen Guilan.
63. Xin Fengxia, *Yishu shengya*, 93.
64. Tianjin [13], 1–13; Israel Epstein.
65. Tianjin [21]; Chen Pei, 25–26; Chen Guilan.
66. Xin Fengxia, *Yishu shengya*, 2. Among the 132 households surveyed by Feng Huanian in 1927–28, three had funerals. One for an aged mother cost the family 23 yuan (about one-ninth of the total annual income); one for a young child cost less than five yuan. The third funeral was for the head of a household, but since he died in another province the family did not pay the major share of the costs. One household covered in this survey received presents of more than 60 yuan when the father of the house died. Feng Huanian, 503–4, 528.
67. Ji Kailin.
68. The numbers were 2,910 and 1,543 respectively. Wu Ao [4], and [1], 39–41.

CHAPTER EIGHT

1. Chen Ta [Chen Da], "Analysis of Strikes in China," 846.
2. Dong Zhenxiu, "Zhongguo gongchandang zai Tianjin," 4; interview with Liao Yongwu, Tianjin History Museum, Nov. 19, 1980. An was a native of Fengrun county, Hebei; he and Yu taught at the Beiyang College of Law and Political Science (Beiyang fazheng zhuanmen xuexiao) in Tianjin while starting the workers' school. In 1923 An was transferred to teaching work in Hangzhou; he was killed in the 1927 coup. Dong Zhenxiu, 22.
3. Dong Zhenxiu, 7, 12, 27–28; Liao Yongwu, Nov. 19, 1980.
4. Wang Lin, *Bozhong*, 3; Liao Yongwu, *Tianjin wanbao*, Oct. 23, 1963; Si Chengxiang, "Canjia Tianjin zaoyi geming," 69; "Yijiu erwu nian Tianjin," 42.

5. "Yijiu erwu," 42–44; 48.

6. *Ibid.*, 43–44; Liao Yongwu, *Tianjin wanbao*, Oct. 23, 1963; Wang Lin, 4–5; Si Chengxiang, 69–70; interview with Zhang Quanyou, former Bao Cheng Cotton Mill worker, Jan. 7, 1981.

7. "Yijiu erwu," 44–45; Liao Yongwu, Nov. 19, 1980; Zhang Quanyou.

8. Wang Lin, 6; Liao Yongwu, "Wusa fenglei hua Tianjin," 93; "Zhao Shiyan shenping shizi," 86–87; "Yijiu erwu," 46; Si Chengxiang, 72–75; Dong Zhenxiu, 13–14; Mian Er, *Changshi*, 30–32.

9. "Yijiu erwu," 45; Wang Lin, 15–25; Dong Xunru, "Yong bu momie de yinian," 58. Another account of these events is given in *YSB*, Aug. 11, 1925, reprinted in Zhongguo [5], 199–201.

10. Si Chengxiang, 76–77; "Yijiu erwu," 47.

11. Si Chengxiang, 77; "Yijiu erwu," 47; Xiang Ruizhi, "Ji yijiu erwu," 116–21; Liao Yongwu, Nov. 19, 1980; Mantetsu tōa keizai chōsa kyoku, *Shina no rōdō undō*, 78; Dong Zhenxiu, 14, 26–27.

12. "Yijiu erwu," 47; Wang Lin, 27–29; Dong Zhenxiu, 14–15; Naitō Juntarō, *Zai Shina keizai sōgi* [Economic Conflict in China] (Tokyo: Toasha, 1925), 144; *North-China Herald*, Aug. 22, 1925, 202.

13. Si Chengxiang, 78; Xiang Ruizhi, 118, "Yijiu erwu," 47.

14. "Yijiu erwu," 47; Si Chengxiang, 78; Wang Lin, 29–32; Zhang Quanyou; Chen Zhi; *North-China Herald*, Aug. 22, 1925, 202.

15. "Yijiu erwu," 47–48; Wang Lin, 33–38; Si Chengxiang, 78–80; Xiang Ruizhi, 118.

16. *North-China Herald*, Aug. 15, 1925, 159.

17. *Ibid.*, Aug. 22, 1925, 202; "Zhao Shiyan shengping shizi," 85; "Yijiu erwu," 48–49; Wang Lin, 39–47; Si Chengxiang, 80–81; Naitō, 146–47; Xiang, 119–21; *North-China Herald*, Oct. 22, 1925, 202.

18. "Zhao Shiyan shengping shizi," 85; Si Chengxiang, 81.

19. Dong Zhenxiu, 16–17; "Zhao Shiyan shengping shizi," 96–97.

20. "Zhao Shiyan shengping shizi," 96–97; Si Chengxiang, 83; Dong Zhenxiu, 17; Liao Yongwu, *Tianjin wanbao*, April 26, 1963; "Zhao Shiyan shengping shizi," 97; *Gongren xiaobao* (Workers' Tabloid), Jan. 25, 1926; *Gongren shenghuo* (Workers' Life), Nos. 8–10 (Jan. 15, 1926), 10–12.

21. *Gongren shenghuo*, Nos. 8–10 (Jan. 15, 1926), 34.

22. *Ibid.*, 16–23; Si Chengxiang, 84.

23. Dong Zhenxiu, 20–22; Si Chengxiang, 88–89, 92–98.

24. Mian Er, *Changshi*, 37–42.

25. *Ibid.*, 39–40; Wang Lin, 48–54; for an account of a 1926 strike at Bei Yang, see Si Chengxiang, 86–88.

26. Dong Zhenxiu, 20; Si Chengxiang, 86–92; Xiang Ruizhi, 121.

27. Liu Weiwu, "Kangzhan qianhou Jinshi gongyun," 10; Si Chengxiang, 98; Gongshangbu laogongsi bian, *Shiqinian gedi gonghui diaocha baogao*, 2–3; He Zechun, 26, 3–4, 43; *NWSS*, 3, No. 18 (May 5, 1930), reports that in 1929 union members totaled 29,542.

28. He Zechun, 45–46, 74–76.   29. *Ibid.*, 66.

30. *Ibid.*, 36; Wu Ao [1], 127–32.   31. He Zechun, *passim*.

32. "Report on the Investigation of Tientsin Trade Unions (Kuomintang Report)," Aug. 1932, cited in Cheng Haifong, China Correspondent Monthly Reports (Feb. 1933), C1809/000, 28.

33. Tianjin [28], 131–36.

34. *Ibid.*, 91–105; Tianjin [5], 10–11.

35. Si Chengxiang, 98.

36. Li Hanyuan, "Guanyu Chen Diyun beibu jingguo." The events leading to this series of arrests are a matter of dispute. Two accounts by CCP worker activists assert that the arrests began when two party officials, former workers themselves, began to extort money and steal from other CCP members. In desperation, the provincial Party Committee ordered the two killed. When the municipal government investigated the murders, the wife of one victim and the mother of another identified a number of CCP members as suspects. The GMD government used this opportunity to sentence many of them, including Peng Zhen (Fu Maogong) to long prison terms. But Li Hanyuan, the head of the government Special Agent Division at the time, denies that the murders, which took place in the French concession and were out of his jurisdiction, had anything to do with the identification of the CCP network. Si Chengxiang, 99–107; Zuo Zhenyu, "Yijiu erjiu niande yuzhong douzheng."

37. *Hongse Zhonghua*, No. 50 (Sept. 10, 1932), 20–28.

38. Wu Ao [4]. The corresponding statistics for 1932–36 are: 1932, 47 disputes (nine strikes); 1933, 25 disputes (five strikes); 1934, 35 disputes (three strikes); 1935, seven disputes (no statistics on strikes); 1936, 14 disputes (no statistics on strikes). These ranged from 2.3 percent to 14.83 percent of the national total. *CYB 1933*, 365; *CYB 1934*, 249; *CYB 1936*, 320; *CYB 1938*, 326; 1934 totals are from Cheng Haifong, "Visit to Peiping," 11.

39. Tianjin [27], 56–57, 59–69, 74–76. For an account of 1932 Bao Cheng strikes over economic issues and the quality of union representation, see *Fangzhi zhoukan*, 2, No. 10 (1932), 254–56; No. 13, 320–21; No. 14, 342–43.

40. Du Wensi, 25; *CYB 1934*, 257.

41. *CYB 1934*, 260.

42. *Ibid.*, 259; Mian Er, *Changshi*, 49–50; Zhang Jiagui, Jan. 17, 1981; *Fangzhi zhoukan*, 3, No. 24 (1933), 766.

43. Zhang Quanyou; *YSB*, July 15–17, 1935; May 15, Sept. 23, Nov. 22, 1936, 5.

44. *YSB*, Jan. 12–16, 19, 20, 22, 26, 27, 29, 30, Feb. 25, March 18, 19, April 17, May 19, June 23, 1935; March 22, 25, April 11, May 20, June 8, 22, 26, July 16, Aug. 29, 1936, 5.

45. *YSB*, Jan. 26, 27, 29, 30, 1935, 5.

46. *YSB*, Jan. 20, 21, 1935, 5.

47. *YSB*, Feb. 1, 10–13, 15, 17, 24, 26, 28, March 1, 5–7, 1935, 5.

48. *YSB*, March 8–11, 1935, 5.

49. *YSB*, March 12, 14, 1935; Aug. 6, Dec. 13, 1936, 5.

50. *China Weekly Review*, 84, No. 9 (April 30, 1938), cited in Cheng Haifong, China Correspondent Monthly Reports, (April 1938), C1803/85, 5.

51. Chen Zhi; Zhang Chunfeng.   52. Han Ruixiang, April 1, 1981.

53. Han Ruixiang, Jan. 17, 1981.   54. Liu Weiwu, 11.

55. Tianjin [4], 181–82; Cheng Haifong, China Correspondent Monthly Reports (Sept. 1946), C1803/176, 41–42.

56. Han Ruixiang, April 1, 1981; Ji Kailin.

57. *Gongren zhoukan*, Nos. 8–9 (Jan. 15, 1947), 7.

58. *Huabei laodong*, 1, No. 8 (Feb. 15, 1947), 17.

59. *Gongren zhoukan*, Nos. 8–9 (Jan. 15, 1947), 9–21.

60. *Tianjin shi zhoukan*, 1, No. 3 (Dec. 28, 1946), 3–4.

61. Cheng Haifong, China Correspondent Monthly Reports (Oct. 1946), C1803/177, 13; (June 1947), C13-2-77, 39; *Tianjin shi zheng tongji yuebao* [Monthly report on statistics of the Tianjin Municipal Government], 3, No. 2, 14; 3, No. 3, 8; 3, No. 4, 10.

62. Cheng Haifong, China Correspondent Monthly Reports (Sept. 1946), C1803/176, 43.

63. Ji Guangzhi, "Jiu Zhongguo shiqi Tianjin gongren," 17.

64. Cheng Haifong, China Correspondent Monthly Reports (Sept. 1946), C1803/176, 41; *YSB*, Dec. 27, 1946, 4; Jan. 7, 1947, 4.

65. See, for example, *YSB*, Dec. 7, 12, 15, 1946, 4.

66. Han Ruixiang, April 1, 1981.

67. Virtually every worker interviewed for this study confirmed these impressions. Han Ruixiang, April 1, 1981, offered one of the most complete appraisals.

68. Interview with Zuo Jian, former underground CCP member, Oct. 9, 1980.

69. Zuo Jian; Santiaoshi Archives, A2 (42.2, 42.4).

70. At the end of 1946, with the outbreak of civil war, the Tianjin Work Committee dissolved and went back under the leadership of the Central Hebei Urban Work Department. Zuo Jian; Santiaoshi Archives, A2 (42.4); Chen Yihe.

71. Zuo Jian; interview with Sun Shaohua, former cotton mill worker and official of the GLU, April 16, 1981. Sun subsequently worked in Cotton Mills #2 and #4, under different names. Su Geng remained in the Liberated Areas until 1949, then returned to Tianjin after 1949 and took charge of women's work in the GLU. She was attacked during the Cultural Revolution and died in 1977.

72. Interview with Yang Chunlin, former wool mill worker and official of the GLU, May 29, 1980.

73. Yang Chunlin.

74. *Ibid.*

75. Han Ruixiang, April 1, 1981; Sun Shaohua.

76. Mian Er, *Changshi*, 123–24.

77. *Gongren zhoukan*, No. 1 (1946), 7; *YSB*, Jan. 10–12, 15, 17, 18, 1947, 4.

78. *YSB*, Jan. 7, 8, 1947, 4; *Gongren zhoukan*, Nos. 8–9 (Jan. 15, 1947), 12; Mian Si, "1947 nian bugao liudi bo," Jan. 6, 11, 13; Chen Zhi.

79. *YSB*, March 5, Nov. 26, 27, 29, 1947, 4.

80. *YSB*, June 1–3, 11, 15, 17, 21, 1947, 4; Nov. 24, Dec. 19, 1948, 3.

81. *YSB*, Feb. 18, 1948, 4.

82. Han Ruixiang, April 1, 1981; Ji Kailin.

83. Li Guilan; Gao Fengqi.

84. Lieberthal, *Revolution*, 28–29.

85. E. P. Thompson, *The Making of the English Working Class*, 9.

86. This was not true during the Cultural Revolution. Whether the uses of these terms at that time accurately reflected workplace struggles is a question well beyond the scope of this study.

BIBLIOGRAPHY

Aminzade, Ronald. "French Strike Development and Class Struggle." *Social Science History*, 4, No. 1 (Winter 1980), 57–79.

An Lifu. *Tianjin shi banyun gongren gongzuo baogao* (Report on work among the transport workers in Tianjin). Beijing: Gongren chubanshe, March 1950.

Arnold, Julean. *Commercial Handbook of China*, vol. I. Washington, D.C.: Government Printing Office, 1919.

Banghui shouce si zhong (Four secret society manuals). Taibei: Xiang sheng chubanshe, 1975.

Bao Juemin. Lecture at Nankai University, Tianjin. July 4, 1980.

————. "Tianjin gangkou fazhan zhi dili beijing" (The geographical background of Tianjin's development as a port). *JJZK*, No. 77 (Aug. 22, 1934).

————. "Tianjin zhi qihou" (The climate of Tianjin). *JJZK*, No. 44 (Dec. 27, 1933).

————. Tour of Tianjin. Jan. 24, 1980.

Barnett, A. Doak. *China on the Eve of Communist Takeover*. New York: Praeger, 1963.

Bell, Donald H. "Worker Culture and Worker Politics: The Experience of an Italian Town, 1880–1915." *Social History*, 3, No. 1 (Jan. 1978), 1–21.

Bi Mingqi. "Tianjin de yanghang yu maiban" (Tianjin's foreign firms and compradores). *WSZL*, No. 38 (Feb. 1963), 69–97.

Bianco, Lucien. *Origins of the Chinese Revolution, 1915–1949*. Stanford, Calif.: Stanford University Press, 1971.

Bonnell, Victoria E. *Roots of Rebellion: Workers' Politics and Organizations in*

St. Petersburg and Moscow, 1900–1914. Berkeley: University of California Press, 1983.

Burgess, John Stewart. *The Guilds of Peking.* New York: Columbia University Press, 1928.

Bythell, Duncan. *The Sweated Trades: Outwork in Nineteenth-Century Britain.* New York: St. Martin's Press, 1978.

Cai Muhan. "'Shenfang Cai' fajiashi" (How the Cai family of Shenfang built a family fortune). *TJWS*, No. 2 (Feb. 1979), 130–41.

Chan, Ming. "Labor and Empire: The Chinese Labor Movement in the Canton Delta, 1895–1927." Ph.D. diss., Stanford University, 1975.

Chang Nan. "Yingguo Huifeng Yinhang de jingji lüeduo" (The economic plunder of the British Hong Kong and Shanghai Banking Corporation). *TJWS*, No. 9 (June 1980), 69–78.

Ch'en, Jerome. *Yuan Shih-k'ai,* 2d ed. Stanford, Calif.: Stanford University Press, 1972.

Chen Pei, ed. *Hebei sheng Wuqing xian shiqing* (Affairs in Wuqing county, Hebei). N.p.: Xinminhui zhongyang zonghui, 1940.

Chen Shiru. "Cao Kun jiazu dui renmin de jingji lüeduo he yazha" (The economic plunder and oppression of the people by Cao Kun's family). *TJWS*, No. 1 (Dec. 1978), 99–112.

Chen Ta [Chen Da]. "Analysis of Strikes in China from 1918–1926." *CEJ*, 1, No. 10 (Oct. 1927), 843–65.

Cheng, Haifong. China Correspondent Monthly Reports. 1927–49. ILO Archives, Geneva.

———. "Visit to Peiping, Tientsin and Tsinan, 21 May–14 June 1935." C1802/3. ILO Archives, Geneva.

Chesneaux, Jean. *The Chinese Labor Movement, 1919–1927.* Stanford, Calif.: Stanford University Press, 1968.

———. *Secret Societies in China in the Nineteenth and Twentieth Centuries.* Ann Arbor: University of Michigan Press, 1971.

Chin, Rockwood Q. P. "Cotton Mills, Japan's Economic Spearhead in China." *Far Eastern Survey,* 6, No. 23 (Nov. 17, 1937), 263.

China. *Trade Statistics of the Treaty Ports, for the Period 1863–1872.* Shanghai: Imperial Maritime Customs Press, 1873.

"Chunjie zhong laoku dazhong yulechang: Sanbuguan manyouji" (The amusement place of the toiling masses during the spring festival: records of a ramble through Sanbuguan). *YSB* (Tianjin), Feb. 1935.

Cochran, Sherman. *Big Business in China: Sino-Foreign Rivalry in the Cigarette Industry, 1890–1930.* Cambridge, Mass.: Harvard University Press, 1980.

Cohen, Paul. *China and Christianity.* Cambridge, Mass.: Harvard University Press, 1963.

Cranmer-Byng, J. L., ed. *An Embassy to China: Being the Journal Kept by Lord Macartney During His Embassy to the Emperor Ch'ien-lung 1793–1794.* N.p.: Longmans, 1962.

Cronin, James E. "Labor Insurgency and Class Formation: Comparative Perspectives on the Crisis of 1917–1920 in Europe." *Social Science History,* 4 (1980), 125–52.

———. "Theories of Strikes: Why Can't They Explain the British Experience?" *Journal of Social History,* 12, No. 2 (Winter 1978), 194–221.

Deliusin, Lev. "The I-Kuan-Tao Society." In Jean Chesneaux, ed., *Popular Movements and Secret Societies in China, 1840–1950*. Stanford, Calif.: Stanford University Press, 1972, pp. 225–33.

Deng Qinglan, ed. *Tianjin shi dierci gongye tongji* (Second set of Tianjin industrial statistics). Tianjin: Tianjin shehui ju, 1935.

Deng Zhongxia. *Zhongguo zhigong yundong jianshi* (Short history of the Chinese workers' movement). Beijing: Renmin chubanshe, 1953.

Dierci Zhongguo laodong nianjian (The second China labor yearbook). Beiping: Shehui diaochasuo, 1932.

Ding Gu. "Zhongguo gongye de liudong ziben de wenti" (The problem of circulating capital in Chinese industry). *JJZK*, No. 14 (May 31, 1933).

Dong Changyan. *Tianjin mianfen gongye zhuangkuang (gongye congkan diyizhong)* (The Tianjin flour industry [industrial series no. 1]). N.p.: Hebei shengli gongye xueyuan gongye jingji xuehui, 1932.

Dong Quanfu and Liu Shenzhi. "Cao Kun jiazu yu Heng Yuan Fangzhi Youxian Gongsi" (The Cao Kun family and the Tianjin Heng Yuan Spinning Company, Ltd.). *WSZL*, No. 44 (Aug. 1963), 85–114.

Dong Xunru. "Yongyu bu momie de yinian" (An indelible recollection). *TJWS*, No. 10 (July 1980), 49–68.

Dong Zhenxiu. "Zhongguo gongchandang zai Tianjin de zaoqi geming huodong" (The early revolutionary activities of the CCP in Tianjin). *TJWS*, No. 10 (July 1980), 1–29.

Drake, Noah Fields. *Map and Short Description of Tientsin*. N.p., 1900.

Du Lijun. "Bai E zai Tianjin" (White Russians in Tianjin). *TJWS*, No. 6 (June 1980), 150–77.

Du Wensi. *Ping Jin gongye diaocha* (A survey of the manufacturing industries in Beiping and Tianjin). Beiping: Gongji yinshu ju, 1934.

Dublin, Thomas. *Women at Work*. New York: Columbia University Press, 1979.

Duplessis, Robert S., and Martha C. Howell. "Reconsidering the Early Modern Urban Economy: The Cases of Leiden and Lille." *Past and Present*, 94 (Feb. 1982), 49–84.

Eberhard, Wolfram. *A History of China*. Berkeley: University of California Press, 1977.

Eley, Geoff, and Keith Nield. "Why Does Social History Ignore Politics?" *Social History*, 5, No. 2 (May 1980), 249–71.

Ellis, Henry. *Journal of the Proceedings of the Late Embassy to China*. Philadelphia: A. Small, 1818.

Fairbank, John K. "Patterns Behind the Tientsin Massacre." *Harvard Journal of Asiatic Studies*, No. 20 (1957), 480–511.

Fang Xianting [H. D. Fong]. "Tianjin mianhua yunxiao gaikuang" (A survey of the transportation and sale of raw cotton in Tianjin), Part 2. *JJZK*, No. 76 (Aug. 15, 1934), n.p.

———. "Zhongguo mian fangzhiye zhi weiji" (The crisis in the Chinese cotton spinning industry). *JJZK*, No. 8 (April 19, 1933).

———, and Chen Zhenhan. "Zhongguo gongye xianyou kunnan de fenxi" (An analysis of current difficulties in Chinese industry). *JJZK*, No. 26 (Aug. 23, 1933).

Feng Guoliang and Guo Tingxin. "Jiefangqian Haihe ganliu zhili gaishu" (A general description of bringing the main stream of the Hai River under control before Liberation). *TJWS*, No. 18 (Jan. 1982), 25–38.

Feng Huanian Xiansheng jiniance (Memorial volume to Mr. Feng Huanian). *Minguo shiliunian zhi shiqinian Tianjin shouyi gongren jiating shenghuo diaocha zhi fenxi* (An analysis of the investigation of the livelihood of Tianjin handicraft workers' households, 1927–28). Tianjin: Li Rui, Hua Wenyu, Wu Daye yinzeng, 1932.

Feuerwerker, Albert. *China's Early Industrialization.* Cambridge, Mass.: Harvard University Press, 1958.

———. *The Foreign Establishment in China in the Early Twentieth Century.* Ann Arbor: Center for Chinese Studies, University of Michigan, 1976.

———. "Industrial Enterprise in Twentieth-Century China: The Chee Hsin Cement Co." In Feuerwerker et al., eds., *Approaches to Modern Chinese History.* Berkeley: University of California Press, 1967, 304–42.

Fong, H. D. [Fang Xianting] [1]. *Cotton Industry and Trade in China*, Vol. I. Tientsin: Chihli Press, 1932.

———[2]. "Cotton Mills and Raw Cotton Supply in Tientsin." *Chinese Economic Monthly*, No. 7 (April 1924), 1–6.

———[3]. *Hosiery Knitting in Tientsin.* Tientsin: Chihli Press, 1930.

———[4]. *Industrial Organization in China.* Tientsin: Chihli Press, 1937.

———[5]. "Industrialization and Labor in Hopei, with Special Reference to Tientsin." *Chinese Social and Political Science Review*, 15, No. 1 (April 1931), 1–28.

———[6]. *Rayon and Cotton Weaving in Tientsin.* Tientsin: Chihli Press, 1930.

———[7]. *Tientsin Carpet Industry.* Tientsin: Chihli Press, 1929.

Fox-Genovese, Elizabeth, and Eugene Genovese. "The Political Crisis of Social History: A Marxian Perspective." *Social History*, 10, No. 2 (Winter 1976), 205–20.

Gao Bohai. "Tianjin maiban Gao Xingqiao fajiashi" (History of the family fortune of Tianjin compradore Gao Xingqiao). *WSZL*, No. 44 (Aug. 1963), 202–26.

Gao Erfu et al. "Jiefang qianxi yanyan yixi de Tianjin gongshangye" (The last gasp of Tianjin industry and commerce on the eve of Liberation). *TJWS*, No. 5 (Oct. 1979), 58–76.

Golas, Peter J. "Early Ch'ing Guilds." In G. William Skinner, ed., *The City in Late Imperial China.* Stanford, Calif.: Stanford University Press, 1977, 555–80.

"Gongce wenti" (The problem of public toilets). *Tianjin shi zhoukan*, 6, No. 7 (March 20, 1948), 12–13.

Gongren shenghuo (Workers' Life). Tianjin. Jan. 1926. Tianjin lishi bowuguan, #GF 1036.

Gongren xiaobao (Workers' Tabloid). Tianjin. Jan. 25, 1926. Tianjin lishi bowuguan, #GF 1748.

Gongshangbu laogongsi bian. *Shiqinian gedi gonghui diaocha baogao (gongshang congkan, laogonglei zhiyi)* (1928 report on an investigation of unions [no. 1 on labor in the series on industry and commerce]). Nanjing: Nanjing gongshangbu zongwusi bianjike, 1930.

Grove, Linda. "Managerial Practices among Traditional Merchants and Modern Capitalists in North China" (forthcoming article).

———. "Rural Society in Revolution: The Gaoyang District, 1910–1947." Ph.D. diss., University of California, Berkeley, 1975.

Gu Jinwu. "Shilun jiefang qian Tianjin Santiaoshi zibenzhuyi boxue de ruogan te-
dian" (A preliminary discussion of some special characteristics of capitalist ex-
ploitation at Santiaoshi in Tianjin before Liberation). Mimeo. Tianjin: Nankai
Daxue jingjixue xi, 1979.
Guo Rongqi. "Wode xueyi jingguo" (How I studied acting). *TJWS*, No. 14
(March 1981), 206–23.
Gutman, Herbert G. *Work, Culture, and Society in Industrializing America*. New
York: Knopf, 1976.
Haimson, Leopold H. "The Problem of Social Stability in Urban Russia, 1905–
1917." *Slavic Review*, 23, No. 4 (Dec. 1964), 619–42; *ibid.*, 24, No. 1 (March
1965), 1–22.
Hamilton, Gary G. "Regional Associations and the Chinese City: A Comparative
Perspective." *Comparative Studies in Society and History*, 21, No. 3 (July 1979),
346–61.
Hanagan, Michael P. *The Logic of Solidarity: Artisans and Industrial Workers in
Three French Towns, 1871–1914*. Urbana: University of Illinois Press, 1980.
———, and Charles Stephenson. "The Skilled Worker and Working-Class Pro-
test." *Social Science History*, 4, No. 1 (Winter 1980), 5–13.
Hao Yen-p'ing. *The Comprador in Nineteenth Century China: Bridge Between East
and West*. Cambridge, Mass.: Harvard University Press, 1970.
He Chengruo. "Ni Sichong zai Anhui he Tianjin de touzi" (The investment of Ni
Sichong in Anhui and Tianjin). *TJWS*, No. 13 (Jan. 1981), 187–91.
He Lian. "Bai yin zhengshui yu miansha zhengshui zhengcishang zhi maodun"
(The policy contradiction in collecting taxes on silver and increasing taxes on
cotton yarn). *JJZK*, No. 88 (Nov. 7, 1934).
———. "Zui jin Tianjin tongyuan diejia zhi yuanyin ji qi yingxiang" (The reasons
for the recent fall in the price of copper in Tianjin and its effect). *JJZK*, No. 6
(April 5, 1933).
He Zechun. *Kaocha geji gonghui zong baogao* (General report on the investigation of
labor unions at every level). Tianjin: Zhongguo Guomindang Tianjin tebie shi
zhixing weiyuanhui, 1929.
Heng Yuan Fangzhi Youxian Gongsi zong bangongchu ji gongchang zhangcheng
(Regulations for the general office and factory of the Heng Yuan Textile Com-
pany, Ltd.). N.p., n.d.
Hersey, John. "Homecoming," *The New Yorker* (May 10, 17, 24, 31, 1982).
Hershatter, Gail. "Flying Hammers, Walking Chisels: The Workers of Santiaoshi,"
Modern China, 9, No. 4 (Oct. 1983), 387–419.
———. "The Making of the Working Class in Tianjin, 1900–1949." Ph.D. diss.,
Stanford University, 1982.
———, and Emily Honig. "Hard Times Cotton Mill Girls: Women Workers
in Shanghai's Cotton Spinning Industry, 1895–1927." Ms., June 1977.
Hobsbawm, E. J. *Labouring Men*. Garden City, N.Y.: Anchor Books, 1967.
Hochstadt, Steve. "Social History and Politics: A Materialist View." *Social History*,
7, No. 1 (Jan. 1982), 75–83.
Hommel, Rudolf P. *China at Work*. New York: John Day, 1937; reissued, Cambridge, Mass: MIT Press, 1969.
Honig, Emily. *Sisters and Strangers: Women in the Shanghai Cotton Mills, 1919–
1949*. Stanford, Calif.: Stanford University Press, 1986.

————. "Women Cotton Mill Workers in Shanghai, 1919–1949." Ph.D. diss., Stanford University, 1982.

Hsiao Liang-lin. *China's Foreign Trade Statistics, 1864–1949.* Cambridge, Mass.: Harvard University Press, 1974.

Huang Wansheng and Yi Jizuo. "Shilun Zhongguo wuchan jieji juxianxing" (A preliminary discussion of the limitations of the Chinese proletariat). *Shehui kexue,* No. 5 (1980), cited in *Qingnian bao,* Jan. 11, 1981, 3.

Huang Xiangting. "Sanshi nianlai yingshang Ren Ji Yanghang zai Tianjin de lüeduo" (The plunder of the British firm William Forbes and Co. in Tianjin during the last thirty years). *WSZL,* No. 44 (Aug. 1963), 193–201.

Huashang shachang lianhehui mianchan tongji bu (Department of statistics on cotton production of the Chinese Cotton Millowners' Association). *Zhongguo mianchan tongji* (Statistics on Chinese cotton production). N.p., 1929.

Hummel, Arthur W., ed. *Eminent Chinese of the Ch'ing Period (1644–1912).* Taibei: Ch'eng Wen, 1972.

Humphries, Jane. "Class Struggle and the Persistence of the Working-Class Family." *Cambridge Journal of Economics,* 1 (1977), 241–58.

"Japan Developing North China Cotton Industry." *Far Eastern Survey,* 5, No. 17 (Aug. 12, 1936), 185.

Ji Guangzhi. "Jiu Zhongguo shiqi de Tianjin gongye gaikuang" (A survey of Tianjin industry in old China). *BGCQ,* 2, No. 2 (April 1960), 16–29.

————. "Jiu Zhongguo shiqi Tianjin gongren zhuangkuang" (The condition of Tianjin workers in old China). *BGCQ,* 2, No. 3 (July 1960), 16–30.

Ji Hua. "Ni Sichong zai liangshiye de touzi" (The investment of Ni Sichong in the grain industry). *TJWS,* No. 4 (Oct. 1978), 194.

Johnson, Richard. "Thompson, Genovese, and Socialist-Humanist History." *History Workshop,* 6 (Autumn 1978), 79–100.

Johnson, Robert E. *Peasant and Proletarian: The Working Class of Moscow in the Late Nineteenth Century.* New Brunswick, N.J.: Rutgers University Press, 1979.

Joint Factory History of the Tianjin Carpet Factory and the East Wind Carpet Factory. Ms., May 1959. Factory Archives, Tianjin Carpet Factory #3.

Jones, F. C. *Shanghai and Tientsin: With Special Reference to Foreign Interests.* New York: Institute of Pacific Relations, 1940.

Jones, Gareth Steadman. *Outcast London.* Oxford, Eng.: Clarendon Press, 1971.

Jordan, David K. "The Recent History of the Celestial Way." *Modern China,* 8, No. 4 (Oct. 1982), 435–62.

Judt, Tony. "A Clown in Regal Purple: Social History and the Historians." *History Workshop,* 7 (Spring 1979), 66–94.

Kōain Kahoku renraku bu seimu kyoku (Asian Development Institute, North China Liaison Bureau Political Affairs Office). *Kahoku rōdō mondai gaisetsu* (An outline of the North China labor problem). N.p., 1940.

Koenker, Diane. *Moscow Workers and the 1917 Revolution.* Princeton, N.J.: Princeton University Press, 1981.

Lee, Frederic E. *Currency, Banking, and Finance in China.* Washington, D.C.: Government Printing Office, 1926.

Li Bingzhi. "Diguozhuyi kongzhixia Tianjin haiguan de neimu" (Inside story of the Tianjin Customs under the control of the imperialists). *TJWS,* No. 9 (June 1980), 54–68.

Li Hanyuan. "Guanyu Chen Diyun beibu jingguo de shishi buzheng" (A historically factual supplementary correction on the arrest of Chen Diyun). *TJWS*, No. 10 (July 1980), 130–31.

Li Luozhi and Nie Tanggu. *Tianjin de jingji diwei* (The economic status of Tianjin). Tianjin: Jingji bu Jirechasui qu tepaiyuan bangongchu jiesu banshichu zhu Jin banshi fenchu, 1948.

Li Pu Lung (Li Bulong). *The Brick Industry in Tientsin and the Problem of Its Modernization.* Mimeo. Tientsin: Hautes Etudes; Shanghai: Université l'Aurore, 1940.

Li Ranshi. "Jiu Tianjin de hunhunr" (The hunhunr of old Tianjin). *WSZL*, No. 47 (Jan. 1963), 187–209.

Li Shaomi and Ni Jinjun. "Tianjin zilaishui shiye jianshi" (Short history of running water facilities in Tianjin). *TJWS*, No. 9 (June 1980), 79–106.

Li Shiyu. *Xiandai Huabei mimi zongjiao* (Secret religions in contemporary North China). Chengtu: Studia Serica Monograph, 1948.

Li Zhidao. "Zhongguo shiye yinghang xingshuai xiaoshi" (Short history of the rise and decline of the China Industrial Bank). *TJWS*, No. 1 (Dec. 1978), 54–63.

Liang Peiyu. "Tianjin Yihe Yanghang ji qi maiban Liang Yanqing" (The Jardine, Matheson Company of Tianjin and its compradore Liang Yanqing). *TJWS*, No. 9 (June 1980), 79–106.

Liao Yizhong, Lu Wanhe, and Yang Sishen, eds. "Tianjin Heji Yanghang shiliao" (Historical material on the International Export Company of Tianjin). *Tianjin lishi ziliao*, No. 6 (July 1980), 1–70.

Liao Yongwu. "Wusa fenglei hua Tianjin" (The tempest of May 30 in Tianjin). *Tianjin shifan xuebao*, No. 3 (1975), 91–94.

Lieberthal, Kenneth. "Reconstruction and Revolution in a Chinese City: The Case of Tientsin, 1949–1953." Ph.D. diss., Columbia University, 1972.

——. *Revolution and Tradition in Tientsin, 1949–1952.* Stanford, Calif.: Stanford University Press, 1980.

Lin Kaiming. "Guanyu Tianjin Santiaoshi faren de jidian tantao" (An inquiry into several points concerning the beginnings of Santiaoshi in Tianjin). Ms., Dec. 12, 1962.

Lin Shuhui. "Dierci yapian zhanzheng hou Tianjin diwei de bianhua" (The change in Tianjin's status after the second Opium War). Paper prepared for the Ming Qing guoji xueshu taolunhui, Tianjin, Dec. 1980.

Liu Chin-t'ao. *Egg Industry in Tientsin.* Economic Studies No. 18. Tientsin: Tientsin Institut des Hautes Etudes, 1941.

Liu Guhou. "Tianjin gongshangye de weiji" (The crisis of Tianjin industry and commerce). *SHYK*, 1, No. 1 (July 1929), 42–50.

——. "Tianjin gongshangye zhi niaokan" (A bird's-eye view of Tianjin industry and commerce). *SHYK*, 1, Nos. 5–6 (Dec. 1929), 1–24.

Liu Jingshan. "Hanjian eba Yuan Wenhui de yisheng" (The life of traitor and local tyrant Yuan Wenhui). *TJWS*, No. 18 (Jan. 1982), 202–12.

Liu Weiwu. "Kangzhan qianhou Jinshi gongyun zhi dongtai" (Trends in the Tianjin workers' movement before and after the resistance war). *Huabei laodong*, 1, No. 1 (Jan. 15, 1946), 10–11.

Liu Xinquan. "Huabei shachang gongren gongzi tongji" (Statistics on the wages of cotton mill workers in North China). *Shehui kexue zazhi*, 6, No. 1 (March 1935), 141–58.

Lowe, Chuan-hua. *Facing Labor Issues in China.* Shanghai, 1933.

Lowe, H. Y. [Lu Xingyuan]. *The Adventures of Wu: The Life Cycle of a Peking Man*. Beijing, 1940, 1941; reissued, Princeton, N.J.: Princeton University Press, 1983.

Lu Dangping. "Fazhan Tianjin gongshangye zuidi xiandu de gongzuo" (The minimum degree of work required to develop Tianjin industry and commerce). *SHYK*, 1, Nos. 5–6 (Dec. 1929).

———. *Tianjin gongshangye* (Tianjin's industry and commerce). Tianjin: Tianjin tebie shi shehui ju, 1930.

Lu Luyuan. "Bei Yang shachang yu Zhu Mengsu" (The Bei Yang Cotton Mill and Zhu Mengsu). *TJWS*, No. 6 (Dec. 1979), 128–42.

Luo Yusheng. "Wutai shenghuo liushi nian" (Sixty years of life onstage). *TJWS*, No. 14 (March 1981), 170–95.

MacKinnon, Stephen R. *Power and Politics in Late Imperial China: Yuan Shi-kai in Beijing and Tianjin, 1901–1908*. Berkeley: University of California Press, 1980.

Malone, Col. C. L. L'Estrange. *New China, Part II: Labour Conditions and Labour Organizations*. London: Independent Labour Party, 1926.

Mantetsu tōa keizai chōsa kyoku (Manchurian Railway Economic Investigation Bureau). *Shina no rōdō undō* (The Chinese labor movement). Tokyo: Doshoten, 1926.

McDougall, Mary Lynn. "Consciousness and Community: The Workers of Lyon, 1830–1850." *Journal of Social History*, 12, No. 1 (Fall 1978), 129–45.

Mendelsohn, Ezra. *Class Struggle in the Pale: The Formative Years of the Jewish Workers' Movement in Tsarist Russia*. Cambridge, Eng.: Cambridge University Press, 1970.

Mi Luzhai. "Yan Xishan yu diguozhuyi de junxu maoyi neimu" (The inside story of the trade in military supplies between Yan Xishan and the imperialists). *WSZL*, No. 49 (Jan. 1964), 66–77.

Mian Er (Cotton Mill #2). *Changshi 1918–1949* (Factory History 1918–1949). Ms., Sept. 15, 1958. Tianjin: Factory Archives, Cotton Mill #2.

Mian Si (Cotton Mill #4). "1946 nian ben chang jianjie he diaocha" (A brief introduction to and investigation of this mill in 1946). Tianjin: Factory Archives, Cotton Mill #4.

———. "1947 nian bugao liudi bo" (Record of announcements for 1947). Tianjin: Factory Archives, Cotton Mill #4.

Minami manshū tetsudō kabushiki kaisha (South Manchuria Railroad Co.). *Hokushina kōjō jittai chōsa hōkokusho: Tenshin no bu* (Report on the investigation of the actual condition of factories in North China: Tianjin). N.p., 1938.

Montgomery, David. "Strikes in Nineteenth-Century America." *Social Science History*, 4, No. 1 (Winter 1980), 81–104.

———. "To Study the People: The American Working Class." *Labor History*, 21, No. 4 (Fall 1980), 485–512.

Naitō Juntarō. *Zai Shina keizai sōgi* (Economic conflict in China). Tokyo: Tōasha, 1925.

Nankai Daxue [1] jingji yanjiusuo bian. *Nankai zhishu ziliao huibian (1913–1952)* (A compilation of Nankai index data, 1913–52). Beijing: Tongji chubanshe, 1958.

——— [2] jingji yanjiusuo bianji. *Tianjin shi shehui diaocha ziliao* (Material on a social investigation of Tianjin). Mimeographed scrapbook, 1931.

——— [3] lishixi 1956 nianji bian. *Tianjin diqu Yihetuan yundong diaocha baogao*

(A report on the investigation of the Boxer movement in the Tianjin area). Mimeo. Tianjin: n.p., 1960.

—— [4] *liushi nian* [Sixty years of Nankai University]. Tianjin: Nankai Daxue, 1979.

—— [5] zhengzhi jingjixue xi (Nankai University Department of Political Economy). "Guanyu jiefang qian Tianjin Santiaoshi zibenzhuyi boxue qingkuang diaocha ziliao" (Investigative material on the conditions of capitalist exploitation in Tianjin's Santiaoshi before Liberation). Mimeo., March 1972.

National Government of the Republic of China, Commission of Financial Experts. *Project of Law for the Gradual Introduction of a Gold-Standard Currency System in China.* N.p., 1929.

Nieuhoff, John. "The Embassy of Peter de Goyer and Jacob de Keyser from the Dutch East India Company to the Emperor of China in 1655." In John Pinkerton, ed., *A General Collection of the Best and Most Interesting Voyages and Travels in All Parts of the World*, Vol. VII. London: Longman, Hurst, Rees, Orme, and Brown, 1811.

"Pekin Tenshin shisō dantai chōsa" (An investigation of ideological organizations in Beijing and Tianjin), Part 2. *Chōsa Geppo* (Investigation Monthly), 2, No. 6 (June 1942), 385–460.

Peking and the Overland Route. Shanghai: Thomas Cook, 1917.

Pleck, Elizabeth H. "Two Worlds in One: Work and Family." *Journal of Social History*, 10, 2 (Winter 1976), 178–95.

Pollard, Sidney. "Factory Discipline in the Industrial Revolution." *Economic History Review*, 2d series. 16, No. 2 (1963–64), 254–71.

——. *The Genesis of Modern Management.* Cambridge, Mass.: Harvard University Press, 1965.

Qiao, Hong. "Ming Qing yilai Tianjin shuihuan de fasheng ji qi yuanyin" (The occurrence of floods in Tianjin since the Ming and Qing periods and their causes). *BGCQ*, 2, No. 3 (July 1960), 86–95.

Qing hong bang kao yi (An investigation and explanation of the Qing and Hong Bang). Taibei: Shidai haiyuan yuekanshe, 1973.

Qing pu jiyao (A summary of the Qing Bang "Genealogy"). Tianjin: Chong yi wu xue she, 1932.

Rasmussen, O. D. *Tientsin: An Illustrated Outline History.* Tientsin: Tientsin Press, 1925.

Reddy, William M. "Skeins, Scales, Discounts, Steam, and Other Objects of Crowd Justice in Early French Textile Mills." *Comparative Studies in Society and History*, 21, No. 2 (April 1979), 204–13.

Reid, Alistair. "Politics and Economics in the Formation of the British Working Class: A Response to H. F. Moorhouse." *Social History*, 3, No. 3 (Oct. 1978), 347–61.

Ren Pu. *Santiaoshi.* Tianjin: Baihua wenyi chubanshe, 1964.

Rodgers, Daniel T. "Tradition, Modernity and the American Industrial Worker: Reflections and Critique." *Journal of Interdisciplinary History*, 7, No. 4 (Spring 1977), 655–82.

Rowe, William T. *Hankow: Commerce and Society in a Chinese City, 1796–1889.* Stanford, Calif.: Stanford University Press, 1984.

——. "The Qingbang and Collaboration Under the Japanese, 1939–1945." *Modern China*, 8, No. 4 (Oct. 1982), 491–99.

Ruan Weijing. "Mei shang Da Lai Yanghang zai Zhongguo de lüeduo" (The plunder of the American firm Robert Dollar Company in China). *WSZL*, No. 49 (Jan. 1964), 1–20.

Rui Chongzhi. "Tianjin ditan gongyede xingqi he fazhan" (The rise and development of the Tianjin carpet industry). *TJWS*, No. 1 (Dec. 1978), 64–79.

Scott, Joan W. *The Glassworkers of Carmaux*. Cambridge, Eng.: Cambridge University Press, 1974.

Selden, Mark. "The Proletariat, Revolutionary Change, and the State in China and Japan, 1850–1950." In Immanuel Wallerstein, ed., *Labor in the World Social Structure*. Beverly Hills, Calif.: Sage Publications, 1983, pp. 58–120.

Sewell, William, Jr. "Social Change and the Rise of Working-Class Politics in Nineteenth-Century Marseille." *Past and Present*, 65 (Nov. 1974), 75–109.

———. *Work and Revolution in France: The Language of Labor From the Old Regime to 1848*. Cambridge, Eng.: Cambridge University Press, 1980.

Shaffer, Lynda. "The Chinese Working Class." *Modern China*, 9, No. 4 (Oct. 1983), 455–64.

———. *Mao and the Workers: The Hunan Labor Movement, 1920–1923*. Armonk, N.Y.: Sharpe, 1982.

Shanghai shi mian fangzhi gongye tongye gonghui choubeihui. *Zhongguo mianfang tongji shiliao* (Historical statistical material on Chinese cotton spinning). Shanghai, 1950.

Sheridan, James E. *China in Disintegration*. New York: Free Press, 1975.

Shiba, Yoshinobu. "Ningpo and Its Hinterland." In G. William Skinner, ed., *The City in Late Imperial China*. Stanford, Calif.: Stanford University Press, 1977, 391–440.

Shorter, Edward, and Charles Tilly. *Strikes in France, 1830–1968*. Cambridge, Eng.: Cambridge University Press, 1974.

Si Chengxiang. "Canjia Tianjin zaoqi geming huodong de huiyi" (Reminiscences of joining early revolutionary activities in Tianjin). *TJWS*, No. 10 (July 1980), 69–108.

Skinner, G. William. "Mobility Strategies in Late Imperial China: A Regional Systems Analysis." In Carol A. Smith, ed., *Regional Analysis, Vol. 1: Economic Systems*. New York: Academic Press, 1976, 327–64.

Smith, Steven R. "The London Apprentices as Seventeenth-Century Adolescents." *Past and Present*, 61 (Nov. 1973), 149–61.

Song Yunpu. *Tianjin zhilue* (An outline record of Tianjin). Tianjin: Tianjin xie cheng yinshua ju, 1931.

Spector, Stanley. *Li Hung-chang and the Huai Army*. Seattle: University of Washington Press, 1964.

Staunton, Sir George. *An Authentic Account of an Embassy from the King of Great Britain to the Emperor of China*, Vol. I. Philadelphia: John Bioren, 1799.

Stevens, Catherine. "Peking Drumsinging." Ph.D. diss., Harvard University, 1973.

Strand, David. "Peking in the 1920's: Political Order and Popular Protest." Ph.D. diss., Columbia University, 1979.

———, and Richard R. Weiner. "Social Movements and Political Discourse in 1920's Peking: An Analysis of the Tramway Riot of October 22, 1929." In Susan Mann Jones, ed., *Select Papers from the Center for Far Eastern Studies*, No. 3, 1978–79. Chicago: University of Chicago, 1979, pp. 137–79.

Sun Hua. "Ling xin" (Getting paid). *Gongren zhoukan*, Nos. 8–9 (Jan. 15, 1947), 18–19.

Sun Jingzhi. "Yuanlong zhoubudian yu 'Qingxiutang Sun' de xingluo shimo" (The rise and fall of Yuanlong Silk Store and Mr. Sun of the Qingxiu Clan). *TJWS*, No. 2 (Feb. 1979), 118–29.

Sun Limin and Xing Gongxian. "Tianjin Rizujie gaikuang" (Survey of the Japanese concession of Tianjin). *TJWS*, No. 18 (Jan. 1982), 111–51.

Tao Ling and Lydia Johnson. "A Study of Women and Girls in Tientsin Industries." *CEJ*, 2, No. 6 (June 1928), 519–28.

Tawney, Richard. *Land and Labour in China*. New York: Harcourt, Brace, 1932.

Tenshin Nihon shōgyō kaigishō (Tianjin Japanese Chamber of Commerce). *Tenshin gaikan* (A general view of Tianjin). Tianjin: Japanese Chamber of Commerce, 1927.

———. *Tenshin shōgyō annai furoku* (A supplement to the guide to Tianjin commerce and industry). Tianjin: Japanese Chamber of Commerce, 1939.

Thomas, S. Bernard. *Labor and the Chinese Revolution*. Ann Arbor: Center for Chinese Studies, University of Michigan, 1983.

———. *"Proletarian Hegemony" in the Chinese Revolution and the Canton Commune of 1927*. Ann Arbor: Michigan Papers in Chinese Studies No. 23, 1975.

Thompson, E. P. "Eighteenth Century English Society: Class Struggle Without Class?" *Social History*, 3, No. 2 (May 1978), 147–50.

———. *The Making of the English Working Class*. New York: Vintage, 1966.

———. "Time, Work-Discipline and Industrial Capitalism." *Past and Present*, 38 (1967), 56–92.

Tian Hongshi. "Tianjin gaishu (yijiu yijiu yiqian)" (General description of Tianjin [before 1919]). *Tianjin lishi ziliao*, No. 3 (March 1, 1965), 1–13.

"Tianjin [1] Bao Cheng shachang shixing sanbazhi" (Tianjin Bao Cheng Mill implements system of three eight-hour shifts). *Tongji yuebao*, 2, No. 4 (1930), 3–4.

"Tianjin [2] chan er fengsu" (Tianjin birth customs). *SHYK*, supplement (March 20, 1930), 1–6.

"Tianjin [3] de yanghang maiban" (The compradores of Tianjin's foreign firms). *Tianjin wenshi cankao ziliao jianji zhi liu* (Brief selections from Tianjin cultural and historical reference material, no. 6). Tianjin, Aug. 1975.

"Tianjin [4] fangzhi jianshe gongsi Tianjin fen gongsi bian. *Tianjin zhongfang er zhounian* (The second anniversary of the Tianjin branch of the China Textile Industries Corporation). Tianjin, 1947.

"Tianjin [5] geji gonghui diaocha gaikuang" (A survey of the investigation of Tianjin unions at different levels). *SHYK*, 1, Nos. 5–6 (Dec. 1929), 1–26.

"Tianjin [6] gongren shenghuo chengdu ji qi jin sinianlai shenghuofei zhi bianqian" (The standard of living of Tianjin workers and the changes in the cost of living during the past four years). *Jingji yanjiu zhoukan*, 19 (July 6, 1930).

Tianjin [7] jinbu ribaoshe bianyin. *Tianjin gongshangye congkan 3: Wujin jiqi nongju jingying de fangxiang* (Tianjin industry and commerce notebook 3: The direction of management of hardware, machines, and agricultural tools). Tianjin, 1951.

Tianjin [8] Nankai Xuexiao shehui shicha weiyuanhui. *Tianjin Nankai Xuexiao shehui shicha baogao* (The social observation reports of Nankai School in Tianjin). Tianjin, 1930.

Tianjin [9] shachang shiye jinkuang (Recent developments in Tianjin cotton mill enterprises). *Fangzhi zhoukan*, 5, Nos. 22–23 (June 15, 1935), 561–64.

"Tianjin [10] shi 25 nianfen renkou chusheng zhuangkuang" (Fertility in the Tianjin population, 1936). *Jicha diaocha tongji congkan*, 2, No. 5 (May 1937), 1–8.

"Tianjin [11] shi 25 nianfen renkou siwang tongji yiban" (A partial look at mortality statistics for Tianjin in 1936). *Jicha diaocha tongji congkan*, 2, No. 4 (April 1937), 6–20.

Tianjin [12] shi fangzhi gongye ju bianshi ju. "Jiu Zhongguo shiqi de Tianjin fangzhi gongye" (The textile industry of Tianjin in old China). *BGCQ*, 2, No. 1 (Jan. 10, 1960), 86–110.

"Tianjin [13] shi hongbaihuoye shangqing xiguan diaocha" (An investigation of the business conditions and customs of the wedding and funeral goods trade in Tianjin). *SHYK*, supplement (March 20, 1930), 1–13.

"Tianjin [14] shi hualiubing fangzhisuo" (Tianjin venereal disease prevention and treatment center). *Tianjin shi zhoukan*, 1, No. 8 (Feb. 1, 1947), 9.

"Tianjin [15] shi jiaohang jianjie" (A brief introduction to the Tianjin transport guilds). *Tianjin shi zhoukan.* Part 1: 2, No. 2 (March 15, 1947), 7–8; Part 2: 2, No. 3 (March 22, 1947), 6–7.

Tianjin [16] shi jingjutuan gai bian. *Liu hao men* (Gate #6). Tianjin: Baihua wenyi chubanshe, 1965.

Tianjin [17] shi lishi yanjiusuo Tianjin shi yanjiushi. *Tianjin jianshi* (A short history of Tianjin). Tianjin: Tianjin shi lishi yanjiusuo, 1979.

Tianjin [18] shi lishi yanjiusuo ziliaoshi zhengli. "Tianjin de jiaohang" (The transport guilds of Tianjin). *Tianjin lishi ziliao*, No. 4 (Oct. 1, 1965), 1–29.

Tianjin [19] shi shehui ju bian (Tianjin Bureau of Social Affairs). *Guohuo yilan* (A look at Chinese-made goods). Tianjin: Tianjin shi shehui ju bianyin, 1929.

Tianjin [20] shi zhengfu tongji chu bian (Tianjin Municipal Government Office of Statistics). *Tianjin shi zhuyao tongji ziliao shouce—dierhao: gongshang zhuanhao* (Handbook of major statistical materials for Tianjin—No. 2: special number on industry and commerce). Tianjin: Tianjin shi zhengfu tongji chu bianyin, 1948.

"Tianjin [21] shi zhi fengsu diaocha" (An investigation of Tianjin customs). *Hebei yuekan*, 1, No. 3 (March 1933), 1–22.

Tianjin [22] shiji diaochadui Santiaoshi zaoqi gongye ziliao diaochazu bian (Santiaoshi early industry investigation group of the Tianjin historical sites investigation team, eds.). *Tianjin shi Santiaoshi zaoqi gongye ziliao diaocha* (An investigation of material on early industry in Tianjin's Santiaoshi). Mimeo. Tianjin, 1958.

Tianjin [23] shiye ju. *Tianjin xian shiye diaocha baogao* (Economic survey of Tianjin county). Tianjin: Tianjin shiye ju, 1925.

"Tianjin [24] tebie shi funü jiuji yuan jiuji funü yi lanbiao" (A list of women given relief by the Tianjin Municipal Women's Relief Institute). *Tianjin tebie shi shehui ju yi zhounian gongzuo zong baogao, 1928–1929* (Report on the work of the Tianjin Municipal Bureau of Social Affairs during the first year, 1928–29). Tianjin: Shehui ju, 1929.

Tianjin [25] tebie shi gongchang lianhehui huiwu jiyao (Summary of the business of the Tianjin Special Municipality Factory Federation). Tianjin, 1943.

Tianjin [26] tebie shi gongshu (Government Office of the Special Municipality of Tianjin). *Tianjin tebie shi gongshu 27 nian xingzheng jiyao* (Government Office of the Special Municipality of Tianjin, administrative summary, 1938). Vol. II. Tianjin, 1938.

Tianjin [27] *tebie shi shehui ju minguo shiba nian gongzuo baogao shu* (A report on the work of the Bureau of Social Affairs of the Special Municipality of Tianjin in 1929). [Tianjin], n.d.

Tianjin [28] *tebie shi shehui ju yizhounian gongzuo zong baogao (minguo shiqi nian bayue zhi shiba nian qiyue)* (Report on the work of the Tianjin Municipal Bureau of Social Affairs during the first year [Aug. 1928–July 1929]). Tianjin: Tianjin tebie shi shehui ju, 1929.

Tianjin [29] tebie shi tebie xingzhengqu gongshu bian (Government Office of the Special Administrative District of the Special Municipality of Tianjin, ed.). *Tianjin tebie shi tebie xingzhengqu gongshu Zhonghua minguo 30 nian nianbao* (Annual report for 1941 of the government office of the special administrative district, Special Municipality of Tianjin). [Tianjin], 1941.

"Tianjin [30] zujie jiankuang" (A brief survey of the Tianjin concessions). *Tianjin wenshi cankao ziliao jianji zhi san* (Brief selections from Tianjin cultural and historical reference material, no. 3). [Tianjin], 1972.

"Tientsin Slowly Emerging as a New Textile Center." *Far Eastern Survey*, 6, No. 1 (Jan. 6, 1937), 11.

Tilly, Louise A. "*I fatti di maggio*: The Working Class of Milan and the Rebellion of 1848." In Robert J. Bezucha, ed., *Modern European Social History*. Lexington, Mass.: Heath, 1972, pp. 124–58.

————. "Paths of Proletarianization: Organization of Production, Sexual Division of Labor, and Women's Collective Action." *Signs*, 7, No. 2 (Winter 1981), 400–417.

————, and Joan W. Scott. *Women, Work, and Family*. New York: Holt, 1978.

————, and Charles Tilly, eds. *Class Conflict and Collective Action*. Beverly Hills, Calif.: Sage Publications, 1981.

Von Laue, Theodore H. "Russian Peasants in the Factory, 1892–1904." *Journal of Economic History*, 21 (1961), 61–80.

"Wages in Tientsin Industries." *Chinese Economic Monthly*, 3, No. 10 (Oct. 1926), 418–23.

Wales, Nym [Helen Foster Snow]. *The Chinese Labor Movement*. New York: John Day, 1945.

Wan Xinquan. "Tianjin shi shuijian gaikuang" (A survey of Tianjin taxes). *Hebei yuekan*, 1, No. 4 (April 1933), 1–4; *ibid.*, 1, No. 5 (May 1933).

Wang Da. "Tianjin shi gongye" (The industry of Tianjin). *Shiye bu yuekan*, 1, No. 1 (April 1936), 109–218.

Wang Huaiyuan. "Jiu Zhongguo shiqi Tianjin de duiwai maoyi" (The foreign trade of Tianjin in old China). *BGCQ*, Part 1: 2, No. 1 (Jan. 1960), 65–85; Part 2: 2, No. 2 (April 1960), 29–44. Part 3: 2, No. 3 (July 1960), 98–109.

Wang Jinghang and Zhang Zesheng. "Yu Yuan shachang de xingshuai shilüe" (A brief history of the rise and decline of the Yu Yuan Cotton Mill). *TJWS*, No. 4 (Oct. 1979), 172–79.

Wang Jingyu, ed. *Zhongguo jindai gongyeshi ziliao, 1895–1914* (Source materials on the history of modern industry in China, 1895–1914). 2 vols. Beijing, 1957.

Wang Lin. *Bozhong: Tianjin gongyun shihua* (Seeding: History of the Tianjin workers' movement). Tianjin: Tianjin tongsu chubanshe, 1953.

Wang Qingbin et al. *Diyici Zhongguo laodong nianjian* (The first China labor yearbook). Beiping, 1928.
Wang Xirong et al. "Jiefang qian Santiaoshi tugong de xuelei" (The blood and tears of Santiaoshi apprentices before Liberation). *Lishi jiaoxue*, No. 2 (1965), 42–46.
Wang Xiushun and Zhang Gaofeng. "Tianjin zaoqi shangye zhongxin de lüeying" (A flickering image of Tianjin's early commercial center). *TJWS*, No. 16 (Aug. 1981), 61–73.
Wang Yunsheng and Cao Gubing. "Ying Lianzhi shidai de jiu *Dagong bao*" (The old *Dagong bao* in the era of Ying Lianzhi). *WSZL*, No. 9 (Sept. 1960), 1–44.
Wang Zijian. *Minguo 23 nian de Zhongguo mian fangzhiye* (The Chinese cotton textile industry in 1934). N.p.: Guoli zhongyang yanjiuyuan shehui kexue yanjiusuo lao gao, n.d.
Wang Zishou. "Tianjin diandangye sishi nian de huiyi" (Memories of forty years in the Tianjin pawnshop business). *WSZL*, No. 53 (Nov. 1965), 35–58.
Wei Bogang. "Tianjin Hengbin zhengjin yinhang yu Wei jia liangdai maiban" (The Yokohama Specie Bank of Tianjin and two generations of compradores from the Wei family). *TJWS*, No. 18 (Jan. 1982), 153–81.
Wei Kejing. "Tianhou gong de bianqian" (The changes at the Temple of the Heavenly Empress). *Tianjin ribao*, Feb. 8, 1981.
Willmott, W. E., ed. *Economic Organization in Chinese Society*. Stanford, Calif.: Stanford University Press, 1972.
Wolf, Margery, and Roxane Witke, eds. *Women in Chinese Society*. Stanford, Calif.: Stanford University Press, 1975.
Wright, Tim. "'A Method of Evading Management'—Contract Labor in Chinese Coal Mines Before 1937." *Comparative Studies in Society and History*, 23, No. 4 (Oct. 1981), 656–78.
Wu Ao [1]. *Tianjin shi fangshaye diaocha baogao* (Report on an investigation of the Tianjin spinning industry). Tianjin: Tianjin shi shehui ju, 1931.
——— [2]. *Tianjin shi huochaiye diaocha baogao* (Report on an investigation of the Tianjin match industry). Tianjin: Tianjin shehui ju, 1931.
——— [3]. *Tianjin shi mianfenye diaocha baogao* (Report on an investigation of the Tianjin flour industry). Tianjin: Tianjin shi shehui ju, 1932.
——— [4] et al. *Tianjin shi shehui ju tongji huikan* (Statistical issue of the Tianjin Bureau of Social Affairs). Tianjin: Tianjin shehui ju, 1931.
Wu Huan. "Guanyu wo fu Wu Diaoqing de huiyi" (Some recollections of my father, Wu Diaoqing). *WSZL*, No. 49 (Jan. 1964), 228–35.
Wu, Leonard T. K. "The Crisis in the Chinese Cotton Industry." *Far Eastern Survey*, 4, No. 1 (Jan. 6, 1935), 1–4.
Wu Shicheng. "Tianjin zhi zhibi" (Tianjin's paper currency). *Shangxue yuekan* (July 1935), 27–33.
Wu Ziguang. "Jingji konghuangzhong Tianjin duiwai maoyi zhi shuailuo" (The decline of Tianjin's foreign trade during the Depression). *Hebei yuekan*, 2, No. 12 (Dec. 1934).
Xia Shaoquan. "Guanyu Zhou Xuexi, Yang Weiyun he Hua Xin shachang ziliao de buchong" (Supplement to the material concerning Zhou Xuexi, Yang Weiyun, and the Hua Xin Cotton Mill). *WSZL*, No. 31 (July 1962), 320–22.
Xiang Ruizhi. "Ji yijiu erwu nian za Yu Da shijian de qianqian houhou" (Remem-

bering the ins and outs of smashing Yu Da). *TJWS*, No. 10 (July 1980), 116–21.

Xiao Zhuwen. "Tianjin Yingmei Yan Gongsi de jingji lüeduo" (The economic plunder of the British and American Tobacco Company in Tianjin). *TJWS*, No. 3 (June 1979), 166–94.

Xin Fengxia. *Reminiscences*. Beijing: Panda Books, 1981.

———. *Xin Fengxia huiyi lu* (Record of the reminiscences of Xin Fengxia). Xianggang [Hong Kong]: Sanlian shudian, 1980.

———. *Yishu shengya* (A career in the arts). Vol. 2 of *Record of the Reminiscences of Xin Fengxia*. Xianggang [Hong Kong]: Sanlian shudian, 1982.

Xu Jingxing. "Tianjin jindai gongye de zaoqi gaikuang" (A survey of early Tianjin modern industry). *TJWS*, No. 1 (Dec. 1978), 124–61.

Xue Buqi. *Tianjin huozhanye* (The Tianjin warehouse industry). Tianjin: Xin lianhe chubanshe, 1941.

Yan Yiwen. "Sishi nian maiban shenghuo huiyi" (Recollections of forty years of compradore life). *WSZL*, No. 38 (Feb. 1963), 69–97.

Yan Zifeng. "Yan Xishan jiazu jingying de qiye" (The enterprises managed by the Yan Xishan family). *WSZL*, No. 49 (Jan. 1964), 46–65.

Yang, Lien-sheng. *Money and Credit in China*. Cambridge, Mass.: Harvard University Press, 1952.

Yao Xiyun. "Tianjin shidiao de yanbian" (The evolution of current Tianjin tunes). *TJWS*, No. 14 (March 1981), 160–69.

Ye Qianji. *Tianjin mianhua xuqiu-jiage xiangguan zhi yanjiu* (Research on the interrelationship of demand for raw cotton and price in Tianjin). [Tianjin]: Nankai Daxue jingji yanjiusuo zhengzhi jingji xuebao danxing ben, 1935.

Ye Wuxi and Shao Yunrui. "Liu Shaoqi 'Tianjin jianghua' zai pingjia" (A reevaluation of Liu Shaoqi's Tianjin talks). Mimeo. Tianjin: Nankai daxue lishi xi dangshi jiaoyanshi, 1979.

Yi Sumin, ed. *Qing bang kao shi* (An investigation and explanation of the Qing Bang). Taibei: Chang yan chubanshe, 1978.

"Yijiu erwu nian Tianjin fangzhi gongren douzheng jingguo (bawei laogongren zuotan jilu) (The course of the 1925 Tianjin textile workers' struggle [record of a discussion among eight old workers]). *BGCQ* (Oct. 10, 1959), 42–49.

Yokohama shōkin ginkō chōsaka (Yokohama Specie Bank Investigation Section). *Tenshin menka oyobi men kōgyō* (The raw cotton and cotton industry of Tianjin). N.p., 1919.

Yu Henian. "Tianjin Tianhou gongkao" (A study of the Temple of the Heavenly Empress in Tianjin). *Hebei yuekan*, 3, Nos. 6–7 (1935).

Zai Pekin Dai Nippon teikoku taishikan (Imperial Japanese Embassy in Beijing). *Kahoku ni okeru kōtsū unyu rōdōka chōsa* (An investigation of the laborers in the transportation business in North China). N.p., 1941.

Zai Tenshin Nippon teikoku soryojikan (Japanese Imperial Consulate-General, Tianjin). *Sangyōjo yori mitaru Tenshin to Hokushi no keizai jōsei* (The economic condition of Tianjin and North China as seen through a look at industry). N.p., 1938.

Zan Daotu. "Yi Guan Dao de zui e neimu" (The evil inside story of the Yi Guan Dao). *WSZL*, No. 47 (Nov. 1963), 210–25.

Zelnik, Reginald E. *Labor and Society in Tsarist Russia: The Factory Workers of St.*

Petersburg, 1855–1870. Stanford, Calif.: Stanford University Press, 1971.

———. "Russian Workers and the Revolutionary Movement." *Journal of Social History*, 6, No. 2 (Winter 1972–73), 214–36.

Zeng Tiechen. "Tianjin zhi jiqiye" (The machine industry of Tianjin). *SHYK*, I, Nos. 3–4 (Oct. 1929), 1–34.

Zhang Gaofeng. "Quanyechang yidai de bianqian" (Changes in the Quanyechang area). *TJWS*, No. 16 (Aug. 1981), 74–92.

Zhang Heqin. "Jinmen qutan cangsang lu" (A record of the vicissitudes of the folk performance world). *TJWS*, No. 14 (March 1981), 116–59.

Zhang Shou. *Jin men za ji* (Tianjin miscellany). Tianjin: n.p., 1884.

Zhang Shouchen. "Huigu wode yiren shengya" (A look back at my career as an actor). *TJWS*, No. 14 (March 1981), 196–205.

Zhang Xuyu. "Wo shi yige fangzhiye de gongren—shuo jiju dui fangzhiye de ganxiang" (I am a textile worker—let me share a few of my thoughts on the textile industry). *Huabei laodong*, I, No. I (Jan. 1946), 12–14.

Zhang Zhong. "Shen Kuo tan Tianjin" (Shen Kuo talks of Tianjin). *Tianjin ribao*, Jan. 15, 1980.

Zhao Shixian. "Junfa Wang Zhanyuan jingying gongshangye gaikuang" (A survey of the industrial and commercial activities engaged in by warlord Wang Zhanyuan). *TJWS*, No. 4 (Oct. 1979), 163–71.

"Zhao Shiyan shengping shizi" (Historical material on the life of Zhao Shiyan). *WSZL*, No. 58 (1979), 36–162.

Zhen Ji. "Shengli qian Tianjin jixie gongchang gaikuang" (A survey of Tianjin machine factories before the victory). *Huabei gongkuang*, No. 2 (June 1946), 107.

Zheng Qinan. "Jingji bu jieshou Dongya Yancao Gongsi gaikuang" (A survey of the takeover of the Dongya Tobacco Company by the Ministry of Economics). *Huabei laodong*, I, No. 6 (June 1946), 14.

Zheng Yufu. *Tianjin youlan zhi* (Record of travels in Tianjin). Zhonghua shudian, 1936.

Zheng Zhizhang. "Tianjin Taigu Yanghang yu maiban Zheng Yizhi" (The Butterfield and Swire Company in Tianjin and the compradore Zheng Yizhi). *TJWS*, No. 9 (June 1980), 107–24.

"Zhengdun jiaohang" (Reorganize the Jiaohang). *Tianjin shi zhoukan*, 4, No. 6 (Sept. 27, 1947), 3–4.

"Zhongfang Tianjin dierchang gaikuang" (A survey of Tianjin cotton mill #2). *Huabei laodong*, I, No. 7 (Jan. 1947), 24–26.

"Zhongguo [1] gongye de liudong ziben de wenti" (The problem of circulating capital in Chinese industry). *JJZK*, No. 14 (May 31, 1933).

"Zhongguo [2] laodong jieji shenghuofei zhi yanjiu" (Research into the living expenses of the Chinese laboring class). *Jingji yanjiu zhoukan*, No. 3 (March 17, 1930).

Zhongguo [3] zuojia xiehui Tianjin fenhui bian (Chinese Writers Association, Tianjin branch). *Hai he hong lang* (Red waves on the Hai River). Tianjin: Baihua wenyi chubanshe, 1960.

——— [4] zuojia xiehui Tianjin fenhui bian (Chinese Writers Association, Tianjin branch). *Yehuo shao bujin: Tianjin mianfang wu chang lishi* (Wildfire forever burning: A history of Tianjin cotton mill #5). Baihua wenyi chubanshe, 1959.

——— [5] zuojia xiehui Tianjin fenhui bian (Chinese Writers Association, Tianjin branch). *Yijiu erwu nian de fengbao* (The tempest of 1925). Tianjin: Baihua wenyi chubanshe, 1959.

Zhonghua quanguo zonggonghui bian (All-China Federation of Labor), ed. *Banyun gongren gonghui gongzuo cankao ziliao* (Reference material on the work of the Transport Workers' Union). Beijing: Gongren chubanshe, 1950.

Zhu Chunfu. "Beiyang junfa dui Tianjin jindai gongye de touzi" (The investment of Beiyang warlords in Tianjin modern industry). *TJWS*, No. 4 (Oct. 1979), 146–62.

———. "Zhou Xuexi yu Beiyang shiye" (Zhou Xuexi and Beiyang industry). *TJWS*, No. 1 (Dec. 1978), 1–28.

Zhu Mengsu. "Tianjin Bei Yang shachang yange ji qi yu Jin Cheng, Zhong Nan liang hang de guanxi" (The evolution of the Bei Yang Cotton Mill in Tianjin and its relationship with the Jin Cheng and Zhong Nan banks). *WSZL*, No. 49 (Jan. 1964), 195–200.

"Zui jin Zhongguo [1] renkou de xin guji" (A new estimate of the recent Chinese population). *Shehui kexue zazhi*, 6, No. 1 (March 1935).

"Zui jin Zhongguo [2] zhi renkou tongji" (Recent Chinese population statistics). *Tongji yuebao*, 1, No. 1 (1929).

Zuo Zhenyu. "Yijiu erjiu niande yuzhong douzheng" (The 1929 prison struggle). *TJWS*, No. 10 (July 1980), 122–30.

INDEX

Library of Congress Cataloging-in-Publication Data

Hershatter, Gail.
  The workers of Tianjin, 1900–1949.

  Bibliography: p.
  Includes index.
    1. Women—Employment—China—Tientsin—History.
  2. Tientsin (China)—Industries—History. I. Title.
  HD6200.Z6T544 1986   331.4'0951'15   86-1270
  ISBN 0-8047-1318-9 (alk. paper)